I0577262

James Martineau

A study of religion

Its sources and contents. Vol. 2

James Martineau

A study of religion
Its sources and contents. Vol. 2

ISBN/EAN: 9783337260507

Printed in Europe, USA, Canada, Australia, Japan

Cover: Foto ©Lupo / pixelio.de

More available books at **www.hansebooks.com**

A STUDY OF RELIGION

MARTINEAU

a

London

HENRY FROWDE

New York

MACMILLAN AND CO.

A

STUDY OF RELIGION

ITS SOURCES AND CONTENTS

BY

JAMES MARTINEAU, D.D., LL.D.

LATE PRINCIPAL OF MANCHESTER NEW COLLEGE, LONDON

Πότερον οὖν δὴ ψυχῆς γένος ἐγκρατὲς οὐρανοῦ καὶ γῆς καὶ πάσης τῆς περιόδου γεγονέναι φῶμεν, τὸ φρόνιμον καὶ ἀρετῆς πλῆρες, ἢ τὸ μηδέτερα κεκτημένον;

PLAT. *Legg.* x. 897 B

VOL. II

Oxford
AT THE CLARENDON PRESS

New York
MACMILLAN AND CO., 112 FOURTH AVENUE

1888

CONTENTS OF VOL. II.

CHAPTER II.

§ 1. *Right, as universally valid.*

As the Causal aspect of the Divine nature is opened to us by our own Will and carried out into the sphere of nature, so must we expect the *Moral* aspect to be disclosed to us by our Conscience, and applied to the relations of human life. It is Mind only that can read mind: it is Character only that can construe character; and in suffering our ethical intuitions to speak as religious interpreters, we invest them with no other prerogative than they already exercise in revealing to us the inward springs of action in our fellow men. Our order of inference therefore is still the same, from self-knowledge to divine knowledge; only that we shall now measure a different part of the base from which we work. Against the frequent objection that this is anthropomorphic logic I hope an adequate defence has already been made. The objection is in fact a piece of sheer idealistic scepticism, requiring us to treat our whole inner life as merely so many personal phenomena, and to deny that they can teach us anything beyond themselves as egoistic changes. If *there be* a world beyond the Ego, —material for Perception, moral and spiritual for the Conscience,—evidently it can be apprehended only through its relation to these powers: if it is there to speak at all, it is to them that it must speak; and to insist on its relativity to them as a reason for discharging it from existence, to distrust its voice because it is only their hearing, is to treat its self-proclamation as sufficient evidence of its non-existence, and render it impossible for it to report itself to our faculties, however real its being or intimate its presence. If you prefer to suppose that your nature deceives you, and in presenting you with what is 'other than yourself,' entertains you with dreams which are a part of yourself, there is certainly no guarantee against the possibility of such illusion: in order that you should seem to be in a universe of things, surrounded by persons, and in presence of God, it is only necessary that you should be what you are and think as you do: this would secure the semblance to you, though there were no such reality and you were alone in space. All your self-consciousness is relative, and postulates the *otherness* of the objective term of the relation: if you arbitrarily deny that postulate, I have nothing to say for it except that it is natural, inherently involved in the very law of thought itself. We have to trust something, before we can know anything; and to assume the *unveracity*, instead of the *veracity*, of the primary relations of thought is to proclaim universal agnosticism, and reduce all intellectual procedure to the analysis of personal phenomena. For reasons already assigned, we take the opposite course, and accept what each faculty reports as to its correlative term. That report is what we call *an intuition.* We have seen what it gives us in the case of *volitional* experience, viz. an *objective causality*: by a parallel presentation in the case of *moral experience*, we shall find that it gives us an *objective authority*; both alike being objects of immediate know-ledge, on the same footing of certainty as the apprehension of the external material world. This statement, however surprising to those who are unaccustomed to look into the ultimate grounds of human cognition, is deliberately made. I know of no logical advantage which the belief in finite objects around us can boast over the belief in the infinite and righteous Cause of all.

The fundamental form which the Moral Intuition assumes has been fully expounded in a previous treatise on the theory of Ethics[1], and can here only be recalled by a few words of recapitulation. Whenever two incompatible springs of action simultaneously urge us, there is an attendant consciousness of superior excellence in one of them; an excellence, not in point of pleasure or advantage which it were wise to take; not in respect to seemliness and beauty which it were tasteless to decline; but in the scale of *right*, which, in carrying our assent, commands our obedience. All these kinds of superiority it is open to us to disregard, but at the cost, in the first two cases, merely of personal *inferiority*; in the third, of a mysterious and haunting *disloyalty*. Accusing ourselves of this, we are aware that our offence is not a private mistake to be settled with in our home accounts, but looks beyond ourselves and infringes rights that are not our own; and we are visited by more than shame at failure or regret at folly; we are cast down in severe compunction under the very different sense of *guilt*. The element of value which differentiates the springs of action to the conscience, being totally unlike either the hedonistic or the æsthetic, has made a language for itself, which can be translated into no other: the superior terms in the scale do not court us by their charms and graces, but claim us by their *authority*; tell us that we *ought* to follow them; that they are *binding* on us; that they are offered to our option by a higher than we; and that in neglecting them we *sin*. To conform our voluntary life to the preferential scale of obligation, as its parts emerge into consciousness, is our *Duty*, for the observance of which we are *responsible*. This is the circle of ideas in which the Conscience lives and moves, and which supplies the moral

---

[1] Types of Ethical Theory, vol. ii. Bk. I. chapters 1 and 4.

nature with a sphere of cognition special to itself. They are intelligible to all men : they flow into every language and give it half its force and fire : they are the preamble of all Law, and the pervading essence of the higher religions. Hear the testimony of Michelet, as he sums up the results of his extensive legal researches ; ' I have studied,' he says, ' the symbols embodying the human sentiment of Rights, under the two points of view which embrace their infinite diversity, viz. their Age and their Nationality. Still, however great their variations, Unity prevails. If in the secondary forms the difference is great, it disappears in the most important. It is an impressive spectacle to see the chief legal symbols reappearing in all countries throughout all ages. There are few nations in which we do not find the marriage rite by mutual purchase (co-emptio), by the sacrificial cake (confarreatio), and conveyance of estate by delivery of a straw, of tenancy or measurement of land by the throw of a missile and riding the bounds, and alliance by libation of blood.'

' These symbols, never broken in transmission but to reappear further on, remind one of the Zend or Sanskrit words which, though without representatives in the German, turn up again in cognate or derivative tongues, in the Greek, for instance, or the English.

In truth, except to one who regards the human race as the great family of God, the central unity of his creative work and purpose, there must be something magical and dismaying to the mind, in alighting upon these voices which, out of hearing of each other, yet answer so exactly from the Indus to the Thames.'

' It is one of the features of our age, that humanity has begun to recognise a harmony in its diversity of language, law and manners, and to find in it its own self-conscious unity. This sense of humanity as one, i. e. as Divine, is to me the surest pledge of our religious re-awakening.'

'To me it was a sublime experience, when first I heard this universal chorus. So world-wide an accord, if surprising in languages, was profoundly touching to me in the expressions of Right. Reversing the sceptical inferences of Montaigne, who ferreted out so curiously the usages of all nations to detect their moral discordances, I was filled with admiration at their harmony. A miracle opened on my perception. From my little momentary existence I saw, I touched, unworthy though I be, the eternal communion of the human race[1].'

These ideas then are uniform in all men ; the seeming discrepancies of ethical judgment clearing themselves away as we push back the comparison from external actions to the internal springs, and see that the same problem is really present to the differing minds. In proportion as the springs of action have strength within us according to their worth, are we at peace with ourselves and conscious of a secret harmony. And by the same rule it is that we estimate each other ; pouring indignation on the man whom no call of compassion can snatch from his selfish ease ; watching with enthusiasm the hero from whose lips no terror can extract a betrayal or a lie ; looking up with reverence to the saintly mind in which all discords cease and the higher affections reign without dispute.

Now what means this scale of relative excellence which gives an order of rank to our impulses, and frames them into a hierarchy? Why cannot they change places, or take turn and turn about? Since they exist, have they not, one and all, a right to be? and are they not then all on a footing? What entitles any one of them to put on airs towards its companions and show them the door? Is

---

[1] Origines du Droit Français cherchées dans les Symboles et Formules du Droit Universel, par Michelet, Introduction, civ., cv. : Paris, 1837.

not this a usurpation?   And if not, what is the nature of the right?

One step in the determination of this question can be taken without challenge. The moral order is not arbitrary, in the sense of being a personal accident, an individual prejudice, got up by the subject himself and alterable fortuitously or at will. When you read of a tyrant who, travelling in winter and afraid of frost-bite, cut open a horse to warm his feet in him, your abhorrence of the wretch for preferring his comfort to his humanity is not a matter of taste, like your preference of pheasants' feathers to peacocks' or of peaches to pine-apple : it is neither, like these, contingent in yourself on sensible conditions, nor reversed or absent in others' minds : it exists irremoveably in each, and with consensus in all ; attended by the feeling, which belongs to no personal judgment, that to think otherwise would involve an unspeakable shame, the guilt of taking sides against an everlasting Right. It is the peculiarity of all properly moral verdicts, that they are not the expression of individual opinions which we work out for ourselves by sifting of evidence ; but the enunciation of what is given us ready-made and has only to pass through us into speech. We may indeed debate within ourselves the claims presented in this or that example of outward conduct, because the choice of action has to be determined not only by the principle that issues it, but by the effects that follow it : these are amenable to the calculus of the understanding, without resort to which the action cannot be *rational* ; but so long as the prior problem is before us, of securing the right spring of conduct, we have nothing to seek by logical process, but only to give forth what we find. Here, where alone truly *moral* judgment resides, we are but organs of what is deposited with us ; to pretend that we are concerned with its fabrication and must speak diffidently of its probability, is quite out of

place : the real arrogance lies in mixing ourselves up with
it and delivering it as *our* opinion ; the true humility, in
simply repeating the sentence which it has been given us
to know. In other words, the Moral Law (for such is the
'Canon of principles' taken as a whole) is *imposed by an
authority foreign to our personality*, and is open, not to be
canvassed, but only to be obeyed or disobeyed.

§ 2. *Right, by Social Vote.*

Of that foreign authority a plausible account is given by
writers who treat it as an embodiment of 'public opinion,'
an ideal aggregate of sentiment made up of all the praise
and blame which men bestow on what helps or hurts their
interests. Nothing, it is said, is so important to us as the
estimate formed of us by our fellows : the saddest heart
grows light with their approval, and the most joyous sinks
before their frown ; and when they have coined all language
in the moulds of their fancy, and sent it forth to circulate
the gold of their admiration and the brass of their contempt ; when we have had through life to think through
the inheritance of their thought, and have gained no idea
of life and conduct, through conversation, through books,
through art, without the colouring of their love or hatred ;
nay more, when we have been born with our very organism
predisposed, by the habits of generations, to repeat their
feelings with a strength enhanced ; what wonder if we are
subject to modes of judgment which we know to be not
our own, and in which we recognise a decision larger and
more august ? That which they have stamped as wrong,
what magic glass have we to reverse into the right ? What
is our puny voice against the solemn roll of all the ages ?
If we even tried a different tone, we should have to repent
and fall into the great accord. This massive vote it is
which is the objective shadow overawing your heart : your
sense of 'responsibility' is the secret dread lest you offend

it, and draw its darkness on you ; and your 'remorse' is the despair of an exile driven from the commonwealth of sentiment by folly of his own. The essence of this explanation is, that Social Rule, constituted out of accumulated reckoning of human interests, makes the Moral Law, and enforces it by fear, sympathy, and heritage on the individual mind. The single Conscience is the product of the cumulative Public feeling ; and that feeling, in its original ingredients, is *prudential,* aiming, with more or less consciousness, to secure advantages and patronise the disposition to reproduce them. The countless threads of the universal self-love weave themselves into the sense of duty of which we are conscious, one by one.

In thus sending the individual to the Public school for his rudiments of ethical sentiment, our psychologist is apt to forget that this school itself is already composed of individuals, who either have or have not a moral sense to begin with. If they have, if the Rule which they render venerable is one which they venerate, then the Conscience which they create is but an extension of their own, and they are themselves examples of the very phenomenon which they are cited to call into being. They too inwardly bend before an authority foreign to themselves, whisper the secret to each other, and report it to their children. And we need not doubt that this transmitted moral experience gains in depth and volume as it passes from life to life ; for all *natural feeling* potentially sleeps in every mind and springs up in response to some appeal ; and as words of admiration and abhorrence gather around character and conduct in literature and history, and the voices of a thousand witnesses give courage to our own, the Sense of Right cannot fail to obtain a range and speak with a decision greater than before. This is but the unfolding of a given nature from its germ to its maturity,—the growth of the seed-scale into the cedar of Lebanon. But if the constituent

individuals are to be conceived as made of only self-love
and passions all equal in their rights, and if all that they
can do is to insist upon what they like, then from such
materials a million years will no more generate a conscience
than they will raise a cedar of Lebanon from a chalk stone.
We have learned to make light of the boundaries of *species*;
but no evidence yet carries us through such a transition
in aliud genus. I can understand how 'Society,' taking the
individual in hand, can create a *Must* for him ; but not
how it can create an *Ought* ; and as self-interest, by which
alone it works, does not begin to be anything else by length
of days, but only becomes a swifter thought and easier
habit of the same type, it is useless to borrow millenniums
in order to turn it into Duty.   Those who have at command
a stock of fears and hopes may doubtless, if they can adequately agree on what they want, extort obedience from
one who would not spontaneously do as they desire, and
may vote into existence a rule from which there shall be
no escape : but what relation is there between this coercion
of Law and a conviction of Conscience?   By making it a
man's *interest* to be *disinterested*, do you cause him to forget himself and put any love into his heart ? or do you only
break him in and teach him to turn this way and that by
the bit and lash of a driving necessity ?   Even if we set to
work the overtasked doctrine of the association of ideas,
and avail ourselves of the Hartleian 'law of transference'
which hands over the attractions of the primitive pleasures
to their causes, and enamours us of things at first indifferent;
if we suppose ourselves thus to grow *fond of the dispositions*
which *lead to actions* which *win approbation* which *promises
or symbolizes favours and rewards* ; still we make no
approach to any moral idea ; we are only fascinated instead
of forced ; a new taste or affection is formed which leaves
the original tendency far behind ; but should it ever be
baffled by some rude return of the 'old Adam,' there is no

reason here why we should feel such a thing as *compunction*, more than in any other case of disappointed affection. Surely it is not enough to say, with Mr. Darwin, that this is due to our having indulged the intenser momentary impulse which has now faded, at the cost of a persistent feeling which has returned to its usual force. This difference may exist without inducing any sense of sin : if, in some whim of colour-fancy, I choose for my drawing-room a wall-paper to which I permanently prefer another previously rejected in the same lot, I may be sorry for my mistake ; but my regret has in it no tincture of *remorse*. Nor does it seem to me true that, as this explanation requires, self-reproach arises only as an *after-thought*, on the return of a more durable feeling in place of a temporary one. If you are afflicted with a disputatious nagging temper that always bids for the last word, may you not, in some altercation with your friend, persist in saying rude and stinging things, while all the time you are inwardly ashamed, and your heart is weeping with the very love which you are bruising? In such case, it is not that you are successively occupied first by the transient and then by the permanent tendency ; but that of two, which are both present and alike permanent, you simultaneously surrender yourself to the more importunate, and remorsefully condemn it as the worse.

It is chiefly in the school of Hobbes that psychological attempts have been made to deduce the moral sentiments from the self-regards of collective man, and resolve all objective authority into Social opinion. There is no neater or better defended exposition of the doctrine than that in which it is given by James Mill, in whom the logical vigour, analytical precision, and firm consistency of that school appear to me to culminate : though the later treatment of the same topics by his son and by Bain has a greater scope and ampler illustration, it is watered down, in order to wash out its blots, into a comparatively flaccid condition, too yielding for either attack or defence. In his ' Fragment on Mackintosh ' (p. 389), Mill assumes that ' pleasure to the agent is the end of all action,' and divides all 'useful acts' into two classes, viz. those which, being agreeable to the agent, he will perform of his own accord ; and those which, being otherwise, he must be artificially induced to perform. Now, having a strong interest in extorting these latter, we have hit upon an artifice successful for the purpose ; we annex rewards to these actions and penalties to their neglect ; or, we may find it sufficient to hold out hopes of reward and fears of penalty; or even simply to *praise* on the one hand and *blame* on the other ; these minor methods operating on the mind as *symbols of a disposition* to give pleasure or pain. To visit conduct thus is to exercise ' *the moral senti-ments* '; which are therefore a contrivance adopted for securing beneficial actions that would else have no cause of existence; a social ' *demand* ' set up, in order to secure a ' *supply*.' When this device of praise and blame has become established and been often enough applied to us by others, we learn to practise the trick upon ourselves ; we find our-selves approving or disapproving our own conduct, and playing the part of judges towards all that issues from our will. This, however, is only a secondary extension of judicial feeling, a borrowing of the demeanour of our fellows towards us by way of rehearsal, to test the look of what we do ; but ' the words *moral* and *immoral* were applied by men, primarily, not to their own acts, but the acts of others.' Had they not judged us, we should never have been able to judge ourselves: it is by ideally assuming their position and clothing ourselves with their sentiments that we become objects of self-reflection, and fancy ourselves tried by some other tribunal than theirs.

If we reduce this theory to its shortest terms, it resolves itself into three constituent propositions :

(1) Self-love, or the idea of a pleasure to one's self, is the sole spring of action.

(2) Joint or collective self-interest sets up a public demand for actions not pleasant to the agent; and this public demand is *moral sentiment.*

(3) An ideal adoption, by the individual agent of this public demand, is *Conscience.*

A thorough scrutiny of this theory would require a whole treatise on Moral Philosophy. For our purpose it will be sufficiently answered by showing

I. That the first proposition is not true :

II. That if it were true, yet would the second proposition be false :

III. That even though the first and second were true, yet the third would be inadmissible.

I. For the disproof of the first proposition I must be content to refer to the chapter in 'Types of Ethical Theory' which treats of the Springs of action [1]. Reasons are there given for distinguishing a *Primary* class, whose characteristic it is to be *disinterested*, that is, to impel us forward upon an action or an object suited to that part of our nature, without preconception of the experience it will bring : the object is not wanted because it gives pleasure ; it gives pleasure because it is wanted. We cannot begin to act with a view to our own feelings until we have had them and learned how to procure them ; and this is a lesson of experience which only long activity, supplied from a different source, is qualified to give. No moral quality attaches to this absence of self-regard from our primary impulses ; it simply detains them on the *instinctive level*, prior to their admission into the voluntary life ; and belongs alike to the animal propensions and to the highest tendencies of human nature. But when, in surveying the Primary

---

[1] Types of Ethical Theory, vol. ii. Bk. I. ch. v. 1.

springs of action, we reach the *personal affections*, this disinterestedness means that we have forms of *altruistic love*
which are original, and not the product of double distilled
self-consideration ; and at this point it is that the fact, if
such it be, assumes its bearing upon moral theory. If there
be a Parental, a Social, a Compassionate affection, just as
much *given* in our nature as the self-seeking desire, there
are more elements to go into the ethical organism of
thought than James Mill has allowed. And that it is so,
the plainest facts of life, not only human but simply animal,
incontestably declare. Watch the swallow's nest when the
young bird has been hatched, or go to the kennel excited
by the arrival of new puppies ; and if you do not learn a
lesson of maternity that laughs away your doctrine of self-
love, you must be very philosophical ; nay, if you can take
Hartley, Mill or Bain, and read on the spot their psychological history of the devotion to offspring, without any
sense of its humorous effect, your gravity must be truly
scholastic. And if you study a community of beavers, or a
rookery, by the light of Hobbes's Leviathan, or Mill on
government, I shall be surprised if you discover even why
the creatures like to be together, and do their work with a
stimulating mixture of co-operation and rivalry. We have
no hesitation in speaking of the family and the associative
affections in these tribes, as instinctive ; and to deny them
such a character in man, is an arbitrary refusal to follow
the obvious pointing of analogy. Neither in human consciousness, nor in the phenomena of animal life, is there the
slightest ground for assigning priority to the self-seeking
desires, and treating all extra-regarding affections as derivative from them. Instead of admitting that pleasure sets
up all our springs of action, I affirm that the springs of
action set up all our pleasures.

II. Next, were this starting point of Mill's ever so well
secured, it would not help him to his second position, viz.

that by aggregation, the self-love of each man will establish
a common rule, and flow into a common moral sentiment
for all.   By the hypothesis, the actions which this rule is to
produce are those in which the interest of the individual
agent is at variance with that of his fellows ; and they take
him in hand to remedy this clashing by putting artificial
pressure on him, through the hopes and fears which are at
their command.   And when you represent the conflict as
lying between a consentaneous multitude, intent upon a
given thing, and a solitary agent who does not want to
concede it, it seems an easy task for the major power to
enforce its will, and to provide for future cases by giving
notice that the coercion will be repeated, if necessary ; and
such notice it is, covering a whole class of actions, that
Mill identifies with a moral law.   He thinks that, because
men like to be benefited, nothing is more natural than for
them to set up a rule demanding useful services, to applaud
him who renders them, and make him who withholds them
smart for his reluctance.   And so it would be, if the voters who
create the rule could be sure of always occupying the position
which now recommends it : could they but entrench
themselves through life as recipients of services from others,
their self-love would be quite competent to the framing an
altruistic law.   But there is no such stereotyped relation
between the many and the one ; every man of the majority
is liable to change places with the neighbour from whom
he extorts the sacrifice : the rule which he makes in his
own favour to-day may be pressed against him to-morrow ;
and before he passes it he has to think, not simply whether
he likes to be benefited, but just as much whether he likes
benefiting ; for to *this* he commits himself by the very vote
which he gives to bind another.   As human relations are
reciprocal, and each person performs as many acts as he
receives, the debtor and creditor account of such a rule
answer to each other, and there is not even a balance on

his side.   Is it then so certain into which urn he casts his
bean ?

In order to represent the problem truly, we must picture
to ourselves not a united multitude on one side and an
individual or a few on the other ; but two persons, planted
on the stage in a position to become respectively benefactor
and beneficiary ; in the midst of a theatre of neutral spectators or dikasts ; all present being assumed to be furnished
with no spring of action except self-love, and to be aware
that, except by contravening this principle, the benefit
proposed cannot be rendered.   Suppose that, under these
conditions, the benefactor makes the sacrifice and gladdens
the heart of his beneficiary : what will be the effect on 'the
house'?   You say, the spectators will clap ; and so they
will, if they are made as you are ; but if you will cut yourself down to Mill's pattern, and think how things would
look in the eye of a solitary, all-interpreting self-love, you
will be at a loss for a reason to justify such applause.   Why
should they praise Andrew for doing good to Luke ?   Do
you say, because they may be in Luke's case next week,
and would be glad of such treatment ?   Yes ; but they
may as probably be in Andrew's place, and not be so glad
to incur his sacrifice.   Or do you say, they sympathise
with Luke's gain of pleasure ?   Without pausing to wonder
how any such feeling can run the blockade of self-love,
which by hypothesis was to be close and absolute, we must
ask, why not sympathise with Andrew's loss of pleasure ?
Perhaps you will reply, this also they do, in due measure ;
but inasmuch as the gain on the one side exceeds the loss
on the other, does their preponderating feeling go with the
beneficiary's advantage.   If, however, that sympathy follows
this preponderance, and takes proportion from it, their
maximum of praise will be given to Andrew when, at the
smallest cost to himself, he purchases the vastest benefit to
Luke ; and if ever he makes a great effort to give his friend

a little relief, their approval becomes a minus quantity. It is needless to say that our natural admiration is measured by the reverse rule ; being hardly stirred at all by a trifling outlay for a mighty gift, but intensely moved by the self-forgetful love which would venture all to ward off a transient danger or sorrow from another,—offering the full young life to save the remnant of the old,—or spending the rich and noble nature to redeem the base. The more a man gives up in order to render a service to others, and the less importunately urgent that service is, the more do we appreciate his conduct. I conclude then (as I have elsewhere said) that for our jury of selfish spectators to resolve on applauding the benefactor would ' involve the renunciation by public vote of the very principle on which alone that vote is assumed to be taken[1].'

There are other evidences of the incompetency of self-interest to create the law and sentiments of Right. Canons of approbation and disapprobation, it is said, are voted into existence, in order to eke out the deficient supply of spontaneous useful actions. The more therefore this deficiency is experienced, the more active will be the fabrication, and the more urgent the pressure of these rules : in proportion as spontaneous services cease, and the stagnation of selfishness threatens to become universal, will the compensating artifice be set to work, and laws of duty grow stringent, and moral opinion become loud. In short, morality, as we have said, would carry its tides hither and thither by the scale of demand and supply. But does social experience conform to such a rule ? Is general self-seeking found to be the prelude to Stoical rigour and ethical enthusiasm ?

---

[1] Types of Ethical Theory, vol. ii. Bk. II. Branch I. ch. i. ii. § 2. I might perhaps have contented myself with referring the reader to the discussion of Mill's theory contained in the section here cited. But he will not, I trust, be displeased to have the case reproduced with variations of method and pleading.

Does prevalent neglect of mutual services oscillate by re-action into disinterestedness and the sense of responsibility? On the contrary, in the moral life, like tends to generate like with a rapidity frightful in one direction, glorious in the other. Selfishness produces selfishness; benevolence answers to benevolence; the one is simply repulsive and establishes universal insulation; the other is attractive and flows into social coalescence. The former, instead of stimulating us to repair its own defects and cultivate by a forced growth what it does not itself supply, induces us perpetually to lower our demands upon each other, and, by tacit conspiracy against inconvenient pretensions, to treat the very idea of disinterestedness with more and more of cynical contempt. And even if, in descending to this state, we pass through a stage of exaction, when the vigilance of each against the encroachments of the rest raises eager complaints and peremptory demands, the success with which they are brought to bear upon some reluctant will tends only to make it more recalcitrant, and remove it further from any spontaneous reproduction of serviceable acts. And where, on the other hand, is the standard of moral demand for beneficent action at its highest point? Is it not where it most freely arises of its own accord, and least requires any artificial appliances of social pressure?—among communities in which works of mercy and willing sacrifice are habitual? There surely it is that such acts enter most largely into the ideal of the perfect life, and are secured by the strongest guard of moral sentiment. Yet precisely there, because they never fail to come of themselves, the very cause of moral sentiment, according to Mill, is cut off, and its appearance would be impossible. The principle of his analysis must be reversed: it is not the need, but the supply, of disinterested service that multiplies it in action and invests it with enthusiasm in thought.

Again: if beneficent acts were elicited, when not recommended by self-interest, through the exhibition or suggestion of hope and fear, those persons would secure the most of them who had command of the largest army of hopes and fears.   For the amplest and most constant outpouring of disinterestedness we should have to resort to the palaces of the affluent and powerful, and, throughout society, to the patrons in the midst of their clients ; for it is upon inferiors that coercive rules can be brought to bear ; it is for inferiors who can be made amenable that they are framed.   How completely is this at variance with fact !   *Services,* no doubt, the rich and great can readily procure ; but *friends, disinterested helpers,* are not usually supposed to throng around their persons as their most congenial resort.   The importance of their favour, the value of their praise, constitute a hindrance, instead of an aid, to the growth in their vicinity of any true social and moral sentiment ; so that all good offices rendered to them are suspected of selfishness, precisely because they have so copiously at their disposal the very instruments which are said to conquer it.   And conversely, where are the centres of attraction that draw to them the most constant flow of self-forgetful acts ?   In the cradle of the infant, the infirmary of disease, at the couch of sinking age,—wherever lie the poor sufferers who have neither good nor ill at their disposal, whose only power is in their helplessness, and whose sole return of praise is in their eye of trust and smile of thankfulness.   This is just what we should expect, if Pity were the ever-ready medicine of nature for human ills, set to flow at the very look of a weakness or a wound that needed it ; but would be impossible, if it were the last transformation of refined self-interest, elaborated by social artifice into a useful superstition.

For these reasons I submit that, with the datum of individual self-love, we cannot reach the moral law and judicial sentiment which we apply to the conduct of others.

The ethical facts of life evidently rest upon a wider and a different base.

III. Finally, even if this theory gave a true account of the origin of rules of conduct, and of our judgments upon others, it would not explain our self-judgment, that is, the phenomena of *Conscience*. Here, the fact from which we start is, that we approve or condemn others, and others approve or condemn us. The fact at which we have to arrive is, that we approve or condemn ourselves ; and the problem is to find a path of transition from the one to the other. I affirm that no such path can be found.

If indeed you interpret conscience into bare *fears*, and take self-judgment to mean no more than the consciousness of what men think of us and are inclined to do to us, there is no difficulty in showing how this state of mind comes about from the supposed antecedents. It is merely that the human criticism of conduct, which we have learned to understand, we perceive to be directed upon ourselves, and we feel the smart of others' displeasure, or the satisfaction of their good-will. Here there is nothing more than the recognition, *as a fact*, of others' opinion, favourable or un-favourable ; there is no self-judgment : for this it would be necessary that, besides knowing what others think, we think the same ourselves. To conscience we do not come, till we visit our behaviour with approval or with blame, as the critical observer visits it : this is the phenomenon of which we seek the explanation.

It evidently cannot have the same origin that Mill assigns to the spectator's praise and blame, viz. the deter-mination to extort actions which would not else be issued. No such device of patronage and discouragement can we play off towards our own acts, in order to eke out the defective inducements to their performance or suppression : even if we could invent such fictitious feelings, we should have no reason for allotting them to this rather than to that, were not actions already discriminated as fit or unfit to receive them. The supposition involves a conscience behind the conscience, and so defeats its own end.

Not having a parallel source with others' sentiments about us, our self-judgment must be derivative from them; it must be that we imitate, with respect to our own conduct, the demeanour which we observe or believe in our neighbours towards it, and play the echo to their voice. This accordingly is the order of origination accepted by the moralists whom we are reviewing. The world's presumed sentence upon us is the determining prototype of all our inward awards of censure or approval : we transpose ourselves into the bystanders' position and observe ourselves thence : we understand how they must feel towards our behaviour : we sympathise with their view : we adopt it : we administer to ourselves the same punishment or reward which would await us at their hands ; and this is what we call the compunction or satisfaction of conscience. It could have no existence, were there not bystanders to judge us first. Nay, so dependent are we, it is said, on the external aspect for our power of estimating conduct that, in difficult cases, we cannot inwardly decide on the right course, except by imagining how this or that alternative would look, if it were taken up and realized. So we plant before us a representative or duplicate ego, as an artist sets his lay-figure ; and, opening our wardrobe of resources, dress him up in our own moral clothes, and, adjusting him into suitable attitudes, retire to the critic's distance to see how far they are becoming to one who is thus placed ; and according to the happy or disappointing fit, we take the costume or change it. The inward decision is but the copy of the outward.

Now in order that this analysis should be true and adequate, there is one condition obviously necessary, viz. that the objective and subjective principles of judgment should *not conflict.* They must be of the same kind, and capable of concurrence ; or the one kind could never take counsel of the other, receive help from it, and adopt it as decisive. I should never shift my position into yours in order to judge myself aright, unless your view were assumed to be my own, only clearer and freer from refraction. Even if I had no view at all corresponding to yours, I might possibly borrow yours mimetically, and act as if I had it ; but only if I were blank towards it, and it met in me with nothing to contradict or resist it. In the doctrine which James Mill represents, this condition is violated. The individual judgment and the social are not in harmony, but at variance; and the resultant is not their sum but their difference. Interest, he tells us, is the sole guide of action : if all interests harmonised, there would be no rules of conduct ; it is only in the case of clashing interests that moral judgment comes into play ; so that whenever I conform to an obligation on which others insist, I have to surrender my own point of view in order to adopt theirs. Instead of reconciling the two and reading their verdicts as identical, I sacrifice one of them to avoid collision with the other ; or, if I have refused the sacrifice, then, putting myself by an effort of ideal sympathy into the place of the bystanders, I make confession to this effect, 'Yes, *if I were you*, I should find fault with this act of mine.' This concession, of a right of censure on the part of others, is all that can be extorted from my assumption of the spectator's station ; and this is not *self-blame* ; for, as *I am not you*, but occupy the antago-nistic position to you, the hypothesis fails which alone would turn it into self-blame. It is not therefore *conscience* which is thus explained ; for the self-condemnation which it involves hinges upon no '*If*,' and least of all is conditional on Ego being a non-Ego, but fastens with terrible grasp upon the past reality of my own Will : it needs no change of place with any public, but rather sinks into solitude and becomes more articulate as the voices of men cease to be heard. The question is, why, *remaining in propriâ personâ*, that is, at the very opposite point of clashing interest to that which justifies the critic, I blame myself, just as he blames me, only with the intenser bitterness of contrition. There is no collision of judgment between us : disapprove me as he may, I have anticipated him, and he can only tell me the story which I have already heard in silence ; and the whole power of rebuke depends on its simply giving external voice to the inward shame and grief of conscious sin. Far from having to take the observer's place before I can condemn my own wrongdoing, my recognition of guilt is more apt to enliven itself by the inverse transposi-tion : what exclamation can be more natural, on witnessing a moral offence, than this, ' How I should reproach myself, if I were he ! ' And what makes us put it in this way, if it be not that, in order to have the disapprobation of wrong keen and clear in my thought, I must take my stand *within the mind of the offender* ; and that, till I get out of the spectator's station, and identify myself with the agent's consciousness, I am at one remove from the native home of all compunction ? While this is the order of originality and intensity between the private and the public sentence, the two are distinguished by no other contrast, and bear no marks of contrariety. In the agent and in the spectators the sincere conscience has but one verdict to give ;—a fact which, through all the conflict of interests, constitutes a reserved and secret source of moral harmony. This is intelligible, if the moral scale is indigenous in each of us, and needs only interpretation to be concurrent in all. But it would be impossible, if, in its very essence, morality expressed nothing but the opposition between the indivi-dual and his community, and embodied only the pressure of the latter against the will of the former. For these reasons I find nothing satisfactory in the attempt to construe the solemn authority of duty into the incubus of social necessity.

Though however our present moral intuitions are thus far provided with no adequate history, we are not entitled to infer that they can have no history at all. And before we can use them for any ontological purpose, there remains a wider question for discussion : suppose them to have some other mode of genesis,—which may perhaps be hit upon after many unsuccessful attempts,—and to have reached their present state through an indefinite series of infinitesimal changes, in the earlier stages of which their existing characteristics were not noticeable at all ; would this discovery discredit these characteristics, and abrogate the 'foreign authority' which they seem to carry? In other words, if the evolution theory should find the antecedents of Conscience, not only, like the psychologists, within the life of the individual, but through all prior generations till beyond the range of ethical phenomena altogether, should we thereby lose the right of drawing conclusions from our own moral constitution to a corresponding governance of the world ? Is it necessary, for such conclusion, that the human conscience should *have no growth*, but appear at once in ready-made perfection ? To judge from the alarm excited by the modern doctrine of development, this is the prevailing assumption. How little it will bear examination, a few obvious considerations will show.

(1) However far you may carry your belief in the originality of conscience, you cannot (unless indeed you have recourse to the hypothesis of the pre-existence of souls) assign it a date earlier than that of the man in whom it is planted ; nor can you exempt it from the process of genesis and growth by which he is brought to the birth and gradually matured. Quick and unerring as are now the decisions of the solemn Rhadamanthus within him, there was a time in his history when he was quite blank to right and wrong,

and the rudiments of moral good were as foreign to him as
to the kitten or the calf. Nor can you say that the transition from the earlier to the later condition was effected *per
saltum* at any moment assignable or unassignable, so that
at a stroke the blind man saw, and the dumb spake. On
the contrary, no change can well be more gradual than the
dawning of moral light upon the consciousness, or more
certainly dependent on two concomitant conditions, viz. a
certain stage of physical development, and the presence of
certain mental or disciplinary influences to play upon the
inchoate susceptibilities as they emerge. The infant is
there, tossed about as the mere plaything of his own
instincts, long before the will is born which is to set them
in order and hold them to their relative place ; and, after
it has appeared, it is entrusted with a very little through a
probationary term, ere it is made master over its ten cities.
These indisputable facts constitute an evolution of conscience in the individual by increments scarcely perceptible,
starting from zero, and accumulating to the full proportions
of a responsible nature. And this history in no way disturbs our faith in the validity of those moral intuitions into
which it lifts us at last.

(2) Would, then, the case be essentially altered if the
same person lived on and enlarged his inward and outward
experience through thousands of years ; winning new
springs of action and finer discernment of their claims?
Is not this progressive education of the moral nature
a recognised element in the ideal image of the heavenly
life? Nay, is continuity of life conceivable at all without
such process of expanding growth? In the case of the
intellectual faculties, it is impossible to conceive of their
existing and operating at all without constant increase in
their range and refinement : their very life is itself development ; nor do we throw doubt on the latest apprehensions of the Reason, on the ground that they have

been reached through inferior antecedent stages. They
are none the less accepted as light, from their emerging
out of darkness. A confidence precisely similar does a
conscience merit, which in like manner has had its beginning and passed through its day of small things to its ripe
sense of duty. And if this is true in principle, it can make
no difference whether the evolution be long or short, compressed within the term of a generation or spread over
reaches of geological time. There is something intelligible
in an objection to phenomenal variation at all, in the
longing to find some eternal entity on which to rest secure.
But when once you are in the region of genesis, it is
childish to lay stress on the *rate and measure* of change,
complacently accepting it if brief and rapid, but panic-
stricken if it slowly march through the ages.

(3) But perhaps it makes a difference that, instead of
the same person continuing his education through many
a millennium, he is removed, and the process passes
through a series of descendants, each of whom, while
forming a link in the continuity, has his separate individuality. If we try to define the difference thus introduced
into our previous hypothesis, it resolves itself into two
elements; (1) Of the modifying conditions, physical and
psychical, which conduct the evolution of growing character, the former are transmitted by inheritance and suffer
no interruption by the change of generations; while the
latter, the training by persons around,—must be begun
over again with every child, and will be for the most part
a repetition of what has been done before, instead of carrying on the process from the point which the parent had
reached. The continuity therefore is reduced by one half;
holding on to the line of the bodily constitution, but
broken off on the mental side by the fresh start of education which each young nature requires. (2) While one
long-lived individual could register or remember the steps

and story of his growth, or at least be aware of them as
they pass, the interposition of death cuts the self-knowledge short by change of persons: each new comer is
unconscious of his predecessor's history, though carrying
its vestiges in his organism. He relates his autobiography
as if it were complete between its beginning and its end;
though it is but a chapter of a larger and interminable
life. The latter of these differences may hide from him
the antecedents of his present intuitions, and induce him
to regard them as indigenous to his insulated nature. But
if they were so, this suddenness of origin supplies no more
ground for taking them as true, than would exist if they
came by degrees, and had a history before they arrived
at him. The immediate judgments involved in the exercise of my own faculties I have in any case to trust;
whether they got there in my time or before, is a matter
of no significance; and it will not frighten me in the least
to show me an ancestor in the 5000th generation *a parte
ante*, who had no notion of them: I shall be sorry for his
venerable ignorance, but shall not put out my own light
in filial sympathy with his darkness. If we were to throw
away our ultimate psychological trust and to play with
the hypothesis that perhaps nature may deceive us, her
trick might just as conceivably be practised upon us at
a stroke within our own constitution, as elaborated with
persistent unveracity trailing on through all the ages.
Nature is as worthy of trust in her processes as in her
gifts. And as the later stadia of her developments rise
above the earlier, we have less reason to fear error in their
issues than in their elements; and instead of going back
to the rudiments of conscience for the measure of its truth,
may confide rather in the final oracles of its experience.

My protest, then, against James Mill's theory is not that
he evolves conscience, instead of treating it as innate; but
that what he evolves is not conscience at all; and that

the process by which he obtains his product, in missing the real conscience, exhibits it as an illusion, and eviscerates moral language of all its meaning. If he merely insisted that sensation came before reflection, instinct before will, snatching at pleasure before foregoing it, and found the order of sequence among such phenomena, his mode of exposition would be legitimate. But when he treats affection as self-love under a mask, and duty as interest artificially created, and admiration and reverence as an outlook for future favours, and contrition as the false fancy of a possibility lost, and resolves all that is more than this into an unreal and sentimental halo, then, even supposing his psychology to be right, he is measuring the end by the beginning, and assuming that no new thing has arisen between them, only that the old elements have been playing hide and seek with each other. To this it is that I must object. The growth of the human mind is not like a process of cookery or chemistry, in which ingredients are compounded, and under every transformation may be recovered by analysis without anything over: as it advances it is not only *other* than it was, but *more*; and, to come to our present problem, *conscience*, as compared with its antecedents, is a fact altogether fresh, having a language of its own, which is not to be construed back into the blunt maxims of ruder faculties. In short, I admit that a new thing may come by degrees. I deny that what comes by degrees cannot be new.

We may dismiss, then, the doctrine that the foreign authority which imposes the Moral Law is nothing but the gigantesque shadow of Social opinion looming fearfully upon our thought. The springs of action are not differenced merely by men's interested preferences among them; but have an order of claim which is sealed in the constitution of things, and belongs to them wherever they appear on the theatre of a voluntary nature. It is admitted on all hands that these inherent differences between right and wrong, being more than subjective fancies, are reported to us and urged upon us by *some objective power* with which their validity is identified; and the self-interest of Society is not that power.

§ 3. *Right, as the Divine in the Human.*

Whither then must we turn to find our informant? How do we come to know the scale of moral differences?

It is not enough for us simply *to have* the springs of action operative within us. The brutes have several of them without attaining to any moral knowledge. And we might remain equally in the dark, though subject to them all, if they occupied us one at a time, so as to challenge no comparison; or if, being present together, they stood related to our feeling only by their intensity. But this is not all that they have to say to us: while affected by their degree of intensity, we are also conscious of their competitive worth. This is a perfectly distinct relation to our feeling: a concomitant immediate apprehension or intuition which it is equally impossible to escape and to explain. Am I told that this is not philosophy, but mystery? I reply, It is *both*; and the mystery is no more than we have to encounter in dealing with any other mode of communication between an object and the subject. The cognitions we gain through the ordinary exercise of the Senses are perfectly analogous, in their mode of origin, to those which come to us through the moral faculty. In the act of Perception, we are immediately introduced to an *other than ourselves that gives us what we feel*: in the act of Conscience, we are immediately introduced to a *Higher than ourselves that gives us what we feel*: the externality in the one case, the authority in the other, the causality in both, are known upon exactly the same terms, and carry the same guarantee of their validity. I grant that that guarantee resolves itself, as it must in all cases of first-hand knowledge, into the postulate of the veracity of our faculties; but I affirm that nothing more is needed for this moral revelation than the same fundamental faith on which all our physical knowledge rests. The dualism of perception, which sets ourselves in the face of an objective world, and the dualism of Conscience which sets us in the face of an objective higher mind, are perfectly analogous in their grounds. The religious intimation is not contained in the mere fact, that there is a graduated worth among our inward springs of action; but in the further fact, that the superiors among them lay claim to our will with an authority that is above us, and that presents them as mere delegates of itself. For our æsthetic faculty also there is given a differential scale of beauty, higher and lower; but here, the gradations remain upon the level of ideal facts, and do not rise into imperative Law, subjecting us to a transcendent relation that asks the sacrifice of ourselves. It is the specific sense of *Duty* that constitutes a dual relation and cannot belong to a soul in vacuo, and must be for ever a disconsolate and wandering illusion, till it rests with Him to whom the allegiance is due. In other words, the Moral Law first reaches its integral meaning, when seen as impersonated in a Perfect Mind, which communicates it to us, and lends it power over our affections sufficient to draw us into Divine communion. How else could it transcend our whole personality as it does, and haunt us with tones from beyond and above? If our humanity were at the summit, and, in passing further, we emerged into blank silence, how could these subduing voices flow thence upon the heart? They attest a speaking nature there, that bids us feel as it feels and become the organ of its thought; a nature that, appealing to us from a superhuman height, cannot be less than a conscious will, but simply a personal and holy Mind; and that, reporting

to us a Law which holds for all thinking and voluntary
beings, is universal and supreme.   Here at last and here
alone does the objective authority of what the inward conscience tells find its explanation and its home ; and hither
it is that we are brought, in proportion as our self-knowledge is deep, and our moral ideal is lofty and complete.
I care not whether this be called an *immediate vision* of
God in the experiences of conscience ; or whether it be
taken as *an inference* drawn from the data they supply.
It is the truth contained in them : with one man it may
be only implicitly felt in their solemn and mystic character;
with another, explicitly and immediately seen emerging
from them as they come, and making him the Seer of God
rather than the reasoner about him.   In any case, the constitution of our moral nature is unintelligible, except as
living in response to an objective Perfection pervading the
universe with Holy Law.

There are certain aspects of our inward and outward
experience which are so accordant with this interpretation
of our conscience, that it may gain some fresh light by
being brought into their presence.

For our true moral life and education, we are dependent
on the presence of some nature higher than our own ;
without which the mere subjective feeling of relative worth
among the springs of action would rarely pass from knowledge into power.   All the Dynamics of character are born
of inequality, and lie asleep amid unbroken equilibrium.
To mingle only with those on the same level with ourselves and encounter nothing but ethical self-repetitions,
is the surest way to stunt the possibilities of growth ; nor
does any activity of the retired and solitary mind, though
given to subjects deep and high, avail to carry its affections
to greater altitudes.   If your whole past could be laid open,
where would you find its moments of purest consecration,
of fresh insight into duty, and willing love to follow it?

Not, I believe, when you were criticising a creed or con-
structing a philosophy, though with the simplest aim at
truth: not when working out the contents of some comprehensive precept, though you owned its obligation: not
when some crisis of danger brought you face to face with
the alternatives of an eternal state, though you deemed
them solemn and at hand: but when first there stood near
you some transparent nature, nobler, simpler, purer than
yourself, that fixed your eye and compelled you to look
up. This loving wonder at some impersonated goodness
is the sole attraction to which we rise: this it is which
sprinkles us with a wave of true regeneration. Let me
privately watch one who healthily does what, in sickness
of will, I ignominiously neglect, and he becomes to me as
a glance of heaven, pursuing me with a just severity.
Or let me sit by some worn-out sufferer, from whose
features the lines of pain cannot efface their sweet composure, and listen to the tones of settled trust, passing like
music across the fretfulness of happier lives; and it is in
vain, when I go home, to hide myself from the Omniscient
look: the inner meaning of existence has burst upon me:
the meanness of my selfish cares astonishes me with
shame: and I sink upon the compassion of God to make
my own mind nobler, and my brother's cross more light.
Nor, for the exercise of such influence, need it be a greater,
if only it be a better, spirit that appeals to us. Even the
guileless suggestions of a child's conscience, or the reveren-
tial efforts of his will, have often extorted penitential tears
from parents who had forgotten such simplicity and truth.
Among those who have had any deep moral history at all,
there are probably few who, on looking back to the sources
of their first high faith, do not see the sainted image of
some companion or guide, whose like they never think to
meet again, and through whose spirit, to the end, they will
not cease to gaze at life. To others, less happy in their

living friendships, the new birth may have come from some image of ideal excellence in the pages of biography or fiction; for though here the voices and stir of reality do not beat upon the ear, conception does the work of the eye, and the story tells upon the heart, like scenery still speaking, though silent, to the deaf. In all these cases, the same principle holds; that the inward suggestions of conscience remain dreamlike suspicions and do but cleave the air, so long as they play around our own centre; and first start upon their feet and go forth to conquer, when they come to us in their objective power, and so step before us in the conflict. We need this assurance that the moral differences we feel have their verification in reality, ere we commit ourselves freely to them. The personal consciousness of them is not, simply as such, an integral knowledge, but only the sign that points to something signified; and the faith of conscience hovers with us, meaningless and incomplete, till it rests upon a realized Righteousness.

The contents of this fact are not, I think, adequately appreciated by those who see in them no more than the 'force of example.' The operation of example is mechanical only: the subduing influence of which I speak is spiritual. Example plays upon the tendency to imitation: the ascendency of the greater soul over the less is won by touching the springs of reverence. Example acts downwards as well as upwards, and enables the evil to contaminate the good: the attraction with which we have here to do ever lifts us above ourselves, and taken in reverse becomes a mere repulsion. Example operates *piecemeal* upon the habits: while the enthusiasm awakened by a loftier mind is a universal energy flooding the whole soul. If you live with a family orderly, temperate, and frugal, you insensibly acquire their ways, with perhaps no active moral conviction even on those very points, and without disturbance to any selfishness or irritability that may have

characterised you before.   But if you are intimately thrown
with one in whom you recognise a greater spirit than your
own, to whose gentle or majestic excellence you go into
captivity, his power over you takes no single line of direction, but speaks through all the dimensions of your
nature : it does not set you on copying him, but bends
you low before the Holiest of all ; so clearing away the
whole film of conscience, that duty stands with all its
obligations before your eye at once, and life is seen no
longer in section only, but in its deep moral perspective.
It is here perhaps that the main difference lies between
the Will ethically obeying, and the heart spiritually surrendered,—between morality and religion. Morality applies
itself successively to several points of duty: religion, fairly
awakened, seizes all at once.   Morality, intent on one
obligation, is apt to be betrayed upon another : religion,
demanding harmony above everything, achieves the whole
more easily than a part, and takes the discords out of
opposites.   Morality proceeds from action towards the
soul: religion issues with the soul into action.   Thus, the
inspiring power of mind over mind goes far beyond the
moral contagion of example: it rests upon the reciprocal
correspondence of the inner and the outer moral world,
in the verifying response of real truth to the ideal foreshadowings of the conscience.

Consider then what is implied in this fact of moral
dynamics,—that, unless acted upon by a higher nature,
we never rise.   It will perhaps be said, this is the gospel
of ' hero-worship,' and only shows that admiration,—of the
greater by the less in indefinite gradations,—is the great
lever of character that lifts the elementary masses of society
and forms its shapely pyramid.   To bring the law into
play, all that is needed is a certain range of inequality in
human minds, conducting into the weak the power of the
strong, and holding all together by the magnetism of

natural dependence: we are carried no further by all this than the story of our humanity. Be it remembered, however, that this law applies, not to our particular selves alone, not merely along the ascending steps of moral and mental elevation, but just as much, nay, even with intenser force, at the summit levels where the culminating saints and heroes stand. They too are human: and are they then cut off by their position from all dependence? Do they never look up, or, if they do, only to grow dizzy with the empty space? Is their sympathy all downward? and do they spread their hands dispensing, as gods, their self-created or self-existent goodness on a venerating world? On the contrary, to none is such an attitude more repugnant, and even odiously false. That they are what they are, because they are carried out of themselves by that which transcends their will, is their profoundest consciousness; of all dependence, theirs is the deepest and the most clinging; of all faces, theirs the most habitually upturned; and the less they encounter any higher visible righteousness, the more flows in upon them from an invisible Highest of all[1]. And thus, through the hierarchy of moral ranks, we are led up to a supreme objective Perfection, without which these grandest and loveliest natures could never be. We cannot leave the climax incomplete: for even angels to pass up and down the ladder which has its foot on earth must have its point of rest in heaven. Even on the testimony of the sensational philosophy it is no unexampled process by which we are thus inevitably conducted from finite experiences to transcendent beliefs: for the method by which it conducts us to the idea of immeasurable space is not dissimilar. It is true, we are told, that we have no ex-

---

[1] Nor are minds of a different order unvisited by such experience. Amiel says : ' J'éprouve avec intensité que l'homme, dans tout ce qu'il fait ou peut faire de beau, de grand, de bon, n'est que l'organe et le véhicule de quelque chose ou de quelqu'un de plus haut que lui.' Journal Intime. T. II. p. 221.

perience of an infinite line: but we have experience of
a longer and a longer, with always a possibility of a longer
still; and this, worked out in all directions, suffices to
assure us of the infinitude of space. Similarly, from the
indefinite experience, in moral life, of a better and a better,
with yet a possibility of a better still, we rise into the
assurance of an infinite perfection. And as in the one
case the infinite space is the condition of all the quantities
limited from it, so in the other is the infinite perfection the
cause of all the partial and broken reflections of it in
created minds.

But are the indications of an objective Divine Holiness
communing with our nature confined to men of superlative
nobleness? and, below this height, is it only man that acts
on man through the force of admiration? This momentary
concession I must now withdraw. Large as the operation
is of some leader's mind upon the led, it is by no means
co-extensive with the advance of character; and many
a struggle upwards, whether by patient steps or by some
flight of conversion, takes place, where no visible master-
touch infuses the needful energy. Nay, it is not uncommon, in such cases, to find a strong aversion to what is
called 'hero-worship,' a jealousy of all pretensions set up
for human excellence, and a scrupulous guarding of the
heart from fervent admiration, as an idolatry: the mind,
protecting itself from too much sympathy by a zone of
loneliness around it, seems to gain an unborrowed consecration. This however is simply the history of those
who, though far down, it may be, on the scale of goodness,
yet resort with their aspirations straight to the same source
that draws and lifts the summit minds: they pass by the
intermediary aids, and fly at once to the supremely holy.
The principle is still the same: they find in their religion
the living and realised ideal which presents itself to others
within nearer and human distance: but if to them it were

a *mere* ideal, if it were *not* living, if it were *not* real, if its
presence did not touch and penetrate them with new light
and love, do you think it would snatch them from their
low level and plant them in the air of a higher life? No,
nothing is so sickly, so paralytic, so desolate, as 'Moral
Ideals' that are nothing else: like a pale and beautiful
estatica that can only look down, and whisper dreams, and
show the sacred stigmata, they cannot will or act or love ;
and their whole power is in abeyance till they present
themselves in a living personal being, who secures the
righteousness of the universe and seeks the sanctification
of each heart.   The whole difference on which I have
dwelt between morality and religion hangs upon this conviction of an Eternal Holiness in correspondence with the
individual conscience.   Not infrequently indeed it is admitted that this conviction exercises an unrivalled moral
power with which perhaps it would be dangerous to dispense; but it is added that from the efficacy of a belief
we cannot legitimately infer its truth.   That depends, I
should say, entirely upon the nature of the belief.   In the
case of a derivative doctrine, which has found its way into
some elaborate system of philosophy or theology, it would
certainly be absurd to judge it by its apparent practical
operation, instead of by its logical claim of connection with
undeniable premisses: here, where the tests of correct
reasoning are at command, we must hold its goodness to be
conditional upon its truth.   But in the case of an intuitive
belief, the implicit contents of which admit of more meagre
or full interpretation, the conditions of judgment are different.   If, when you spread out all that the natural
consciousness finds in it, it performs a great and healthy
part in life; while, on being reduced to the minimum that
will save its name at all, it is palsied, and, trembling itself,
moves nothing else; surely it is allowable to prefer the
version of common sense, and leave the pulseless analysis

to its fate; and let its goodness be the determining condition of its truth. In the sphere of the 'Practical Reason,' where we have to do with the postulates of conduct, rather than with the axioms of the intellect, it is impossible to avoid a teleological principle of judgment. The primary moral ideas, the fundamental data of conscience, are not there on their own account, but are invested with a *function*: they are *for the sake* of right action and right character; and if, when construed in one way, they win their end, while, construed in another, they lose it, we gain assurance at once that the former is the true one: just as, in settling the meaning of a doubtful element in a machine, we at once accept that which proves alone consistent with the instrument's effective work. On this principle, we are entitled to say that conscience reveals the living God, because it finds neither content to its aspirations nor victory in its strife, till it touches his infinitude and goes forth from his embrace.

Nor is it only in its forward pressure and ideal aims that the conscience leads us to him. In its retrospect also, nay, in its very failures, it brings us to his presence; no longer, it is true, under the inspiring aspect of Infinite Perfection, but in the solemn character of our Moral Governor and Judge. According to the complexion of our voluntary acts, so variously right and wrong, we are conscious of good or ill desert; or, if we exclude the former, as possible only in relation to men, at least of different degrees of ill desert. These words however express relative conceptions: deserve what?—for *merit*, *reward* or at least approving recognition: for *demerit*, a *retribution* of pain and displeasure. Whence then are these to come? for they are not phenomena of physical nature, but transitive acts or expressions of beings related to us and owning the same rule of righteousness; and if we have incurred these acts or expressions, we have thereby

invested someone with the right to direct them upon us.
The execution of the penalty naturally vests, you will say,
in the recipient of the wrong. And no sooner, accordingly,
does the boy disobey his parents, or the servant deceive
his employer, than he knows himself subject to their indignation, and expects or flies their retributive justice:
they are his superiors, and with the word of judgment carry
also the arm of power. Even when the injury passes from
equal to equal, the penal sentence still takes effect; for
evil doing makes cowards of us all; and the offender, un-
manned by his fault, cowers before the victim whom he has
made fearless with resentment. In these cases, our nature
itself is armed with adequate force to vindicate the equities
of which it is conscious. But if, betrayed by some passion,
we insult or wrong the weak, who have the right to strike
but are bound hand and foot before us,—the captive that
hangs upon our mercy, the child that can reproach us only
with the flush of wonder and the burst of tears, the faithful
dog that licks the hand which smites him,—here, there is
at once the keenest demand and the utmost miscarriage of
justice; and the moment of deepest shame is that of most
complete impunity. This anomaly suffices to show that
the phenomenon is a fragment,—a relation of which one
half is presented and the other hid. Our compunction
assures us that, the demerit being a hideous reality, the
correlative penal power can be no empty fiction: and that
the answer which cannot come from the visible victim is
but held in reserve by an invisible witness. Was there
ever a guilty conscience that believed in the flatteries of
success, and sincerely expected to escape? Such delusion
may belong to the torpid and blind who are not yet born
into the true moral life; but not to the contrite who read
themselves aright: no false peace can chase away the
divine shadow that haunts them: haste as they may, it
overtakes them: 'the wicked fleeth, though no man

pursueth.' Thus the very consciousness of justice un-
satisfied gives rise to a faith that we see not the whole:
that the Righteousness obviously meant and largely embodied in the constitution of the world has yet to complete
itself in the unseen; where silent watch is kept over the
rights of them that have none to help them. Did we
wrong only our equals and our superiors who could bring
us to account, the moral Law might (in this relation) have
seemed to us complete within the limits of human life,
and have carried us to nothing that is divine. But the
dependents whom we dare to injure have power, by their
dumb looks, to call up for themselves an Almighty Protector,
and reveal to us an Eternal Equity. It is in the exercise
of our trust over inferior natures that we feel the presence
of a superior; and discover that we are in a system where
the meanest being has sympathy from the Highest, and
every insult to the smallest creature become a defiance of
a Supreme Providence.

That the divine secret of life, its relation to One infinitely
Holy, is really wrapped up in these moral experiences, is
confirmed by the marvellous effect of a bold and penetrating appeal to them. Stories of religious conversion may be
ridiculous to the cynic and mistrusted by the philosopher;
they are however indubitably true, not only of scattered
instances, as of an Augustine and a Loyola, but of rude
masses of unawakened men, suddenly lifted out of disordered dreams into the clear light of heavenly reality and
the enthusiasm of a devoted will. And how are these
wonders wrought? Is Reasoning the exorcist whom the
evil spirits obey? Are they frightened out by the lash
of disproof? Or do they slowly retreat before the persuasion of self-interest, and the pressure of better tastes?
In order to effect the change, must we believe that things
are as they look,—that nothing is present but animalism,
no sense of right and wrong, no susceptibility except to

the momentary impulse, and only hopeless blindness to invisible relations? If we thus begin at the beginning, it will never have an end. But it is notorious that if, with faith intense enough, you will assume the 'sense of sin,' and speak to its agony of shame, you will not only find a conscience there, but fling it down at the feet of a God never seen before: the same moment which brings the inward moral history into its true light, throws it also off the merely human stage and makes it part of a divine drama. Whoever gives full credence to the consciousness of guilt finds himself estranged, not only from the just sympathy of men, but from an ever living Righteousness that searches their hearts and his. This is exactly what we should expect, if our life were under the Divine Moral Government, and our nature framed for responsive communion with an Infinite Perfection; but would be wholly unintelligible if the conscience were as strictly limited to social uses, as the laws of economy and the conventions of speech.

For consider, finally, what is the alternative, if there be no objective Divine authority of which the moral law is the expression. That it is not any human authority which hides itself behind an awful mask and speaks to us, we have already seen. And there is no third superior power that can overshadow our personality and prescribe our Duty. Nothing then remains but to pronounce the sense of responsibility a mere illusion: the fiduciary aspect of life must disappear: there is no trust committed to us, no eye to watch, no account to render: we have but to settle terms with our neighbours, and all is well. Purity within, faithfulness when alone, harmony and depth in the secret affections, are guarded by no cautionary presence and aided by no sacred sympathy: it may be happy for us if we keep them; but if we mar them, it is our own affair, and there is none to reproach us or put us to shame. Nay,

not even can we reproach ourselves ; for our moral freedom
stands or falls with our relation to a supernatural mind ;
and, in the absence of this, we lie, no less than the winds
and waves, under nature's necessity, and can never be
other than we are : so that the remorse that racks the
guilty conscience must be discharged as a 'superseded'
and 'fallacious feeling'[1]. The measure also which the
natural conscience takes of wrong acts and dispositions
must be discarded ; for when they drop out of relation to
a Divine Perfection, and take their place among facts that
could not be otherwise, moral evil merges into natural, and
sums itself up in the sufferings it entails, and wears itself
out when these are spent, like sickness for the convalescent.
To add to the intensity, or prolong the duration, of the
inevitable pains, still more to introduce others that ficti-
tiously swell the amount, is a gratuitous enlargement of ill.
When the conscience therefore shivers in the returning
shadow of old sins, when, not having suffered enough at
the hands of circumstance, it plunges into self-inflicted
penances, when, oppressed for half a life by the secret of
an unsuspected crime, it makes spontaneous confession at
last, that it may not miss its righteous retribution ; these
superfluities of anguish must be flung away in contempt
as mere superstitions. Yet surely they are among the
most pathetic and solemn of human experiences ; not as
pitiable infirmities, but precisely because they are the
outburst of a truth, and the self-vindication of a moral
law, which resolution cannot suppress or weakness defy.

We rest therefore in the conclusion that, both in the
aspirations of conscience which lift us upwards, and in its
recoil of horror that arrests our fall, we are under the
action of an Infinite objective Perfection, that would win
us to sympathy with itself.

---

[1] Belsham's Elements of the Philosophy of the Mind and of Moral
Philosophy, 1801, p. 284.

§ 4. *Implicit Attributes of God, as apprehended by Conscience.*

The form which Theism assumes when developed from this source widely differs from that which is given by the principle of Causality. There, the Divine scene was outward, in the cosmos : here, it is inward, in the human soul. There, the Divine agency was seen in natural law : here, it is seen in the moral. There, consequently, its order was that of invariable necessity : here, it is that of variable possibility and freedom. There, it presented its intellectual affluence of purpose and resource : here, it reveals its supreme idea and character. Can we then, ere we quit this fresh field, gather up the results of the new insight which it gives us, and attach to the thought of God the additional predicates by which it is now enriched ? They are easily drawn out from the preceding analyses and reasonings.

I. God, relatively to us, is identical with *our Highest*, the supreme term in the hierarchy of spiritual natures; blending in himself the superlatives of all that we reverence as great and good ; the eternal life of Moral Perfection. And, conversely, our moral idealism turns into reality in him, and wins for itself the scope of space and the solidity of the universe, and, forbidding the last word to physical laws, reveals the ulterior ends which they subserve. When we resort to the conscience as his interpreter, we have but to lay out before us the elements of ideal perfection, and we have the attributes which we may ascribe to him. Whether or not they may seem to conflict with the outward facts of the world, and whether, if they do, the conflict can be closed, can be considered hereafter. Certain it is that, *till we are contradicted*, we are carried by our moral nature into conceptions of God which are the transcendent forms of our own aims and prayers ; and these must be defined, before they can be corrected.

(1) We cannot but ascribe to him *Benevolence towards sentient beings.* Of this the indications are unmistakeable in the order and relative authority which he has given to our springs of action. Not even the most elementary propensions which we share with the brutes, however susceptible of selfish distortion, give the least encouragement to solitary monopoly of good : they have more or less obvious reference to a united scheme of life, involving mutual consideration. The spontaneity of young animals only half breaks out, till they meet and spend it in their play ; and the cattle in the field will grow thin on good pasture, unless they browse together ; exhibiting an incipient fellowship, even in the activities most limited to the needs of the individual organism. Again, the only repulsive elements of our nature, the *Passions*, are strictly defensive, and sleep till some invasion of evil wakes them, and subside when it has passed by : they are no aggressive force sweeping an enemy's country, but only sentinels on the watch at home. On the other hand, the attractive impulses, viz. the *Affections*, are the positive powers, the daily elements, of life, prescribing its most constant work, and directing it to the service of others, with or without our own. And the greater the weight that is laid on human love, the stronger becomes the inward tension to lift it : see the utter devotion of the mother to her infant, with its incessant claims of helpless dependence : and the patient vigils and tender offices of compassion in the private sick room or the public hospital ; involving abstinences and weariness which would be dreadful but for the elastic force of self-forgetful affection, which glorifies imprisonment and turns a slavery into a joy. Nor is it only the larger, it is also the higher, place assigned in us to the attractive than the repulsive tendencies, that speaks

their meaning in our existence. Often has the uplifted arm of anger dropped relentingly before the beseeching look of misery, or, in striking the blow, crushed the heart that wields it with insufferable shame! If we allow our fears a hearing against the impulses of disinterested love, and turn away from our friend in his hour of peril, with what a bitter secret do we move about in our security, and find reproaches in the genial sunshine of the world! The self-protecting and self-seeking mind defeats its ends by pursuing them, and is the very nest of morose complaints and consuming cares; while the enthusiasm of self-forgetful sacrifice moves with a free joy, and even in dark hours brightens its path with its own inward glow. The one makes discord with nature : the other brings out and enriches its harmonies. Well, then, from this constitution of our humanity is there nothing to be learned of its Author? Are its laws without relation to the Lawgiver? Are we made to approve and reverence what He regards with aversion or indifference? Is Pity implanted in us by the Pitiless? Are the variegated tissues of sympathy woven by One whose infinitude admits no colours of affection and is empty of all pathetic sympathy? Nay, in giving us compassion is He not, *ipso facto*, compassionate, providing countless channels through which remedial blessings flow? In grouping us around centres of love is He not loving, inventing for our life what most sweetens and elevates it? Whether therefore we look at our nature as the reflection, or simply as the effect, of His will, we must admit that will to be benevolent.

(2) We must recognise in the Infinite Disposer *Justice towards moral beings*, i.e. a treatment of them according to character. We reach Him only at our highest ; and that point is not yet touched, when we have simply risen from the level of selfishness to disinterested altitudes. The social affections are not the final crown of excellence ;

nor is the benevolent aversion to the spectacle of suffering
worthy to assume an absolute ascendency in any spiritual
nature.   Wherever it completely dominates within us, we
are enfeebled for our trusts ; the nerve of authority is
relaxed : stern responsibilities are declined ; and in education, in government, in the whole administration of life,
peace and good will are purchased at any price of indulgence.   This good-natured existence is little more than
half-way to the perfect life ; and short indeed of wing
must be the conscience that can alight and dwell there.
It might be realised by a mind insensible to truth, to
beauty, and at least to many forms of goodness ; and
not till these become powers and mingle with the prior
springs of action, does a true moral order become possible,
and justice find its conditions complete.   When all the
elements of character are assembled, and we look on men
as conscious of their relative claims and free to follow
them, the sentiments which rise within us, as we watch
the drama, are far other than the benevolent, and far
higher : it is not as suffering, but as acting, that we now
contemplate the persons around us ; and wherever their
nature becomes the theatre of strife, and a conflict arises
for the suffrage of their will, we take sides in the moment
of suspense, and cheer them on to the heroic preference,
and are thrown into indignant sadness by their mean
defeat.   Of this deep interest in the game of human action
it is an inherent element, that we assume it to be rendered, and to be due, to real differences ; that it is not any
arbitrary taste of ours which is pleased or offended ; that
what we admire is in itself admirable, what we reprobate,
in itself culpable : we expect the echoes of our own feeling
from all living voices, and seem to hear its reverberations
in the very nature of things.   In our own case, we know,
by determinate consciousness of relatively good or ill
desert, the truth of these ethical judgments : they verify

themselves, in the case of others, by responsive sympathy : and the consensus of all substantiates the law of man as the law of nature. Hence the conscience of mankind refuses to believe in the ultimate impunity of guilt, and looks upon the flying criminal as only taking a circuit to his doom ; and is almost tempted to envy the suffering saint, already touched, in the midst of shadows, with a dawning light of heaven. Unless therefore we are made upon one pattern and the scene of things upon another, though we are compelled to *assume* a consonance, the universe is a commonwealth of minds morally governed, and is under a supreme Righteousness, of whose premo-nitions and awards our own secret insight and judicial afterthought are the reflection. If you still insist that this may be superstitious externalisation of consciousness, if you dispute the passage from the subjective to the objective sphere as unverifiable, if you choose to treat moral differences as phenomena of an animal species with no prototype beyond, I cannot disprove your assertion, any more than you can prove it. Dreams, no doubt, can simulate realities ; and a life-long dream would detain us in illusions that never break ; but we do not, on that account, prefer to consider ourselves deceived. There is no objective belief that has more than a subjective guarantee : and we have no less reason to accept our conscience as delegate of a Sovereign Righteousness, than to regard the dimensions of our body as limited from universal space. What paradox can be greater than to deduce the pheno-mena of character from an agency that has none ? Can you obtain the colours from a ray that has no differences in it ? If the cause of all be neutral, and unsusceptible of moral polarity, how could it set up in us the intense attractions and repulsions that sway our life ? Without the solar glow of the central equity, what is there in the cold dark vacancy to kindle in us the enthusiasm of

Right? As surely therefore as moral effects must flow from a moral source, may we read in our own ethical discriminations the reflections of an Eternal Justice.

(3) On similar grounds we advance a further step, and attribute to God *Amity towards like minds*, however vast the moral dimensions of their distance. The administration of proportionate approval or disapproval is in itself prospective, and looks to an ulterior and higher relation. It is in place during the contingencies of the still tempted and wavering will, trembling between defeat and victory : it belongs to the stage of conflict, when the best impulses are not always the strongest, and it is doubtful whether the wing of resolve or the gravitation of desire will gain the mastery. It is only at the end of this prior suspense that the words 'Well done!' break forth as a crowning joy. But the character may reach an altitude at which such strife is surmounted, and no spring of action retains any disordered strength, and only harmony prevails within. When the natural flow of life takes the very form required by the holiest ideal, and that which might be duty comes from the inspiration of love, we feel ourselves in presence of a divine spectacle, which transcends approval and is unapproachable by reward ; we yield it our reverence: we draw towards it in spiritual kinship: and, but for our great distance, should bring it the offering of our love. This difference between the inward battle and the final peace modern language marks by the distinctive names of 'hero' and 'saint': but it had not escaped the acuteness of Aristotle, who will not allow to the self-denying man more than the negative praise of ἐγκρατής (abstinent or continent), so long as there is in him anything that opposes and withstands (ἐναντιούμενον καὶ ἀντιβαῖνον) the higher prompting, and reserves the unqualified terms σώφρων and ἀνδρεῖος for him in whom reluctant fidelity has ascended into congeniality and joy [1],

---

[1] Ὁ μὲν γὰρ ἀπεχόμενος τῶν σωματικῶν ἡδονῶν καὶ αὐτῷ τούτῳ χαίρων

and all things are in accordance with reason (πάντα
ὁμοφωνεῖ τῷ λόγῳ)[1]. As this is the end which was intended to emerge when all resistance was cleared away,
and in view of which the probation was followed with
helpful sympathy, he who attains it is received into a
serene affection, venerating in observers that stand below,
supporting and uplifting from the supreme Witness.
Sanctity of character is in itself harmony with God,—
the human form of similitude to him,—and carries in it
the communion by which, among minds that live together,
like understands like, and the perfections of one meet and
quicken the aspirations of the other. If then conscience,
in its struggles, represents what God is for and what he
is against, no less, in its heavenly calm, does it bespeak
the living unison of his spirit with our own ; nor does
there seem the slightest reason for distrusting the conviction of devout faithful persons in all ages, that they
were habitually sustained and kindled by a Divine communion, exalting and transcending their own personal
strength. The wonder surely would be, if it were otherwise. How should related spirits, joined by a common
creative aim, intent on whatever things are pure and good,
live in presence of each other, the one the bestower, the
other the recipient of a sacred trust, and exchange no
thought and give no sign of the love which subsists between them? Outwardly, there may be 'no speech nor
language'; but when religious experience affirms that, in
the silent colloquies of the heart, it is not all soliloquy,
but that Divine words also flow in and break the loneliness, who will say that such belief is unnatural or even
mystical ?

So far then as God is apprehended by us as *the Highest*,

σώφρων, ὁ δ' ἀχθόμενος ἀκόλαστος· καὶ ὁ μὲν ὑπομένων τὰ δεινὰ καὶ χαίρων
ἢ μὴ λυπούμενός γε ἀνδρεῖος, ὁ δὲ λυπούμενος δειλός. Nicom. Eth. II. iii. 1.
[1] Ibid. I. xiii. 16, 17, 18.

he becomes invested with these three attributes: bene-volence towards sentient beings: justice towards moral beings who are under probation: amity towards beings that have attained a moral harmony. Other predicates might doubtless be named, but these, relatively to us, con-stitute the chief elements of Divine perfection. They are all, be it observed, additional to what we found ourselves able to say of God as Cause ; and indeed, stand so clear of it, that we shall have to assure ourselves by adequate evidence that they really belong to the same subject. For the moment, we assume this, and add them on to the contents of our prior conception.

II. But the revelations of our moral nature do not close here. In being identified with the supreme moral ideal, God is the summit of each of our consciences, taken one by one, and overshadows every transient life with an eternal sacred authority. This is a separate secret for you and me, and would subsist as a private understanding between the human spirit and the Divine, though they were alone together. In time, however, we discover that this secret of each repeats itself in all : we had hid our own contrition ; but, coming unexpectedly on our brother, we surprise him in like tears: we had gone aside for our lonely devotions, but from the next closet we overhear the murmur of the same prayers : we had been born again under the quickening power of some holier son of God, and timidly knocked at his door to make confession of dis-cipleship and ask his help: when lo ! others are there before us, and the vision and the voice so searching to one are heavenly to all. And so it breaks upon us, that the revelation of the All-perfect, though the deepest of all personal experiences, is not simply individual, but human : not a confidential whisper into each ear, but one tone, or rather one harmony, vibrating through the universal medium of spiritual existence. Here then is a new fact,

that He stands in *one relation to all of us*, giving the same
warnings, ordaining the same strife, inviting the same
affections, breathing the same inspirations. Hence the
knowledge of Him and the life in Him emerge from
the level of a solitary faith, and become a principle of
union interpenetrating the social attachments, interpreting
their intensity, and steeping them in new and fairer
meanings. Every natural group of human beings, in so
far as it gives rise to a secondary or corporate personality,
with its system of duties and of rights, is modified and
consecrated by this fact, its duties becoming more solemn
and its rights more inviolable : nor, by any artifice of
analysis, can a State remain purely secular for a Nation
that has once entered on a higher life. Once bend before
the authority of God, and you can reserve nothing from it :
it covers every obligation : it is not that it creates another
and separate sphere of duties, and adds a department
to the claims upon the human will ; but that it transfigures
and elevates the work and affections of every relation, be
it domestic, social, or political. The moment the two
truths are apprehended, of the spiritual unity of our nature,
and of the All-righteous as its Source and Head, the idea
inevitably follows of our united human life as constituting
a *kingdom of God* ; for it has no binding laws that are not
His : no offences, that are not sins : no just penalties, that
are not expressions of His will : no noble passages of
history, that are not the march of His advancing Providence. The Theocratic conception of Society rests upon
indestructible foundations in our nature, and must for ever
return, unless that nature becomes atheistic. The mischiefs
it has occasioned are due, not to falsehood in its principle,
but to defects in its application. Instead of giving us too
much that is divine, it has given us too little : setting up
some exclusive pretensions for an order of men, or for a
particular faith, and waging war on all else, as if it were

profane ; and failing to recognise the sacred possibilities
involved in the remaining elements of life and other forms
of religion.   Take away these miserable limits : embrace
in the compass of the Divine sway, not a priesthood or a
sect or a ' holy nation,' but the world in its whole breadth
and its long drama ; and surely, from this gathering of all
peoples and all thoughts beneath the eye of God, no excuse
can be drawn for selfish pretensions or wanton wrong: and
the sense of a more august citizenship will be gained, than
can arise from any secular partnership of interest or terms
of contract.   It is from this side,—from the recognition of
a common base of moral conviction and inward reverence,
—that the aspiration, so often reappearing, after an ideally
constituted Society proceeds,—a society which, in its ranks
and arrangements, shall be conformable to the hierarchy
of moral good, and which shall reproduce on earth, as
Plato said, the perfect commonwealth of which the model
exists in heaven.   As the unity of Reason in all men is for-
ever tending to an ascent of the sciences into more comprehensive conceptions, pointing towards some one dominant formula that would yield them all, so the unity of
Conscience in all wakes the prophecy of One acknowledged
realm of Divine Law, harmoniously working towards a
human perfection analogous to that of a higher world.
Nature constitutes throughout one intellectual organism :
humanity, one moral organism : and as God is the in-
forming thought of the one, so is He the spiritual authority
of the other.   In recognition of the former, we raise the
University: as symbol of the other, we dedicate the Church ;
neither of which fulfils its essential idea, till it places us
at an altitude whence the whole domain of knowledge
on the one hand, of duty on the other, can be surveyed
in its relations, and seen suffused with the Divine and
blending light.

E 2

CHAPTER III.

Unity of God as Cause and God as Perfection.

§ 1. *Inseparability of Attributes.*

We have now sought an origin for our primary religious ideas on two sides of our nature, the intellectual and the moral ; and found an infinite Will, first in the principle of Causality, then in the intuitions of Conscience. On looking back upon the ground we have traversed it cannot fail to strike us, that the two lines of thought are separate throughout ; the one running through outward nature, the other through the inward life : the one tracing the genesis of phenomena, the other, a scale of immutable relations : the one following the chain of means and ends, the other interpreting the contrast of right and wrong. The attributes with which, respectively, the processes invest the Divine nature, are similarly distinct : in the one case intelligence, power, self-existence ; in the other, benevolence, justice, holiness, and sovereign government of men. The actual religions of mankind have had widely different characteristics, according as they have been worked out from one of these sources or the other ; the Nature-worships which have been suggested by the spectacle of the cosmos missing the high moral idealism to which nations may rise, when they seek God in the experiences of humanity and along the course of history. If then the two directions we have followed lie so much apart as they advance, are we sure that they have any contact at their close ? Each brings us to the presence of an eternal

Being ; but are these beings one and the same? What we find true of the Creator, may we affirm of the Righteous Judge? And what we say of the Holiest, may we apply to the Architect of Worlds? Or must we, like some of the Gnostic sects, relegate the Demiurgic function to some other being than the All-perfect, and relinquish the attempt to prove his work Divine? To this question we must briefly address ourselves: first giving reasons why we must identify the Causal with the Holy God ; and then examining the difficulties which obscure our recognition of an infinite moral perfection in the constitution and administration of the world.

Notwithstanding the different impression left upon us by the outward physical order and the inward moral law, it is impossible to refer them to separate sources : for

I. We ourselves unite, in our own persons, a subjection to both, in a way which baffles all attempts to discriminate them as two factors, combined as the result of partnership. We are on the one hand *natural objects,* passing, no less than the tree, through the cycle of birth, growth, and decay; with clear relations to the scene around us, through organs that communicate with it and instincts that use its elements ; and with just such complex structure as best illustrates the adaptive art of creative intelligence. Of all the products that may be cited in evidence of causal Thought in the universe, the human body is the most telling and complete. On the other hand, we are also *moral beings,* invested with a *trust,* therefore treated as *causes* and lifted out of the mere series of effects ; and so planted above nature and ranged with the supernatural, like God Himself. And in this capacity it is that, instead of being surrendered to the stronger, we are supplied, as the rule for our causality, with the consciousness of the better and the worse through all the impulses that urge us ; and in our treatment of this rule does our personality

mainly declare itself. In one and the same Self therefore
are blended, not only passive pleasures and pains, but
clamorous instincts pushing to the front, with a regulative
and judicial Will capable of repressive and selective
action : from neither element by itself, only from the
co-operation of the two, can *character* arise and manifest itself. It is obvious, therefore, that the moral phenomena presuppose the physical as their condition ; and
that till Nature has drawn her briefs and urged her pleas,
there is nothing on which sentence can be pronounced.
Our probation, as moral, consists in managing ourselves
as animal ; and He that has devised the trial must have
created the test. The very Ego to which He offers it is
a unity of the natural and the spiritual.

II. But not only is one of the two constituents of our
own person found within nature, and the other beyond ;
our instinctive springs of action are themselves waked up
by the external world, and have reference to aspects and
changes there. It is on the assaults of harm or danger
thence, that the Passions start up and mount guard. It
is at the spectacle of the wounded and suffering there, that
Pity is moved and hastens to soothe and save. And there
it is that all the network of human relations is woven,
which determines the pattern of our affections, and the
order of their work. The truth which Wonder longs to
know, the beauty which we follow in all things with instinctive quest, the justice which draws us to faithful and
noble men, all speak to us from the visible scene in which
we live, and use the symbols of nature to carry their higher
meaning to our hearts. Conscience, with all its insight,
can think nothing and do nothing in empty space ; it
waits for the data of life and humanity ; and all its
problems are set by the conditions of the world. Vainly
therefore should we endeavour to charge the moral order
upon one Cause and the physical upon another ; they are

organically blended in their real existence ; which however is enabled, by their copresence, to be for ever rising into the ideal. If in one view there seems to be an opposition between man and nature, so that the moralities of the one are but a battle with the evils of the other, and if, from this struggle of character with fate, there is some temptation of feeling to frame a dualistic hypothesis, of a world set up by conflicting powers, in another view the apparent opposites return to real concurrence, inasmuch as, but for the natural ill, there could not be the moral good, and all that adorns life and throws a fragrance on its air has its root in the dark soil formed by waste and decay. The drama of human virtue is everywhere relative to the stage of human existence ; and though the one is a spiritual and and the other a material creation, the interpretation of each is to be sought in the other.

III. That external nature is not foreign to the system of moral laws is further evident from the fact that, to a considerable extent, it administers their retribution and enforces their discipline. Not only does the constitution of things arm mankind with vast resources for giving effect to their sentiments of approval or displeasure towards the conduct of their fellows, but the very organism of the individual agent contains provisions for checking passion and punishing excess ; and follows the neglect of conscience by the wasting of health. I know it is said that this is not wonderful, since it is just the injury to health which constitutes excess, and without it there need be no limit to indulgence. But no considerate moralist, even if he estimates right and wrong by the canon of consequences alone, will consent thus to consult merely physical effects, and disregard the inward operation upon character, and the outward upon social obligations : and if he owns any scale of relative worth in the springs of action themselves, he will utterly refuse to shift his valuation of them with

their variations in result, and will insist that the lower
remain lower in the midst of impunity, and the higher
are still higher at whatever cost.   If this be so, then the
ruined health of the intemperate, the repulsive physiog-
nomy of the selfish, the comical elation of the vain, are
literally judgments of physical nature, exposing men for
their offences to the lash of pain, or hanging on them the
ticket of degradation, or setting them in the pillory of
ridicule.   Here then, it is plain, the natural and the moral
systems are one, and play into each other's hands.   Nor
can we mistake the *order* of their co-operation : the natural
laws lend themselves to the service of the moral, and undertake to represent and in part carry out their penalties.
The *end* therefore towards which they look and work, is
ethical, and the Divine Causality places itself at disposal
of the Divine Perfection : the eternal Thought moves in
the lines of the eternal Holiness.

§ 2. *Conflicting Moral Aspects of the World.*

The idea of God furnished by the inward sources of
divine knowledge now stands in its chief lineaments before
us.   It is justly said, however, that every objective belief
supplied by the mere movements of our own faculties will
fail of practical power, and remain a mere πρόληψις ἔμφυτος,
—a native presage,—till it is carried for verification into
the sphere of outward things.   This we have already done
in regard to the intellectual Divine attributes, in our notice
of the teleological aspects of nature : and there is now a
similar test to be applied in regard to the moral perfections
predicated of the Supreme Mind.   Is the constitution of
the known universe such as we should expect from the
benevolence and righteousness of an Infinite Being?   Does
it exclude what must be at variance with the purposes of
such a being, and provide for only that which must be
congenial to them?   It is impossible to put these questions

without a consciousness, almost appalling, of the obstacles to a satisfactory answer. With the critic who arraigns the creative skill and thinks the solar system or the human eye a bungling piece of work, it is easy to be simply amused without disturbance: but whoever asks us about the problem of evil, and especially of sin, touches a chord of secret sorrow, and subdues us to a grave anxiety. It cannot be denied that in various ways the phenomena of life are disappointing to our ideal of a moral administration of its affairs. But in order to estimate aright the conclusions which they justify or enforce, we must screen ourselves from partial impressions by embracing the problem as a whole, and surveying the conditions on which it has to be worked out.

In approaching this question, we must keep steadily in view the kind of scheme which alone we are entitled to expect; else we shall be in danger of applying inconsistent tests, and stipulating for incompatible excellences. We seek to know, whether the system to which we belong corresponds with the *righteousness* ascribed to its Author. Well then, by hypothesis it is to be a *moral* system, and must comprise the requisites for the formation, the exercise, and the discipline of *character*. Character however consists (so far as it is good) in right choice; for which the opportunity does not exist, unless wrong choice be simultaneously possible. There must therefore be left a certain range of contingency, surrendered to the free will of finite beings, and leased out to them as the scene of their probation; whatever else be set fast and secured against failure and imperfection, here is a field that must remain open to the possibilities of moral evil. The establishment of this risk, so far from contradicting the holiness of God, is its immediate and indispensable expression; and only shows that He does not necessitate a good, of which the very essence flies at the touch of necessity. Though, however, the possibility of wrong cannot be excluded, it may be variously limited ; and we may fairly ask that the limits be not so wide as to endanger the equilibrium of the moral world, and cancel its superiority over an *unmoral*. As, in our home, the wisdom of education lies in a just balance between allowing the child an unrestricted range of transgression, and never trusting him to a step that may go astray, so, in the righteous administration of the world, we expect to see an adequate control over guilty aberrations reconciled with ample scope for the highest nobleness.

Another caution to be observed in estimating the scheme of things arises from the fact, that it is not a stationary fabric, complete and given once for all ; but rather a perpetual creation, all whose constituent factors are on the move and yield new products on innumerable lines. It exhibits, therefore, a series of changing values, on any one of which it would be arbitrary to dwell as its just exponent : for this would be to treat as *an end* that to which the chief significance attaches as a *means*. If an intelligent observer, flitting through space, had come across the whirling fire-cloud that once occupied, we are told, these regions of the universe, he would hardly have known what to make of it, and might think that whoever put it there was at all events no friend to life, and was determined to render his realm too hot to hold it : yet, if he came back to-day, he would find the same tracks alive with teeming globes. You judge the oak, not in the acorn, but in the forest of a hundred years. And so, in order to appreciate the system of relations which constitute our world, we must look mainly at the ends to which it is tending, rather than at its momentary state : *these* it is which give its true idea, and can alone interpret the meaning of the originating Mind ; and the imperfection of what is may be but the fulcrum which falls beneath the onward step to what is

yet to be. I am far from pleading for any immunity from
criticism, on behalf of the apparent flaws and ills of life :
only, where they are temporary and instrumental, they
should be measured against the purpose they subserve,
and wait for their condemnation till it has been shown
that the end is not worthy the means employed to reach
it. In the light of these rules, let us pass in review (1)
the provisions which admit suffering : (2) those which
admit sin : (3) the apparent abandonment of human history to the conflicts of rude force.

A. Admission of Suffering.

The first of these difficulties affects the whole empire of
sentient life : the other two are special to the government
and destination of Mankind.

a. Doctrine that Pain is no evil.

By one class of Theists the difficulties are summarily
dismissed with the absolute dictum, that there is no such
thing as evil at all ; and that to ask why things are not
better is absurd in a system which is already the best.
That there is anything amiss in nature or life is an
illusion (it is said) incident to our point of view : could we
stand clear of this aberration of vision, we should perceive
nothing but unmixed good. If we ask these happy believers how they have come to detect this illusion in themselves, and what guarantees to them that, in spite of
appearances, all is well, they reply, ' We know that God
is wise and good, therefore that all is good:' they thus
employ their own *a priori* idea as a solvent in which all
concrete facts and impressions shall be reduced and disappear : instead of recognising a double truth, on the one
hand of thought, on the other of experience, and owning
the need of bringing them into harmony. Thus, Dr.
Hedge, having raised the question, ' How reconcile the
existence of evil with the being and rule of a wise and
good God, almighty to effect what love proposes and

wisdom plans?' says, 'there is but one answer to this
question. What love proposes and wisdom plans must
needs be good. This fundamental truth of practical reason
is the only solution of the problem. In the view and
intent of a Being of infinite wisdom and goodness, there
can be no evil. Such a Being sees and knows and does
only good. What we call evil, therefore, the evil of our
experience, when referred to its source, has precisely the
same character with that which we call good. If God is
good, and if all that is proceeds from him, there is no evil.
Suffering, distress, privation, woes of every kind: but no
evil. All is good in its origin and purpose, and must
eventually approve itself as good in human experience.'
'To the question, then, how evil consists with the goodness
of God? I answer flatly, it does not consist with the goodness of God. One or other of these conceptions must be
abandoned. Either there is no God, such as we figure
him, or there is no evil. Pain and suffering in abundance,
but no evil. For only that is really and absolutely evil
which is evil in its cause and effect, in its origin and end;
evil in its issues, evil for evermore. Nothing in God's
universe answers to that condition [1].'

If no more is meant here than an appeal to religious
trust, if, in the presence of two conflicting impressions, we
are simply told to hold fast our faith in the Divine goodness and treat all that contradicts it as we should treat
an insinuation against a friend, no truer words of practical
piety can be spoken. But to call them a 'solution of the
problem' seems to claim for them too much: they simply
deny it, or give it up, and try to float off from it by cutting
away the moorings of a well-anchored word. Pain, privation, failure, wrong, we are not, it seems, to call 'Evil,'

---

[1] Ways of the Spirit and other Essays, by Fred. Henry Hedge,
Boston, 1877, pp. 243, 245.

though it is precisely to characterise these and take them in as its contents that the word has come into use ; and though, when these are expelled from it, nothing remains to which it will fit. You will not allow the word to be employed till you find some suffering or sin that for ever was and for ever will be what it now is : and meeting with no such impossibility, you say that there is no evil. Wonderful feats are performed by abstract terms : but by no such wave of their magical wand can this problem be spirited away. It can dispense with the word evil altogether, and keep close in its statement to the phenomena which are admitted to be abundantly present in the world, under the two heads of pain and guilt. The infinite cause of all we are impelled to believe perfect in love and holiness : to love, the infliction of pain, and to holiness, the presence of guilt, is repugnant : yet into the Divine creation both have made their way. It is vain to deny the contrariety between the predicates of the Cause and these phenomena of the effect ; and the problem requires, not that we should simply affirm the one and deny the other, but that we should find some mediating conceptions that relieve the contradiction, or that take up both the opposites to some higher point of view, in which they may merge and harmonise. Not deeming it legitimate therefore to cancel and discharge this question by the decree of an imperial optimism, I cannot excuse myself from dealing with its perplexities in the concrete, and attempting some just measure of the grievous phenomena of the world. I will consider first the case of natural suffering ; and then that of moral evil. In human experience they appear in close connection with each other : in order to make a separate estimate of the first, it will be necessary to attend to it chiefly as affecting the lower animals. Among them no moral effect can be produced by pain : how is it then that they are subject to it?

b. Doctrine that animals are Automata.

It is no longer necessary, except as a matter of history, to notice the mythological hypothesis that the first sin is answerable for the entrance of disorder and death into the whole sentient world. The geological record, of ages indefinitely earlier than the human, conclusively attests the operation of death and of animal war prior to the conditions of moral probation ; and, in doing so, has rather relieved the Divine Cause of an imputed wrong than assailed any element of His perfection : for to visit the guilt of one race upon the constitution of all would only show, if it were a fact, that neither Reason nor Right had any place in the government of this planet. So strongly was this felt in the seventeenth century, even by those who never dreamt of disputing the alleged fact, that orthodox theologians eagerly took refuge in the paradoxical doctrine of Descartes, that, with the exception of man, all animals were mere automata, at the blind disposal of purely physical agencies, especially of heat generated in the heart as a central furnace. ' This will do,' they thought, ' for machines do not feel : and if this anæsthetic is administered to all the brutes, we may do what we like with them, and let the Creator distort and kill them, without hurt to them or to his beneficence.' There was certainly much temptation to this reasoning in Descartes' assertions[1], that what we call sensations,—as of warmth and cold, and propensions, such as of hunger and thirst,—belong to the body which is only a mechanism, and not to the soul, which alone is conscious, and that the lower animals have only bodies and not souls. If so, these states are, in such natures, nothing but material movements and impressions, and therefore not sentient conditions at all. ' The brutes do not feel : this proposition,' says Kuno Fischer, ' stood so

---

[1] Les Passions de l'âme, Partie I, Art. xxiv.

high in the esteem of the Cartesian school, that they used it to justify vivisection[1].' By an easy extension of the same argument, they could use the doctrine to defend vivisection on a larger scale by the Divine hand. The theological adherents of the school display a curious zeal in denying the sensibility of animals, spurning the imputation, as if it were a stain upon their innocence. 'Have they then eaten the forbidden fruit?' exclaims Malebranche, evidently thinking that in charging consciousness upon them we should wrongfully taint them with original sin. So singular an opinion betrays, it must be confessed, a gloomy estimate of their lot: it cannot be a happy fate which becomes defensible only by remaining unfelt.

The most express and effective exposition of this doctrine is found in a treatise of Bossuet's, almost forgotten, though, of all his writings, one of the most worthy to be remembered; *de la Connaissance de Dieu et de soi-même.* He devotes an important chapter to the investigation of the animal nature as compared with the human. In analysing the latter, he starts with the three elements on which the triple scholastic division rests, into body, sensitive soul, and rational soul; external objects (1) act upon our organs: (2) produce sensations: (3) followed by reasoning about them and choice among them. But, of these, the last is often omitted, and the phenomenon is complete in the other two: showing, in spite of the absence of Reason and Will, wonderful adaptations to conditions which are present. Anger, for example, gives us strength, and fits us for a dangerous encounter: fear adds fleetness to the feet, if we can fly, or, if we are falling from a height, flings out the hands before us to break the shock; and, in hunted creatures, often prostrates them in faintness, so that they are supposed to be feigning death as a means of

---

[1] Geschichte der neuern Phil. I. i. cap. xi. p. 532. 2te Auflage, 1865.

escape[1]. Such automatic actions seem to be common to us and to the brutes, and we naturally construe them alike in both cases: we *feel* them as well as *do* them, and conclude that other creatures do so too. But this is a hasty inference: and we see plainly how misleading is the analogy on which it depends, when we turn from the sensitive to the rational aspect of such instinctive activities. What can be more like reflective intelligence than the ingenious structures and adaptive habits of the lower animals? Yet we know that, though their skilled works are executed, they are not excogitated, by these busy artizans. The absence of mind is indicated by the incapacity for using language or other signs of thought; and by the uniformity of the animal skill, so different from the progressive learning of man. The insect or the bird in its ingenious work is evidently the organ of an intelligence not its own; and as you explain its simulation of art without resort to a rational soul, so may you explain its simulation of feeling without resort to a sensitive soul. It is true that, in training and modifying the habits of animals, you have recourse to what you understand to be the administering of sensations. A *man* you can influence by immaterial ideas, of truth, of virtue, of order and proportion, of immutable laws, &c.; but to a *dog* you offer a bit of bread to eat, or, if you catch him tasting the partridge which he ought to bring you, you beat him with a stick, and mould him by its blows to better ways, as a blacksmith the iron with the hammer[2]. From one another also animals receive new impressions and dispositions: the young bird receives in its brain the impression of its mother's flight; and this impression, being like that which is in the mother, necessarily brings about the same act. But if this is called learning, all nature learns: and nothing

---

[1] Œuvres de Bossuet (Bausset, 43 vols, 1815–1819), Tom. XXXIV, p. 313.   [2] Pp. 326, 328.

is so docile as wax, which so well preserves all the characters which the seal makes upon it.   The bird learns to
repeat a song: echo does the same: and if two lute-strings
are in unison, the vibrations of each will bring response
from the other; and no less exclusively organic is the performance of the living songster[1].   There is not the slightest
occasion to suppose that the beaten dog feels, that the
young bird sees or hears, as we do: the mechanical impression of objects upon the organs of the body suffice for
the whole effect, the history of which is as follows: the
heat of the heart animates and propels the blood towards
the head: ere it reaches the brain, the thicker liquid elements are arrested by reticulated tissue, through the pores
of which only an etherial residue, called the 'animal spirits'
can pass : these finer constituents are distributed from the
brain through all the sensory nerves of the body, and in
turn are stimulated into movement from the periphery to
the cerebrum by the action of external agencies, such as
light, sound, pressure, &c.: the change thus conveyed to
the cerebrum is there handed over to the motory nerves
(i.e. those which supply the muscles), and sets up the
corresponding action.   In order to provide for the immense number of different impressions and movements,
recourse is had to possible varieties in the animal spirits
according to their velocity, the composition of the blood
which gives them forth, and the several channels through
which they flow ; whereby, in spite of the uniform machinery, modifications sufficiently numerous may, it is
said, be easily imagined[2].   An animal thus fitted up
will be the theatre of a series of received centripetal
changes propagated through it from external things: and
of a consequent series of centrifugal movements delivered
forth upon the outward scene: we may call the one *im-*

---

[1] Pp. 330, 331.   [2] Pp. 357, 358.

pressions, and the other *actions*, or, if habitual, *dispositions* : but these words must be limited to a material sense, as when we speak of an *impression* on clay, the *action* of a watch, a *disposition* of threads upon a loom, and must not be understood as including any sort of feeling on the one hand, or conscious energy on the other. 'This doctrine,' says Bossuet, 'takes credit to itself for a more precise solution of the problem,' than that which refers the animal problem to 'sentiment,' i.e. sensations of pleasure and pain; 'because it has not to explain how the animal soul is neither spiritual nor immortal, dispensing as it does with anything more than the blood and animal spirits. It says that the movements of animals are not given forth by sensation, and that, to explain them, it is enough to suppose the organisation of parts, the impression of objects on the brain, and the direction of the spirits to set the muscles into play. In this it is that instinct consists : it is nothing but the moving force by which the muscles are moved and worked[1].' In man this automatic arrangement is supplemented by a rational soul, which, being immaterial, has no extension : but which is brought into vital union with the organism in the pineal gland. *There* is the terminus of all the movements of the animal spirits ; and thence proceed all the messages to the muscles ; and from the presence of the soul at that point, both processes are rendered *conscious* in the human case. Of the conscious phenomena thus arising, all that are cognitive and involve thought and will, the soul would have in its own separate existence : but the sensations, with the passions arising thence, it has merely in virtue of its union with the body. The body could not have them without the soul ; nor the soul without the body ; they result from the temporary relation of the two. Thus, 'the advocates of this view,' says Bossuet, 'maintain that sensation can never, any more

---

[1] Pp. 359, 360.

than reasoning, come from body: but then (unlike the scholastics who provide for it by a separate sensitive soul) they assign sensation to no other seat than that to which they assign reasoning: because sensation, while not in itself apprehending truth, has, according to them, no function except to excite the part which is cognitive. And they contend that sensation serves no purpose for either explaining or causing bodily movements ; because, far from causing, it follows them : so that, in sound reasoning, we must say, 'such and such a movement takes place, therefore such and such sensations ensue :' and not, 'there is such and such a sensation, therefore such and such a movement ensues[1].'

Though the bishop avoids mentioning the name of Descartes, and does not expressly commit himself to the philosophy which he expounds, no reader can doubt his approval of it, or his complete mastery of its bearings. I have dwelt upon his version of it because, more than any other with which I am acquainted, it brings out distinctly the absolute denial of all sentiency to the animals, and accepts the whole meaning of the mechanical analogy with automata. This feature of the doctrine was from the first attributed to it by *its opponents*. Thus, Henry More writes to Descartes in 1647 : 'of all the opinions of yours from which I dissent, there is not one which, whether from weakness or from tenderness of temperament, more revolts me, than the truculent and barbarous sentiment advanced in your " Method," by which you divest all the animals of life and feeling (*sentiment*) : or rather, you maintain that they have never had any ; for you will not allow them to have ever been alive. Here, the penetrating light of your mind causes me less admiration than dismay : terrified at the destiny of the animals, I am less engaged by this ingenious subtilty of yours, than by that cruel and slashing

[1] P. 361.

weapon with which you appear armed, to take away at a
blow life and feeling from almost all animated nature, and
metamorphose them into marbles and machines[1].'

---

[1] Œuvres de Descartes, Cousin, Tom. X. pp. 187–8. Henry More
adds some well-selected examples of animal action, with a view to
test the theory: 'Is it possible,' he says, 'that parrots and magpies
should imitate our sounds, if they could not hear with their organs
and apprehend what we say? You say, they do not understand the
word which they pronounce by imitation : but how can you deny that
they utter their own want, viz. the gift of food which they expect from
their master by this means? They mean then to beg for their food
on the strength of their having so often got what they want by talking.
And otherwise, would singing birds give so much attention to hear
what is addressed to them, if they had neither sensation nor reflection? and could foxes and dogs show such subtilty and sagacity?
How comes it that threats and commands repress animals when they
give signs of fierceness? When a hungry dog has stolen something,
why does he fly and hide himself as knowing that he has done wrong,
and moving with fear and distrust, make up to nobody as he goes,
but slink away from their track, and drooping his head seek a retired
spot, with prudent precaution to avoid punishment for his offence?
The innumerable anecdotes told to prove that animals have an
allowance of reason must surely be admitted to show that at least
they have sensation and memory. It would be endless to quote here
the stories to this effect : but many of them, I know, are too conclusive for the acutest ingenuity to escape their force.
 ' But I quite see that the inducement with you to reduce the animals
to machines lies in your mode of proving that our souls are immortal.
Assuming that body is incapable of thought, you conclude that
wherever thought is, *there* must be an entity other than body, and
therefore immortal. Whence it would follow that, if the brutes had
thought, they would have souls consisting of an immortal entity.
 ' But tell me, my keen philosopher, I pray, since your argument
leaves you the choice of either stripping the brutes of all sensation or
endowing them with immortality, why do you prefer to make them
inanimate machines, rather than animate material bodies with imperishable principles (*animabus*) of life : all the more, because the
former opinion is by no means agreeable to the phenomena of nature,
and never heard of until now : while the latter has been sanctioned
by the wisest of the ancients, as Pythagoras, Plato, and others?
Besides, there is nothing which could more confirm the Platonists in
their belief of the immortality of animals, than that a man of so fine
a genius as yourself should be driven to treat them as insensate
machines for fear of making them immortal.' For the *Latin* letter,
see Garnier's Descartes, vol. iii. p. 288.

But it is not only among opponents of Descartes that he is thus interpreted. So early and devoted a representative of his school as Father Malebranche eagerly embraced the doctrine in this form as part of his inheritance as a disciple, and acted on it in a way that did not commend it to men of simpler instincts : ‘As for Father Malebranche,’ says the Abbé Trublet, ‘he was profoundly convinced of it, and, having more courage than his master, held to it undismayed. Why was this? Because the automatism of the brutes, though revolting alike to sense and reason, accords very well with faith, and even favours and supports it in regard to so essential a dogma as that of the spirituality of the Soul. On the subject of this strong conviction of Father Malebranche’s, M. de Fontenelle used to relate that, on his calling one day to see Father Malebranche at the Oratory in the Rue St. Honoré, a large pregnant bitch belonging to the house came into the hall where they were walking, and began to fawn on Malebranche and throw herself at his feet. After some fruitless attempts to get rid of her, the philosopher dealt her a great kick which made her howl with pain, and drew from M. de Fontenelle an exclamation of compassion. What! said Father Malebranche, coldly, don’t you know that the thing does not feel[1]?’ And in Pascal’s writings the idea is welcomed as a means of relieving the Divine goodness from the burden of animal suffering. In modern text-books of the history of philosophy, the doctrine is constantly mentioned as one of the characteristics of Descartes. Thus in Krug’s Dictionary of the philosophical sciences it is stated that, among the arbitrary assumptions

---

[1] The Abbé adds in a note : ‘Among the papers of M. de Fontenelle I have found a short piece upon Instinct, arriving at the conclusion that the brutes are endowed with thought, and are not machines.’ Suite sur M. de Fontenelle, par M. l’Abbé Trublet : Mercure de France, Juillet, 1757, p. 78, Paris.

of the system, must be reckoned the hypothesis of vortices through which he framed a cosmogony, the selection of the pineal gland as the probable seat of the soul, whence it operated in conjunction with the animal spirits, and the assertion that the animals were mere automata,—*living but insensible machines*,—because else their souls would have to be free and immortal like the human[1].'

After this testimony on the part of both critics and disciples, it may appear rash to affirm that Descartes' doctrine has been interpreted rather by what it logically ought to be, than by what it actually is. But if we judge it by his own statements, we shall find, not only distinct admissions of particular states of feeling in animals, but a direct disclaimer of the opinion imputed to him, that they have neither life nor sensation. The evidence is as follows.

(1) He habitually illustrates the sense in which he calls the animals machines by the parallel case of our own instinctive actions, and maintains that, on this involuntary field, where thought is not required, they often surpass us: 'some of them,' he says, 'are stronger than we are, and others have at disposal natural intrigues that may deceive the keenest men. But the only actions, I conceive, in which they imitate or surpass us are those in which our thought is not concerned. For it often happens that we walk and eat without at all thinking of what we are about: and so it is without use of reason that we repel things hurtful to us, and ward off blows aimed at us, and that, if we were to try ever so much, we could not help flinging out our hands, when surprised by a fall. I believe that, in the absence of thought, we should eat like the brutes, without having learned: and they say that sleep-walkers sometimes swim across rivers where they would drown

---

[1] Art. Descartes, i. p. 433.

if they were awake[1].' In insisting upon this analogy, Descartes intends to exclude *thought and will* from the brutes; but he leaves *feeling* undisturbed; for the involuntary actions which he cites, whether executed in waking condition or in sleep, are prompted by felt impulses, as well as attended by sensations in their performance.

(2) Descartes distinctly ascribes to the animals *passions and affections* which have their natural signs and lead to various movements. His favourite distinction between us and the brutes is, that we have proper language (la parole) for the conveyance of thoughts; while they have only signs related to their wants and passions: except for this difference, we are as much machines as they. 'Though the movements of passion in us,' he says, 'are attended in our case with thought, because we have the thinking faculty, yet it is very plain that they do not depend upon it, since they often take place in spite of us; and consequently they may occur in the brutes, and even more strongly than in us, without implying that they have thought. In short, on examination you will find no one of our external actions involving a thinking soul, or requiring our body to be more than a self-moving machine, with the exception of words or other signs corresponding to matters that present themselves, without having relation to any passion. I say "words or other signs," because mutes make use of signs, as we do of the voice; and I require them to correspond with things, in order to exclude the case of parrots, while saving that of crazy people, in which the language still corresponds with the subjects in hand, though not in a rational way; and I stipulate that these words or signs shall be unrelated to any passion, in order to exclude not only cries of *joy and distress*, etc., but also all that may be artificially taught

---

[1] Œuvres de Descartes, Cousin, ix. p. 423.

to animals. For if you teach a magpie to say '*bon jour*'
to his mistress when he sees her coming, you can only
do it by making the utterance of these words obey the
movement of some one of his passions : viz. here it will be
the stirring of his hope of something to eat, if you have
been accustomed to give him a morsel when he utters his
words. And so, all the things that you make dogs or
horses or monkeys do, are only movements of *their fear,
their hope, or their joy*, which can be made without any
thought[1].' On another occasion, repeating the argument
from the exclusive use of language by man, he again refers
the natural expression of animals to the stimulus of internal passion : 'my chief reason,' he says, 'for thinking
the animals destitute of intelligence is, that although, in
the same species, some, as in our race, are more perfect
than others,—a fact particularly observable in horses and
dogs, which have very unequal powers of retaining what
they learn,—and although they all make pronounced
natural movements of *anger, fear, hunger*, and the like,
either by the voice or by other bodily actions, yet no
animal has ever been observed to advance far enough to
employ genuine language[2]. Again he says, 'As to the
signs which dogs make with their tails, these are only the
movements that *accompany an affection*, and these I think
we must carefully distinguish from language, which alone
is a certain sign of the thought which is hid in the body.'
And that in this department, of natural expression, he
makes no distinction between us and the brutes is evident
from the sentence which immediately precedes : 'this
summer I hope to publish a short treatise on the passions,
in which it will be clearly seen how all the movements of
our members, concomitant on our passions or affections,
are produced, not by our soul, but only by the mechanism

---

[1] Pp. 424, 425.   [2] Tom. X. p. 207.

of our body [1].' Throughout these passages, and as the very pith of their meaning, the animals are presented to us as inspired by anger, fear, hunger, hope, joy, distress, and as performing their expressive actions from impulses similar to our own. How then is it possible to maintain that Descartes supposed the animals to be insensible?

(3) Further, he directly,—totidem verbis,—disclaims this opinion : ' for brevity's sake,' he remarks, ' I say nothing of the other grounds for denying thought to the brutes. I must observe however that it is of thought, *and not of life or feeling*, that I speak : for I do not deny *life* to any animal, making it consist only of the heart's heat : nor do I refuse them *sensation*, so far as it depends on the organs of the body. Under these conditions, my opinion ought less to be regarded as cruel to the animals, than as kindly to men, who do not give in to the superstition of the Pythagoreans' (viz. of the migration of souls into the bodies of animals); ' for it acquits them of all suspicion of wrong in eating or killing animals [2].'

It is then perfectly evident that Descartes' denial of ' *sentire* ' to the brutes applies simply to the *cognitive*, not to the *feeling* element of sensation. His meaning will come out more clearly from the comparison of two remarks of his, apparently at variance. ' It is,' he says, ' *the soul* which sees, though by the intervention of the eyes.' According to this, the brutes, being without soul, would not see. But again, we find him saying, ' The animals *see indeed*, but not as we do when aware that we see (dum sentimus nos videre), but only as when, under pre-engagement of mind, the images of external objects are painted on the retina, and their impressions on the optic nerve, without our being at all aware of them, determine, it may be, different move-ments in our limbs : in which case we are moved just

---

Ibid., p. 240.   [2] Tom. X. pp. 207, 208.

as automata[1].'   Here it is plain that the denial of *sentire*
is the denial, not of an impression of sense, but of self-
knowledge of it.   In conformity with this, Descartes distinguishes three stages of sense (du sens) : (1) the movements
excited by external objects, e.g. the rays of light, say from
a stick, in the nerves, and thence the brain : this first degree
du sentiment we have in common with the brutes.   (2) The
immediate effect of this in the mind, through its close
union with the affected organ, is the consciousness to ourselves (*perception*) of colour and light in the case of the
stick, as in other cases of pain, hunger, thirst, sound, smell,
taste, heat, cold : and here (i.e. with self-knowledge of
sensations), the function of *Sense* in man stops.   (3) The
judgments we form about the *objects* whence the impressions come, viz. that they have colour, size, position,
distance, &c., are properly acts of the understanding, and
are recognised as being so, except in cases of custom from
infancy, where the intellectual process seems fused into the
sensible[2].   Here we have *sensation pure and simple* as the
animal function : *self-knowledge of it*, as the function of the
human senses : *objective knowledge from it*, as the function
of the human understanding.   It must be observed, however, that *pain, hunger, and thirst*, which, in the passages
previously cited, were placed among the '*passions*' *of
animals*, now appear under the head of sensations *specially
human*.   This is an instance of an inconsistency and wavering of which Descartes could never rid himself.   With his
dualism, of body which had only *extension and movement*,
and soul which had only *thought*, he did not know what to
do with *feeling*.   The division between the two members of
his dualism he fixed between the brutes and man, in whom
first Soul appeared upon the stage.   The brutes have
undeniably sensations and propensions : these then do not

---

[1] Compare Tom. X. 63 (1647), and VI. 339 (1637).
[2] Tom. II. p. 356.

belong to Soul, of which the brutes are destitute, but are mere mechanical processes : but if so, they are nothing but material movements, i.e. not feelings at all, but only *sham* sensations and propensions. Feeling then, being beyond the resources of body, takes refuge with the soul. The essence of the soul is its thinking power, its cognitive self-consciousness, its knowledge of its own states, and those of the body with which it is connected as well as of other bodies. Among these states,—since man also is an animal, —are the very same hunger, thirst, and other propensions which have just been shown to be the action of an insensible mechanism. But we, who alone are permitted to see what they are, know them to be sensations and felt impulses : and as it is not the knowledge of them that makes them so, and they could not be known as feelings, unless they were so, they had this character prior to its discovery, i.e. in the animal nature without soul : this however is a purely corporeal structure : therefore it is not beyond the bodily resources to have real sensations and propensions. From this contradiction there is no escape : it is the inevitable result of striking out everything between matter that is only mechanical and spirit that is rationally self-conscious: at whichever door feeling and passion apply for admission, they must either be driven away, or be let in surreptitiously or by mistake, with liability to be detected and turned out. Hence, the language of Descartes is far from self-consistent on this point. In his Second Meditation he absolutely identifies *Sentir* and *Penser* : the usual impression of light, of sound, of heat, or even the dream of it, he says, is what we mean by *sentir* : and ' that is strictly nothing else than *penser*[1].' To the Soul, therefore, which alone can think, does it belong. Yet in the sixth Meditation, he refers certain of our sensations to the intimate union of the soul with

---

[1] Tom. I. p. 255

the body, without which they would have no existence.
'Nature teaches me,' he says, 'through the feelings of pain,
hunger, thirst, &c., that I am not only lodged in my body
like a pilot in his ship, but that I am closely conjoined
with it and so blended as to form one whole with it. Were
it not so, I should not, when wounded in the body, feel
pain on that account, being but a thinking thing, but should
perceive the injury by the understanding only, as a pilot by
eyesight perceives that anything is broken in his vessel.
And when my body was in need of food and drink, I
should simply have knowledge of the fact ; without being
served with notice of it by the indistinct feelings of hunger
and thirst : for in fact all these feelings of hunger, thirst,
pain, &c., are nothing but certain indistinct ways of thinking, which proceed from the union, and depend on the mixture of the mind with the body[1].' Neither of these would
admit the animals to sensation ; for both of them require a
soul : and, in order to justify the frequent ascription of
feeling to the brutes, there ought to be yet another variation
of opinion, viz. that sensations, as animal processes, are
merely corporeal. This third view also Kuno Fisher
detects in Descartes ; but I do not find it in the passages
where it is said to lurk : they do indeed trace through the
body the series of organic movements by which the action
of external objects, or the disturbance of internal parts,
propagates itself along the nerves to the brain ; but they
distinctly say that the end of this mechanical process is
that the *soul feels*[2]. Descartes indeed gives a rule for
settling what is to be attributed to the body, what to the
soul : and the rule is this ; we are to assign to the body
whatever we perceive to be possible to bodies *wholly in-*

---

[1] Tom. I. p. 336.

[2] Kuno Fisher's Descartes, 2nd ed. 1852, p. 532 ; Cousin's Descartes, Tom. IV. pp. 57, 58 ; Les Passions de l'âme, Art. 23, 24
'L'Âme les sent.' 'Ils *donnent à l'âme* deux sentiments.'

animate (tout-à-fait inanimés) : the rest to the soul[1]. This leaves no room for sensation outside the soul.

It is therefore equally certain that Descartes left the animals in possession of sensations and propensions ; and that his philosophy provided them with no title to these. He himself carried their automatism no further than that of the somnambulist, or any person who loses self-consciousness in some other consciousness, and is disposed of for awhile, neither by will, nor by any insensible machinery, but by possession of some intense feeling. But his followers, completing his logic, and parting with his common sense, reduced the brutes to their mechanical rights, and exhibited them on the stage as puppets and pretenders. In charging this opinion on the master, the disciples contributed nothing in the way of evidence : the doctrine rests upon his authority, but he did not hold it. Curious as its history is, its philosophical merits are not such as to give any real relief to our

---

[1] Cousin's Descartes, Tom. IV. p. 39 ; Les Passions de l'âme, Art. 3. Descartes laid himself open, by defect of steady precision in his language, to some misconception of his doctrine of organic automatism. It was easy to misconstrue his meaning into the proposition 'the animals *do not feel*.' But when, along with this, Professor Huxley attributes to him also the affirmation 'the animals *do reason*,' it is difficult to account for a statement so often contradicted by the philosopher himself. 'As is well known, Descartes'. . . .'maintained that all animals were mere machines and entirely devoid of consciousness. But he did not deny, nor can any one deny, that in this case they are reasoning machines, capable of performing all those operations which are performed by the nervous system of man when he reasons.' (Huxley's Critiques and Addresses, 1873, p. 282.) What then are we to make of the evidence adduced by Descartes to prove that the brutes differ from man, 'not by having less reason than he, but by having absolutely none at all :' and that 'their surpassing us in some things, instead of making good their claim to mind, shows that they are quite without it, and that they are disposed of by nature through the adjustment of their organs : just as a clock made up of wheels and springs can count the hours and measure time more correctly than we with all our wits?' (Discours de la Méthode, Cousin, i. pp. 188, 189.)

problem. We cannot excuse ourselves from reckoning
with the sufferings of the animals, on the plea that they are
all a sham ; and from seeking in them some better significance than this histrionic no-meaning.

Without attempting to drown this whole question in the
sense of mystery, or to silence objections by insisting on
our incompetency as critics of the universe, we may fairly
ask at the outset what we are entitled to claim, ere we
admit the benevolence of God. To the demand for happiness in a sentient creature *some limit* must be set : inasmuch as the creature is finite, and by hypothesis has
a nature terminable in time, restricted in range, imperfect
in quality. Whatever portion of good be assigned to it,
the question therefore might always be raised, 'why not
more ?' and could never be set at rest till the finite became
infinite. Perhaps you will say, it is not of the limited
measure of good, but of the mixture of evil, that you
complain. Are you then prepared to contend that, of the
two modes of bestowing a given portion of happiness, viz.
to deal it out with even uniformity, and to pour it forth
in waves of elevation and depression beyond the average
level, the former alone can be the object of benevolent
Will ? If not, then the mere interruption of enjoyment by
pain, the alternations of hope with fear, of repletion with
want, of health with sickness, can justify no protest ; and
your objection has still no place, unless you can show that,
when the additions and subtractions have all been made,
the balance is on the wrong side. This *preponderance* of
pain is the point on which the argument hangs, and on
which accordingly the pessimist bestows his labour. Have
we then any common measure, or any hedonistic notation,
enabling us, in any given case, to make the reckoning and
strike the balance? It is easy to descant exclusively on
the positive side, and paint the living world in the rosy
tints of a summer morning : or exclusively on the negative

side, and exhibit all things shivering in the night of wintry
storms : but is there any exact test to adjudicate between
these extreme valuations ?　Usually, it has been assumed
that we have such a test in the *willingness to live.*　So
long as this continues, existence, it has been supposed,
must be worth having ; and as soon as the scale turns the
other way, you will know it by the wish to die.　By this
rule, however, the pessimist could never make out his
case : for it is few, indeed, among the tenants of this teeming world, that would give him their vote by electing to
perish.　So, he insists that the clinging to life is no rational
judgment, no *insight* into the preferable, but a mad passion,
working irrespectively of the individual interests, for the
greatest conservation of vitality in nature : every creature
is its subject and its victim, fascinated by its own miseries,
and vehemently resisting the deliverance which lays them
to rest.　Once rescued from this delusion, and looking on
its lot with the calm eye of reason, it would see, as well as
feel, the bitterness of existence, and decline the dreadful
gift.　'The boundless clinging to life,' says Schopenhauer,
'cannot be attributed to knowledge and reflection : in the
view of these it is an insanity ; for the objective value of
life is a very dubious affair, and it is questionable, at least,
whether it is preferable to non-existence : nay, if experience and reflection are called to council, non-existence can
hardly fail to win.　Knock at the graves, and ask the dead
whether they would rise again : they will shake their
heads[1].'　If they be very dyspeptic dead, perhaps they
will ; else, should you be surprised if one were to say,
'Yes, try me again, and I will do better :' and the poet
to exclaim, 'just for a few years, to write my last cantos :'
and the statesman, 'well, I *should* like to see this passage
of history played out :' and the mother, 'let me only come

---

[1] Die Welt als Wille und Vorstellung, 3to Aufl., 1859, B. II. p. 529.

back till my wandering boy's return :' and even Schopenhauer himself, 'a little time I did certainly want to finish my proof that life is an unhappy dream ?'   And can it be denied that these answers would be as reasonable as they are natural ? do they not pitch upon real elements of worth in life? and are they not a fair sample of the interests and reasons which attach us to it ? and is it not true that, in proportion as these interests and reasons drop away, the aspect of death becomes placid and the wish to linger disappears ?   If so, our estimate of life varies in the ratio of its value, and may be taken as a fair measure of the good which it contains : and we are not the blind subjects of a cruel illusion, circling, like the moth, around a light that dizzies and consumes us.   Not that I deny the love of life to be instinctive, in us, as in all creatures : but, on its becoming self-conscious and submitted to reflection in our nature, it proves to be accordant with the measures of reason ; and justifies our assuming it, in the animal cases which we cannot similarly scrutinise, as an accurate expression of the eligible contents of existence to the creatures evincing it.   At all events, if this standard is disowned, there is no other to which we can appeal : and the conditions of the controversy between the prophets of hope and of despair must remain altogether indeterminate.

In passing under notice the sufferings of animals, it will be convenient to consider first, those which are incident to the structure of the organism itself; and then, those which arise from the relation of the organism to the scene of its history.

C. Pains from the Organism itself.

The possibilities of pain inherent in the organism are of two kinds : those which normally recur through life in the shape of *wants*, and which *work* the organism ; and those which at last set in, when the organism can no longer be worked.

a. Pains of Want.

The former of these already receive their explanation in the words which describe them : *they work the organism.* Hunger, thirst, fatigue, serve not only as heralds, punctually to announce a need, but as guides and incentives to supply it : nor is it conceivable that living power should be set in action at all, without a disturbance to the equilibrium of content. This class of pains is strictly self-corrective, and reacts into the corresponding pleasures : the tired animal sleeps, the thirsty drinks, the shivering creeps into shelter, the threatened flies or stands upon its guard. Reason itself, were it universal, would be a poor substitute for this sharp reminder. If each creature had to study its own case, and, like an outside physician, prescribe its diet and its meals, where to rest, and how and where to build, how long would it be before it slipped into some fatal forgetfulness, like the patient kept alive by art, and blundering among his medicines? As it is, the uneasiness of appetite or passion sets it upon tentatives for relief, and trains it to mastery over the resources of its world. It is curious to notice the opposite uses to which this law may be put by the differing tempers of its interpreters. Life, the pessimist tells us, is a continuous horror, a perpetual flight from pain : it is the goad from behind that spurs all its energy : it is to escape from itself that it is precipitated forward ; and though panting and spent, it cannot stop, for the ground caves in at every step ; and its whole story is made up of exhausting effort, in recoil from inflicted suffering. Take the same fact in front, look at its *whither* instead of its *whence,* and how different the aspect it assumes : Yes, we say, Life *is* a constant *escape* from suffering, a triumph over it by energy, a leaving of it behind, as a shadow that cannot overtake the swift and strenuous : and in this victory the creature learns that its true function is, not to *enjoy,* but to *achieve,* to command its field, and press into its own perfection. This is the true end that draws it forward into the future; and towards which its way is beneficently sped by a lesser content with the present. In proportion as the conquest of uneasiness by activity is better than the inertness of unbroken ease, are the pains to be welcomed which wake up faculty into existence. Take away from the animal all appetites, all passions, all affections, and what sort of creatures do you leave? whither will they move? what call will they answer? at what sound will they start? what will quicken and kindle their eye? You doom them to torpor, in which they hybernate instead of live. Do you think to stir them by pleasure and spare them pain? You may separate the names, but not the things; for they denote changes, and each is the transition from the other. You cannot have attraction where repulsion is made impossible, or joy where you forbid grief, or love where anger cannot come: these are polar forces, and must either enter in pairs, or stay away. I cannot say that, among the infinite reserves of things, there is no alternative possibility; but, so far as our range of conditions goes, the objection to pain is an objection to sentient life, and proposes not to reform, but to abolish, all but the vegetable realm of natural history. It would leave the beauty of the world without a witness, and its affluence without participants.

The variable and unequal strain, which constitutes the motive power of animal existence, is seen upon the largest scale in what is called the 'struggle for life' between races needing the same field, and nearly matched in their claims for its possession. Both the good and the evil of the law of want seem here to be most conspicuous. On the one hand, the way in which every advantage gained, in organism or instinct, secures its permanent hold and enriches the earth with higher forms, strikingly marks the pressure of nature towards the ulterior perfection, and betrays the ideal aim that works beneath her physical procedure. And, on the other hand, the cost at which the victors win their race, the baffling of the slow, the perishing of the weak, sink into the heart of the generous observer, and make him complain that nature is pitiless, and heeds not any suffering that enhances the glory of her works. This very complaint, however, is in itself a homage to the worth of life, and no pessimist could urge it without answering himself. Is it a *cruel* feature in the competition for existence, that the halt and feeble lose their footing on the world, and are exiled from life? Is it an evil which they thus incur? Then the life which they miss must be a good ; and it is a hardship *not* to find and keep a place within its teeming fields. If animal existence be not worth having, why invite our compassion for those that lose it ? Even on the opposite assumption, that, in spite of draw-backs, it is better to be alive, this plaintive plea for the beaten armies of nature has its ground more in imagination than in reality. The creatures that cannot compete, that are more ugly, or more awkward, or less swift or strong, than their rivals, do but suffer the fate of any dwindling minority, which may accomplish its ultimate vanishing without any great discomfort to its members, taken one by one. The extinct races whose only representatives are in our geological museums have suffered no agonies in their generic death, but have been quite unconscious of their interesting rarity ere they disappeared : and the last Dodo of New Zealand had no cause to envy the first. While the 'struggle for life' serves, for the whole organic world, as a principle of continuous advance, conducting each type towards its limits of perfection, it is simply, for each individual, the putting forth of all its faculties, which makes the best of the life it has. May we not say then, that it accomplishes the maximum of good with the minimum of evil, and pushes on a perpetual conquest, without leaving any vanquished aware of their defeat? And when we remember, that every attainment of an instinctive end is on that very account a pleasure, that all animal action is directed upon such ends, and that, for once that it is frustrated, it has a host of successes, how is it possible to doubt the overflowing preponderance of enjoyment, that is purchased on the cheap terms of an impelling want and a forfeited inertia?

β. Pains of Decline.

The sufferings which set in when the organism can no longer be worked, present a more difficult problem: for they have no future and cannot be prospective. What comes near the beginning, in the way of hardship, has time to clear itself and set forth its reasons in its effect: but when the most tragic scene is the last, there seems no room for relief, and we wonder why the winding up should be so sad : had nature provided it with an anæsthetic, what harm would be done?

I cannot deny that the phenomena of disease among the lower animals are perplexing facts, which at present admit of no satisfactory explanation. Why, in one season, the cattle should be smitten with a spreading malady, which they must be slain in order to arrest; and, in another, the grouse pine away into skeletons and strew the moors with their dead : why, when the body's natural term approaches, the failing organs should be susceptible of so many forms of painful decay, so that, if all that are at the last stage were brought together, the scene would be like a battle field at evening when the fight was done, I do not find that any wisest thinker is able to tell. But neither do I know that we should expect to tell ; for these are precisely the phenomena in which the known marks of intention fail, which are evidently *not the ends* for which the organs are constructed, which even constitute the dis-

appointment of those ends : for which accordingly it is as
unreasonable to seek a 'Wherefore,' as to ask the runner
why he falls, or the boatman why he shoots Niagara.
They are present, it is plain, *in spite of* the normal purpose
of the structure they disturb ; relatively to which they
must be regarded as *undesigned* imperfections, however
they may be embraced within some larger project in
whose paramount good their partial evils vanish. Do you
ask, what business have 'imperfections' in the work of an
infinite Being? Has he not power to bar them out? Yes,
I reply, if he lives out of his boundless freedom and, from
moment to moment, acts unpledged, conducting all things
by the miscellany of incalculable miracles, there is nothing
to hinder his Will from entering 'where it listeth,' and all
things will be 'possible to him.' But, if once he commits
his Will to any determinate method, and for the realization
of his ends selects and institutes a scheme of instrumental
rules, he thereby shuts the door on a thousand things that
might have been before ; he has defined his cosmical
equation, and only those results can be worked out from
it which are compatible with the values of its roots. If
the square of the distance gives the ratio of decreasing
gravitation, the universe must forego the effects which
would arise from the rule of the cube. If, for two transparent media, the index of relative refraction is made
constant, the phenomena are excluded which would arise
were it variable. Every legislative volition narrows the
range of events previously open, and substitutes necessity
for contingency ; and a group or system of laws, in
providing for the occurrence of one set of phenomena,
relinquishes the conditions of another. It is vain therefore
to appeal to the almightiness of God, unless you mean to
throw away the relations of any established universe, and
pass into his unconditioned infinite : in the cosmos, he
has abnegated it ; and there is a limit for what you may

demand from it as within its compass. The limits, it is true, which are assigned to its play are *self-imposed* : but, in order to any determinate action at all, *some* limits had to be assigned: and, unless you can show that to a different scheme better possibilities and a less mixed good would have attached themselves, a tone of complaint which can only be justified by such comparative criticism, is out of place. Most of the sufferings now under our notice arise from some troubled relation between the animal organism and the scene in which it is placed : ungenial seasons, desolating winds and floods, an atmosphere charged with germs of disease, a frost that creeps into the heart of the old, a marsh vapour that spreads the fever-bed for the young, are the visitations that make a wreck of life. And these are the occasional results of that scheme of physical laws which, while preparing the theatre of animal existence and favouring its development, yet goes beyond it and steps from world to world, negociating for other interests also, and contemplating more enduring good. In launching a power commissioned to a million ends, still more in adjusting together twenty different lines of power, whose crossing and confluence is to work out these ends, it is surely conceivable that the Creator's Will, while subjecting his means to steady rules, may realise some elements of his design less absolutely than if they had stood alone. To every finite method (and to create is to enter the sphere of the finite), this partial disability, this unequal approximation to the ideally perfect, inevitably clings : if it is made inflexible, it must sometimes start a conflict between its universal means and its partial ends: if it is left fluid, it is no longer a method at all. The problems how much should be yielded of one design to serve another, and at what cost of purpose persistence and exactitude of rule should be secured, can be surveyed and solved only by a Mind that commands the whole field of the actual and the possible. They are entirely beyond the reach of any calculus of ours. It is enough for us to see that they exist, and that under them appear to lie the very cases which most embarrass us in the pathology of nature. In some such consolations as these almost every philosophy has taken refuge ; unable otherwise to harmonise its entrancement with the divine beauty of the world in front, and its feeling of the dark shadow, as of some fate, behind. When Plato says that the Creator, having to mix together necessity and thought, made the universe as like to himself as he could : when Aristotle distinguishes the inner form from the outer matter of the world, identifying the Divine perfection with the former, and deriving all imperfections from the latter : when Leibniz tells us that this is the best world possible, but that, being an assemblage of finite natures, it cannot but have its relative ills, and that, in duly balancing the well-being of the whole with the interest of each part, God had to solve a problem in maxima and minima ; they all recognise limits of possibility, on which, and not upon the Divine Will, they charge all natural evil.

This general doctrine dispenses with the necessity of seeking for some end in view, to justify each type of suffering ; and leaves only the question, whether it is better to permit it, or that the system of sentient nature should not be. And this question settles itself at once by the simple fact, that the class of pains with which it is concerned is by hypothesis *exceptional and terminal*, breaking in upon the usual order, or finishing the functions, of life ; and is therefore inconsiderable, in comparison with the well-being of which it is the price. Nor are the cases, taken as they arise, without alleviations and palliatives which greatly relieve their aspect. It is an old common-place, not worthless even in practical consolation, still less in theory, that, if pain is sharp, it will also be short : and no one can

have observed any permanent form of crippled life, without
wondering at the compensations of nature and the reconciling adaptations of habit.   In the lower animals too,
accident and disease carry with them only the pangs of
present sensation ; not the ideal torture of memory and
fear, of imaginary self-wreck, of broken schemes, of anxious
affections, of vain regrets, which enter into the corresponding afflictions of men.   And as to the final collapse of the
worn out organism, with what face can any creature ask
that, *living* being so pleasant, *unliving* should be so no
less?   That it feels the cold on going out does but prove
how warm its house has been.   You cannot have opposites
giving you the same experience : if it be sweet to behold
the light, sweet it cannot be to lose it : if to thirst be
a distress, to drink will be relief.   The uneasiness of death
is the necessary correlative to the happiness of life.

  d. Pains from relation to the environment.

  a. From the physical elements.

  I turn now to the sufferings which arise from the relations of the animal organism to the theatre of its existence ; and to the physical elements around it.   To this
class of liabilities I have already incidentally alluded ; and
little remains for me to say of them.   The difficulty which
they raise may shape itself into either of two questions :
' Why are the laws established for this theatre of existence
such as to admit of animal catastrophes?' or, 'Why, the
laws (for whatever reason) being such, are animals allowed
to be exposed to them?'   To the former question it would
be idle to attempt to reply : the great cosmic laws under
which our planet is moved and moulded are entirely
beyond our criticism ; for how can we have any alternative
to propose?   We slowly read the order which they produce, and record it in our sciences, which exhibit the intellectual structure of the world : but the reasons which
determine it into being, as against other possibilities, we

must assume to be sufficient and not pretend to scan. The physical system then we take as given, and consider only why sentient beings are not withheld from the misery it may inflict.

No disasters have a more appalling aspect, or seem to make more cruel sport of life, than those produced by the earthquake, the volcano, the geyser,—convulsions that contradict the very solidity of the world. We cannot wonder that rude tribes, but too familiar with the sweeping vengeance of oriental conquerors, saw in these events the Divine retribution on the sins of men, and so brought them into rough harmony with the sense of right: or that, when this explanation too obviously failed, its loss left the heart oppressed, as by a mystery of wrong. It could not be otherwise, so long as these phenomena were regarded as part of the *moral* government of the world, and as ordained each for its own special end. But this is an instance in which relief is gained by recognising the co-existence of a physical with a moral order, so that the latter has not the *sole voice* in the history of nature, but is sometimes silent while events are determined by other conditions. The disturbances of which we speak are, all of them, indications on the earth's crust of its past genesis and present relations: they declare the story incomplete: they are remnants of the process of planet-making, which still goes on; which has advanced far enough to offer some habitable lands, but not far enough to secure them all against caving in. Among the various problems presented by the cooling of the globe and the condensation of its surface, none could be more momentous than this: at what point of the process should life be permitted to appear? should it be postponed so long as the equilibrium was unstable, though the strata were laid and relaid, and the atmosphere was spread, and the continents were raised, and the rivers flowed, and the valleys were scooped, and all was ready as a well-dug winter garden-plot to receive its seed? Or would wisdom rather be impatient of these millenniums of barrenness, and give orders of immediate possession to life, notwithstanding its partial liability to collapse? If the latter, is not the decision like that of the general who, intent on some great enterprise, marches his army across lands that may be partially mined, rather than keep it sleeping in its tents through a possible campaign? Is it not better for organic nature to occupy its territory at once, and make good the earlier stages of its history, even though here and there one of its battalions should perish on the way? Even in the countries most exposed to them, these catastrophes are so infrequent, that scientific travellers have often exhausted their patience and spent half their lives in the vain hope of seeing them; and the sum total of their injuries sinks into insignificance, compared with the measureless amount of the unimpaired vitality from which it is a deduction. There is nothing in it to deter a beneficent Creator from opening the story of sentient existence, ere yet the crust of the earth has settled in its last security.

But even if our planet were already solid to its centre, there is another class of destructive paroxysms to which its surface would remain exposed: storms that rend the forests, floods that drown the plains, the untimely frost that nips every growing promise, the sudden avalanche that buries the growing fields and the warm life of the valley in its snows. To these also the same principle applies. If you ask me to find for them a place in the *moral order* of things, and tell you the end for which each is ordained, I have no answer to give. But if the question be, how, with these things in the physical order the moral order is yet compatible? I need only beg you to look beyond these particular phenomena to the system in which they appear, and which cannot be judged by them alone.

They occur in conformity with atmospheric and meteoro-logical laws which alone render life possible, and under shelter of which every breathing thing exists and moves and grows and sees the world and feels the sun : so that the same rules which are death-dealing for an hour or a day are life-giving for ever.   If we are to judge truly of the expression and significance of nature, surely we must look on her face not in the convulsion of a passing struggle, but in its permanent aspect of composure or of joy.   The real question is simply this ; whether the laws of which complaint is made work such harm, that they ought never to have been enacted ; or whether, in spite of occasional disasters in their path, the sentient existence of which they are the conditions has in its history a vast excess of blessing.   Can any one who really applies this test pronounce that it was incumbent on a wise and bene-ficent Being to refrain from instituting the terrestrial laws ?

A third class of ills, incident to the relation between the animal organism and the scene of its existence, presents more difficulty ; because, fastening on living bodies and touching nothing else, it seems directly aimed at them, instead of merely catching them on its way over some wider sweep : I allude to epidemic or endemic maladies. The difference, however, between this case and those already noticed is more apparent than real ; and, were it not that the causes of an inroad of disease are invisible in the air or in the water, so that we see it first in its effects, it would not strike us so exclusively as a physiological blow dealt out of the dark.   Once let its external sources come clearly into view, and, as they approach, give notice of the danger that impends, and this kind of destruction would no less plainly belong to the physical order than the deluge or the hurricane.   The same considerations therefore really apply to both ; only, in the case of extensive disease of a given type, there is this peculiarity ; that the general law of

which it is the expression is physiological rather than
physical, and, though involving a play between the outer
elements and the organism, has the greater part of its conditions in the latter : *there* it is that the complex and
delicate equilibrium lies, which some simpler external
agency suffices to overthrow.   Hence it is that epidemics
prevailingly take (as if by selection) the members of some
one species, which have all the same constitution of body,
and offer therefore the same ready receptacle to the mor-
biferous agency from without.   A form of malady which
runs a fatal course among cattle will have no effect upon
the birds of the farm yard.   It is in virtue of their unity of
constitution, that multitudes of creatures summarily suc-
cumb to an unpropitious influence ; their sufferings in
common are an expression of their *sympathy of kind*.   But
from this same sympathy springs almost everything that
gives interest and value to their existence ; their instinctive
affections, their gregarious life, the sport of the young
among them, the sagacity of the old, their combined action
in danger, their doubled content with the pasture, the sunshine, or the shallow river, when enjoyed in company.   In
short, the decree by which they die together is the same
that ordained them to live together ; in estimating it, we
must take it as a whole, and consider whether we should
reckon it as a gain, either to dispense with the kinship of
animals and fling them into lonely separation, or even, to
split the law of alliance in two, so as to arrest the sympathy
of nature at the limits of enjoyment, and, as soon as they
suffer, terminate their association and isolate them in distress and death.   Is it mere empty sentiment to say that,
under a law which ties together the kindred lives of the
same tribe, and carries the unity of type through all the
incidents of their history, a higher idea, a clearer moral
expression, shines through the order of nature, than would
be given if, the centres of sympathy being weakened, each

organism declared its independence, and went apart with its securities and dangers? As it is, the very constitution of the world, ere it reaches the level of responsible existence, already prefigures the social conception to which it tends, and rebukes from afar the selfishness of man, when he tries to set up for himself and escape his share in the common lot.

β. From the predaceous method of life.

The liabilities of each animal race are not all due to the physical elements: others, of a more constant and formidable character, arise from its relation to hostile tribes. There is perhaps no feature in the order of nature, which less easily harmonises with an ideal perfection of moral rule, than the Law of prey, which makes each race of creatures, through vast provinces of natural history, the devourer of some other. The natural desire we feel to free the caught fly from the spider's web, or to rescue the mouse from the owl's beak, constitutes an involuntary protest against the method in which the animal commissariat is managed: and, after closely following the habits of the predaceous families, and engaging our imagination with the terror of the hunted victim, the agony of the capture, the atrocity of the death, we are tempted to say that the sweet face of nature is hypocritical, and that the calm loveliness of the woods and ravines does but hide innumerable torture-halls and battle-fields. From such impressions I own that I cannot always entirely free myself: yet that they arise from a partial and narrow view of the phenomena, and cannot be justified on a rational survey of the whole case, will appear, I think, from the following considerations.

It is a great exaggeration to affirm, that animated nature is a scene of universal war. There is no war except of each tribe against those on which it is appointed to subsist: and it is worth while to observe how extensive are the exemptions which this limit creates. The herbivorous families have no victims, and, but for their enemies, would live at peace with all. And the carnivorous tribes are not omnivorous, but select, in their tastes and their antipathies; so that they are foes only to a few species, and leave all others undisturbed. And however savage they are, when stimulated by hunger and heated by the chase and brought into the conflict, it is by sudden paroxysm, directed against a race of strangers, that suffer from it only in that passing encounter: the herd of deer that loses a victim to the pursuing panther, turns in its flight into some fresh pasture, and grazes, and forgets. And then this temper, so terrible in the fight, can be quite sheathed at home, and is in no way incompatible with gentle affections and faithful cares towards the kindred and companions of the daily life. And if kindly terms are established among creatures that spend their time together, it matters comparatively little that, in raids upon an enemy's territory, bursts of fierce passion have their hour. The immunities therefore from the cruelty of appetite are large: its crises are short; and by far the greater part of life, both to the hunter and the hunted, is untroubled by it. And, among the modes of death, there is no reason to suppose that to become the victim of animal voracity is more painful than to perish by disease, or pine away by exhaustion. Sharp and quick extinction may shock the observer by its startling contrasts: but, to the sufferer, the surprise is an economy of pain. To imaginative creatures it might be otherwise: they might torture themselves with life-long dread of the last struggle: and such ideal diffusion of possible calamity it is, that makes the human measure of pain so different from the merely sentient. But where there is no anticipation, and the unsuspecting victim strolls at ease, or keeps merrily on the wing, up to the moment of its fate, the sensibility is spared to the uttermost. I believe that, in our shrinking from this law, we illegitimately import into our conception of the case elements, which are indeed inseparable from any analogous human experience, but which have no entrance into the history of the lower terrestrial races.

It behoves the critic of this predaceous system to balance against it the alternative that must take its place, if it be removed. Withdraw altogether the carnivorous habit, and the whole stock of the world must become graminivorous: 'all flesh will be grass.' I will not attempt to trace the vast results of such a change upon the economy of the globe,—the modification of organic types on land, the emptying out from the seas of almost all their life ;— but will be content with a single question : How would you dispose of the bodies of the dead animals? If you say, there are plenty of vegetarian tribes already, and they give us no trouble in their death, you forget that for this we have to thank the carnivora, that carry them into their larder and spare us the burden of their interment : and, especially, that Man himself undertakes a commission to clear out nearly the total numbers of the oxen, sheep, and deer. But if no creature would touch muscular fibre, or adipose tissue, or blood, and all animated nature had to be provided with cemeteries like ours, we should be baffled by an unmanageable problem: the streams would be poisoned, and the forests and the plains would be as noisome as the recent battle-field. Nature, in her predatory tribes, has appointed a sanitary commission, and in her carrion-feeders a burial-board, far more effective than those which watch over our villages and cities : and one of the great difficulties of our crowded civilization is due to the fact, that there is nobody to eat us. Yes, it will perhaps be said : but, in order to have an herbivorous world, we might ask for the corresponding alteration in the laws of putrefaction, so as to leave nothing for us to remedy or prevent. We are thus carried to a deeper change, as indispensable to the proposed reform,—no less than a reconstitution, on new

bases, of the whole chemical legislation of the universe.
The hypothesis, enlarged by this condition, breaks into
dimensions so little measurable, that no available method
can work it out to any determinate result ; and we may
leave it with the remark that, however easy it may be to
picture to ourselves a world clear of this or that imputed
blemish, we constantly find, when we attempt, by reasoning
out the conditions, to make provision for its departure,
that it is inseparably interwoven with the pattern of the
whole, nay, that if its thread were withdrawn, some of the
most delicate lines and finest colours of the tissue would
unexpectedly disappear.

There is however another alternative, which amuses the
fancy of some of our humane cosmical reformers. The
true euthanasia for all mortal beings would be, they think,
to pass away, without previous decline, by instantaneous
apoplexy : and, if this were universal, there would then be
no objection to letting the bodily remains of the lower
animals be turned to account as food for the living.
Nature would thus be the only executioner, and no animal
would be eaten alive. The carnivorous races need not be
ordered off the stage : notice would simply be served upon
them that, henceforth, they must resort to the dead-meat
market, instead of hunting for themselves. How they
would receive such change, and whether, with the cessation
of the chase, their fierce temper could be trusted to subside
and die away, may well be doubted. Perhaps the old
prophecy would be fulfilled, and ' the lion would really lie
down with the lamb.' But, remembering how the vultures
behave before and after the breath is out of the body
which they watch, I should rather fear that, around every
tempting carcase, there would be enacted no very amiable
scene ; and that, in the competition for a meal, battles
would be witnessed not less ferocious than those of the
chase ; with this unfavourable difference, that now they

would rage not between strangers and natural foes, but among members of the same race and kindred, pressed by the same wants and invited to the same meal. The barbaric element therefore would not be eliminated from the living world : nor would any improvement be secured by its change of form. As no further alternative remains, we are entitled to conclude that no case is made out against the existing law which supplies the subsistence and regulates the relations of the animal races.

(*c*) Pathology of Human Life.

So far as we too, by our constitution, fall under the cognisance of zoology, our case is included in the foregoing plea. But the pathology of our life has a further range of its own: and of this our problem requires us to take separate account. I have already noticed the limitation of animal pain to the moments of its actual presence to Sense, and contrasted it with the ideal misery that may affect us through long periods exempt from physical pain. It would seem that, if this difference can be urged in favour of the brutes, it must be reckoned as making against us; and that our lot must be less compatible with creative benevolence than theirs. This however would be a very erroneous inference, drawn from premisses far too narrow : as I hope the following considerations will show.

The additional dimensions which suffering gains in us beyond the limits of animal sensibility are contributed by the intellectual endowments. It is because we can look fore and aft from the point where we stand, because we have ever with us the possible as well as the actual, because the visible has no power to blot out the invisible from our thought, that with us no pang can be born and perish in a moment : it sends us notice of its approach : it leaves with us many a vestige on its departure : far beyond the term of total eclipse it spreads a broad penumbra of mournful twilight. Memory seems to have the cruel

property of stripping trouble of its transitoriness ; as foresight betrays its secret, and will not let it hide itself till
the instant of surprise ; and, if it be uncertain and contingent, and might therefore never touch us were we blind,
imagination snatches away the chance of escape, and
realises it even when unreal. The longest shadows of
life are cast by the light of thought from low altitudes
above a far horizon, and disappear for those who live
always under the vertical sun of the present moment. All
sorrow is certainly loss that refuses to go away into the
past : all anxiety, privation that will not wait for the future :
and we should be spared both, did we forget everything
and anticipate nothing. What then is the just inference
from this ? Would you renounce your Reason that you
may be saved your tears ? Would you quit your many-
chambered mind, and shut yourself up in a single cell, and
draw down its blinds, that you may suspect no storms and
see no lightning, and know nothing till you are struck ?
No : you would not part with your prerogative, even
though it did no more than multiply your troubled moments. But this is less than half the tale : the ideal
suffering which is added to our nature is balanced and
over-balanced by an ideal happiness of which it alone is
made susceptible. The capacity of thought takes up into
it all the elements of our experience, and gives them a
boundless spiritual extension : and if, in this enlargement,
there is any change of their proportions, it is that the
ideal forms rather soften the shadows and glorify the
lights : so that the inner life is sweeter than the outer,
and supplies the truest balm for the wounds of the actual.
It is evident that, while we suffer in the dark, we can see
no way of escape : that intellectual consciousness is the
condition of whatever control we may obtain over our
distresses : that only by their continuance in thought can
we distinguish their kinds, investigate their causes, discover

their remedies ; and that, by occupying the mind, they put
themselves into the hand of a master. It is the self-knowledge of suffering that opens all the resources of sympathy,
whether direct, in face to face intercourse with living con-
solers, or indirect, through the literature and art which
preserve the pathos and the heroism of humanity. From
these things you must part, if you would decline your
human heritage of pain. That heritage is the *consequence
of intellect*; and cannot be resigned without forfeiting all
that intellect brings.

But further, suffering is the *postulate of our moral nature*:
the structure of which, in some of its essentials, would be absolutely unmeaning without it. Among the Primary springs
of action, which set all the problems for our conscience, is
there not one whole class,—viz. the *Passions*,—that are
relative to what repels and hurts us ? So that we are
made to the pattern of no world without alloy, but are
sent into a field assumed to have its open or its ambushed
foes ; and are supplied with sentinels that may bid us wake
and take up timely arms. Nor is this the only indication
that life is *meant* to have its paths of pain,—not to be all
laid out as a sunny Paradise, but to contain its cypress
groves where few rays penetrate. If fear, antipathy, and
anger are our ready protectors against harm to ourselves,
what is compassion but a natural provision of healing for
the distress of others ? We come into the world, therefore,
already furnished with activities which have no other
function than to repulse ills that approach ourselves, and
draw us to those which visit our fellows ;—a constitution,
which at the same time presupposes suffering, yet, far
from making it *an end*, meets it with *a remedy*, and shows
how the face of nature turns towards it with regretful
looks. In these springs of action we have our credentials
and commission to contend against it : and in the play
which we allow to them, and the application we choose

for them, consists a large part of the responsibilities of life.
No one can be brave, without regulating the importunities
of fear; or generous, without setting the true limit to
anger ; or just, without subordinating Pity to the sense of
Right.   The very elements that make up the cases of duty
are thus, in innumerable instances, relative to the presence
of suffering, and, in its absence, would themselves disappear.   It holds a place therefore among the data of the
moral life, and is essential to this highest term in the ideal
of humanity.   And so the maxim of Richard Rothe is
verified : that ' in this world all Good, even the fairest and
noblest,—as Love,—rests upon a ' dark ground,' which it
has to consume with pain and convert into pure spirit [1].'

But suffering is not only the postulate whence our moral
nature starts ; it is also *the discipline* through which it gains
its true elevation.   I do not say that, by the mere incidence of pain, the torpid conscience is awakened, or the
close affections opened and the slavery of selfishness
escaped : no sentient experience can necessitate a moral
result : and in low types of mind, where the insight is
small and the voluntary power is weak, it is quite possible
for the character to dry up and harden and contract, when
brought to the furnace of affliction.   Nor do I doubt that,
for many men, the school of action fairly serves to purify
and invigorate their will, though they ride through life on
the crest of the world's wave and never sink into the
hollows.   But, though some can do without it, and others
do nothing with it, yet it is true that, for the greatest and
best, you must seek among those who have abounded in
hardships and been passed through the fire.   Ease and

---

[1] Stille Stunden, Aphorismen aus Richard Rothe's handschrift-
lichem Nachlass, Wittenberg, 1872, p. 136.   In dieser Welt ruht alles
Gute, auch das Edelste und Schönste wie die Liebe, auf einem ' fin-
steren Grunde,' den es unter Schmerzen aufzehren und in lichten Geist
umzeugen muss.

prosperity may supply a sufficient school for the respectable *commoners* in character : but 'without suffering is no man *ennobled*[1].' Every highest form of excellence, personal, relative, spiritual, rises from this dark ground, and emerges into its freedom by the conquest of some severe necessity. In what Elysium could you find the sweet patience and silent self-control of which every nurse can testify ? or the fortitude in right, which the rack cannot crush or the dungeon wear out ? or the courage of the prophet, to fling his divine word before the wrath of princes and the mocking of the people ? I know it is said, that these would be superfluous virtues there, their worth being wholly relative to the evils which they minimise. But is this true ? Is the soul which has never been subdued to patience, braced to fortitude, fired with heroic enthusiasm, as harmonious, as strong, as large and free, as that which has been schooled in martyrdom ? No, the least part of these conquests is in their immediate mastery of the besetting ill : they add a cubit to the moral stature : they clear the vision : they refine the thought : they animate the will : so that there is not a duty, however simple, that does not win from them a fresh grace, or a mood, however common, to which they do not give a richer tone. And if to our own chastening we must acknowledge this personal debt, it is equally certain that the sufferings of others speak with an indispensable appeal to our affections, and wake us into a disinterestedness else impossible. Not that we are without sympathy with happy lives also ; but as they need nothing from us, they are only a pleasant spectacle, and do not stir us from our passiveness, and the affection remains superficial for want of striking root in effort of the will : for, until you serve and strive, you cannot truly love. It is in the presence of sorrow and

---

[1] Stille Stunden, p. 210, Niemand wird ohne Leiden *geadelt.*

privation that we most forget ourselves: and in many a
home the crippled child or the disabled father has trained to
tenderness and considerateness the habits which would else
have been self-seeking and frivolous[1].   The noble army of
benefactors of mankind whose names tradition will not
forget, consist of men and women whose hearts have been
smitten with some great compassion, and who have given
their lives 'a ransom for many.' And here too it is vain to
say that, in a world without affliction, we could well spare
them.   It would be but an insipid place.   Take away
these figures from the stage of history, and who would
care to sit its drama through?   Has their biography no
interest on its own account?   Are they mere organs for
discharging this or that evil from the world, and have they
no measure but as instruments for this one end?   On the
contrary, it is their own depth of character, rather than
their special work, that comes home to us with power; so
that the end they had in view often affects us less than the

---

[1] *The Widow's Mite.*

A widow—she had only one!
A puny and decrepit son;
  But, day and night,
Though fretful oft, and weak and small,
A loving child, he was her all—
  The Widow's Mite.

The Widow's Mite—ay, so sustained,
She battled onward, nor complained,
  Though friends were fewer;
And while she toiled for daily fare
A little crutch upon the stair
  Was music to her.

I saw her then; and now I see
That, though resigned and cheerful, she
  Has sorrowed much:
She has, He gave it tenderly,
Much faith; and, carefully laid by,
  A little crutch.
    London Lyrics, by Frederick Locker, 1878, p. 43.

great personalities which it created. More readily still
must it be admitted that, but for its sorrow, the heart
would seldom find its rest in God : for even the cynic feeds
his humour on the fact that men betake themselves to
religion, when they have lost all else. As usual, he sees
aright, but gives the meaning wrong. He thinks it some
mean fear, that wrings forth the sufferer's prayer,—some
snatch of despair at a dismal refuge, like a plank in ship-
wreck, or a hideous meal in famine ; and takes it in proof,
that religion is nothing but the lowest dregs of life, when
the generous wine is all drained off. And so it would be,
if there were no truth in it, and the sole reality lay in the
temporal well-being : to fall through the comforts into the
pieties of life would then be to exchange the substance for
the shadow, and to cheat away misery by opiate dreams of
superstition. But if, through and behind the finite which
we are and see, there is the infinite reality of God in us
and around us unseen, if the former engages all our action,
and crowds upon us appeals to our affections, while the
latter lies around us as the spaces of a cathedral on which,
like the workman in it, we have no time to gaze ; then
surely it is intelligible without reproach, that, in the suspense of activity and through the tears of love, we should
lift our eyes and look down the great perspectives, and
ponder the sacred emblems, and find on what holy ground
we stand. So long as we are abandoned to the customary
play of phenomenal causes, we rarely quit the surface of
either our own nature or the world : but when we are
thrown out of the swift current and laid aside in the sorrow
of some great change, the inner and the outer deeps are
opened, and we sink at once into ourselves and God.
Instead of passing away from reality, we now first reach
it ; and the foot which had been planted on the wave,
rests at last upon the rock. Whether it be that the fading
of external things brings out the inward lights, or that the

surrender of all aims and desires itself delivers us into the
Divine hand, it appears certain that the truest piety is to
be learned only in the school of suffering : and, strange to
say, its usual characteristic is in a certain brightness and
restfulness of spirit, free from the plaintive tone of painless
religion : its faith is not shaken, but confirmed, by the
shock. It is the observer that whimpers, while the victim
sings, 'Though he slay me, yet will I trust in him.'

In another way also are we disciplined by pain. Whence
comes the permanent uneasiness and discontent that are
apt to haunt even favoured lives, and that trace the lines
of care on every thoughtful human face? From the
constant presence of unrealised ideas. The sense of short-
comings, of broken purposes, of blighted visions, follows
everyone with a shadow darker than the sun's, and brings
many a chill on the most genial hours. This is the one
comprehensive human affliction into which innumerable
minor troubles may be resolved ; and it consists in a
perpetual transcendency of conception beyond performance, a law of acceleration for the advance of thought
beyond the rate of movement practicable for the will: so
that in morals, in art, in literature, and in the State, action
is disappointment and achievement poor. Yet to this
very law we evidently owe the whole impulse which saves
both the individual and society from a stationary existence.
But for this felt interval between what is and what ought
to be, who would stir from his position of content? who
resolve to make the future better than the present? what
should prevent the whole world from being arrested where
it is, and becoming a stereotyped Chinese empire? In
truth, what we often call 'the struggle of life' and regard
as the competition of men with each other, is in no small
measure due to this restless ideality, and is rather their
attempt to overtake their own conception, and render more
nearly perfect the work which they perform. Doubtless,

the two incentives act together: but, without disturbed equilibrium between thought and deed, competition would have no effective engine of operation. This characteristic pain is therefore the very spring of all progressive good; and justifies the ancient aphorism, 'Dei omnia laboribus et doloribus vendunt.' If you ask me why they are not given us *gratis*, I hold my peace, till you show me whether that would have been better for anything but our ease; and whether, in case of such gift, the *thanks* would have followed.

The human sufferings which I have noticed all enter distinctly into the plan of our nature, and play an assigned part in it. If there be any residue to which this account does not apply, I can only regard them as not objects of separate intention, serving a preconceived end, but as included among the admissible consequences of some eligible general law.

B. Admission of Sin.

Let us now turn our attention to the provisions which admit *moral evil* into the world.

In treating of this old and terrible perplexity, some care is needed to keep it clear of passionate exaggeration, and present it in a form sufficiently exact for true appreciation. To judge from the threnodies of the modern pessimist, he is chiefly impressed by the *miseries* which vice and wrong produce. Would he then prefer that they should produce happiness? or would he have it make no difference to the external well-being of mankind, whether greed and license prevailed, or disinterestedness and purity? Surely the entail of natural evil upon moral is the indispensable expression of a righteous administration of things: and the Divine holiness, instead of requiring its abatement, rather forces us to ask whether it is strict enough,—whether there is not too much impunity,—whether justice does not halt too long and far behind the fugitive from the law of

Right. I have dealt already with the phenomena of pain
and reviewed them in their several aspects : but the one
class of them which I have not felt called upon to notice,
because it was impossible to make a difficulty out of them,
is that of natural penalties for guilt. Sin being there, it
would be simply monstrous that there should be no
suffering, and would fully justify the despair which now
raises its sickly cry of complaint against the retributory
wretchedness of human transgression. The *incidence* of
such wretchedness may doubtless be at times open to
wonder and criticism : it may fall upon the innocent, and
so seem to miss its proper aim. But its existence and its
amount are only what must be expected in a state of
being in which character is to bear its consequences. The
question which presses upon us is not, 'how does it consist
with the *benevolence* of God to admit so much morally incurred *pain* ?' but 'how does it consist with the *holiness* of
God to admit so much *unholiness* in human life ?'

There is a contrast worth noticing between this difficulty
and those which we have already discussed. In encountering *them*, we were haunted by *the fatalism of nature*,
and cried out against the inexorable sternness with which
her laws marched on, regardless of all that they crushed or
sacrificed : we deprecated the determinate persistency that
had but one path and would never swerve from it. But, in
the present case, we are disposed to find fault with the
contingency left unclosed in our humanity, and protest against
its opportunities of going wrong ; to ask why we were not
so hemmed in, as all to keep 'the narrow way that leads
to life.' While the former complaint was of too much
necessity, this is of too much *possibility*. Both objections
assume that there is nothing which we may not ask from
the omnipotence of God, and that no petition can be
unreasonable, addressed to such a being. This, however,
we have seen, would no longer be true, when once he

had quitted his unconditioned infinitude, and instituted a cosmical existence: for every *definite* system, having its own scheme of phenomena, must exclude such eligible options as lie beyond. And, by parity of reasoning, I must now submit, that every *contingent* system, having its own range of alternatives, must admit such ineligible options as lie among the variations: if there is to be liberty for the worse, there cannot be necessity of the better. It is absurd to treat these limits to our demands as a denial of the divine Almightiness: it is not a question about the power of doing, but of the compatibility of being and the consistency of thought: no force can break the nexus of reason, and the most trivial of contradictions may defy omnipotence. Notwithstanding the supreme causality of God, it is rigorously true that only in a very restricted sense can he be held the author of moral evil.

He is no doubt the source of *its possibility*; having set up the created wills, in which it originates, and planted them on a scene where they may make the false step as well as the true. Whoever commits a trust to others thereby opens a possibility of moral evil; but we do not on that account regard him, if the trust be violated, as the author of the unfaithfulness; unless indeed he has burdened the assigned duty with unmanageable conditions. But, if at the outset he has secured both the knowledge of the right and the power over it, we do not charge him with the wrong, on the mere ground that he has not rendered it impossible. He might certainly have done so: but only by substituting mechanism for free agency,—by locking up, for example, his bills and money in an iron strong room during his absence, instead of leaving them to his cashier to meet and present his claims as they fall due: at the cost, therefore, of barring out the honesty and the dishonesty together. It is only by abstaining from pre-determining necessity, and allowing play for preferential choice, that he leaves room for the exercise *of character* and the testing of fidelity. In virtue of this abstinence, he is at once the *cause of the existence of character*, and *not the cause of what that character shall be*. Similarly, a universe which no sin could invade, neither could any character inhabit : and, in insisting that every access be shut against moral evil, we ask the holiness of God to cancel its own conditions, and take away the alternatives which reveal and reproduce it. It is *because he is Holy*, and cannot be content with an unmoral world where all the perfection is given and none is earned, that he refuses to render guilt impossible and inward harmony mechanical : were he only benevolent, it would suffice to fill his creation with the joy of sentient existence ; but, being righteous too, he would have in his presence beings nearer to himself, determining themselves by free preference to the life which he approves : and preference there cannot be, unless the double path is open. To set up therefore an absolute barrier against the admission of wrong, is to arrest the system of things at the mere natural order, and detain life at the stage of a human menagerie, instead of letting it culminate in a moral society.

While however, to avoid this extreme, some range of contingency must be admitted, it would again be inconsistent with righteousness to leave that range unlimited. Among the conditions under which character is formed, unless there be some constants mingled with the variables, and unless to the degenerative tendencies, when they set in, some check is provided, a total moral anarchy and dissolution may ensue, and a hell on earth be formed instead of an incipient heaven. It cannot be left to mere created natures to play unconditionally with the helm of even a single world, and steer it uncontrolled into the haven or on to the reefs ; and some security must be taken for keeping their deflections within tolerable bounds. So that again the problem seems to lie between two extremes, — of absolute mechanism and absolute contingency,—and to fall under the method of maxima and minima: being virtually this; how to provide the free conditions of *character*, with the best security for *its tending upwards*. We are ourselves only pupils in the great school in which this problem is answered, and are doubtless but incompetent critics of its solution: but some of the elements in the computation are within the reach of our estimate, and serve at least to show that none of the essentials have dropped out of the account.

If in every mind the springs of action had strength in exact proportion to their worth, and in their application were directed by correct judgment of their effects, the best forms of conduct, and nothing else, would spontaneously arise. They would arise, however, not by reason of their goodness, but by reason of their force, with no more virtue in them than in the growing of the clover or the incubation of the bird. 'Nothing takes place morally,' says Rothe, 'except what takes place *through one's own self-determination*: and this it is that converts it from a mere taking place into an *action*[1].' To provide for this we are endowed with Will, the possession of which elevates us from mere sensitive theatres of phenomena and organs for the transit of force, into personal agents capable of being causes. But this power would still be latent, and without means of asserting itself, if no discrepancy were ever permitted between the order of strength and the order of worth among our springs of action: the voluntary suffrage could only superfluously decree what would equally happen without it. In order to give scope for the intervention of Will, there must arise some conflict

---

[1] Stille Stunden, p. 186. Das moralische Geschehen ist das Geschehen kraft eigener Selbstbestimmung. Eben deshalb ist es kein Geschehen, sondern ein Handeln.

between the intensity of one impulse and the higher worth
of another : were we left at the disposal of instinct, we
should be carried off by the first : but, appealed to by the
claims of the other, we throw our causality into it, and
stop the abduction which threatened us.   It is only under
these conditions,—which constitute what we call *temptation*,
—that personal self-determination can step upon the field
and show the difference between natural events and moral
agency : we must begin therefore with a certain disorder
among our springs of action, some native elements of
rebellion of the forces against their relative rights : else,
our Will can have nothing to do, and self-made character.
that is, character at all, will be impossible.   But unless the
measure of that disorder is kept within limits, the most
disastrous results may ensue : a vehement discrepancy
between the scale of strength and that of worth will raise
the temptation to a high pitch, and set the will too
strenuous a task for frequent victory ; and, through its
continual yielding to overmastering lower impulses, a de-
generacy will set in, which passes with accelerated speed
into indefinite depths.   No moral governor could so order
the world as to leave it exposed, through the will of his
creatures, to such a possibility.   And the question therefore
is, whether the range and intensity of temptation are
practically unlimited ; or are placed under such restraints
as to forbid their predominance, and mark the destination
of the world as a scene of growing righteousness.   I submit
that, in the constitution of our nature, there are manifest
safeguards, controlling the tendencies to corruption, and
securing the advantage to the higher forms of character.

(1) Temptation, we have seen, arises from want of concurrence between the scale of strength and the scale of
worth in our springs of action ; and puts a strain upon us
proportioned to the extent of the interval between them.
What then are the conditions on which the amount of

possible deviation depends? Evidently it will be at its
maximum, where both series consist throughout of variables:
the discrepancies would then be in effect indefinite, and
the coincidences as few as in the simultaneous dealing of
two shuffled packs of cards. But if you fix one series, and
throw all the variables into the other, you gain, not only a
vast reduction in the number of intervals, but a station, not
itself liable to shift, from which to measure them, instead
of leaving them momentarily relative. Now this limiting
provision is exactly what we find in our own nature ; its
springs of action have variable intensities in different
persons ; but the same order of relative authority in all :
respecting the *de jure* power there is a universal consensus :
but the *de facto* sway is in no two the same. Having in
a former treatise given evidence that conscience, no less
than reason, has this uniformity in men [1], I must be content
to assume it here, and to point out only its consequences
on the problem which engages us. It is plain that the
constancy of the moral order gives it an immense advantage
over the prudential (that is, the sensitive or individual), an
advantage that may go far to compensate its intensive faintness of appeal. It would incur the greatest danger, were
there a similar constancy in the other scale, so that men were
all stirred together by the same temptations, and led to con-
spire against the rule which resisted them. But, as it is, they
do not want the same sins, and they do respect the same
excellences : their inclinations diverge ; their admirations
converge ; and though no one can look unabashed, and without something to hide, at the face of the moral law, yet that
pure and steady eye subdues them all, and melts away the
courage of defiance. This want of consent among us in the
relative strength of the several impulses, is the great security
against the permanent dominance of any, the great hope of

[1] Types of Ethical Theory, Part II, Bk. I, ch. ii. 2, pp. 77, 78, second
edition.

the regulated subordination of them all : he who has sent conscience among them, as the delegate of his righteousness, has so prepared the way, that it can easily execute its commission, '*Divide et Impera.*' The difficulty of uniting many men in a permanent alliance for a common object increases as that object appeals less and less to any disinterested affection or high inspiration, and rapidly proves itself insuperable, when it sinks into a mere scramble of greediness and vanity. You have but to compare a 'Catilinarian conspiracy' with a 'solemn league and covenant,' and the difference is conspicuous between the precarious combinations of profligate selfishness, and the organised solidity of conscience and of faith :

ἐσθλοὶ μὲν γὰρ ἁπλῶς, παντοδαπῶς δὲ κακοί[1].

(2) In the dynamics of a moral being, a change is ordained to take place which works in the same direction, and increases his advantage over every unregulated nature. His original distinction is, that, instead of being disposed of by his impulses as they come uppermost, he is endowed with a certain personal causality, which can lend itself to one impulse and suppress the action of another. At the outset, this power of Will is small, and the conscious self only half wakes up from the dream of nature ; but every exercise of it clears it and augments its strength : nor would anyone readily believe, till well-experienced in faithful energy, what stormy passions will subside, what wild gales will die away in whispers, if he will but calmly fling upon them the word of faith and power. In rightly directed will there is an ever-gathering force, which renders the earlier foes contemptible, and impossible achievements possible : as it is by 'doing just things that,' according to Aristotle, 'we become just, and by exercising self-restraint that we acquire self-

---

[1] Arist. Eth. Nic. II. vi. 14. Quoted from an unknown author, perhaps Theognis.

restraint [1]' so it is, inversely, by putting forth volition that we gain the faculty of will [2]. This self-determination is the essence of personal power: it is this that makes the man, and enables him to command instead of serving the scene in which he is placed. No doubt there are instances in which this superiority to the play of surrounding influences and internal fluctuations is exhibited by men of no great moral elevation: but, for the most part, the great school for creating it is the school of duty: there it is that we are braced to resistance, wakened to energy, inured to sacrifice, and find ourselves by conflict with ourselves: so that the supreme proficients there go forth to be masters in the circle of their life. True to their own order of reverence, and having no concern but to go with the right impulse, they have no inward variance by which you can distract them, but remain indomitable where they stand, and move unswervingly to what they mean. The whole resources of their nature being well in hand, their creative and controlling agency is raised to the highest pitch, and by its persistency diplaces a thousand obstacles which would baffle weaker and more wavering purposes. Thus it cannot be denied that the life according to conscience lifts the human characteristic to its highest altitude, and subjects the whole realm of instinct to the self-determining will.

Take the reverse case, of a mind only occasionally heeding the worth of its impulses, and more often surrendered to their intensity. That it is not always so, but that sometimes the better mood prevails, itself tells a story of inward self-variance that scatters half the natural strength: and, while this lasts, many a compunction will do its best to

---

[1] Arist. Eth. Nic. II. iv. 5. Εὖ οὖν λέγεται ὅτι ἐκ τοῦ δίκαια πράττειν ὁ δίκαιος γίνεται, καὶ ἐκ τοῦ τὰ σώφρονα ὁ σώφρων.

[2] Durch die eigene Selbstbestimmung des Subjects geworden sind nämlich auch das Vermögen der Selbstbestimmung, die Tugend und die concrete Weise der Selbstbestimmung, das pflichtmässige Handeln. Rothe, Stille Stunden, p. 186.

provoke the languid moral power into the effort of resistance, ere it is too late. But the habit of yielding loosens
all the compactness of the mind : every instance opens a
new leak through which its store of energy oozes away : in
the movements that seem voluntary there is less and less
of creative choice : instead of a self-assertion there is a self-
abandonment to the chance-pressure of the moment, and
the mind may be turned hither or thither by skilfully playing on the instinctive springs. Thus, neglect and misuse
entail an internal dying away of Will, till the possibility of
self-determination practically vanishes, the moral life is to
all intents and purposes expunged, and the human constitution reverts to the simply zoological. Power is thus being
always lost by those in whom the conscience sleeps, and
always gained by those who form themselves by the higher
law ; so that the tendency is for the human causality to go
entirely over to the faithful and heroic among men, the rest
falling away on to the borders of the animal types, that
sooner or later are sure to find their subordinate place. For
character to lose its hold on the affairs of men and serve
the anarchies of impulse is no more possible than for the
sheep to drive the shepherds.

Moreover, however great the evils incident to the lower
forms, whether of savage and undeveloped or of degenerate
life, we must remember, in estimating the range of *sin* in
the world, that they belong to the class more of *natural
evils* than of *guilt. Moral probation* there is none, except
where there is a conflict between an order of worth and an
order of intensity in the springs of action : and while the
latter has the field to itself, both before the former dawns
upon the consciousness and after it has sunk away and set,
responsibility is absent, and sin impossible. The freedom
of choice which is the condition of the moral life may have
yet to be gained, and may be easily lost : it is only in the
mid-period between these extremes that duty and its viola-

tion have their range: and whatever ills of conduct precede and follow are indistinguishable from the maladies of
nature and the sufferings of physical disorder.   The forfeiture of freedom, the relapse into automatic necessity,
is doubtless a most fearful penalty of persistent unfaithfulness ; but, once incurred, it alters the complexion of all
subsequent acts : they no longer form fresh constituents in
the aggregate of guilt, but stand outside in a separate record after its account is closed.   There is thus a provision,
awful, but conclusive, for stopping the history of sin, and
incapacitating the agent for indefinitely committing more.
The first impulse of the prophets of righteousness, when
they see him thus, is to cry ' he cannot cease from sin,' and
perhaps to predict for him eternal retribution : but, looking
a little deeper, they will rather say, ' he has lost the privilege
of sin, and sunk away from the rank of persons into the
destiny of things.'

(3) Though there is in all character a certain *infection*,
which might lead us to fear an unbounded spread of selfishness and corruption from every centre where they strike
root, yet a natural check is found to moral desolation in
the conflicting and self-destructive nature of its effects.
Both right and wrong affections intensify and reproduce
each other by their mutual play: but in doing so, the
former attain, the latter defeat, their aim.   Between persons, disinterested sympathy constitutes the joy which each
wishes for the other ; and the more it is deepened, the more
does it give : while envy and ill-will, miserable in themselves, plant a guard round the good they want, and put it
further out of reach, the intenser they become.   All the
lower passions miss or spoil what they seek, by their eager
or wrongful grasp ; and nowhere, probably, is there more
bitterness in life, than where there is care only for its
sweets.   A dissolute society is the most tragic spectacle
which history has ever to present,—a nest of disease, of

jealousy, of dissension, of ruin and despair,—whose best hope is to be washed off the world and disappear. Nor can any selfish desire, be it for honour, gain, or power, seize the helm and disown its subordination to what is higher, without making enemies resolved to impede or disappoint it: it has no secure and peaceful home, but lives on a battle-field, ever on the watch against surprise. It is intent on taking more than it gives;—a thing not possible except by giving more than you would take. In short, the moral order being a harmony of each individual within himself and with society, every deviation from it is a discord, the parts of which clash, and cancel instead of supporting each other: and the forces which are additive in the one case are subtractive in the other. All dominant evil therefore is, in the last resort, doomed to natural suicide, and we have a divine guarantee against a perpetuity of corruption.

C. Triumphs of Force in History.

Here, by a natural transition, we are brought to the third and last difficulty in the moral aspect of the world, viz. the apparent abandonment of human history to the conflict of rude force.

It is no doubt easy, in the immense complexity of historical phenomena, to select the materials of many a tragedy, and amid the ruins of the past to fix attention upon fragments of beauty dashed by the hand of violence, and noble forms that protest in vain against a resistless barbarism. The conspicuous changes which constitute the crises of nations, and are set forth as the drama of the world, are the collision at last of causes that have long converged and have now to try their strength; and they necessarily assume the form of interfering energies, the greater of which is most manifest in the line of future direction. In the clash of this repeated strife, the observer who feels everything and analyses nothing is apt to lose

his head, and declare that confusion reigns and all things
here go by *might* alone. He is moved by the pathetic
struggles of perishing or exterminated tribes. He ad-
mires in a Hannibal the baffled heroism of an extinguished
country, and in the victims of an Alva the fruitless martyr-
doms of a crushed faith. He turns his head away, as city
after city of his favourite Greece opens its gates to the
Macedonian troops. He is terrified at the tramp of Goths
and Vandals along the Roman causeways, and into the
stately palaces and courts of the Italian cities. He looks
into the slave-quarter of a patrician's estate, or of a planter's
coffee-ground, and is embittered by the pretence of justice.
He hears the bell of St. Bartholomew's night, and, thinking
over what it denotes, despairs of a race whose very religion
consists in quenching the humanities. He concludes that
the law of the strongest everywhere prevails ; that the play
of the world is a scrambling lottery, where the prizes are
seized by the least scrupulous mind and the most greedy
hand, while all the blanks are drawn, amid the laughter of
the shrewd, by hesitating conscience and pious simplicity ;
that the very idea of right has no place except in the mind
of man, and that *there* it is utterly powerless to remedy
the wrongs of nature.

As soon as the tumult of these compassionate impressions
subsides, it becomes apparent how great a confusion of
thought is involved in them. That, in a competition, the
weakest must go to the wall, and the strongest prevail, is no
melancholy fact, characteristic of our world, but a mere
verbal or analytical proposition, true of all possible worlds,
like the statement 'the warmer you are, the less cold you
will be.' By 'weakest' we mean 'that which goes to the
wall': by 'strongest,' 'that which prevails': this is the
test or measure of strength ; the predicate and the subject
being but two words for the same thing, the assertion
is empty of all information. Alter the world as you will,

make it exactly to your own mind, still 'that which prevails' will be 'the strongest,' and 'all things will go by might.' In order to give these propositions the bad sense which they are intended to bear, you must restrict the words 'might,' 'strength,' &c. to 'physical force,' as distinguished from influences which affect minds by the persuasion of thought, and incentives to will: and *then* the assertion, in gaining a significance, loses all its truth. If the greatest fund of strength, thus understood, secured the victory, the earth would be ruled by the elephant or the buffalo, and man would be serving them as their mere slave retinue; and though you may say that only by borrowing and appropriating other stores of force than his own is he their master, it is by his wits and not by his muscles that he is enabled to borrow; and his ascendency is throughout an example of intellect coming to the rescue of weakness. But, besides the skill to utilise the dynamics of nature, there must be also the power of adding together the small contributions of individual strength and intelligence, and making them into an integral mass with combined movement for a given end: superior art would be of little avail, without organising ideas and community of aim. And, among these organising ideas and common aims, not all are of equal efficiency. Who would compare the impulse that carried the Persian host across the Hellespont with that of the three hundred at Thermopylæ? Does not every general know that to breathe into his troops a high conviction of justice and indignation is worth an army of reserves? What then becomes of the alleged tyranny of brute power? Material force, instead of being all in all, is the mere tool at the disposal of intellectual faculty, of social cohesion, of superior arts, of moral vigour, of inspiring enthusiasms. It would be too much to say,— as it would be too much to demand,—that in the conflict of history nothing good has ever failed, and no conspiracy

of evil gained its crown: it is not essential to moral
government that every truth and right, however incipient
and small, should at once be victor against all odds; but
only that it should not be weighted in the race, and in
a fair field should be enabled to carry off the prize. And
I think it possible to show that, in human affairs, each
lower form of character is intrinsically weaker than its
immediate superior; so that the tendency, in the strife of
parties, of politics, of races, of religions, and consequently
of all historical development, is towards higher conditions
and a more complete equipment of right with strength.
No more can be attempted here than a mere general
program of argument by which this position may be made
good: a topic so vast and vague as the tendency of
human life upon the earth it is difficult to drive within
any definite lines at all; and the only hope of any
reasonable result must lie in finding some law of our
moral constitution which, as the constant element amid
all variables, is the determining factor of the whole
problem.

This dominant law do we not detect in that conscious
scale of worth and authority on which our springs of
action dispose themselves? To answer this, it will suffice
to place that scale before us in broad sections, without
descending into the details: and to say that there are
four types of human life, well marked in the course of its
personal or social ascent, viz. (1) that of *instinctive appetite
and passion*, in which there is the least remove from the
condition of other animals: (2) that of *self-conscious pursuit
of personal or social ends*, involving the first exercise of
will: (3) that of *conscience*, in which these ends are taken,
not as we *like*, but as we *ought*: (4) that of *Faith*, in which
the conflict is transcended between what we like and what
we ought, and duty becomes Divine. As the individual
passes through these successive stages, he leaves behind

him one source of weakness after another, till he rises
to the full stature of his power. In his first impulsive
life he knows no restraint, and under the incentives of
passion has his paroxysms of vivid energy: but his limitless
nature, meeting with no certain arrest, betrays him into
excess: his fortuitous inclinations thrust him upon divergent and wavering directions, that bear him nowhither :
not being able to forget, he cannot live for the moment
and have done with it, but feels the smart of variance with
himself; and the wild freedom which began with so
smooth a sweep begins to grate and jar, and dies away in
hesitating pain. As the self-conscious life is thrown to the
front by this very pain, the will wakes up and learns to
rein-in the ruinous spread of blind propensity, and train
the contending instincts to run in company : by the mere
shrinking from the remembered misery of recklessness,
some harmony is introduced among the clashing tendencies
of nature : and under the measured checks and stimulus of
self-interest, a unity of movement is given to the activities,
which more or less turns them all to account, and prevents
their cancelling each other. Thus, the life of Prudence
saves the waste of the life of Passion, and reduces its
energies to an economy. But at the same time, we must
observe, it introduces no new force: it is rational, not
kinetic : its whole operation is to control and not to
propel : and hence the self-regarding vigilance of ex-
pediency terminates with the negative merit of preventing
loss. Its caution has in it nothing that is creative ; and
happily shows its want of intensity by being easily swept
away before some flood-tide of affection that bears us right
away out of ourselves, and plants us amid higher incentives,
separated by quite other differences. Once born into the
moral life, we discriminate the springs of action which
solicit us, by a mark which is not only *intellectually dis-
cerned*, but *authoritatively felt*; which adds something

therefore to the dynamical conditions otherwise present to us ; which presses, not only with a restraining tension on one spring, but with an impelling on the other: so that whilst enthusiasm is impossible to prudence, it is congenial to conscience. I admit indeed that the moral perceptions may often stop short with their critical and judicial function, so as to deal, almost as much as prudence, with mere limitation and inhibition, and to render the scrupulous mind little less feeble than the selfishly cautious. But this negative aspect of conscience belongs only to its rudimentary and rationalistic stage, while it is still in the bondage of fear, and has its downward look : when its wings of love have grown, and its eye is drawn to the heavenly light, it springs into an ideal air, and finds new vigour as it rises. There is therefore more power in the moral life than in the rational : the harmony which it introduces is not partial, like the sentient, but ultimate and complete ; and it effects its end, not by repression only, but by inspiration. Still, repression there is, so long as conscience is called in to decide between rival desires, even though its decision be always obeyed : and the harmony is kept unbroken, not by leaving every chord to vibrate, sure that it will throw in its tone at the right place, but by laying the silencing hand on all that would speak in discord if left alone. The nature therefore is all truly regulated, but not all used : its right order is purchased by some sacrifice of force, some of which has to be spent in holding down a portion of the rest. And this sacrifice is not escaped, till the competition of impulse ceases by the absolute concurrence of the scale of intensity with the scale of excellence : then, at last, there is no movement to suppress, no resistance to overcome : the natural and the moral efficiency, the human instinct and the Divine prompting, coalesce, and by adding the native currents to the winds of heaven, create an incredible swiftness of advance. In this highest stage of character, the harmony is not only exact, but full, played no longer on some thin selected stops, but with everything thrown open on the great organ of the mind ; and the volume of power attains its maximum. It is obvious that, of these four stages, the first is characterised by freedom without regulation ; the second and third by regulation at the expense of freedom ; the fourth by the coincidence of freedom and regulation. And each person, it is plain, respects himself, or becomes more at one with himself, as he passes from each of them to its successor ; reducing some warring inconsistency, satisfying some haunting claim, ridding himself of some gnawing uneasiness ; and, on this account also, standing forth in greater vigour, clear of all enfeebling self-contempt. To the lower states some cowardice and hesitation for ever clings : but whoever goes over entirely into the identification with the Divine righteousness feels no detentions, and is borne along in simple lines, without even the need of courage. Thus it is that, in the individual personality, God has invested goodness with strength.

Now the rule which determines our self-respect determines also our respect for others : the internal scale of moral relations being the same for all, the critical estimates of conscience are impartial and universal. For one who is a mere creature of impulse we may have, under happy conditions, the admiration due to any fair and fine type of natural being ; but none of the feelings which are appropriate to *character*,—no approval, no reflected shame, nothing that stirs us to aspiration or humbles us in self-reproach. At best, he is no more to us than a perfect animal, that by beauty and symmetry pleases our naturalist tastes. Some advance on this mere æsthetic satisfaction is made at the next stage : if we meet with some prodigy of prudence, his aspect speaks more home to us ; we own the presence of one who is 'no fool,' and perhaps are

doubtful whether he would say the same of us : we do not
deny that we have something to learn from the skilled
order of his life, so sure to be steady and decorous and
keep out of scrapes : nay, if we happen to be a little
random in our ways, and he be a highly finished model,
we may look upon him with a wonder like that which we
direct upon genius in some unknown field, as a poet might
pay a distant homage to a great mathematician whose art
is to him a mystery. But the deference which we render
is essentially intellectual, and if it kindles any emulation, it
partakes of the nature of ambition, not of affection or
veneration. In order to awaken this, we must change the
scene, and seek the companionship of one who has taken
on him the vows of conscience, and under their constraining influence lives,—not merely a wiser, but a higher
life than ours, having tamed what is still wild in us, and
sweetened what remains a bitter fountain in our hearts,
and calmly confronted the laughter or the frowns that
have broken down our sense of right. Nothing can so
convict us of infirmity, yet kindle us to the hope of higher
courage, as the story of incorruptible confessors and the
'noble army of martyrs': nor does any breath so fan the
blaze of moral enthusiasm as the purifying wonder whether,
in like straits, we too could meet unflinching that last
agony. Yet this moral enthusiasm may be transcended
when we look up to one who, like God, 'cannot be tempted
to evil'; one who needs no victories, because he feels no
conflicts ; whom neither suffering will bring nearer to sin,
nor blessing secure more perfectly to holiness ; whose
saintly affections live above the storms that may rend and
wreck his sentient nature, and never lose the calm sunlight
through the fiercest and darkest night. Every nation with
a history has traditions of its sages, its heroes, its saints :
but, whilst it boasts of its Solomons, and is fired by its
Maccabees, it sits at the feet of its holy prophets and sons

of God ; and, for the highest things, 'hid from the wise and prudent,' thankfully turns to the very 'babes' of sanctity.

If this be the order in which we award our respect to others, it is also the order of their power over us ; for the sentiments which in our hearts we entertain towards them are the real sources of their influence upon us : the two modes of expression describe the same relation, and differ only by looking at it from its opposite ends. The measure of our confidence in another, as having insight, strength, holiness, greater than ours, is the measure of his as-cendency as our leader and guide : in every crisis that would perplex and shake us if we stood alone, we enlist under his banner, we march in his train. As this is the universal law of attraction and cohesion among the inter-dependent human multitudes, it follows that, by their natural affinities, men are grouped around the centres which ought to hold them, and from which issues precisely the suasion most fitted to lift and enlarge their nature. And, of the associations thus constituted, each will be commanding, in proportion as it gathers round a nucleus of higher principle. If it be simply self-protective and interested, like a trading guild or a commercial company, it may organise a thousand petty economies and save indefinite waste, and lift a high head among its rivals on the field of gain. But, once convict it of *monopoly*, and throw it therefore into collision with the *sense of justice*, and you have struck it with certain though it may be tardy blight : the taint of wrong will eat, like a canker, into the timbers of its stately fleets : its inflated dividends are punc-tured ; and long-headed men, saying nothing, will quietly sell out. As with free trade, so with free labour. Far within living memory, the slave interests of the western nations were among the most powerful, the best consoli-dated, the most defiant and self-complacent, that the world had ever seen, deceiving themselves with specious piety,

and hung over with labels from holy writ. But the word
went forth that ' man cannot hold property in man ' ; and
that word could no more return void than the seed upon
the prepared ground : the stirrings of pity, the claims of
right, gained upon the ear through all the clamour of
interest and usage : not that they were louder, but sweeter
and more solemn, and left the heart quite differently
attuned.   The social conscience, once rendered sensitive,
could not be thrown back into paralysis : it accepted its
new commission, and has ever since been setting free the
captives of human greed and cruelty.   And, in doing this,
it has exemplified the ascendency not only of Right over
selfishness, but of Faith over both ; for, in the process,
Religion has gone over from her biblical examples of servitude to her native alliance with the lot of freedom and
the life of duty ; and the demand that the fetters of the
slave should be struck off has been made, not on the mere
plea of human equity, but in the name of God, and under
the inspiration of a divine and redeeming love.   Mission-
aries, sent out to teach contentment and obedience, returned
to claim emancipation : having found that one whose will
is not his own cannot be addressed as if responsible ; that
where the human characteristics are suppressed, the human
virtues are impossible ; that the Christian ideal of life
presupposes a brotherhood which servitude denies ; that
the communion between the children of God and the
Father in heaven can live only where the spirit of both are
free.   When the movement had fairly caught this fire, and
not only pressed the State with the doctrine of equality,
but kindled the Church with the ' enthusiasm of humanity,'
it became invincible : a memorable proof that, among
societies of men, Faith wields a force greater than conscience ; as conscience than prudence, and prudence than
passion.

The history of the individual is an epitome of the

development of mankind. *Races* repeat in their experience the successive stages of personal character, and exhibit among them the same relations of graduated strength: each stage, as it is reached, gaining an advantage over its lower predecessor, and conferring fresh resources for social combination and obedience. The impulsive or instinctive period is the time of petty wars and small communities, ruled by the methods of an extended family or clan. Conquest, fusion, and alliance may widen the boundaries, while weakening the natural ties, by substituting social partnership for consanguinity with its blending traditions and affections ; and where conditions favourable to coloni- zation and commerce are added, we see, by the case of the Phœnicians, how vast a portion of the earth's surface may be covered by a network of interests woven by the industry of one people. In citing that people as a sample of utili- tarian civilization, I do not mean to deny to them the higher strata of character: they had doubtless their gallery of heroes ; and there were few accessible climes that did not know something of their temples and their gods. But the genius of their race, and the impulse to its diffusion, were mercantile enterprise : nor can we charge Plato with wrong in treating them as the typical embodiment of the *gainful desires*[1]. Can we say that, under this instigation, they rise to any majestic place in the history of the world? Their alphabet indeed has had a wonderful life ; but how little a part of the tale it has told has been their own ! It was the quick-witted Greek who moulded it into melody, and subdued it to the flexibility of thought. Compared with his little Athens, what have those bankers and carriers and factory-builders of antiquity bequeathed, in memory of their existence? When the time arrived for them to come into collision with the grave and vigorous Roman, no

---

[1] Rep. 436 A.

individual genius, no prowess, could avert their fall before
the sterner moral solidity against which they were flung :
the commercial civilization, which was great on the ex-
changes of the world, went down before a law-giving and
law-abiding people, whose mission it was first to codify the
social conscience of the human race. Estimate as we
may the particular rights and wrongs of the Punic wars,
prefer as we may the greatness of Scipio or of Hannibal,
the real essence of the drama lay in the strife of national
character, in the antipathy between the epithumetic and
the ethical elements of rule : and the victory fell to the
higher organising power. Yet, when that mighty Rome
had, by centuries of military police, embraced in her order
all that was not barbarous of three continents, and opened
a field for sympathies large and human, the strength and
tenacity of its universalism were put to a test which they
could not bear. An unnoticed competitor for the homage
and allegiance of all hearts stole in at the background of
the scene ; insisting also on a common law, administered
in no Prætor's court ; but, far more, on a blending affection
such as fellows in suffering, in exile, in hope, may naturally
feel ; speaking with equal voice to the conscience of the
woman and the man, the bond and the free, the client and
the patron; and by glad hymns and tender prayers making
the presence felt of an everlasting Love, the home and rest
of all trustful spirits. In Christianity, a spiritual universality stepped forth to try its strength on the field of the
legal and political ; and, though long despised, and more
than once driven into retreat and threatened with extinction, it asserted its superior vitality by slipping across the
boundaries of empire, raising its altar in opposing camps,
and quietly surviving the shocks of revolution. As the old
order caved in and made a disastrous ruin, the new religious
organism lifted its head and grew : and whether we judge
the inward unity which it created, by its intensity or its

duration, it far transcended that of the great secular
empire which first spread its field.   Whatever may be said
in derision of the dissensions of theology, and said truly
within the limits of the minor phenomena, there is no
uniting principle so deep, so wide, so enduring, as the
enthusiasm of religion ; which, relatively to the minds
possessed by it, is also the highest.

If then it be true that, in the individual mind, among
social groups, and in the races of mankind, the several
types of character exercise an influence proportioned to
their high level in the scale, there must be a perpetual
tendency of power to pass into the hands of the most
worthy: the vanishing elements must be those which can
best be spared, the advancing ones those that are most
wanted ; and, in any struggle long and large enough to
escape local tides of force and occupy the general surface
of history, the presumption is in favour of the cause which
wins.

No doubt, this general law attaches superior strength to
the better type, only in virtue of its *quality*; and does not
provide for its existence in greater quantities than its
inferiors ; and, in order to its effective prevalence, both
factors must be rightly adjusted.   If there should be,—as
there often is,—a vast numerical preponderance of men in
the lower stage, passion, in spite of its relative weakness,
may outvote prudence ; and prudence, conscience ; and
conscience, faith ; and many a noble cause may be lost
because, as yet, there are too few ready to answer its appeal.
Not only is this undeniably possible ; it is even the usual
course of human experience in its earliest attempts to rise.
The first chapter in every story of regeneration is tragical,
and not unfrequently so quenches hope that no sequel
seems conceivable.   On some solitary soul, or some small
band of friends in council, the oppression of an old wrong,
or the inspiration of a new truth, has descended : but when

its missionary comes before the multitude, and pours out his enthusiasm upon them, they stand agape and think him mad: or, even if he gathers some 'little flock' to whom 'it is the Father's good pleasure to give' this new 'Kingdom,' this does not prevent his being crucified out of the way, and their being hunted from city to city and filling up the measure of his sufferings.   The inevitable rush of interest and passion, to stamp out the threatening spark in the stubble of corruption, may overwhelm those who have kindled it, but is itself a foreboding of the coming blaze. The very cross which brings the darkest despair upon the present may lift its head into the light, and become the sacred ensign of the future.   If the appeal of the new life be true, the statistics of the hour are of small account: it has a secret advocate in every mind, and will be for ever enlarging its minority, touching its very persecutors with repentance, outliving its inveterate foes, and winning young souls at once by its inherent beauty and by the pathos of its first sacrifice.   Can any one name a good cause which, —not locally, but in the world at large,—has perished and had no resurrection?   Intervals of suspended animation there may be: but the final mortality of the 'better part' I must utterly disbelieve.   When we say of the baffled reformer, 'he was born *before his time,*' we confess our assurance that 'his time' must come, and betray the fact that, for us at least, it has already come.   The unequal numbers, therefore, which may rob the superior type of its natural advantage, do not invalidate our law: they resolve themselves into a mere demand for *time* in order to render its operation visible; and all apparent exceptions will be found within the interval in which that time is being gained.

It might be otherwise if there were such fixed differences of race among men that the preponderance of an inferior caste of character were permanent and irreducible.   The

ruder forms of physical strength would then measure themselves, in compact and unbroken mass, against strength
intellectually guided and morally moved : and the limit
might easily be reached of the advantage possessed by the
latter ; and brute force might win the freehold of the earth.
But since all men, however actually low, are potentially
claimed by the higher functions of character, and only
waiting to own the universal law, the consolidation of
power at the bottom of the scale is for ever precarious,
broken up by constant desertions, and weakened by inward
misgivings in the presence of a natural superior which is
the image of its future self. The very constitution of our
nature thus affects its elementary representatives with a
secret half-consciousness of fighting in a losing game. And
if, in spite of this, they are still numerous enough to conquer some civilized state, the first thing they do is to begin
to learn from it ; so that in their very victory they change
sides, and their barbarism capitulates. It is this persistent
and universal capacity for development which deprives the
mere census of human character of its most discouraging
significance.

The very facts which are adduced in evidence of the
reign of unscrupulous force in human affairs appear, under
this light, to admit of a very different interpretation. The
great courses of history, if we can but rise above their din
and crash to look calmly down on them, exhibit a clear
ascending movement, from which we must not allow our
attention to be withdrawn by the many pathetic episodes
interspersed throughout the drama. The poet and the
novelist borrow many a touching story from the sad fate of
the American Indians, exiled from their hunting grounds,
dwindling in numbers, corrupted by the civilization they
can neither adopt nor resist, and doomed ere long to become a mere study for its archæologists. And we certainly
cannot say that all is good on the area which they have

vacated. But would any one really prefer to see them in possession, as of old, of the continents now occupied by the European immigration? and defend their right of exclusive use of the whole western world for their own game-preserves to the end of time? Have the forests fallen in vain to make room for the New England villages, with their churches, their school-house, their industries? It would need a Rousseau to obtain a momentary hearing for the cause of these lost tribes, and even he would confute himself by the very splendour of his pleading, which forbids us to regret the substitution of literary art for the dumb monotony of life without a record. It cannot be denied that the instinctive stage of existence has here made way for a higher.

Of the reverse order, however, an example is said to be afforded by the humiliating submission of Greece and the East to the rude soldiery of Macedon. What was Pella, that its ruler should lay his hand even on Thebes, whither he himself had been sent to school, and still more on Athens, the intellectual light of the world? Was there ever a more melancholy descent than that of the city of Miltiades, Pericles and Phokion, the home of art, of philosophy, of history and poetry, into subserviency to a race untouched by the Hellenic genius, and without legitimate link with its traditions? How great was the disaster is evident from the fact that *there* Greek history ends and has no more to say. Doubtless, the disappearance of Greece from the drama of the world constitutes an immeasurable loss, and presents at first view all the aspect of a blight thrown upon a superior civilization by an inferior. But, in attributing this change to the Macedonian ascendency, we render too much honour to Philip, and invert the order of cause and effect. Had the spirit and habits of Miltiades' time still survived, the astuteness of Philip would have been as unavailing as the hosts of

Xerxes: and the pleadings of Demosthenes, instead of
dying without response, would have been forestalled by
action. Dissensions among the states, the exhaustion of
protracted war, the growth of public corruption, the canker
of private vices, had induced a general decay of character
and impotence of will, which gave the advantage to a more
resolute and disciplined people moved by a single mind ;
and intellectual and artistic skill, deserted by moral vigour
and consistency, had no arms against the prince who knew
his own mind and was proof against dialectic and intrigue.
It was the weakness of the southern cities that opened the
channel for Macedonian influence, and even charged it
with a civilizing function which it unconsciously exercised.
The creative period of the Athenian intellect had nearly
done its work and drew to a close in that very generation :
its quickening products needed now a distributing agency
that should bring them to bear upon the education of mankind ; and this agency was supplied by the second stage of
the Macedonian advance, which carried European sway to
the banks of Indus : it was the whirlwind of Alexander's
conquests that drew after it on the morrow the free breeze
of Attic thought to freshen the languor of the East. In
doing this, he gave a better life than any which his sword
destroyed, and planted more than he displaced : were it
only that he made the Greek language the medium of intercourse throughout the empire which he bequeathed, he
must be reckoned as a benefactor of the first magnitude,
though not of the highest order ; since it is impossible for
any people to become familiar with that marvellous instrument without vast accessions of intelligence and feeling,
amounting in the Asiatic mind to a re-birth into a new
world. Thus, in the light of a considerate interpretation,
the change of power which seemed at first a descent into
relative barbarism, vindicates its beneficence, as giving
universal diffusion to the noblest literature and most

stimulating historic life that the world has ever witnessed ; and *that* at the very moment when its vivifying influence was complete.

The office which Macedon performed for the East, as a carrier and postmaster of Greek culture, Rome accomplished for the West ; absorbing into her own education and habits, reproducing in her literature, and diffusing with her language and throughout her provinces, the ideas and tastes to which her ancient ruggedness had already yielded. Nor was she merely the messenger of this foreign gift : as the great administrative organiser of heterogeneous tribes and dependencies, she erased the temporary and exceptional from the principles of government, and brought a larger portion of mankind to live under one Law, than had ever before a partnership of rights. This unification was doubtless gained at a great cost of extinguished nationalities : but who can find among them any that can be the subject of serious regret ? any, from which the world could expect a characteristic gift that has been lost, or a higher order than that which supplanted it ? After Italy had been won and found its centre of gravity on the Tiber, the submissions to Rome were for the most part made by countries whose national life had either run its course and been worn out, or had not yet found conditions stable enough for it even to begin ; and no boon could, at such a time, be more opportune than to secure a vast and tranquil area of unity, where no one should be out of reach of a common justice or without some breath from the common atmosphere of thought. A more marked instance of such an overbalance of good, in unity over independence of parts, is seen in our Indian empire, where it is but too possible to cite examples of high-handed wrong towards suppressed principalities, and awaken sympathy for superseded modes of life ; yet quite impossible to wish for any reinstatement of the past, or deny the preponderant benefits conferred by the ascendency of a just and uniform controlling power.

But if the dominance of Rome was so great a good to the world, must we not admit its fall to be a disaster equally great? and how are we to be reconciled to the frightful spectacle of plunder and massacre in her fields and cities by greedy barbarians who knew no law but the sword? Amid many differences, the story is, in its rationale, not dissimilar to that of Greece. Rome was not overthrown till she had become other than the Rome that earned her empire. *Then* she had been superior to the Eastern nations in vigour, and to the Western in order and obedience: now, she had appropriated and outstripped all the dissoluteness of the former and the turbulence of the latter; and had become the mere traditional custodian of a civilization which had no longer any charm for her, except in its intoxicating dregs. Her provinces groaned under the extortions of their governors: her capital was at the mercy of reckless and venal prætorians: a senate without authority, citizens without duties, a palace without control, left no worthy incitements open to counteract the downward tendency of idleness and luxury: and to a generation whose moral strength and susceptibilities were sapped by private vices, even the lofty example of Marcus Aurelius appealed in vain. The home population of freemen, thinned and enervated by licence and untouched by patriotism, could no longer recruit the armies of the empire; and the stalwart mountaineers of Pannonia and Illyria, and peasants from the forests of Germany, were not likely long to remain ignorant of their strength, or to look with untempted eyes on the opulence which they defended,—on the harvests of Lombardy, the olive-grounds of Etruria, the vintages of Calabria, and the princely villas that rose amid them all. But for these so-called 'barbarians,' it would seem as if all energy would have rolled away from European society.

Had we only the testimony of Jewish and Christian observers, we might suspect that we were listening to the exaggerations of enthusiasm : but, with singular unanimity, the Pagan literature, whether grave or gay, leaves the same impression of a corruption of manners, paralleled perhaps in the history of Eastern nations, but hitherto unknown in the Western world.   There was no hope for our nature, but in dispossessing the degenerate heirs of the old civilization, and beginning anew with the healthier races that were waiting outside for their turn in the moral and historical life of mankind.   Christianity itself could not find scope to develop more than half its power, till it came in contact with other than the Greek and Latin minds : the Teutonic genius was needed to give full response to its inwardness and spirituality.   There is reason therefore to say, that the earthquake which shook down the ancient polity and culture was no fortuitous outburst of bad force ruining the good, but a subsidence of worn-out strata already denuded of all fruitful soil, and an upheaval of new formations, charged with fertilising capacity for the growth of purer beauty and larger life.   The passage from ancient to modern history exhibits the forfeiture of empire by corrupt and unfaithful trustees, and the delivery of the world into more capable and hopeful hands.

But whatever happy interpretation may be found for these large and complex changes in human affairs, it is surely impossible to construe such simple phenomena as slavery and persecution into anything but the sheer triumph of force over right : and as these are almost constant facts, how, it is asked, can any just rule prevail in a scene where they have played so great a part?   The question is apparently asked, either on the assumption that all causality remains with God and none is lent out to other minds, or in forgetfulness of the relations between the ordainer of a trust and its recipient.   God kidnaps no slaves : he burns no

heretics : these are human doings : and, except that they lie
within the scope of the freedom he has permitted, he has no
share in them : nor has he left them possible, without setting
his face against them.   You think perhaps, ' why stop with
forbidding them ? why not *prevent* them ?'   But this is just
what you may ask about any other crime ; and is simply
the old suggestion that by dispensing with a moral world
he might have excluded moral evil : what, in that case, he
would have included that was worth having, only the brutes
could tell.   As it is, there are two Agents from whose concurrent or conflicting Wills all history arises : and in
estimating the character of each, we must not charge upon
one the preference shown by the other, but look simply to
his own end in view and the plain drift of his activity.
When duly careful of this distinction, we may often find
a curious contrast between the separate motives of individual men and the aggregate effect of their action :
they mean one thing, and do it ; but, along with it and
through it, they do many another which they never meant,
which may even work in the opposite direction, and finally
cancel their own achievement.   The crimes of persons, and
even of society, are sometimes absorbed by surrounding
conditions, or thrown into unintended conjunctions which
precipitate their poisonous elements, and find a use for
what remains.   The human perpetrator we judge by the
intention to which he directs his will : the Divine governor,
by the sanction or discouragement given to that type of
action in the long tendencies of time.   As between man
and man, Slavery is nothing but a wrong,—a doing to
another, in the arrogance of strength, what we would not
have done to us.   But, as between God and man, in their
protracted relations through history, it has undoubtedly
turned to account the inequality of races, and placed the
inferior in natural tutelage to the superior ; disciplining
them to habits of industry that would not be spontaneously

formed ; accelerating their gradual ascent into intelligent
sympathy with higher forms of life and character ; till,
at last, their claim to stand on the platform of humanity
becomes so clear, that conscience is forced to own it and
strike the fetters from their limbs.   In the education of
tribes, as in that of individuals, the self-regulated will is the
last acquisition, and in neither case is it made without
compulsion : and had men never served each other of
necessity, they would never, beyond the family or the clan,
have served each other voluntarily.   But the very fact that
society outgrows the institution, and learns to trust all its
work to the free springs of character, and is touched with
shame that it was ever otherwise, show what is the idea at
the heart of nature ; i. e. the aim of the Providence of God.
He takes sides against the wrong, and is for ever engaged
in wearing out its power.   He has given such advantage
to liberty of service as to secure its victory.

Our abhorrence of persecution,—the slavery of the
spiritual world,—is less easily soothed by such considerations.   Yet here also it is strictly true that, in the earliest
training of the mind to habits of Reverence, coercive
authority could not be dispensed with ; and that, but for
the steady ideal sphere of awe which it held before and
around the thoughts of men, the higher elements of
character would have had no time to grow.   It would be
a ridiculous pedantry to apply the protestant pleas of
private judgment to such communities as those of ancient
Egypt and Assyria: it is not till experience has accumulated
materials and set up an independent capacity of thought,
not till comparison of religious ideas becomes possible and
inevitable, that new duties enter from the side of *Truth*,
and render the old discipline impossible.   And, with the
duty on the one part, arises also on the other the crime of
denying and resisting it.   It is this survival of coercion
after conscience has been born to supersede it, this pre-

tension of the baser to suppress the nobler, that shocks and revolts us in persecution ; and when it dares, against its spiritual foe, to rush into deeds of blood and fire, it seems as if Justice had fled from earth to heaven. But this very cry of despair overtakes and recalls Justice in her flight. One Huguenot massacre may be celebrated by a *Te Deum* and a Jubilee at Rome; but the horror it excites elsewhere makes another impossible : the eyes of Christendom are opened to its wickedness, and penitence and mourning out-vote the savage joy. In the autobiography of many a person you may have read, how, after years of heedless and unwatched life, some surprise of temptation, plunging him into undreamt-of guilt, has startled him into self-knowledge and self-recoil, and proved the turning-point of his career, setting his face thenceforward to whatever things are pure and good. So too is the conscience of mankind educated in part by the awakening shock of great crimes ; and if the heart is larger that has conquered hate, than that which knows not what it means, and the charity deeper, that can be tender to another's reverence as well as true to its own, it is surely credible, that the outgrown persecutions of the world may have ennobled the love that rises above them, and given firmer tone to the energy which discards them. In order to read the character of God in the tendency of things, we must undeniably compare their end with their beginning : and the moral sense which, in its dim and dark age, plays the inquisitor, but, emerging into its luminous period, flings its instruments of torture relentlessly away, plainly proclaims the Divine intent to supersede all lower force by the ascendency of reason, right, and love.

History, thus interpreted, is no record of the triumph of rude strength : but, on the contrary, attests the ever advancing superiority of the higher terms in the hierarchy of powers.

BOOK III.

REVIEW OF OPPOSING SYSTEMS.

THE Theism which we have thus far vindicated has been reached by following out two distinct lines of thought, each taking its commencement from a primary axiom of our cognitive nature. The first proceeds from the principle of Causality, which the Intellect carries with it into all its interpretations of external phenomena: the second, from the sense of Duty, by which the Conscience reads a sacredness in life, and puts a divine construction on a large portion of our internal experience. Under the guidance of the former, we have resolved the natural world into an effect of one wise and mighty Will: under the guidance of the latter, we have discovered our own affinity with a supreme omnipresent Righteousness. And, from the relation between these separate messages of transcendent truth, it is quite evident that they are separate only to our different modes of apprehension, and that their predicates meet in one Being, perfect alike in Thought and Holiness. With this concurrence of our leading intellectual and leading moral intuition in the same discovery, we may well be content. I do not say that there are no other sources in the human mind whence religion may spring: nor do I forget that speculative theology offers different proofs from these, and that historical mythology detects elsewhere also the germs of such beliefs as they investigate. But so far as the proofs have validity still, or the germs in question have any life that can avail for us, they will be found, I believe, if not identical with the sources I have named, either largely blended with them, or resolved into them by easy analysis. At present I will not pause to remark on other modes of reaching the same end. We have too many opponents yet before us to spend profitable time in criticising and setting right our friends : it will be better to keep pretty close to the paths on which we have hitherto advanced, and notice only the aberrations to which, at certain points, they are found to tempt. In working out, on the first line, the relation of God to Nature, an easy deviation leads to Pantheism ; and, on the second, the relation of God to man may be so conceived as to issue in Necessarianism, or, as it is now more usually called, Determinism. Neither of these doctrines is compatible with the form of Theism which we have deduced ; the former invalidating all personal, and the second all moral relations between the human and the Divine mind. Our position therefore is still imperfectly secured, till we have justified it against these possible deflections, and exhibited its exact bearings with regard to them. Having had occasion to review the former system, as a whole, in a separate monograph on the parent and prince of modern Pantheists [1], and again on its ethical side, in a more recent work [2], I need not do more in the following chapter than supplement the former notices, by a more express treatment of the theory in its bearing on religion.

---

[1] A Study of Spinoza, 2nd edition, 1883.
[2] Types of Ethical Theory, 2nd edition, 1885, vol. i.

CHAPTER I.

PANTHEISM.

THIS word is so often applied to a mode rather of feeling than of thought, to a passionate or tender mingling with the divine beauty of the world, that it may seem to mark a temperament more than a system, the immediate vision of the poet, and not the reflective interpretation of the philosopher. The atmosphere thrown around us by the lyrical music of Shelley, the descriptive painting of Theodore Parker, and even the lucubrations of Professor Teufels-droeckh, seems so crossed by flashing colours and filled with a universal glow, as to defy the presence of form and melt away every line that seeks a station there. The same however may be said of all inchoate speculation : it is the meditating afterthought which reduces to method a prior consciousness of immediate feeling : and the determining work of philosophy finds its material in the indeterminate flood of human experience. It is not only in poets and mystics that the Pantheistic characteristics present themselves : they have also crystallised into systems, forming a well-marked group in the history of thought, though widely differenced from each other. The tendency which gives rise to them is so foreign to our prevailing English genius, that it is not easy to awaken much sympathy with it, or to give a clear impression of the theory it has created. It will perhaps help us to this end if we broaden the contrast between Theism and Pantheism, by first enumerating the features of the former in their extreme type, and then noticing how they provoke a transition into the relief of opposite conceptions.

Though this reverses the historical method which for most
purposes has obtained in our day a just preponderance, yet
it has the advantage which the historian has often desired
for himself, viz. that he could tell his story *backwards*, from
the familiar scenes and attitudes of to-day, to the ages
gradually growing stranger as they recede: for, instead
of transposing ourselves at a single spring into the lost
feelings and faded speech of a civilization we cannot recon-
struct, we can appeal to passages of experience conspicuous
in others, if not remembered in ourselves.

§ 1. *As Reaction from Deism.*

In reasoning out the principle of Causality we were
necessarily brought to treat the universe of phenomena as
an *effect*: we were led to a *Source* or beginning of things :
our problem was to fix upon the *right* ἀρχή. Three
claimants presented themselves for our choice, each emerging from a different field of nature, and supported by
the pleadings of a powerful school : '*Matter*,' construed by
the hylomorphists, declares itself competent to all : '*Life*,'
disowning the lineage, proclaimed by the biomorphists to
be the universal energy of the conscious and unconscious
world : and '*Will*,' protesting that it alone supplies us with
the very idea and meaning of Causality, insists on its right
as paramount. In deciding for the last we so far cast
in our lot with the anthropomorphists as to say, that not till
we reach the highest type of familiar being, do we obtain
the clue of causal knowledge. The question which we
settle in making this election is a question of *origination*,
and nothing more : all comes at first from the Divine Mind,
and is constituted according to the conceptions of that
mind. But that nativity of things, that conversion of
inward conceptions into outward laws, is a long time ago ;
and it is but a faint and far off homage that we can pay to
so archaic a fact. Is there nothing to be said about

the continuous universe and current series of things? We that feel the throbbing pulses of the hour, and pass between cloud and sunshine, cannot put back our religion to the birthday of the solar system, but would know how to think of this contemporaneous course of nature. Living, moving, having our being in it, what is it that we are in contact with? Does it contain anything divine? or is it a huge mechanism, long as Time, separating us from the efficient will of God? On these questions the mere causal argument is dumb, until it changes its problem, and seeks something else than a reply to the *Whence* of this frame of things. So long as Theism engages itself with simply settling its 'First Cause,' there is nothing to prevent its laying down the relation of God to the universe in the following way:

(1) The world was created in time: prior to which, its Divine Cause existed from eternity without it. In course of time it will perish, like everything which has a beginning; after which, its Divine Cause will exist to eternity without it. It is a fruitful interlude between two sterile immensities.

(2) In setting it up, the Creator willed its order into being once for all; depositing in its materials the properties which would execute his purpose spontaneously, without need of his returning to it again. In other words, it is a vast magazine of 'Second Causes,' which enable it to go of itself, and would do their duty though he were asleep.

(3) The creation thus organised is finite, while its Maker is infinite: so that, beyond its limits, his presence boundlessly extends, and is in only external relation to it.

(4) Like all that is finite, the world is imperfect, never, at its best, realising the perfect idea of its Author, and reaching that best, only as a brief acme, gained by slow growth and lost by lingering decay. Meanwhile, these broken rays of good enter the scene from a radiance absolutely pure, the Uncreated Light of lights.

Thrown into this form (which, as a mere doctrine of origination, it could hardly fail to assume), Theism establishes a series of antitheses between the universe and God: in time, in space, in causation, in excellence: and the tendency is to overshadow the world by the contrast of a transcendent glory, and depress it with a conscious insignificance. The sense of ephemeral life, of overwhelming law, of hurrying death, of twilight knowledge, and only fancied power, settles upon the heart of such a faith, and drives it upon artifices of self-relief. The provinces of the Natural and the Supernatural are sharply marked off from one another, in date, in seat, in agency: the former belonging to second causes, to the cosmic interlude, and the scene of physical existence: the latter, to the action of the First Cause, before, after, and outside the regular ordering of the world: so that the supernatural can never be human; and the natural, except in its first institution, can never be divine. In short, the legislating mind of the universe, and its executive media, are kept separate from each other; the one an imperative prefix, that 'spake and it was done': the others, constant servitors, engaged with purely ministerial functions unconsciously performed. What is present with us and around us is only mechanism, running down through its appointed term; and, for any such freshly moving will as is needful for personal relations, we must look, in one direction, further than the dawn of geologic time, and, in the other, to the ' Unseen universe' beyond the equalisation of heat and the death of all things in this.

It must be admitted that the conditions are but rarely present which allow the complete formation of this type of belief. But in the Deism of the eighteenth century we find a sample of their full effect. Not only was the natural theology of that time worked out mainly from the principle of causality; but that principle itself was accepted, not in dynamical sense, still less with its true psychological key, but as a law of succession only among perceptible phenomena.   Mechanical science, having re- cently brought the heavens under its domain, tried its hand at everything, and tyrannised over the conceptions of men, and shaped their whole program of the universe : while the religious life, sunk in languor and talking prose, had no enthusiasm to be hurt and brought to tears by so undivine a world.   Where the same temperament and the same mode of thought prevail in our day, it is seldom deemed worth while to retain a God so nearly superfluous : if all that is wanted is a first antecedent, some less portentous nature, it is thought, may serve as well. And minds that are dominated by mechanical con- ceptions, however they may hold an earlier faith in temporary suspense, will be always tending to such nega- tive result.

But if reflection escapes these limits, it may take a different direction, and set into another form of thought. On closer scrutiny, there is not one of the marks enumer- ated in the Theism just described which does not become questionable ; and cross-examination may even turn their witness completely round.   Let us call them before us, one by one.

(1) Is the idea of *Creation* in time really tenable ?   Can our thought in any way pass from the bare postulate of an infinite lonely Mind, to the subsequent existence of the universe?   By what process or rule of possibility can the absolutely One cease to be one and pass into a duality ? the self-identical become or find what is other than itself? Is it that Mind is in itself a dual existence, inasmuch as it involves at once a thinking subject and an object thought? Yes: but in the primal absence of all save God, both of these are within himself, to whom, by hypothesis, there is nothing external, and can amount only to self-conscious-

ness, without direction on what is *other than himself.* Do
you say that, being not *Thought* alone but also *Will*, he
acts as well as *sees*, and turns the object of inner discernment into outward realisation? If so, you simply put
into the word *Will* a meaning beyond its recognised
function, in order to make it adequate to the requirements
of your doctrine ; for it does not denote any power of
calling up something out of nothing, but only the power
of dealing with the possible, and, within that given range,
determining what was indeterminate before. Action in the
total absence of conditions, the actual conversion of thought
into things with neither time nor space to hold them, is not
within its competency as known to us. And even if it were,
we should still want some account of the change from the
absolute to relative period of God's existence. Why and
when did he begin to create? Was there a defect in his
being without a universe? If so, how did he spend an
eternity without it? Does the universe add anything to
his perfection? If so, how can he prepare to dispense
with it by the extinction of material organisms? By
following out such reasoning as this, we become aware of
difficulties attaching to the doctrine of creative paroxysms,
chronologically separating God from what is other than
God : we begin to think that what once he did he always
does and has for ever done ; that the new which he calls
up is out of the old, and the future of his universe the
harvest of the past. And so, the startling crises which
made the epochs of our former faith break up and diffuse
themselves into a constant life : the thunderclaps roll
away down our horizon, and leave only the whispering air
and the soft light as guardians of a silent fertility. We
pass over to the idea of *perpetual creation*, and let the
Divine presence no longer come in *visits* to the world, but
rest in it for ever.

(2) When once the conception of creative starts is dis-

missed, and the agency which had been concentrated becomes diffused, the distinction is weakened between our 'second causes' and the first.   How are we to conceive of such a Divine act as that of stowing away a given kind and quantum of energy in this or that material ; so that it is parted with by its sole Source, and put out on commission? Can it be anything to the Eternal to compress his act into a moment, and have done with it for the future ? If this is repeated in every instance where a Law of Nature is instituted, and if the reign of law is universal, the whole cosmos is worked by machinery, and, whilst it lasts, there is no living will of God: he has retired behind his deputies, and is scarcely less out of the way than the divinities of Epicurus, whose tranquillity was hardly distinguishable from death.   This surely is the illusion of finite minds subject to the law and successions of Time, and to bodies liable to periodicity and weariness. To an Eternal being, far above these limits, Eternal life, i. e. Eternal action, must be an essential element of perfection : all cosmic power is Will ; and all cosmic Will is His.   The natural forces are numerically distinguished, only because they are assembled in different families of phenomena ; but, dynamically, they pass to and fro : they are subject to the same measure : they are substantively undifferenced : and the unity to which they converge is nothing else than his.   He is the One cause in Nature, acting in various modes : and to all else among physical things that has borrowed the name we may give a free discharge.   We cannot have these 'second causes' idle on our hands : and now that he has clothed himself with the universe to determine its movements, to look at us through its beauty, and to live in its life, all that interposes must take itself away.

(3) Again: were we really justified in saying that creation is finite, while its Author is infinite? However

true it may be that to each created thing there must be
a limit of time for its existence, and a limit of space for its
dimensions, what is there to prevent the *succession* of them
all from being everlasting, and their distribution from being
without end? Whatever reason there ever was for conferring dependent existence, there surely must have always
been: nor can we find any rational demarcation in the
field of space, determining that *here* they shall teem with
being and *there* remain a waste. Why, then, should we
make the effect so little, when the cause is so great?
Why preserve any region of banishment for the latter,
where, for want of effect, it would be cause no more?
Truer far to regard the two as co-extensive, and suffer the
scope of the universe to coalesce with the Infinitude of
God. So here, in another point, the antithesis ceases
between Nature and its Source.

(4) Finally: if nature at every turn has thus rallied
from the shock of its first depreciation, and assumed a
place rather of approximation than of contrast to God,
need we any longer think of it as so imperfect a product,
and use it as the standard type of that which is undivine?
Where indeed are we to look for anything that is other
than divine? If the world falls short of God, it is only as
any passing acts or behaviour of ours may give but a
broken report of us: it is a transient and partial expression of him; but it expresses nothing else: whatever
it shows is an aspect of his thought: whatever it tells,
it tells of him: and since nothing can issue from perfection
but that which is akin to it and an element of it, the
constitution of things can contain only functions of the
best; and its seeming shadows are but visual illusions in
the presence of partial lights. And so we find ourselves
released from our melancholy prison into an optimist
existence: the dark material mass of the world becomes
incandescent with the currents of a Divine life for ever

streaming through it, till the gloomiest spaces flash with heavenly promise.

Thus, one by one, all the marks seem to disappear by which our Theism opposed to each other the Maker and his works. There is no longer any separation between them, in time, or space, or causality, or quality : he who legislates also executes : the natural and the supernatural are one : nor is there any difference between the fiat which institutes and the power which carries out cosmical law, except that the one is the initial and the other the habitual act of the same Will. Nature (as known by us) is taken up into God,—the finite embosomed in the infinite,—and breathes a portion of his mind, and would tell it all, could we grasp the All and interpret every tone. Its essence would be his essence, and nothing would remain over for us to learn of him. Living here and now, we are at no distance from him, and have neither to wait for death nor go to heaven to find him ; and if we are as exiles, it is only that we never draw near to lift the latch of our home.

In this transition, supposing it to be made absolute, we have passed into *Pantheism.* Can we find any single characteristic which sums up its difference from the previous Theism ? May we not say that, in the original form of belief, God was conceived as *transcending* the universe every way, as infinite, as eternal, as source, as perfection : while, in the subsequent, the universe is lifted out of its limits and its transiency, and is identified with his Will in its energy and his Thought in its excellence : so that it is the simple externalisation of his being, and he is wholly *Immanent* in it ? This is the generally received distinction between theism and pantheism, and, subject to some further differentiation hereafter, we may provisionally adopt it. It covers the several particulars of comparison to which we have thus far adverted.

This distinction however will fail to discriminate theism from pantheism without steady adherence to the meaning just given to the words 'transcendent' and 'immanent.' Too often they are used as if they were equivalent to 'external' and 'internal,' as if the contrast in question had reference only to *position here or there*. Of course, if God transcends the universe in the extension of his presence, he must be where it is not, i. e. in space 'external' to it : it would be a contradiction to say that any system of finite objects could use up the infinite. But any existence thus 'external' in virtue of infinitude is not hindered from being internal too, nay, is affirmed to be so by the very same necessity which excludes all outward limits : so that this function of the divine transcendency involves no denial of the divine immanency, and the alleged opposition between theism and pantheism disappears. The same is true if the words 'transcendent' and 'immanent' are applied to the other element of quantity, viz. *Time*. If God, as eternal, transcends the universe in duration, his life before all finite things is no bar to his perpetual life in and among them, but directly involves it : so that the pantheist can say nothing affirmative of his agency there which the theist may not repeat. The conflict begins with the pantheist's *negative* proposition : that beyond the natural order of things and prior to it no divine life or agency can be. It is this *limitation* of the supreme existence, the *denial* of a supramundane cause, which alone the theist is concerned to resist : the one thing with which he cannot be content is the evolution of a God within the genesis and process of the universe. It is simple ignorance, both of the principle and of the history of his doctrine, to charge him with planting all divine agency outside of nature except at her birth-hour, at an indefinite distance from its self-realising purpose in the constitution of living beings. It is sufficient for him, if God be *somewhere more than the contents of*

nature, and *overpass them* in his being, action, and perfection.   Let this condition only be saved, there is no
limit to the admissible identification of what are called
'natural powers' with his, or of organic purpose with his
design.   The pantheist, on the other hand, makes no
return for this concession to his favourite conception of
'immanency': he can allow no 'transcendency': the life
with which he charges the universe has no actual or
possible existence but in the aggregate of finite things:
it speaks its whole being in the cosmic laws.   The
opposition therefore lies between *All-immanency* and
Some-transcendency.

If this be the exact theoretical distinction between the
two systems, it follows that, when theists are found possessed
by the conception of an indwelling God, whose living
thought marks its way in the unsleeping order of nature,
and whose will is self-realising in human life and history,
when they find in the constant duties and the inconstant
lights and shadows of their path a quickening communion
with an invisible source of all beauty and good, they are
chargeable with no inconsistency in thus freely appropriating language deeply tinctured with the immanent
conception.   Doctrines like those of 'perpetual creation,'
and of the 'ordinary action of the spirit,' belong not to the
supernaturalism of their believers, but to their theory of
the universe of law: and with the spirit of them few
writers have been more imbued than Lord Herbert of
Cherbury, the father of that English Deism, which is usually
adduced as the consummated theory of an external
mechanism of the world.   When, on the other hand, a
pantheist like Spinoza has to go beyond the Natura
naturata, and concede a Natura *naturans* related to it as
cause to effect, it is in vain for him to set them forth as
identical by covering them together with the label 'Causa
sui,' and pretend that he has not trespassed upon any

'transcendent' ground. And when Hegel, in giving account of the adaptations of a living structure to subserve a
given end, finds the directing power, not in the individual
being, but in the '*Idea of the species,*' he confesses the end
of this particular life to be not self-realising ; and, to find
the cause, he has to leap off this and every other single
object in nature, in order to catch an ' idea ' which, though
assumed to be immanent in each, is inoperative but as
common to many. In virtue only of such ideal transcendency it is deemed presentable as a cause. Who can
fail to see here also a tacit, but inconsequent, admission
that escape from the transcendent idea is intrinsically
impossible ?

§ 2. *As evolved from Kant's ' innere Zweckmässigkeit.'*

The modern source of the antithesis ' transcendent and
immanent,' as well as of the tendency to confound it with
' external and internal,' is probably to be found in Kant's
critical treatment of the doctrine of ' Final Causes.' He
distinguishes two cases in which a group or series of natural
conditions leads up to an end recognised as eligible and
worth the cost. The first presents itself, wherever a
desirable product is set up by the favouring action of
independent objects, or of prior changes themselves determined by separate laws : the sands, for example, of a
former sea-shore are propitious to the pine-forest's growth:
the winds which sweep over a lonely island bring to it
seeds from distant continents and enrich its flora : the
cattle could not live but for the meadow-grass fed by the
neighbouring river, which again depends in its turn on the
gathered rains or melting snows of the uplands. Here, the
end is external to the means, and forms so small a part of
what they do, that we do not suppose the sea-bed and
beach to be spread for the sake of future pine-trees, or the
atmospheric currents to have been set in motion as a

vehicle for vegetable life, or the clouds and hills to have had their laws computed by the demand for fodder. These objective utilities constitute the class of *adaptations to external ends* (relative oder äussere Zweckmässigkeit)[1]. We regard them, that is, not as letting us into the secret of Nature's plan, but as collateral fruits of it, of which man takes advantage when they appear ; and, were they not there, we should not know what we missed, or at any rate should deem it presumptuous and absurd to pronounce the elements a failure for their absence. The constitution of the natural forces being what it is, irrespectively of them, these benefits are accounted for as incidental results of working processes in a large and neutral mechanism.

It is otherwise with the second class of adaptations, found within the limits of any single living being. Here, the several organs, with their functions, are so related as to stand in reciprocal interdependence which may be read in any order, and to have no self-subsisting individuality apart from each other, and no separate meaning, till taken into view as factors of a whole which at once supplies their interpretation. It is impossible not to regard the several parts of an organism as existing and working, each in its determinate way, for the sake of the living whole which they constitute, and therefore as owing their relations of equilibrium together to some controlling influence from a prior idea of that whole. The respiration, the arterial and venous circulation, the digestive and glandular systems, would amount to a mere arbitrary play of chemical forces, did not the growing, moving, feeling and seeing animal step forth to give their united meaning. Nor is that meaning complete in the individual ; for from him another springs, of which, so far as it is *other*, he may be called the natural cause. But inasmuch as it is *not other*, being a

---

[1] Kritik der Urtheilskraft, § 62 ; Ros. iv. pp. 248 *seqq.*

continuance of the one and the same *kind*, the mere nature-history has had to work under the control of a conservative idea, involving more than individual causality. Such an idea appears again, on behalf of the individual, in what is called the *vis medicatrix naturæ*, the instant assiduity with which the animal organism, when hurt, begins to repair itself, asking only to have the pieces put into right order for it. In all this we have a system of *adaptations to internal ends*, where cause and effect meet within the thing itself (innere Zweckmässigkeit)[1]. The interpretation of nature in this organic field carries in it an inevitable assumption of 'Final causes.' If elsewhere Nature can be supposed to be blind in her activity, here at last she sees her way before her, and is guided by an aim.

Is this Kantian antithesis interchangeable, as is sometimes assumed, with the Hegelian opposites 'Transcendent and Immanent'? It will be found that the correspondence, complete in one term of each pair, fails in the other. The 'internal conformity to an end' with Kant, reappears in Hegel as 'immanent causality': but in the 'external conformity to an end' there is no assertion or implication of 'transcendent causality.' What is it that is 'internal' in the former case? Both the initiating end and the determined means; cause and effect are alike within the organism, the perfection of which is the total object of its own structure and functions, and is self-realising. This is what Kant means by planting a directing aim at its own complete life amidst and before the creature's mechanism and activities. And this is what Hegel means by placing each individual creature at the disposal of the '*Idee* of its species': that *Idee* is the cause that starts its genesis: and what it realises as ultimate effect is but that *Idee* again. What is it that is 'external' in Kant's 'äussere Zweck-

---

[1] Kritik der Urtheilskraft, §§ 63–65 ; Ros. iv. pp. 252 *seqq.*

mässigkeit'? Evidently it is the resulting good, accomplished in and for one being by the constitution of another, involving an interplay between heterogeneous objects, as the synonym 'relative' distinctly expresses. The cause and the effect are here separated ; the former being in the constitution of one, as in the seed which grows the meadowgrass ; the latter, in the exigencies of another, as in the needs and senses of the pastured cattle. In saying of such cases that the causality is not 'external' (i. e. to the seat of the effect), we say that it is not 'immanent'; it matters not which epithet is used. But do we, on that account, say or imply that it is 'transcendent'? Did Kant mean that where causality was not found in the same being as the effect, it must be sought somewhere out beyond nature altogether? On the contrary, he expressly charges the effect, in these 'external' instances, on the natural laws of blind mechanical necessity, and removes it entirely from the category of controlling ends. Treating the useful services it renders as accidental results, he dismisses them as a teleological semblance which deceives us by its analogy to our imperfect exercises of skill. It is obvious therefore that Kant's correlative to 'internal' is wholly different from Hegel's correlative to 'immanent.' Not only does 'transcendent' go beyond the notion of 'externality' into that of *superiority*: not only does its 'externality,' instead of being relative to a single object, carry us outside all finite things ; but, in doing so, it takes us into the very realm of the supernatural which Kant's 'external' excludes and his 'internal' admits : for, when he wishes to mark the blind causal necessity to which he abandons his 'external' category, the word 'Nature' comes first into his thought,— qualified, it is true, by some limiting epithet, saving the word for larger use, when needful : 'the mechanism of nature,' 'mere nature laws,' 'aimless motive forces of nature' ; and the 'intentionality' which he distinguishes from this crude case he describes as a contradiction of nature by herself, inasmuch as its affirmed causality is made up of a rational idea which excludes necessity, and a material process which admits of nothing else[1]. In so far as the 'internal' or 'immanent' end is thus more than nature, it is supernatural, and instead of being the opposite of 'transcendent,' is identical with it.

'Final causality,' planted internally, may be expressed in one phrase: but the meaning of that phrase breaks up, as soon as apprehended, into a plurality of contents. It denotes the governing presence, in an organism, of the end which that organism has to reach. To govern or control is possible only to a dynamic efficient: the 'end' therefore must be regarded as working the organs, or, what is equivalent, forcing them into a particular form. That form then, in order to serve as the rule for the realising power, must be predetermined, and though called the 'end,' must be already there at the beginning. This prior position it cannot itself have ere it exists: the place can be claimed only for the *preconception of the end*, as selected to the exclusion of all other possibles. Such an idea is conceivable only as a phenomenon of some self-conscious and thinking being: and we have to ask where, in this immanent class of cases, we are to find the thinking subject of the directing idea. Must we identify it with the individual animal controlled? Does the creature itself set before it what it is to be, and work its organs by that rule? Not so: in that finite consciousness Theist and Hegelian are agreed that no such aim is to be found, though the processes which realise it tell their story there. Whither then must we turn for the seat of the idea? The Theist replies, 'To the Infinite consciousness, the originating Subject of every thought and purpose planted out into the universe for its accom-

---

[1] Kritik der Urtheilskraft, § 63; Ros. iv. pp. 252, 253.

plishment.' The Hegelian replies, 'To no thinking Subject
at all : for the *Idee* exists before it divaricates into subject
and object, and develops itself in things as well as thoughts,
moving beneath the floor of consciousness ere it emerges
into intellectual light.' Stopping short in these dark cham-
bers where as yet no mind is, he lets the idea remain unconscious, though all the while it is directing processes of
power to its predetermined end. He cannot even say that,
in this account, he is only offering us a *self-realising idea* :
for the thing realised is *an individual*, while the idea is an
'idea of the species': so that there is a margin in the effect
beyond the range of the cause. The possibility of an
immanent agency so paradoxical eludes my grasp. An
unconscious idea, an idea existing, yet not in thought, an
idea busy in the world but present to no Subject, is wholly
unintelligible to me : it is saved from being an absolute
blank only by being an evident self-contradiction. I am
obliged to refer an idea, above all an *aim* (Zweck) to a
Mind which has it, and which, as its subject, is distinct
from the object in which it works ; not necessarily distinct
in place, like one man from another, but distinct as my
own Will from the limbs or the thoughts which it controls.
Without prejudice to the distinction therefore, the intending Mind may be wherever the intention is working itself
out : and least of all can the Theist have any difficulty in
accepting the immanence of his Infinite Subject in every
finite nature which is realising a divine purpose. But in
this copresence, the conscious intent which is missing in
the finite organism is at hand in the Infinite Subject.

The doctrine of 'Final causes' is thus legitimately available for the Theist, especially in its form of 'internal' aim
at an 'end.' If organic nature be the admitted product
and vehicle of determinate causal aims,—aims conceivable
only as phenomena of intending mind : if the flora and fauna
of the world are admitted to be conscious in themselves of

no such phenomena; they are not self-determined but directed to their ends by an intending mind operative through their whole field of nature. The 'immanent' conception thus passes on in the most natural way into the 'transcendent.' By a strange re-adjustment of the same admitted facts, the Hegelian (as we have seen) extorts from the same doctrine of Final causes a disproof of the Theistic position. Throughout organic nature, he says, the end has plainly the command and moulding of the means: just as plainly, this happens without any presence of prospective intention; there is no need therefore for any intending mind: the '*Idee* of the species' can find its way and manage its work unconsciously. The fallacy is obvious. What the conclusion requires is assumed in the premise, viz. that the only consciousness present is that of the finite creature, so that what is absent thence is absent altogether, and may be dispensed with as superfluous. The misfortune is, that this negative proposition leaves the adaptations on our hands, with no causality at all, and utterly blank of all explanation. For, divest the 'idea of the species' of all consciousness, and how can you save its causality? It becomes an εἶδος of Plato, regarded exclusively on its objective side; only that he had the modesty to withhold from it all causality, until it fell into possession of some thinking Subject who could wield it. What sense can we attach to the assertion of a creative or operating power in a specific or generic idea of which no one is conscious? Is it blindly dynamic? then how does it thread its ingenious way through the moving crowd of organic particles, selecting and rejecting by the rule of what is to be? Is it noetic? then how can it stir without knowing what it is about? Are we to think of the marvels of animal instinct as exhibiting nature in a trance, unconsciously performing the skilled feats of a sleep-walker? The illustration, far from ridding us of subjective intention, isolates it as the one causality from which there is no parting; for the somnambulist differs from men awake, by being more absolutely at the disposal of his inner thought and will, undistracted by changes of outward perception: and it is precisely his intense concentration upon an ideal end in view, that bears him swiftly and deftly on the tracks which would lead to it if it were there, but which in its absence may hurl him into death. In short, the objective working of ideas which are present to no thinking Subject can be affirmed in no form of words intelligible and self-consistent. The truth of the Immanent conception is conditional on its consummation in the Transcendent.

§ 3. *Opposite paths of entrance.*

The pantheistic conception, being reached by dropping the contrasted marks of the finite and the infinite factors of the universe, may be approached by either of two opposite paths. Nature may be resolved upwards into the universal Power; or God may be brought downwards into living possession of the whole realm of nature. In the former case we should begin from the scientific list of natural forces, commanding each its natural circle of phenomena, and fulfilling its commission within an assignable boundary: but on observing that, among these, curious relations open up which first indicate their affinity, next give them a common measure, and at last render them even interchangeable, we are led to reduce their number and embrace them in some more comprehensive term. One by one, the Chinese walls which we had built round the provinces of the world crumble away, and throw open to view the undulating sweep and continuous mountain chains of the whole kingdom of nature: and after repeatedly tasting the satisfaction of seeing multiplicity lapse into unity, we can hardly arrest our thoughts short of an entire merging of all secondary energies into a

single primary, the law of which, could we but have its
equation, would enable us to deduce whatever happens in
every field of space.   If the primary, thus inductively
reached and treated as our terminus, be in its conception
purely mechanical or chemical, our theory of the universe
will be *atheistic* ; as is the doctrine of those who, in assuming the self-existence of atoms of different configura-
tion and motion, claim to have data adequate to the evolution of all things.   If our primary ἀρχή present itself to us
not as an inorganic but as a *living* power, though short of
self-conscious and intending mind,—as a ψυχή not a νοῦς,—
pervading the universal frame, our theory will be *pantheistic* : and, according to the *grade* of vitality with which
our imagination endows the world, will range with hylozoic
systems that stop with the plant-life as a type, or with the
biozoic that advances to the analogy of the sentient.
Higher than this it is very unlikely that we shall press
up this inductive path : though the indeterminate limits
of animal consciousness leave the way more or less open
beyond : and the Stoic school, which exemplifies this
method, undoubtedly carried it much nearer to the borders
of theism.   In this instance, however, the natural senses
were not the sole source of the religious conceptions : from
the *moral* side other elements flowed into them, and gave
them an elevation beyond the level of the concomitant
physical speculation.

In the other case, where the universe is taken up into
God by the all-absorbing demands of infinitude, we start
from the idea of the 'Absolute Cause' (or the nearest
approach we can make to it): and, waiting upon its successive self-manifestations in the universe as they break
into ever new differences and multiplied relations, we pass
from province to province of nature without encountering
any shock of arrest, or meeting anything which disowns
the universal power.   It is still the first source that descends

with its ramifications to the last extremities and sustains the life of the whole : and whatever it is in its original essence, that it must also be in its ultimate expression. This is practically decided by the very order of our procedure. It is impossible to begin from the *a priori* end of thought with a *physical* idea : if we are to leave the finite behind and take our stand in the infinite, we must at least include in that datum the functions of *mind* and *will*, even if we do not identify it with these : the highest and substantive term of being, whence are to come all order and beauty and good and all natures capable of apprehending them, cannot be conceived but as comprising these elements of perfection : and we shall therefore read into the universe as its inner essence, even when masked by material disguise, a life of reason in conscious harmony with what we think and venerate as best. Thus it is that intellectual or mystical forms of Pantheism arise ; which, instead of regarding Deity as only the common term or last generalisation of all subordinate life, see nature, however opake to the undiscerning eye, glorified as the garment of God.

While the theories which have their birth in these two methods, *regressive* on the one hand and *progressive* on the other, are thus broadly distinguished in their tendencies, great room is left for variation within each class ; and, in minds not logically compact, even for mixture and alternation of the two methods : so that it is hardly possible to name a single historical system as a sample at once pure and complete of either type. Were we to ballot for a representative of the second, probably every vote would be cast in favour of Spinoza. This choice would be founded, naturally enough, on what he calls his 'geometrical method,' i. e. his attempt to advance from the highest ἀρχή, through its necessary attributes, to the modes under which individual objects and phenomena affect our

senses and imagination. This is certainly the right direction of movement for the nobler pantheism. And if, in
effecting it, Spinoza had started from a Real Being already
charged with all divine predicates in their perfection, and
carried this forward into the generated universe, to be the
animating breath and actuating springs of the heavens and
the earth, he would have fulfilled its promise, and planted
us in a world ruled by thought and thrilled by love akin
to ours, only unerring and supreme, and have left possible
to us a sympathy between the mind of the part and the
mind of the whole. But, instead of this plenitude, ready
to flood all space with infused beauty and good, his ' *Substance*,' out of which all is to come, is kept studiously clear
of all predicates ; under the plea of not hurting its infinitude, you are forbidden to say anything of it but that ' it
exists': the moment you affirm anything further you define
it by a mark, and shut it out from what was open to it
before: you limit it by an exclusion, for 'omnis determinatio
est negatio.' It has nothing, therefore, to share in common
with derivative natures but this indefinite and sterile blank
called ' being': all properties or functions that seem to us
to fill up the worth of this blank,—life, intellect, will, affection,—belong first and only to creatures that are born and
die, and must on no account be ascribed to the Absolute
God. Nay, more : even those two ' attributes' ('extension'
and ' thought '), which we are allowed to treat as belonging
to his essence, are not in any way deduced from it, and
stand in a totally dark relation to it : they figure in the
scheme, only because they stare us in the face when we
begin from the other end and use our senses and observation, and cannot be ignored : but out of the idea of
substance they can no more be evolved than out of each
other ; or than any of the infinite number of other infinite
attributes which, it is said, 'substance' must have, but of
which, in spite of their necessary inherence in it, our

'geometrical method' cannot give us the faintest notion. In short, Spinoza has to make a clean leap in order to clear the chasm between his indeterminate being and the extension and thought which he calls its 'attributes,' and which he wants as his points of departure through the respective realms of matter and of mind ; and if he had arbitrarily taken these up to begin with, as Descartes had done, the whole rational organism of his scheme would have been complete, and nothing would have been wanting to it except an unconnected prefix which hangs over its two chains as a symbol or promise of their unity, but from which no filament passes to either. The Spinozistic *Deus*, therefore, interpreted by the principles of the method, cannot be said to be *in se* either extended or thinking : he is at most only the *possibility* of extension and thought in the ulterior contents of the *Natura naturata*. And when, after experience of them there, we learn, on looking back, to call them 'attributes' of His, we ascribe to him no extension or thought except what belongs to *it* and not to *Him* as distinguished from it : his omnipresence is but the spaciousness of nature and the bulks of things : his 'thinking' is but the total consciousness and mental action of men and other rational created beings ; and in knowing them, we know it all. If, therefore, what we most esteem Divine, and find in the meaning of the word God, be Reason, Beauty, Righteousness, and Love, nothing Divine can be said, in this system, to flow from the Fount of being and permeate its fields and run into its inmost creeks : on the contrary, it is in particular beings, furthest down from the Infinite, that this feature first appears ; the more you retreat back towards the prior Universal whence they are differentiated, the less you have of these qualities which you most revere. And if you are reminded that they were always *potentially there*, and that the cosmos in which they are now actual is still God, you cannot but reply, that they were not in his consciousness till they were in yours, and that, since they are what you mean by the divine, it is only of late that he has developed into God.

I cannot then admit the propriety of treating Spinoza's system as the representative instance of the higher pantheism, and of calling him 'a God-intoxicated man.' There is little to distinguish his first principle from any atomic or dynamic unity assumed as capable of divaricating further down into parallel series of inorganic and self-conscious phenomena. The chief differences between such doctrine and his are, that he will predicate nothing of his ἀρχή, and simply posits it as a self-existent x: and that he does not wait for his dualism till he has travelled some way on the material line, but starts it at the first step from its unity. But, in both theories alike, *Thought* can be attributed to the source of all only ἐν δυνάμει, not ἐν ἐνεργείᾳ; it is a promise for the creation, and not a reality in the Creator. If the characteristics of mind are what we chiefly mean under the term God, then the universe rather *becomes divine* in the end than *is so* in its source[1]. In such a doctrine there is not a breath of the peculiar pantheistic afflatus; it belongs altogether to the severely logical type, and might be held by an absolutely cold and colourless intelligence; and Schleiermacher must have read his own genius into its author's

---

[1] This notion of God gradually emerging as the climax of evolution, is thus broadly presented by M. Rénan : 'Au terme des évolutions successives, si l'univers est jamais ramené à un seul être absolu, cet être sera la vie complète de tous ; il renouvellera en lui la vie des êtres disparus, ou, si l'on aime mieux, en son sein revivront tous ceux qui ont été. Quand Dieu sera en même temps parfait et tout-puissant, c'est-à-dire quand l'omnipotence scientifique sera concentrée entre les mains d'un être bon et droit, cet être voudra ressusciter le passé, pour en réparer les innombrables iniquités. Dieu existera de plus en plus : plus il existera, plus il sera juste.' These words are spoken by one of the interlocutors of a dialogue, and do not proceed from the author in propriâ personâ. Dialogues Philosophiques, Paris, 1876, pp. 135, 136.

mind ere he could burst into the enthusiastic invocation:
'Join me in reverently offering a chaplet to the shade of
the rejected yet saintly Spinoza! penetrated as he was by
the sublime spirit of Nature, the Infinite was his Alpha and
Omega, the universe his only and eternal love. In holy
innocence and deep humility he saw himself reflected in
the eternal cosmos, and in himself too its fairest mirror.
He was full of religion and holy spirit ; and therefore is it
that he stands unequalled and alone, master in his art but
lifted high above the herd of his fellows, without disciples
and without recognition of his rights[1].'

The system of Spinoza was the product of a strictly
scientific mind, intent much more on correctly reading *the
All* than on finding its *God*. He laid the greatest stress on
the distinction, explained in a previous section (Section 4,
p. 250) between the imaginative and the intellectual aspect
of the world : he insisted that the former is an illusion,
treating as an insulated whole that which is only a *mode*
or accident of some attribute of being : and that the latter
alone opens to us some glimpses into the real constitution
of things. He not only looked on the world entirely under
this aspect, but conceived the general laws themselves as
only a temporary or provisional plurality. They were not
independent of one another, like separate volitions of a
self-determining mind ; but linked together by a geometrical necessity, rendering them all deducible from an ultimate
datum, that admitted of no alternative. The highest term
therefore in his system did not differ, except in compre-
hensiveness, from any of the laws, for example, gravitation,
definite proportions, &c., which it comprised : like them, it
was simply a *necessitating principle*, only of universal sweep:
and, as a 'causa essendi,' stood related to all that was
evolved from it, as the defining character or essence of a

---

[1] Reden über die Religion, ii. pp. 47, 48, 4te Auflage, 1831.

circle stands related to all the properties it enables us to
deduce. Towards such a principle no attitude of mind
seems possible, to which the epithet 'mystical' or even
'religious' can be properly applied : and the intellectual
desire to reach such a principle is not what, in the usual
meaning of the words, would constitute a ' God-intoxicated
man.' Spinoza's ideal, and his personal characteristic,
consists in absolute allegiance to truth, in an emergence
from the life of sense and imagination into that of pure
Science, in which the necessary order of the world is
accurately reflected in the Reason. When the individual
thought has thus become the rationally thinkable invested
with consciousness, this perfect consonance he calls, it is
true, ' *the intellectual love of God*' ; and of the tranquillity it
brings he speaks in tones forgetful of his 'geometrical'
severity. But he expressly says that the love is all on
one side, without any answer from the object loved; the
tranquillity is simply the absence of any jar between the
order of thought and the order of things,—a coalescence
between their pulsations in which the individual is lost.
No nature so luminous was ever filled with *drier light*
than his. Pure, veracious, unselfish, as he was, he understood nothing but understanding ; his mind was a limpid
thinking element, the vehicle only of the true, and dissolving away the beautiful and good ; a perfect example of ἀρετὴ
διανοητική; but fixed in a latitude too high and cold to feel
the glow of even a temperate enthusiasm.

Perhaps it is in Malebranche that we find the best
example of a Pantheism, carefully thought out, in which
both elements of the word retain their proper meaning.
Whatever affinities may be traced in his Recherche de la
Vérité (1674-5) with the doctrine of Spinoza, it could
never incur the suspicion attaching to the Ethica (published
1677, the year of the author's death), of having been
originally written without the word 'God,' the terms

' Nature,' and ' Substance ' doing all its work : for the idea of the infinite and perfect Subject of all thought and power constitutes the centre and source of the whole scheme. That idea, found in ourselves, and far transcending our resources, was to Malebranche, as to Descartes, the adequate guarantee of its own validity : it is self-evidencing, and contains in itself, as indeed its very essence, the affirmation of existence. The only problem with him was, how to define the relation between the divine nature and the human, and between both and the world of sensible things. The clue to his solution of this problem is found in his distinction between our 'ideas' and our mere sensations and imaginings ; the former being pure, necessary, invariable thoughts ; the latter, mixed, transient, variable representations : the one, wholly intellectual ; the other, affected by corporeal conditions. Thus, in our conception or memory of the Sun, the circle of its disk, with the boundless space containing it, is appended *in idea*, as what would still be there though we, and even it, were not ; but, the light and warmth are mere feelings of ours, which either might be or might not be. The sphere of the latter is wholly *personal* : my sensations are not yours : each has his own. But the former cannot be appropriated : the universal space is identical in the thought of all ; and so, of all objects or truths that Aristotle calls ἀΐδια it must be said that they are *impersonal*, belonging not to this or that Reason, but to universal Reason : they are in us, because they are in all : they are here now, because they are eternal. But there is no universal and eternal save God : and He therefore is the seat of these ideas ; and in him it is that we see them : ' He is the place of all spirits,' as extension is the place of all bodies. Descartes had allowed no distinction, in the Divine Nature, between necessary and contingent truth : both alike were regarded as matters of arbitrary institution ; God affirms nothing because it is true: it is true because he affirms it. Such dependence of truth upon Will Malebranche will not allow in the sphere of demonstrative certainties: these are self-existent and immutable, identical with the eternal thought of God: and our knowledge of them is a participation in his intelligence. It is otherwise with our ideas of things that might have been different, such as outward objects of perception: these undoubtedly are differenced from each other by divine determination; only the extension which is common to them all belonging inseparably to material existence: while the varieties of motion, into which all distinction of bodies is resolvable, are given, continued, and withdrawn by the will of God. Do we then gain our knowledge of these direct from themselves? Not so; the material world can give only motion, not thought, and has spent its possibilities when it has delivered an impression upon the bodily organs: in God alone do they ideally exist: and that we can *think them*, as well as be corporeally affected by them, is due to his allowing us some participation in his ideas: he communicates to us an intellectual apprehension, concurrent with the organic change. Whether therefore by partnership of the universal Reason, or by ordination of continuous will, He is the light of all our seeing, be it of necessary or of contingent truth.

Turning from the intellectual to the practical side of our nature, we find the same fusion of the human into the Divine persistently carried out. In God is not only all truth for the reason, but also all *good* for the Will: and as necessary truth is the universal element of all thinking being, so is absolute good the universal element of all voluntary being: under this aspect must appear whatever stirs a preference in any agent in the universe. This is the very essence of intelligent activity, just as extension is the essence of body. But as God adds various forms of motion to the geometrical relations of bodies, so does He super-

induce upon the general attraction of agents towards good
a system of particular impulsions, or natural passions,
tending to limited forms or even illusory aspects of good.
Material changes and mental alike proceed from him, and
are in fact modes or incidents of his eternal life. As we
know by admission to his true ideas, which in him are but
a self-knowledge, so do we *will* by sharing his love of good,
which is no other than the love of himself. From him is
all our tendency, whether to *bonum per se*, or to the special
parts of it contemplated by the several desires; all of
which were originally well-ordered, and so related to the
body, through the animal spirits, as to administer its
economy aright; but are liable to go wrong through the
same finite imperfection which, in the intellectual field,
confuses the pure ideas by admixture of sense and imagination. As room is thus left for the discordance between a
true good and a false, and yet our drift towards both is
represented as divinely given, Malebranche cannot escape
the question whether our own will has any part to play.
He endeavours to find one, without prejudice to his
principles, by assigning to it a function simply judicial and
not dynamic: when we are drawn to a limited good that
tempts us, in presence of true and essential good at
variance with it, we must refuse ourselves to the former
power and surrender ourselves to the latter: and though
both are from the sole fountain of power, the latter is as
much higher than the former, as the sphere of spirits in the
universe is higher than that of matter. That the sole
causality of God is really saved by this hypothesis, no one
probably will now maintain: but it marks the author's
eagerness to draw all currents into the one infinite abyss of
perfection.

The feature of Malebranche's system which often strikes
his readers as most expressive of his Pantheism is his substitution of Divine agency for our own in the ordinary

voluntary movements. When I take up my hat to walk out, when I advance to greet a friend, when I fetch a dictionary to look out a word, my purpose in each case is powerless to execute the act, and has no more causal connection with it than the simultaneous tick of the clock ; and did not the Divine will step in at the right moment and do for me what I want, it would remain undone. The doctrine which thus invokes the *concursus divinus* to snatch from us what seems most our own, and deny to us the very skill of our fingers and words of our mouths, is indeed an extreme example of facile resort to the infinite for solution of a familiar problem. The interest however in which it is framed is not exactly the pantheistic desire to get rid of all secondary causation. The principle to which it is pledged and of which it is the result, does not pronounce against all such causation ; but merely says that, *if* it has place at all, it can only be between matter and matter on the one hand, between mind and mind on the other ; and that no mental state can affect a material or *vice versâ* : so that, to establish a uniformly concurrent order between the two, there is need of the only being who is equally related to both, and can keep their successions punctually together. The same doctrine had been taught by earlier Cartesians, who cannot be regarded as pantheistic.

The two types of pantheism which find their representatives respectively in the Stoics and in Malebranche agree in removing all distinction between the natural and the supernatural. There is but one agency pervading the universe. In conceiving that agency, however, you may avail yourself of your previous idea of the natural ; or, of your previous idea of the supernatural ; in either case simply extending it from the part to the whole. The former course is taken by the Stoics : the latter by Malebranche. The one turns religion into a sublimated natural science : the other turns natural science into a theodicy. Without further regard to their separate characteristics, it remains for us, in appreciating their common features, to determine, if we can, the relative validity of Theism and Pantheism.

§ 4. *Relative Validity of Theism and Pantheism.*

The transition from the mechanical form of Theism to Pantheism can hardly fail to appear, at first sight, an escape into a higher view. If anything, in the Natural Religion of the last century, could lay strong hold of the devout imagination, it was the idea of the *Omnipresence* of God ; and were the experiences of early life laid open, during its years of growing fervour and self-discipline, it would probably be found that, both in the orisons of the closet and in the encounter with temptation, the attempt to realise this thought played a great part and wielded the chief power. The consciousness of his spirit whether at noon or night, abiding through every change, calm alike on the restless sea or on the steadfast mountain, with centre here or on the horizon or behind the moon or in the milky way, and radius touching every point of life or thought, holds the mind in sleepless wonder, and renders the risings of passion impossible. Still, in that Divine Infinitude there is a death-like coldness, so long as it is only a passive, though it be an observing presence brooding over every field of thought : it is but Space with eyes, that can never leave us within or without, yet will never help us or so much as return a whisper to our cry. The difference is great, if we may assure ourselves that that Immensity not only looks, but lives : that it is not a presence only, but a power : that the movements of the worlds are his, as well as their distances and numbers : that the lesser and the greater seasons of the earth are a part of his ways : that the speed of the light, and the play of the waves, and breathing of the forests, are his; that 'the balancing of the clouds,' and the gleam and glory of the sun and showers, are the momentary creations of his Art. Fill the geometrical vastness of his being with ever-during energy, pour his causality through time as you diffuse his existence through space, and the solemn impression of a simple omnipresence is quickened into an intenser affection, connecting the whole scenery of experience with him, and making his touch felt in the beauty and the terror, in the joy and the anguish of life. And hence it is that, except in an apathetic age, or among persons of level temperament, the Deistical conception fails to satisfy, and scarcely passes into a religion : once flung into awakening vicissitudes or more impassioned natures, it breaks its bounds and seeks a nearer God 'in whom the spirit may live and move and have its being.' Is this a concession to weakness? or is it an emergence into higher and fuller truth?

That depends, I think we may say, on the extent to which the change is carried. So long as the causality which it makes over to God is taken from outward nature and is *other than ours*, its conversion into an element immediately divine is strictly justified. There is nothing whatever to warrant, in relation to God, the idea of *deputed* cosmical action, through 'second causes' set up as tools, separate from his will and qualified to work of themselves. If they exist, we cannot know them ; for observation and induction, as we have seen, show us nothing but the series and grouping of phenomenal effects ; and the causation to which we refer them is supplied by a law of necessary thought. As that thought is uniform and self-identical in every case, it furnishes no ground for supposing many causes, but gives us a single dynamic idea ; and it has been shown that, when we speak of several nameable causes, we are in reality only *classifying effects*, and referring to now *this*, then *that*, and the *other* order of *phenomena, as caused*,

without any title to assert that each has a cause to itself.
We perceive the phenomena; we believe the causation:
the perception varies from field to field, the belief is the
same through all.   The form in which that belief is given
is that of *Will*; and the only question that can rationally
arise is, whether the action of divine will is most easily
conceived as continuous through the operation it performs;
or as momentary in itself and handing over the prolonged
part of the efficiency to a system of means, inert *per se*, but
charged with delegated power cut off from its source.   The
latter supposition seems to have nothing to recommend it.
If the delegate with which the power was deposited were
another mind and will, which could receive such a trust and
find discipline in carrying it out, the appointment of a
secondary might be intelligible.   But where it is nothing
but a material storehouse or reservoir for the perpetual
dribbling out of that which has been instantaneously put
in, it is impossible to understand why the Will which
measures the delivery should not also make it: the magazine could be useful, only if the source were off and on;
but with a perennial spring, all such artifice is superfluous.
The idea is obviously taken from the analogy of our human
experience, in which we compass our ends by adjusting a
mechanism for their accomplishment, and providing the
weight or heat or tension needful for its working.   The
analogy however has no adequate application to a Will
operating, not like ours, with borrowed energy and a complete tissue of given conditions, but with first-hand resources
and in an open field.   He who draws upon nothing but
himself and lives eternally, cannot be reasonably supposed
either to concentrate or to stay the flow of his power.   And
the more closely we look at it, the more difficult shall we
find it to conceive that each atom of matter, ere it is left to
go its own way, should be instructed and commissioned for
all its future: how to face this way or that and always

move at the prescribed rate and never miss its direction ; and in all respects behave as desired in the countless relations it is appointed to enter.   If the atoms already existed, with their constitution ready-made, so that they served as *data* to which the Creator had to conform, there would then be two dynamic partners in the creative process, and in distributing their functions we might intelligibly leave it to their forces to carry out what his voluntary adjustment of them had provided.   But the separation of volition from execution has no ground where there are no foreign agencies to be consulted, and the directing purpose and efficient power differ only as the intellect and the will of the same Mind.   Both are predicates of One Subject ; and the very distinction which we draw between them is only an analytical contrivance relative to ourselves who have to think of all things, even the Eternal, under the rules of Time.   All external causes therefore lapse into one efficiency ; and are distinguished only in the phenomenal vehicle which that efficiency assumes.

To this view of nature it is objected, that it involves an incessant and universal ' intervention of God ' in the minutest affairs ; multiplying his separate volitions to infinitude ; turning trifles into miracles ; and pulverising the divine agency into a form impalpable to thought. Malebranche himself is sensitive to this objection, and anxious to provide means in his system for reducing the number of ' particular volitions ' involved in the process of conservation as a continuous creation.   His method of doing so is by setting up his scheme of ' occasional causes ' : that is, by establishing it as a rule with the Creator to issue a given phenomenon, of matter or spirit, wherever its fore-appointed antecedent is on the scene ; such antecedent, serving to us as the sign of what is to come, and being to him the occasion of action, may be called the ' occasional cause,' in spite of its intrinsic impotence.   But it is difficult

to see where the economy of this method is to be found.
If each instance of antecedence involves an 'intervention':
if, moreover, the antecedent itself could not appear without
being divinely brought upon the field; if, further, the consecution and concurrence of the 'occasional causes' are
determined by the Supreme will: all rules of nature, and
all their examples, alike require a volition each: and if
infinitude is to frighten us, there is nothing here to save us
from our recoil. But does it really present us with anything from which we ought to shrink? Is there any
assignable reason for parsimony in the expenditure of
immeasurable will? Why may it not disperse itself in
myriad drops, instead of pouring itself forth all in one flow?
It is not in the field of action, but in that of thought, that
we are restive under complexity and for ever pressing our
demand for unity: and in the immanence and boundless
distribution of Divine energy there is nothing at variance
with perfect simplicity of purpose and intellectual symmetry
of method; any more than our own repetitions of will in
each reproduction of habitual action are inconsistent with
a rational system of life. I do not see therefore that
Theism has any interest in reducing the number of Divine
volitions. But if anyone's imagination is troubled by it, he
may perhaps gain relief by considering that we have no real
means of counting them: for who can say whether, in
correspondence with general conceptions and in execution
of them there may not be generic volitions, needing no
repetition and allocation, but sweeping at once through the
whole range of extent and history? Even our own experience is not wholly without analogies that are helpful in
this direction. It is a complicated organism that is placed
at our disposal; and there is scarcely an act of will that
does not call into movement several organs simultaneously,
or run through several links of change to its conclusion:
yet one volition suffices to co-ordinate or regiment the

complex elements of the result. To will the end commands
the means, where both are within the limits of our constitution. The relation of the Universal spirit to the
organism of nature through which he is manifested may
well be such as to embrace indefinitely more within the
units of will, and even to leave behind our whole calculus
of repetition, and substitute a synthesis for each of our
analyses. But, if we have rightly construed the source and
meaning of our causal ideas, the one thing certain is that,
however wide the sweep and durable the continuance of the
laws of physical change, they are intrusted with no causality
of their own, but are only the modes of the Divine action.

The whole external universe, then (external, I mean, to
self-conscious beings), we unreservedly surrender to the
In-dwelling Will, of which it is the organised expression.
From no point of its space, from no moment of its time, is
His living agency withdrawn, or less intensely present than
in any crisis fitly called creative. But the very same principle which establishes a *Unity* of all external causality
makes it antithetic to the internal, and establishes a *Duality*
between our own and that which is other than ours: so
that, were not our personal power known to us *as one*, the
cosmical power would not be guaranteed to us as *the other*.
Here, therefore, at the boundary of the proper Ego, the
absorbing claim of the supreme will arrests itself, and recognises a ground on which it does not mean to step. Did
it still press on and annex this field also, it would simply
abolish the very base of its own recognisable existence,
and, in making itself all in all, would vanish totally from
view. It is precisely by *not being unitary* that causation is
accessible to thought at all; and if our own will does not
exercise it, we are excluded from even the search for it
elsewhere. By *self* we mean the will internal: by 'God'
we mean the will external: by *cause* we mean either: and
as the two former come into our knowledge as terms of a

relation under the category of the latter, it is impossible for either extreme to lapse into the other. It would be a parricidal doctrine of causality that should thus lay violent hands on the conditions of its own existence.

The voluntary nature, then, of moral beings must be saved from Pantheistic absorption, and be left standing as, within its sphere, a free cause other than the divine, yet homogeneous with it. Nor is there any difficulty in saving it : in fact it saves itself ; for no one can exercise his own will and believe it to be another's : and, try as he may to merge his own causality in the Divine, it is still he, and not God, that makes that sublime renunciation. You cannot even declare yourself a pantheist without self-contradiction ; for in doing so you reserve your own personality as a thinking and assertive power, that deals with all else as objective. Here it is that we touch the ultimate and irremovable ground of all certainty ; whence alone we look forth and discover either the $\pi \hat{a} \nu$ or the $\Theta \epsilon \acute{o} s$: and to negative this position on behalf of what it shows us would be like the fanaticism of a fire-worshipper who should put out his eyes to glorify the light. For our present enquiry, viz. how far we are to recognise the Divine agency as immanent source of phenomena in the world, it is sufficient to rest upon this fundamental Duality of causation. The difficulties which arise when we try to adjust the two terms to each other, the self-existent to the created, are doubtless serious, perhaps irresolvable ; but are less than attend any possible alternative, and have no weight against a primary cognition without assuming which they cannot even state themselves. They will more suitably come under consideration, when we deal with the moral side of Theism in its relation to Necessarianism. At present I am content to say that we know ourselves to be the authors of our own voluntary acts, and rightly refrain from attributing them to God. This affirmation is not really inconsistent with our habitual reference of our whole existence and its contents to God : for, unless we deny his power to create a being rational and free, to whom for a season he lends and leaves intact a judging and deciding faculty, he may be the cause of all our possibilities without being responsible for our actualities ; and, notwithstanding the maxim ' Causa causæ causa causati,' our consciousness of an originating activity will be no illusion. Wherever he sets up a proper *self*, the conditions are provided under which he may leave a deposit of power : but not for a moment can insensate matter spare him.

If however the will of rational beings must be allowed a sphere of its own, the concession will have to pass somewhat deeper into their nature. Its decisions are made upon a competition of impulses and a comparison of persuasions and dissuasions, involving exercises of understanding and conscience which are strictly our own. If it is not another that decides, neither is it another that deliberates, that is tempted, that strives and prays. The history of such experience all hangs together : and with the voluntary life itself all the active mental and moral conditions of its play must be reserved to the individual and finite subject. In other words, we must not, even on Divine behalf, tamper with the constituents of man's personality, or alienate from him the normal functions of his intellect, conscience, and affections. This rule guards us not merely from Spinoza's identification of thinker, thought, and thinkable, as a mode of the universal mind ; not merely from Malebranche's doctrine, that our ideas are in God : but from such indeterminate statements as those of Theodore Parker, in which he treats the regular results of the human faculties as an immediate working of God, and regards the Principia of Newton as inspired. He evidently does not *mean* to divest us, either of natural faculties of our own, or of the responsible will to turn them to account ; for he separates

both of these from that 'action of God' on us which he
calls 'inspiration'; laying down the rule, that the latter is
administered in the compound ratio of the two former, depending partly on the 'quantity of our being,' and partly
on the 'quantity of our obedience.' 'Inspiration is the
consequence of the faithful use of our faculties'; which he
enumerates as 'the senses, the understanding, reason, conscience, and the religious sentiment [1].' There is then within
us a personal mind, endowed with powers under individual
direction and capable of *use* for attaining their appropriate
ends, viz. perceptive knowledge, scientific truth, rational
thought, the sense of right, piety towards God. But if such
employment of our capacity as will give us these is the
prior condition of Divine influence, what remains for that
influence to effect? It can only *add* to the store already
earned, by quickening the mental vision or intensifying the
light; introducing gleams of thought, or affection, or a
tension of purpose and will, that would not have been
gained by the unaided faculties. This supplementary *concursus* is conceivable enough, and would harmonise well
with the tendency, so prevalent in the highest order of
minds, to feel that in their supreme moods they are lifted
beyond themselves: but such testimony on their part
means plainly *this*, viz. that the kindling flash of thought
and love that has wrapt them in its fire is something not
from within the limits of their nature; they receive it from
a source *above nature*: from the Spirit of God, where it has
not bound itself up in definitely constituted beings, but
remains still free to flow where it listeth: they declare it,
that is, to be *supernatural.* In that view there is room for
it without prejudice to the integrity of our nature; and
there may be evidence of it in the special character of the
experience, rendering it irreducible to the known laws of

---

[1] Discourse of Matters pertaining to Religion, Boston, U. S., 1842,
pp. 219, 220.

mental suggestion. This only tenable form of the doctrine Theodore Parker, however, appears to reject : the inspiration for which he pleads is nothing exceptional or supernatural, but is universal and constant, immanent in all mind, as the physical agency of God in all matter, identified with the normal operation of its several faculties, so that 'the in-come of God to the soul is in the form of Truth through the reason, of Right through the conscience, of Love and Faith through the affections and religious sentiment[1].' 'Inspiration,' he says, 'is the light of all our being ; the background of all human faculties ; the sole means by which we gain a knowledge of what is not seen and felt, the logical condition of all sensual knowledge ; our human way to the world of spirit. Man cannot exist without God, more than matter[2].' What then becomes of the human personality, when all its characteristics are thus conveyed over to the Supreme Mind ? The very terms in which it is described abolish it. If truth, if righteousness, if love and faith, are all an influx of foreign light, the endowments in virtue of which we are susceptible of them are mere passive and recipient organs on to which they are delivered, and we have no agency of our own. But a *reason* that does no thinking for itself, a *conscience* that flings aside no temptation and springs to no duty, *affection* that toils in no chosen service of love, a 'religious sentiment' that waits for such faith as may 'come in' to it, simply negative their own functions and disappear. Of whom are we to predicate the achievements of genius and character that enrich the world? Is Shakespeare only 'by courtesy' the author of Macbeth? Did Newton *not* excogitate the proof that a projectile must always move in one of the conic sections, but simply suffer it to pass through him as its minister ? When the martyr cries,

---

[1] Discourse of Matters pertaining to Religion, Boston, U. S., 1842, p. 218.   [2] Ibid., p. 219.

'Though he slay me, yet will I trust in him,' does he breathe forth the faith of the finite spirit, or the dictation of the Infinite? Of all these energies Parker's doctrine, by denying them of man, except as the mere conscious *nidus* of them, makes God the real subject: and at times he so little shrinks from this extreme as to speak of God as not only 'omnipresent,' but '*omni-active*,'—an epithet which, if it were more than rhetorical, would carry in it an un-conditional Pantheism. This is far beyond his meaning. To no one was the personality of man, with all the moral truth which it includes, an intenser or more solid reality than to him; vigorous and healthy in himself; and so thoroughly recognised in others, as to be struck by him in many a thunderbolt of righteous anger, and in the lovely summer lightning of many a noble aspiration. But to save the very truths that lay at the centre of his life, it is indispensable to check the wilder excursions of his thought, and restrain it within exacter lines.

The Dual disposition of our universe, between ourselves and all else, acquaints us then with two causes, and no more: and the Divine cause administers all that is not vacated on our behalf. Did we learn nothing of these two except what is contained in their first entrance upon our consciousness, they would be quite co-ordinate except in magnitude: neither would be before or after the other: the antithetic play between them would be upon equal terms. Discovering, however, that we have not always been here, but have been set up in recent times, we have to regard ourselves as phenomena of the other and greater cause: and, falling into this originated position, we qualify our immediate sense of independence with a recognition of prior dependence; and from co-ordinate become *second causes*; and that, in the meaning of *both words*: we are *second*, because there is a first, in relation to whom we are *effects*: we are *causes*, because, in spite of this, we are not

only effects, but are constituted with a will and directing
faculties, which have a store of power at their disposal, to be
thrown on the line of this possibility or of that ; and are not
therefore mere implements or media for executing the
volitions of another.   Is it a paradox to affirm that, notwithstanding our derived existence, we are not *only effects?*   It
would be a greater paradox to deny it.   For how does the
case logically stand ?   It is our own conscious causality that
reveals God's : it is God's causality that has *created* ours :
ours is first in knowledge ; his, in being.   Does this priority
of his take away our causality, and so undo our knowledge ?
Then does this expunged knowledge, as it vanishes, undo
him also, as counter-cause, and abolish his priority.   That
pre-existing Unity of his, which tempts you to own no
other cause, is itself guaranteed to you only by a co-existing duality of causation, and comes out simply as one of
its applications.   We may rest therefore upon the common
consciousness of real human agency : the very argument
used against it having to borrow its assumptions, and
dissolving on their denial.   And so, while there is One
Will in nature, there are two that meet in man.

It must be owned, however, that these realms are more
easily contrasted in words than marked out in fact.   What I
have been treating as the essence of humanity is so little conspicuous in some of our kind, and so wonderfully simulated
by certain other races, that it is a perplexing problem how to
conceive of the Divine agency in relation to such cases, and
indeed to the whole debatable border-land that stretches
between the mechanical and the spiritual.   In the view of
the naturalist, the contents of the world do not dispose
themselves satisfactorily under these two opposing heads.
Not only does Linnæus, for example, arrange them in three
realms, which he thus distinguishes : Lapides *crescunt,*
Vegetabilia crescunt et *vivunt,* Animalia crescunt, vivunt et
sentiunt : but he leaves man to be a sub-member of this last

province, with characteristics therefore of only specific rank,
—hardly entitled, it may be supposed, to fill up one term
in a dual universe. Is it not monstrous, it is said, when
the physiologists are at a loss to agree upon any clear
difference separating man from his congeners, to select just
this scarce visible interval as the supreme and regulative
boundary of existence? It certainly would be so, if in both
instances we were engaged upon the same work, and seeking
to raise a structure on the same *fundamentum divisionis*.
But in classifying for different ends, two enquirers may,
with the best reason, deal with the same materials in ways
that completely cross each other, and pay no attention
to each other's proportions ; the feature which is of superlative consequence to the one, being only insignificant to the
other. In a scale of chemical compounds a slight remove,
a mere altered proportion of carbon and nitrogen, takes us
from the plant to the animal ; and even from the inorganic
to organic the transition, we are assured, is reduced to a
minimum : but to the interior history of the object it makes
no contemptible difference whether it is sentient or insentient, whether it is living or dead. Upon a distinction
trivial in one aspect may hinge, in another, a contrast of
enormous magnitude. Unless this is borne in mind we are
liable to be seriously misled by the scientific maxim '*In
mundo non datur saltus*'; a maxim which, though indolently
assumed as the ground of every theory of evolution, does
not admit of being carried even through the provinces
of Physics and Chemistry. It is but a single degree of
temperature that, handing a body over from solid to liquid,
and from liquid to gaseous, enables it to leap from science
to science and seek the new protectorate of hydrostatics and
of pneumatics. The same small change it is which, in
an instant, brings into play chemical affinities inoperative
before, and with a flash and clap turns the passive volumes
of hydrogen and oxygen into water drops. In like manner,

the law of gravitation, after holding good through spaces
indefinitely vast, turns into sudden repulsion at inappre-
ciable distances, which again gives way to the closer
attraction of cohesion on still nearer approach [1]. And
the rates of ethereal vibration which give luminosity are
strictly limited, and from the extremities of the spectrum
we instantly step into the dark. Where there are two
orders of concomitant change, it is therefore quite consistent
with analogy that, though no term shall present itself
in either series without its correspondent in the other, yet
the intervals of difference should be altogether disparate,
an infinitesimal in the one being answered by a virtual
infinitude in the other. On this ground we may surely
justify the eminent position which we have assigned to the
human Will, without being bound to find in the bodily
organisation a separating feature of corresponding magnitude : and a critic only gives himself an irrelevant trouble
when he introduces us to the anthropoid apes, or any other
of our sylvan relations, and assails our aristocratic prejudice
by demonstrating the closeness of the family resemblance.
We accept all his estimates of physiological resemblance :
but they do not touch our psychological knowledge of the
difference. I call it *knowledge*; because, to learn the
character of animal action, we are not left to inductive
inference alone : the brute is also in the man, and in knowing himself he knows it too. And when we compare their
spheres together, and measure the increments of being
introduced by the rational will and its attendant endowments, with their fruits of language and literature, of
morals and law, of art and science, of history, poetry, and
religion, the interval they establish becomes practically
infinite, and escapes all control from the organic approximation.

---

[1] See Prof. F. W. Newman's Essay on the Atheistic Controversy,
Contemporary Review, Oct. 1878, p. 486.

With the naturalist then we can go in classing Man with the animals in virtue of his analogous organism and his sentient and instinctive functions : but we may nevertheless hold with Descartes, his transcendent separation from them in virtue of his proper personality, that is, his *self-conscious reason and will.* Rightly understood, and expressed in the enlarged terms of modern science, his doctrine, that the animal life is purely automatic, still admits of rigorous defence. I have before shown that it does not deny sensation or passions to the animals ; that it leaves to them internal impulses towards objects suited to their nature ; and only maintains that, in their passive sensibility, they simply have feelings without knowing them ; and, in their active movements, are disposed of by their impulses, without intentional pursuit of an end, or themselves exercising check or choice. It is not sensitive states, it is not motory instincts, that are withheld from them ; but only cognitive apprehension and volitional origination : and in setting these apart, as *sui generis* and referable to a different and spiritual sphere, Descartes assumed a position which philosophy cannot abandon without the certainty of a repentant return. He distinctly saw that though feeling, instinct, will, all manifest themselves in our organism, and all come from some immanent causality, in the last the causality was our own, while in the others it was not : a feeling is something given us : an impulse, something that rises in us and takes us hither or thither : both of them are but changes that happen upon our theatre, and with the ordering of which we have nothing to do : but, in a comparison between a plurality of impulses, a preference among them of the reasonable and right, and a purposed effectuation of the object of choice,—in all this, we are the *Agent*, not the mere recipient or the implement of a change : and the causality we then exercise is all that we ever mean by causality at all. Of a sensation which I have, another may be the source: the movement which I unconsciously execute, another may propel: but of the thinking, the choosing, the willing, which I do, there can be but one subject, and that subject is myself: they cannot be predicates at the same time of two minds, God's as well as my own. It is therefore perfectly possible to admit his agency in the phenomena of the sensitive and automatic life, where the creature exercises no will: and perfectly impossible to charge it with our voluntary acts of reason and conscience. With regard to the former, we and all the lower animal races may be as somnambulists, directed, during the slumber of intelligence and volition, by the fall of impressions on the outer and the succession of images on the inner sense: and the power which determines these wields the whole history. With regard to the latter, we are ourselves awake, and assume the self-direction which plants amid the same materials a new determining cause. Wherever the προαίρεσις is, *there* is the personal agency: if in us, the operative will is ours: if not in us, the operative will is God's.

In thus referring the collective energy of involuntary nature to God, we do but say, in other words, that the pervading power of the universe is not blind and aimless, but works upon ideas and realises purposes ; and, in doing this, traces lines of time-order in eternity, and takes the form of determinate laws of wider or lesser circuit,— physical, chemical, vital, instinctive. Do we thus admit too much that is Divine ? It is a strange objection, seeing that even the 'philosophy of the unconscious' claims no less. In his correction of Schopenhauer, Hartmann declares it impossible to reconcile the evident *pursuit of ends* in the universe with any mere irrational will ; and accordingly affirms that the inner principle of the world is 'so far from being unintelligent and blind, that it is an intuitive and clairvoyant wisdom, determining the contents and directing the processes of nature': it is 'the unity of intelligence and will': it is 'in an *eminent sense individual*': so that it may even receive the predicate of personality; and, if kept clear of humanising additions, is scarcely distinguishable from the immanent God of philosophical theism [1]. That the power of which all this can be said should still be called 'unconscious' may well astonish us. It is explained by the fact that, according to Hartmann, the principle of nature first acted blindly as mere will: and only in the moment of calling things into existence entered thereby upon its intellectual vision, and saw the mistake of creation when it was too late for recall. All that could be done was thenceforth to direct its clear-seeing intelligence to free the world from will, and work it round out of the pure evil of existence into rest and extinction. This return to negation is the only good: and towards this good all the scheme of the universe is directed with the greatest wisdom. This singular theory, of a Creator repenting through an endless day, with infinite skill of reparation, of the one blunder of his primeval night, curiously shows how even the pessimist has to own the intellectual system of the world, and to find excuse for its tending to the only good there is. The whole life of the creation is a working of ideas, an expressing of mind: and to find anything senseless you must quit all that is, and put yourself back before the beginning of things.

The Cartesian line of causal separation between the automatic and the voluntary, which we thus re-adopt, owes its repute, as a paradox, very much to the constant use of *mechanical* language in illustration of the animal structure and functions. The seventeenth century gave an extraordinary impulse to mathematical and experimental Physics:

---

[1] See Pfleiderer's Religions-Philosophie, 1878, pp. 210, 211, with the references there. The pages do not agree with those of the first edition of Hartmann.

and it was in this interest that by far the greater part of the new scientific conceptions and terms was brought into currency. The universal properties of matter, as such, or the variations on them presented by the three forms of solid, liquid, and air, and the general laws of motion and equilibrium, were the favourite objects of study : and the chief inventions aiding the economy of human life were of instruments depending on these laws. Hence the imagination of men ran easily into mechanical grooves : and nothing seemed properly clear, till it could be brought into the likeness of *a machine.* Every regular *consecution* of things was apt to be described as *wheel upon wheel* : every transmission of force, as the operation of a weight or spring upon *clock-work* : and those who denied the free will of man pronounced him *a machine*, or, with the prophet, compared him with clay upon the potter's lathe. Hence the constant resort by Descartes, in expounding his doctrine of the brute nature, to the analogy of *automata*: an analogy which, if hard pressed, would leave two false impressions in no way necessary to the doctrine itself ; viz. (1) of the absence of feeling : and (2) of the *external relation* (as in a spring-box or engine-room) of the efficient power to the members moved. In the present century, chemistry and physiology have nearly overtaken physics, and familiarised us with other modes of energy than the mechanical, and, especially by enabling us to translate molar into molecular force, facilitated the conception of *immanent* dynamics. It is as if, in the time of Descartes, there had been only the *active* and the *passive* voice in which to speak of what the animals do : and, if you did not want to acknowledge them as intelligent subjects by saying, 'they move their limbs,' 'they carry their bodies,' &c., you could only take the passive form, and say, 'their limbs are moved,' 'their bodies are carried' : but now, a *middle voice* was placed at command, enabling us, without determining the agent in any

definite way, to fix *the seat* of the transaction entirely in
their organism, 'they in themselves have a movement of
limbs,'—'a shifting of their bodies takes place.' To the
very conception of animal life, the motory spontaneity
which is thus implied, is essential ; yet it is missed by the
mechanical analogy. But the intelligent direction upon an
end which such spontaneity indicates is not in the creature's
consciousness, which therefore stops short of will : that
completing causal element must be sought in the all-
animating Mind. The spirit of Nature has many 'diver-
sities of operation' : gravitation, the waves of light and
heat, the poles of electricity, the affinities of chemical
elements, the development of life, the play of instinct,—are
his methods of continuous creation ; preparing the materials
and theatre of being : determining its system of kinds :
specialising its individuals : till, the spirit of man arising
to repeat his own personality, he leaves a portion of the
work to him : so that the free and self-conscious end reflects
the free and self-conscious beginning : and as, at first, the
Divine Mind descended into the necessity of nature, so,
at last, from the necessity of nature the human mind
emerges and escapes, an image of the eternal archetype of
beauty, truth, and good.

  The distinction which is thus drawn between the automatic and the self-conscious, though seldom so emphasised
as by Descartes, is as ancient as speculation itself, and
reappears through the whole history of philosophy. The
Greeks marked it by their antithesis of ψυχή and νοῦς : the
former, diffused at least wherever there is life ; the latter,
the universal Reason, whether Divine or human. The
Germans still preserve it in their use of *Seele* and *Geist* :
or, in the Schopenhauer school, in the contrast between
unbewusster and *bewusster Wille.* And it should be observed that, when Descartes denied to the brutes any *âme*
or *anima*, it was an attribute of *Geist* that he meant to

withhold from them : the '*animal spirits*' performing for them the functions of *Seele*. It was not the existence in them of feelings, or the being stirred by instincts and passions, that he called in question : but the reflective *knowledge that they have them* ; and this knowledge it is *Geist* that gives. It would be easy to multiply examples : but I mention only enough to show that there is an evident foundation, in the self-knowledge of thoughtful men, for the delimitation of human nature on which I have been insisting.

To the doctrine thus shaped it may perhaps be objected that, while it admits the Divine action as immediately present in the lower provinces of the cosmos, it excludes that action from the highest, viz. our moral life,—precisely the sphere that is nearest to God and would seem most congenial to him. Are we then to find him in the sunshine and the rain, and to miss him in our thought, our duty, and our love? Far from it ; he is with us in both : only in the former it is his *immanent life*, in the latter his *transcendent*, with which we are in communion. It is not indeed *He* that, under the mask of our personality, does our thinking, and prays against our temptations, and weeps our tears : these are truly our own : but they are in presence of a sympathy free to answer, spirit to spirit ; neither merging in the other ; but both at one in the same inmost preferences and affections.

Did we extend the immanency of God over this higher realm also, so as to render it absolutely universal, the effect would be the reverse of the objector's expectations : instead of gaining something more for the Divine, we should in reality lose it all. For all transcendency would then be gone : no range would be left of free Divine life beyond the pledged order of nature : and this alone it is that gives scope for the conception of a *personal being, living with persons*, and acting on grounds of reason and righteousness.

In proportion as a being *mechanises himself*, and commits all his energy to immutable methods and degrees, he abdicates his personal prerogative, and permits his will to sleep off into a continuous automatism. Without freedom to act freshly out of immediate thought and affection,—that is, without some field unbespoken by habit,—intellect, character, personality, can have no place: and the consciousness of this it is that makes the older Deism appear so cold: it had nothing Divine but the system of 'general laws': and that had its consecration from a long way off, and was a kind of birthday gift, now stale, to the young world from a Creator who had never visited it since. This scheme, however, did at any rate prefix to the mechanised creation a free act of choice and origination: *then* God really *was* personal, though thenceforth the mode of procedure that made him so fell into abeyance, so that it was only retrospectively that the attribute could be assigned to him. But this creative prefix the Pantheistic immanence takes away: so that along the receding track of Time it is vain to seek for any region of transcendency, and unless it be saved by exempting the moral and spiritual life all through from the inexorability of the physical system, the cosmical field will be all filled up with an eternal millwork, with not a cranny left in time or space for the exercise of choice or the play of character. Under the pretence of planting God everywhere, it leaves him nowhere. This fatal effect, of universal necessity, ceases the moment the universality is removed. Let there only be some realm of free Divine action, some transcendent form of life in which the spirit is not bound: and, after learning there the living thought and love of God, we can bear his methodical inflexibility within Nature. It no longer kills out the characteristics of personal existence: it is but the mixture, indispensable to intellectual and moral perfection, of faithful habit with fresh Mind: and from his quickening

touch and converse in the spiritual walks of our experience
we can look without dismay on the unswerving dome of
stars and the river's everlasting flow, and see in them, as
in the customary ways of a righteous life, only the stead-
fastness of promise, not the indifference of Fate.

The field which we thus rescue from pantheistic absorption supplies us with one further inference of no slight
importance. The *personality* of God consists, we have
seen, in his voluntary agency as free cause in an unpledged
sphere, that is, a sphere transcending that of immanent
law. But precisely this also it is, that constitutes his
Infinity; extending his sway, after it has filled the actual,
over all the possible, and giving command over indefinite
alternatives. Hence, it is plain, his personality and his
infinity are so far inseparable concomitants that, though
you might deny his infinitude without prejudice to his
personality, you cannot deny his personality without sacrificing his infinitude: for there is a mode of action,—*the
preferential*,—the very mode which distinguishes rational
beings,—from which you exclude him. Yet we are constantly told that a personal being is necessarily finite ;
that he is an individual, not a universal ; restricted to
a definite centre of consciousness and activity, into which
and from which influences flow that make up his life. In
short, *a Self* implies an *Other-than-Self*, and so gives two
spheres of being, only one of which would be God, while
the other was his negative. According to the division
which we have been defending, this second and antithetic
term is the aggregate of rational and moral beings, represented in our world by Man. Confining our attention
to him, we have actually treated him as a separate cause,
and so have apparently accepted a limit to the infinitude
of God. Is there any reconciliation of these contradictory
aspects of personality? There is none, if you assume that
infinite Will can never abstain from appropriating all its

causality, or divest itself of a portion, in order to fit up another and resembling nature. But surely one who assumes this has already committed the fault which he charges, and discovered something to which his 'rigorous infinitude' is incompetent! If we drop this assumption, then our allowance of independence is itself the result of our dependence : it is *conceded* to us by the author of our being, and, though entrusted for awhile with a certain free play of causality, is referable in the ultimate resort to the Supreme cause : it is included in what he *has caused*, though excepted from what he *is causing.* It takes therefore nothing from his infinitude, but what he himself renounces ; and what is thus relinquished is potentially retained. The self-abnegation of infinity is but a form of self-assertion, and the only form in which it can reveal itself. Whether by setting up other minds with a range of command over alternatives, or by instituting a universe under law without alternative, the Infinite Cause foregoes something of his absolute freedom ; in the one case admitting partners of his liberty ; in the other, establishing for himself a sphere of necessity : and in the latter case, the more comprehensive the sphere, the vaster is the renunciation : and if it extends to the All, so as to leave no margin of transcendency, the limitation reaches its maximum, no possibility but one being anywhere left open. If therefore there be any force in this objection, the Pantheist who brings it is himself exposed to it in a superlative degree. What greater contradiction can there be than to say, in one and the same breath, that a being is infinite and omnipotent, yet cannot put forth preferential power ? And if we are jealous for his infinitude, which shall we be more afraid to grant,—that he lends to a derivative being a little preferential power ; or that he is for ever incapable of exercising it himself?

For these reasons the modern scruples that are felt with

regard to the personality of God appear to me not less intellectually weak than they are morally deplorable. If anyone is fastidious about the *word*, and thinks it spoiled by the Athanasian controversy, let him supply us with a better: but *some* symbol we must have of that Divine freedom in the exercise of Will, the acknowledgment of which makes the difference between Theism and Pantheism, and gives religion its entrance into the conscience and affections of men. As the parts of our nature which thus enter into relation with God are precisely those which make us *Persons* and distinguish us from other 'living *things*,' it is difficult to see why the same term should not be given to the corresponding attributes of rational and moral Will in him: and where the idea is really present and craving expression, I believe that for the most part it will be glad enough of the word. At all events, its contents are just what we rescue from Pantheism. Here it is that the God, immanent through the universe besides, and operating by determinate methods alone, passes into transcendent existence still unpledged, and establishes moral relations with beings whom he has endowed with a certain scope of similar volitional causality. At this point, however, our conclusion, worked out from the causal intuition, encounters a difficulty raised from the moral side. It is said that the preferential power which we suppose ourselves to possess is illusory, and that, on close analysis of the process of volition, it turns out to be but an effect involving no alternative, so that we are the creatures of our past and not otherwise the causes of our future. We are thus obliged, for the protection of our position, to address ourselves to the most perplexing of all questions, the problem, as it is called, of Determinism and Free Will.

CHAPTER II.

DETERMINISM AND FREE WILL.

HITHERTO I have been content, in treating of the grounds whether of Ethics or of Religion, to build upon the assumptions universally made by the consciousness of mankind; aiming only to interpret them accurately, and not attempting to verify them by criteria foreign to themselves. Thus it was shown that the moral judgment which we pass upon ourselves for past conduct takes for granted that, in the moment of yielding to one of two competing solicitations, we might have preferred the other; and that the experience of contrition, the language of praise and blame, the sentiment of justice, the pleas of forgiveness, the reverence for higher virtue, all proceed upon the same belief, that we are not manufactured into good or bad, but, within a certain range of responsibility, are the authors of our own characters. Whether this belief is true, I did not then stop to enquire; but was satisfied to say, that either it was true, or moral judgment was impossible. So too, in the present work, both the lines of argument which have been followed start from the same intuitive assumption: the first in the form, that from the exercise of Will we know what Causality is, and apprehend that of God along with our own: the second in the form, that the authority of Duty is known to us as a relation between our own will as free, and that of a higher and supreme Being. Of that relation we are conscious as a trust, or command of alternative, better and worse, committed to us by a perfect

O 2

righteousness. Beyond the appeal to self-consciousness, I have said nothing in support of these assumptions, on which the whole of both Ethics and Religion is staked. But this appeal is set aside on various ingenious pleas. Our belief in our own independence arises merely, it is said, from a partial ignorance of the complex influences that mould our decisions, and when our inward history is all unfolded and laid bare, each volition will be found to have its place in a regular consecution of phenomena as uniform as those of physical nature, and as little open to the entrance of contingency. The antecedents which we bring into each posture of affairs being what they are, we can no more decide our problems except in one certain way, than water in a frost can refuse to become ice, or an acorn grow into an elm. The insecurity thus introduced into our conclusions it is impossible to leave unnoticed ; and though I can add nothing to so old a controversy, it is incumbent on me so to pass it under review, as to explain why it does not disturb my faith in the principles of the foregoing reasonings.

Though the fascination of this unsolved problem arises chiefly from its profound connection with the very roots of our moral and spiritual convictions, and though, in all logical consistency, these convictions appear to me to stand or fall according to the answer which we give to it, I desire, as far as possible, to keep the weight of this issue at a distance from the discussion. The real life of men, even upon its inner side, is not shaped by philosophical systems, or moved forward on lines of consecutive logic ; and, on either brink of the wide chasm of doctrine which we are about to survey, are seen not only individual champions, but gathered hosts, alike eminent for high-toned character and devoted piety; so that practical experience affords some ostensible support to Professor Sidgwick's opinion, that ethical interests are but slightly affected by our theory of the Will. The advocates indeed on either side arrange themselves in most unexpected ranks. While the austere and lofty Stoic[1], who makes the highest demands on self-command and self-sacrifice, asserts the reign of universal necessity, the prudential Epicurean[2] insists upon free will, and makes his very atoms swerve in order to provide it. In western Christendom, it is the Catholic Church alone, especially in its Dominican and Jesuit schools, that has saved any ability in man to obey the will of God ; while the Augustinian theology, whether sheltered in the Port Royal, or breaking forth into branches of the Reformation, has merged all human power in divine grace and fore-ordination. And, while the history of both is rich in examples of heroic and saintly goodness, an impartial observer, if asked to select and bring together a gallery of portraits marked with the lineaments of moral greatness, would probably search with the most hopeful eye through the camps of the Prince of Orange, of Coligny, of Gustavus Adolphus, and of Cromwell ; for, whatever be the disproportion and æsthetic defects of the evangelical or Puritan type of character, in ethical vigour and religious elevation it certainly has no superior. If in Spinoza and Hobbes, in Diderot and Lamettrie, the doctrine of Determinism has formed part of an anti-theological mode of thought, it is presented, in the masterly vindications of Edwards and Priestley, as the essential life of true religion and implied principle of Christian society. Yet it has never long claimed a church-ascendency without encountering resistance from minds not less penetrating and devout than these : and in Cudworth, Butler, Clarke, Price, and Channing, the standard of revolt is once more raised against an almighty Absolutism, and the protest is renewed, that something of his own must be granted to man, if he is to be worth governing, and

---

[1] Seneca, Nat. Quæst. ii. 45 ; Stob. Ecl. i. 178.
[2] Cicero, De Fato, ii. 10 ; De Nat. Deorum, i. 25.

capable of any similitude to God. There is scarcely any
variety of relation to theology which the doctrines described
in this controversy are not found to assume; and the re-
markable feature recurs in each combination, that our problem plays in it no accidental part; but, in spite of the
contradictory religious conclusions, the opinion favoured,
be it of Liberty or be it of Necessity, is regarded by its
advocate as the essential premiss, and defended as the
turning-point, of the whole scheme. As we are all liable,
on entering this discussion, to become thus bewitched, it
will not be charged upon me, I trust, as an exceptional
sin, if I also am led to affirm the dependence on the doctrine which I vindicate of any clear authority attaching to
either Conscience or Faith. I cannot avoid this, unless I
keep back the very grounds of my own conversion from
the philosophical creed in which I was early established by
the writings of Hartley, Collins, and Priestley; and it will
be no recantation of a reverence for them, if I point out
some inconsistencies of which I have myself had occasion
to repent.

§ 1. *What is the Question?*

It is hardly possible to state the problem with which
this controversy is concerned without employing terms on
the meaning of which there exists a prior divergence. It
might seem therefore an essential precaution to begin with
a series of definitions, settling the exact contents of each
conception involved in the question. It would be easy
enough to do this. But no sooner should we have declared
what we understand by Will, by Cause, by Motive, by
Self, by Choice, by Freedom, by Necessity, than complaint would be made that we had begged the whole
question in each definition; and we should have to discuss
it over and over again upon every word. The two
doctrines are the expression of entire schemes of thought,

which put a different interpretation upon everything in
nature and life of which we have occasion to speak ; so
that language, pushed by them to its ultimate analysis,
ceases to be common to the two ; and they cannot with
advantage converse together, except at a prior stage,
before the words have been pared down and shaped to
the pattern of a system.   It is better therefore to take
them as they speak to the common understanding before
it is driven to philosophical reflection, and to let the more
exact meanings of which they are susceptible come out
into distinct view as we proceed.   Without further preface
then I remark, that our enquiry concerns the originating
cause of voluntary action ; and is mainly this : *whether, in
the exercise of Will* (i.e., *in cases of choice*)[1] *the mind is
wholly determined by phenomenal antecedents and external
conditions ; or, itself also, as active subject of these objective
experiences, plays the part of determining Cause.*   Those
who maintain the first branch of this alternative were
called and called themselves '*Necessarians*,' because, under
the assigned conditions, the sequence of one particular
volition is, in their view, an inevitable event, not less so
than the explosion of gunpowder on the application of a
lighted match, or the fall of a slate blown off into free air
from the roof of a house.   Those, on the other hand, who
maintain the second branch of the alternative were called
and called themselves '*Libertarians*,' because they deemed
it possible, in spite of the assigned conditions, for the mind
not to will, or to will otherwise : it is not obliged to deliver
itself over to a bespoken decision.   It is obvious that these
terms are the offspring of the *dynamic* conception of
causation, in which effect is supposed to be linked with
cause by some constraining objective tie, and not merely

---

[1] The word Will is here used in the first of the five meanings which
have been assigned to it, and which are enumerated supra, vol. i.
p. 210.

in the subjective certitude of our expectations : 'Necessity' denoting subjection to power; 'Liberty,' immunity from it, with ability to use one's own.   The words have evidently come down to us from a date anterior to Hume's essay on ' necessary connection,' or at least to the general acceptance of its doctrine by the English empirical philosophers.   They are wholly out of place in a system which discharges all idea of Force, which abolishes the distinction between active and passive, and resolves Causality into constancy of time-relation between successive phenomena : where nothing has power to *produce* or to *control* another, and each change must be content to play the part of *sign* to what comes next, there is no room for measurements of resistance or claims of freedom.   It is not therefore surprising that J. S. Mill should complain of this language, as leaving a false impression of at least his own position against the pretensions of free will.   He does not mean to tell you anything so disagreeable as that you are coerced or constrained to this or that particular volition ; not the slightest force is put upon you ; it is only that, as an observer of the antecedents, he is sure that nothing else will follow: 'whether it *must* do so,' he says, 'I acknowledge myself to be entirely ignorant ;' ... ' all I know is, that it always does[1].'   No sooner however do you feel the relief of having this incubus lifted off, than you learn, with some little chagrin, that he no less removes it from the material world[2], and assures the weight in the scale that in its descent there is no necessity, but only a sequence ; so that the exemption from Force is impartial, and though you are no more, you are also no less, helplessly brought to your volition, than the wave to the beach and the hail to the ground.   Mill ascribes[3] the common repugnance to

---

[1] Examination of Hamilton's Philosophy, chap. xxvi. p. 501, 1865.
[2] Mill's System of Logic, Bk. VI. ch. ii. § 2, 3rd ed., 1851.
[3] Ibid., § 3.

his doctrine 'almost entirely' to its use of this 'extremely inappropriate term 'Necessity,' carrying in it as it does the idea of some 'mysterious compulsion' or 'irresistibleness'; and thinks that, if it had insisted only on invariable uniformity of succession, its truth and innocence would have been generally acknowledged. What we dislike is, to have human actions referred to 'agencies' as 'uncontrollable,' as 'those agencies of nature which are really uncontrollable,' so as to be no less necessitated than 'death for want of food or air;' and he proposes to discharge this enormous dislike by discontinuing the language of Force in favour of the language of Sequence. He rightly hits the origin of our dislike: he deceives and even contradicts himself in his provision of a remedy. We want, in our voluntary life, to be differenced from physical nature, which we regard as foredoomed to all its changes: he tells us, 'you are under no such constraint as you imagine;' and we are consoled to find our feeling so authoritatively justified. He adds, 'neither is physical nature constrained by any force;' and so, our difference is snatched away again, and our uneasiness returns: if we are left in the same category with rolling stones and forests at the mercy of the winds, nothing is gained by hushing up all mention of force, and describing everything as an unlinked though orderly series. But here he tries a new persuasion : 'it is true,' he urges, 'that your volitions, in their origin, come under the same rule with *some* physical events, viz. those which will certainly happen, unless some change intervenes in the antecedents ; but you must not assimilate them to physical events of the 'uncontrollable' kind, which are sure to come to pass at all events ; and this probably is what disturbs your apprehension.' Are there then *two sorts* of physical events, some only regularly sequent, others delivered by *irresistible might*? Such a distinction, though suggested by such phrases as 'absolute sway,' 'un-

controllableness,' 'irresistibleness,' is inconsistent with the
previous banishment of *force* from all material conjunctions whatsoever.   Mill is thinking of another difference, viz. that some physical events are sure to happen,
subject to a proviso, viz. if no new antecedent strikes in
from an intersecting series, while others are sure to happen,
without any proviso, the antecedents being already complete.   But with what truth can it be said that our volitions
resemble only the former, and are never in the condition
of the latter?   *If* a new motive intervenes, it will modify
our impending decision ; but if and when the preliminaries
have said their say, *actum est*; there is nothing for it but
for the decision to come ; in the sense of being unconditionally certain, it is as 'uncontrollable' as the most
imperious of physical events.   Whether therefore you construe Necessity as *subjective certainty* or as *objective force*,
there is no ground for saying that, in regard to physical
causation, it has one meaning, in regard to moral causation,
another ; and that on this account the word has introduced
an unjust prejudice into the controversy we are considering.

Notwithstanding however this similar relation to both
spheres, the word ' Necessity ' is naturally objectionable to
the disciples of Hume, and must be excluded, as far as
possible, in discussing with them any questions of causation.
The problem immediately before us they are accustomed
to state simply as a question of *uniformity of sequence*;
affirming that, 'under the same circumstances, and in
presence of the same motives, the volition of a given mind
will be the same.'   Were it possible to argue the question
at issue in this form, I would gladly substitute it for the
statement of it which I have already given.   But it seems
to me to be disqualified for discussion by serious faults.
(1) Its hypothesis is impossible ; the 'circumstances' preceding a repeated volition can never be the 'same' with
those which introduced the first, from the very fact that

the first is among them, which it was not before. (2) Its
position, if established, is inconclusive ; i. e. it does not
shut out the rival theory of free will ; for, if the mind have
any latitude of action, it may no less use this to preserve
the uniformity than to break it. Where Necessity reigns,
there doubtless must be uniformity ; but you cannot
convert the proposition, and say, where uniformity is, there
only one thing is possible. The temptation to reduce the
thesis to an assertion of uniformity doubtless is, that it
seems to submit the question to a practical test, which
any observer of facts may apply for himself. This however is an illusion ; and the great difficulty of this controversy is due to the absence of any objective criterion
available for its solution. There are no producible phenomena, no witnesses outside of consciousness, which will
not answer to both doctrines : each has for ages been
propounded as a theory of the world, and has looked all
things, natural and human, in the face, and learned to
think and speak of them in conformity with its own conceptions ; and neither can find an *experimentum crucis*
which the other will acknowledge. The real difference lies
deeper, in the interpretation of our self-consciousness as
active and moral subjects; and in the clue which we follow
in working out our doctrine of causation. No libertarian
can possibly adopt Hume's doctrine ; and a discussion of
the question upon that basis is impossible ; it eliminates at
the outset all the conceptions which constitute the problem,
and leaves such terms as 'free,' and 'necessary,' 'active'
and 'passive,' 'strong' and 'weak,' 'controller' and 'controlled,' 'origination' and 'derivation,' mere verbal husks,
as the refuse of a cast-off philosophy. I am obliged therefore to let the question stand in the form I selected, though
that form includes an antithesis, — of *determining* and
being determined,—which is foreign to the empirical idea
of Causation.

§ 2. *Psychology of Voluntary Action.*

It would carry us too far from our main subject to attempt a systematic exposition of the phenomena of the Will. But, as the chief arguments in the necessarian controversy spring directly from a psychological theory of voluntary action, it is indispensable to sketch the outlines of that theory, before treating of the inferences drawn from it. Originally advanced by Hartley, and worked out in his 'Observations on Man' with rare ingenuity and copiousness of illustration, it has received further elaboration from James Mill, and several important corrections as well as additions from John Stuart Mill and Professor Bain. These latest modifications will be found most compendiously presented in the Notes to their edition of James Mill's 'Analysis of the phenomena of the human mind[1].'

Under all its modifications, the theory of these writers follows the general course of the empirical psychology; assuming that we start with only the animal outfit of sensibility to pleasures and pains, which, on ceasing, leave behind them fainter vestiges in idea; of muscular mobility; and of a tendency in all sensations, ideas, and movements, once associated in a certain order, to recur in the same, whenever the prior term presents itself. The steps which conduct us from these rudiments to the accomplishments of a practised Will are presented by Hartley[2] in the following series.

(1) All muscular movements are at first *automatic*; and so far take place *at random*, that, springing from some

---

[1] Chap. xxiv. Analysis of the Phenomena of the Human Mind, by James Mill, with notes illustrative and critical, by Alexander Bain, Andrew Findlater, and George Grote; edited, with additional notes, by John Stuart Mill, 1869.

[2] Prop. xx.

sensation either administered from without or occurring in
the interior of the body, they partake of the accidental
character of these feelings. Where, however, the feelings
are in constant flow, the movements are regular; e. g. the
heart beats, the lungs breathe, the glands secrete, con-
tinuously. In other cases, the sensational stimulus is only
occasional, and produces the sneeze, the cough, the laugh,
the cry, the contraction of the iris with increasing light.
We begin with being absolutely disposed of by such sensations, persistent or fortuitous.

(2) This distinction, however, between the perpetual
and the occasional stimuli, assumes extreme importance
when taken in hand by the law of Association. The unin-
terrupted movements, as concomitants of all our history,
impartially concur with all its contents, and fall into no
special conjunction with any; so that, whatever power over
them might be gained by accompanying feelings or ideas,
would belong to any one of them, and could never fail to
be present. Such actions therefore remain unintermittent
and involuntary through life.

(3) But the occasionally excited movements fall into
association only with some particular ideas or connected
sensations; on the recurrence of which they therefore
become liable to repeat themselves. A dash of dust or
spray into the eye gives a painful sensation at which the
lids shut; after a few experiences, the mere idea of such
sensations suffices to produce the action; and even the
sight of another person's eye threatened by a blow will
produce a winking of our own. The feeling of actual
fatigue which induces a yawn leaves behind it an idea
qualified to play the same part; so that one suggestive
instance is enough to carry the yawn all round the table.
Closely allied to such instances is the tendency, so marked
in children, to *Imitation*. When the infant, by fortuitous
play of muscular activity, utters a sound, he *hears himself*;

the feelings of the two senses (the ear and the muscles) cling together; and the mere sound, though proceeding from another, will tend to reproduce the vocal act: hence the propensity he has to keep repeating any syllable on which he has been fortunate enough to hit. The essential feature in all these cases is the same: the action falls into connection with an idea, under the command of which it henceforth stands: give the idea, and you ensure the action: it follows with the same certainty as any other term in an associated group, such as the idea of cold at the sight of snow, or of pain at the appearance of blood.

(4) Great as this step is, it does not take us beyond the province of the *involuntary*. The actions which it explains are still such as we issue without design, often without being able to help them. One more distinction will bring us to our goal. Action may become the attendant of many ideas: there is one in particular, associated with which it becomes voluntary; viz. *the idea of a pleasure*, or, in brief, *a Desire*. Some movement, accidentally performed, brings us, it may be, a pleasure or relief, which henceforth becomes connected with it in idea, so that whatever suggests the pleasure suggests the movement too. In this thought of the movement there are two elements, which do not always go together; we may think of its outward *look*, as its sign; and of its *feel*, in the process of execution: the first we might have, if we had only witnessed the act in other persons; the second becomes annexed to it by sufficient personal performance of it. When this has taken place, all the conditions of voluntary action are complete; the mere idea of an attainable pleasure, occurring in the natural train of thought, will bring with it the idea of what we are to do in order to get it; then, the idea of the motory initiative and process; and each link drawing after it the next, by indissoluble association, the operation consummates itself.

It differs from other sequences of action upon idea, such as drawing back your limb when you see another person threatened by a hot iron, or shedding tears at a pathetic story, only in the fact that the antecedent idea is *a wish.* Sometimes indeed the wish does not fulfil itself. When that is the case, it is because the last link is imperfectly secured, and to the mere image of the act experience has not adequately attached the familiar knowledge of its executive procedure; and just there it is that we stop short of the *motive*, and are baulked of the result.

The end in view is not always attainable by a single act; it may require a series more or less protracted, each member of which, though in itself indifferent to us, will acquire an interest from the purpose which it helps to serve. Such a system we learn by heart, exactly as we learn the shorter lesson; and the mental procedure assumes the form into which Aristotle throws it : 'having set before us some end, we consider how and by what means it is to be realized ; if by several, by which of them most easily and best ; if by one, how that one produces the end, and by what means it is itself produced, until we come to the first term of the order of causation, which is the last in the order of discovery ; for in this deliberation we pursue our search, it seems, in a manner analogous to that of geometrical analysis[1].' The longer the series of instru·mental steps interposed between our wish and its accomplishment, the slower will be the process by which the Will matures its power ; and there are manual and mental arts, such as playing the violin and performing arithmetical calculations, which can be acquired only by years of practice. But, by constant repetition, the sequences become so rapid as to vanish from separate consciousness, and complete themselves with a mechanical ease that renders them,

---

[1] Eth. Nic. III. iii. 11.

as Hartley says, 'secondarily automatic.' Thus, the voluntary stage springs from the automatic, and, in the shape of habit, delivers us into it again.

(5) Through all this class of cases, we have to do with some form of outward action. In the control which we also obtain over our inward life, the same principle, viz. the dominant interest of *an end in view*, no less supplies the explanation. By direct command we can will no thought into the mind or out of the mind; for, as the object of our effort, we should be already holding it there. But the consciousness of a chasm, or of an intrusion, in a line of thought, with the desire to get rid of it, will naturally keep our attention, because our interest, fixed on the surrounding and connected parts, and give them the chance of calling up what is pertinent to them, and superseding what is in their way; so that our ruling wish, by summoning its allies and habitual companions into the field, becomes master of the situation, presenting among them what we want, and crowding out what we dislike. For instance, I have forgotten when it was that I called upon a certain friend, and am asked to recover the date. In picturing to myself my arrival at his house, it strikes me that I approached it from the direction opposite to that which I should expect: how was this? It was because I came, not straight from home, but from the Athenæum: what took me there? It was to consult a foreign scientific journal on a matter coming on for discussion next day at a certain society: as that society meets on the second Tuesday of each month, the date was the previous Monday. Similarly, the coherence of thought is maintained by an author as he writes, through the ascendency of his main purpose; the persistent presence of which suggests, as he lays his plan, first the means nearest to it, and then backwards the preceding instrumental steps till the considerations easiest to begin with are reached; whence, by re-

versing the procedure, he moves forward and constructs his organic whole. All these processes are *voluntary*, because their regulative idea is a want or wish, which is so associated with an order of muscular movement or of thought competent to its fulfilment, that the preconception is the sole condition needful to secure the entire sequel.

In its complete form, this theory has not been able to hold its ground ; and large portions of it are already surrendered by the last editors of James Mill's Analysis. Bain withdraws from its cognizance three classes of phenomena which it was supposed to cover ; viz. (1) Reflex actions, through nerves unconnected with the brain, and therefore not requiring sensation for their source ; e.g. respiration, coughing, sneezing, the movements of the heart. (2) The actions which are the outward expression or natural language of the several orders of feeling, as laughter, weeping, starting, shrieking ; these, instead of becoming through their occasionalness dependent on ideas, are from the first organically connected with the emotions to which they are appropriate. (3) The actions of involuntary imitation, such as hysterical convulsions, the contagion of yawning, the spread of groundless panic ; in all of which action follows upon idea, but is not voluntary[1]. Since no one ever affirmed these three kinds of movement to be voluntary, since on the contrary they are adduced by the Hartleyans as express examples of the stages which *precede the voluntary* and illustrate what is wanting to it, it is not easy to see why Bain takes the superfluous trouble of excluding them. Turning however to the phenomena unquestionably voluntary, we find the later Hartleyans not content with James Mill's Analysis. If the action is induced simply as a sequent in a linked series of suggestions, if the certainty with which it follows

---

[1] James Mill's Analysis of the Phenomena of the Human Mind, ed. 1869, vol. ii. ch. xxiv, note 68.

depends on the closeness of association, and if the power
which the first link has of starting the series depends on
the intensity of its interest for us, these conditions, J. S.
Mill remarks, are no more completely fulfilled by a wish
or idea of pleasure to begin with, than by a horror or idea
of pain, in connection with an act of our own as cause ;
and we ought to be found rushing upon misery and ruin
as eagerly as upon the gratification of desire[1]. A reason
therefore is still wanted, why this is *not* what happens ; all
the more, because there are cases which show it to be
possible ; for instance, when the very fear of an awkward-
ness in speech or demeanour makes us commit it, and the
haunting horror of a crime has frenzied the will to its perpetration, and the shuddering at a precipice has been felt
as a temptation to take the fatal leap. Why are these
exceptional cases? The theory requires some addition, to
account for our different demeanour under the excitement
of prospective pleasure and prospective pain,—our movements towards the one, and away from the other.

(6) This addition is provided by Professor Bain in what
he calls the '*Law of Self-conservation.*' He assumes that
there is no occasion, with Hartley, to prefix a sensation to
a muscular movement, inasmuch as it will take place of
itself ; and we are to treat the human being as delivered
into our hands for investigation in a state of *spontaneous*
muscular motion, now in this, now in that isolated part.
This at least is to be our *psychological* datum ; *physiologically*, it has for its antecedent what is called a 'concentrated discharge of nervous energy' from the 'ganglionic
centres'; which, in its turn, is referred to their being well
fed by blood and adequately warmed, etc. Thus born
into a random condition of perpetual motion, we sometimes
hit upon a pleasant variety of it. This, it is said, always

[1] James Mill's Analysis of the Phenomena of the Human Mind, ed.
1869, vol. ii. ch. xxiv, note 67.

heightens the vitality; affecting the whole system, and through it the particular part which has been so fortunate; it therefore goes on with its activity and keeps up the pleasurable result. When, on the other hand, we stumble upon some movement that brings pain, the opposite effect ensues; for all pain is a lowering of vitality: the bodily energy therefore droops, and with it the particular action from which we suffered: it dies away and saves us from meeting our enemy again. This contrasted tendency in pain and pleasure is the 'law of self-conservation': its special claim is, that it accounts for our different behaviour under the accidental experience of what we like and what we dislike. The successful chance coincidence having once been established, a line of communication has been opened between the state of feeling and the appropriate muscular adjustment, along which the molecular movement will in future more readily flow; so that the accidental connection becomes a permanent contiguity, and the voluntary acquisition is complete [1].

(7) Yet, though it is complete, it is, or at least may be, without any intervention of *consciousness* in our experiments. It is at a later stage that this non-essential addition is made to the history. We then *want the pleasure* as an end; and having some experience of muscular motion as sometimes happy in its results, we set it a-going in a random way of 'trial and error'; if with success, continuing it without conscious effort; if with failure, dropping it under the check of disappointment and flattened energy. It is in this additional and later feature that Bain finds for the first time the phenomenon of *effort*. He regards it as consisting in 'trial movements' *for a pleasure*. We are also conscious of it, when a strong motive meets with a

[1] James Mill's Analysis of the Phenomena of the Human Mind, ed. 1869, vol. ii. ch. xxiv, note 68; and Bain on The Emotions and the Will, 1858; the Will, ch. i, especially §§ 6-8.

strong resistance: when, under such conditions, we are said to 'exert ourselves' and show 'great strength of will,' all that is meant is that one motive is matched by another[1].

If this be the true theory of voluntary action, it is obvious that our volitions are dependent, like our memories, on the laws of suggestion, and have their definite place in the trains of ideas, as little variable as that of the letters of the familiar alphabet: that *to will* is to have an idea of pleasure followed by a muscular movement that clings to it, and that whoever wakes up the first secures the second: that 'we' have no more to do with it, than to be the conscious theatre and supply the wielded implements. No room therefore is left for any but the Determinist conclusion, unless the facts admit of some other psychological construction.

Before stating the corrections which this empirical history seems to me to require, I must make one remark on the method by which it is obtained. It is to be a *psychological* history, that is, a report of our felt and self-known experience. It begins with or before our birth: it ends with our term of matured and practised mind. Its earlier incidents, if truly read, will lead up to the latest phase, and draw all that is intermediate into one coherent life. Whether, as interpreted, they really do so, and bring all that we are into the account, can be told only by faithfully consulting the whole volume of our ripest self-consciousness. Not only does this volume contain the problem to be solved; it contains also by far the largest and best known part of the evidence for its solution. The ways in which we now think and feel, the present springs of our actions and processes of intelligence, together with a considerable range of the education of life which has brought

---

[1] The Will, ch. i, note at the end.

us hither, are clear in the view of reflection or memory,
and may be brought to the highest order of certainty.
But, as we recede further back, we pass more and more
into the dark : of our childhood, a few broken gleams from
vivid moments yet remain : of our infancy all trace is
gone ; and of that human period we can affirm nothing
psychological, except by inference or conjecture from
observations newly made on others. As this is a much
more precarious source of knowledge, we are warranted in
saying that our confidence in it should be graduated
accordingly ; and that our imaginary constructions drawn
from it should be severely tested by the immediate contents of our existing or unforgotten self-consciousness.
Instead of this superior deference to our most assured
inner experience, I find a disposition, especially manifest
in the writings of Professor Bain, to take liberties with the
testimony of our present thought and feeling, and put
it out of court, or give it a colouring not its own, on the
ground that it has grown old and is no longer what it was,
and that it is of very little use appealing to so altered a
state of psychological facts. In making out his case the
remark continually occurs, ' It is true that in the mature
condition of the intellect or of the will, we think or we
decide in such or such a way ; but this is adventitious, not
primitive ' ; and so the later is pushed aside as illusory, in
favour of the earlier as the true. Of that ' primitive ' mental
history, on the other hand, he speaks with the utmost
confidence and the most elaborate detail, as if he were
personally cognizant of every sensation, and all that comes
of it, in any new-born creature, and admitted to a private
view of the very beginnings of all the little explosive ' discharges ' and travelling waves, which apparently fill the
interior of the young life. On what evidence can these
changes, for ever hesitating between molecular and mental,
be affirmed and characterized ? On that of external ob-

servation only, directed upon a creature that cannot speak, or even answer inquiry with a responsive look. I do not question the value, within certain limits, of such careful study as Bain has devoted to human infancy, and even newly dropped lambs and staggering calves; but the psychological baby that he is so fond of dandling seems to me to become a sort of fetish to him, from which he expects, and wrings, oracles it was never meant to give. As it cannot contradict him, he has it all his own way; and can so tell the story of what is going on within, when it sprawls and springs and laughs and turns and fumbles with the hands, as to lead up to a foregone conclusion. A large part of his characteristic psychology appears to me to consist of misleading inferences correctly drawn from the contents of a hypothetical infant. The empirical analysis assumes *an amount* of alteration in our ideas from first to last, and takes the benefit of it, which I believe to be wholly unwarranted; and, in trusting the form which they present in our matured intelligence, we are less likely to be deceived, than in reverting to the crude type of even their rightly construed germs. With regard to the Will, we have experience, all through life, of the way in which we gain control over what before was out of voluntary reach: I see no reason to doubt that this *extension* of our power takes place in the same manner with its commencement. This remark will explain why I do not hesitate to appeal rather to our present self-consciousness, than to the imaginary autobiography of infancy. Some preliminary attention, however, we must pay to the initial stages of Bain's theory.

(1) It starts with what appears to me a false relation between the muscular 'spontaneity' from the 'discharges' of 'fed' ganglia, and the primary 'pleasures'; the former being altogether 'random' and indeterminate, till it alights upon one of the latter; which then gives it a definite

direction and reduces it to its service ; presenting already
a sample of the subjection of our nature in the active part
to the sensitive and recipient, and so providing the doctrine
of Necessity in embryo. Subject to some minor quali-
fications, I venture to invert the relation : the first movements, called spontaneous, are not random, but on the
lines prescribed by certain organic wants or tendencies ;
and the first pleasures are simply the satisfaction of these
wants. Life is not a mere wriggling into contact with
something nice, which thenceforth becomes its master ; but
contains within itself its own directing forces, which select
what it is to do, and crown the doing by satiety. To the
principle of such regulated activity Bain himself cannot
object ; for he admits it in two other cases, viz. the associated and rhythmical movements of members that are
partners in the same act, as the two eyes and four legs of
quadrupeds ; and the looks, gestures, and sounds, which
are the natural expression of particular feelings ; and it is
curious that only in the muscular experience which is to
generate the whole does he insist that complete fortuity
exists. I see not the slightest reason for throwing ourselves into this mess of pure accident, unless it be to
secure for the pleasure on which we impinge the credit of
fetching us out again and becoming our law. In the lower
animals there are apparently no muscular movements
except such as either are the outward language of particular passions, or address themselves to particular ends ;
even the 'spontaneous' and wild activity of young creatures
coming under the former head as the expression of ex-
hilaration and the mere joy of being alive. In their case it
would be absurd to assume the haphazard character of
their first muscular contractions, and suppose that, among
the various possible combinations of four (or it may be a
hundred) legs, having hit upon one which confers the
pleasure of walking, an association is established which

induces repetition, and henceforth hands over the muscles to the idea of that pleasure ; or that the duckling depends, for its swimming propensity and power, on the accidental contact with water and the surprise of its agreeableness. And what difference is there in our case, except that, having parents with intelligence to teach us, we are born in a more embryonic state, with the ties of dependence less severed, that is, with less outfit of instinctive skill, and large range for voluntary acquisition ? But every definite natural want which is imperative for life, as that of sustenance, carries in it its own direction to the muscles it uses ; and the infant, from the very first, extracts its own food by a highly complex act. It is however, says Bain, by accident that he *finds* it. Rather is it by the mother's intervention ; and as the act in its very nature is one of partnership, something is left to each ; and it is sufficient, in a *relative instinct*, that in his need he is ready with his part. I know of no muscular movement that does not fall under the same rule. Instead of being fortuitous, waiting to meet its master in some pleasure, it is initiated and shaped by an inward exigency or impulse ; which, in urgent cases, attains its end at once ; in others, gives only an incipient direction, which it leaves us to render precise and perfect by the process of learning.

(2) J. S. Mill expresses his hope that Bain's 'law of conservation' will be finally established ; else, it will remain a mystery why we do not run after pain as well as pleasure. Now the evidence of that law appears to me altogether unsatisfactory. If, as I believe, it is always some want or impulse that spurs us to action, and directs us in it ; and if the satisfaction of the want is what we call pleasure, the disappointment of it, pain ; there is no mystery in our opposite lines of pursuit and avoidance : in one and the same act, viz. yielding to a want, we move away from a pain and towards a pleasure. And if there be besides, i.e.

over and above those which consist in the attainment or failure of a prior want, accidental pleasures and pains on which we stumble at random, they are no sooner experienced than they establish a want, positive in the one case, negative in the other, which, by the aid of memory, acts in future precisely like an original impulse, with the single difference, that now the pleasure is not incidental to the gain of an object, but is itself the object ; and similarly, the avoidance of the pain. But if we set up the direct 'idea of pleasure' in the seat of governance and ignore the prior natural impulses, we can never give account of the undoubted cases in which we *court our own misery*; for instance, for good, when, on the urgency of compassion, we tear ourselves from the sunshine of life and plunge into its cloud of sorrow ; and for evil, when, driven by antipathy or resentment or fear, we torture ourselves with thinking or scheming or suspecting all ill, in a way that would turn the best world into the worst ? What 'pleasure' could there be, what 'relief from pain,' in such modes of activity, but for the antecedent passion which they satisfy?

Inverting the order, Bain works his problem with the datum of chance pleasure and pain ; attributing to the former a vitalizing, to the latter a depressing influence, in virtue of which the one becomes self-continuing, the other self-desisting ; the particular organs concerned partaking of the general change in the whole system, and going on or stopping accordingly. The evidence of any such law appears to me of the slenderest kind ; chiefly this ; that, if you put a nice morsel into your mouth, you get into a sort of hurry with it, and smack and quicken your mastication ; and if, being cold, you come within reach of a fire, you move towards it to get more of its warmth ; as if it were not enough to say that, hunger and cold, constituting wants, and being presented with the means of satisfying them, took the open path to that result. If by increase of

'vitality' is meant added vigour of action, surely it cannot
be claimed as one of the merits of experienced pleasure:
there would even be more truth in the pessimist doctrine,
that all action is the product of uneasiness, and ceases only
for the scant moments when it is laid to rest. Bain, unable to deny this, urges that, in such a case, the stimulus
which moves us is not the malaise itself, but the *relief from
it*, each increment of alleviation sustaining the action which
gives it ; and, no doubt, pending the process, you may describe it either way, as *from* the want or *for* the relief : but,
just when the end is reached and the pleasure at its full, its
alleged vitalizing power disappears and the action drops.
In fact, the largest portion of human pleasures accrues on the
reinstatement of a disturbed equilibrium, which indisposes
us to further action and change ; and it is only while we fail
of this state, and in proportion as we have much to do to
reach it, that we are goaded to exertion ; and the effort which
ceases the moment the want is gone and the pleasure won, is
surely more fitly attributed to the former than to the latter.

If we turn to the other half of the alleged law, still
greater difficulties meet us. Pain, instead of so lowering
vitality as to induce the subsidence of action, is in various
ways its keenest provocative ; and is accordingly resorted
to as the means of animal discipline, and of extorting ex-
ertions else not to be expected. The very examples adduced by Bain in evidence of his law appear to me to
contradict it : 'turning a street corner, we encounter suddenly,' he says, 'a bitter wintry blast ; we feel at once an
arrest upon our movements': on the contrary, I should
expect to see in every passenger, except the physically
incapable, an instantly quickened pace in resolute defiance
of the wind ; and this not, as he afterwards suggests, under
an ideal calculation of relief, but by an immediate waking-
up, defensive no doubt, yet perfectly spontaneous, of natural
energy. 'A painful contact' is said to have 'the same im-

mediate efficacy'; yet a dog upon the hearth-rug, shot at
by a hot coal from the fire, beats his retreat with no feeble
spring. The quickening operation of the goad and the
whip is explained by the singular stipulation that, in order
to depress vitality, the *pain* shall be something other than
'a *smart*'; for without this distinction the law will be
spoiled; which is tantamount to saying, that no pain will
stimulate except the stimulating sort. What can be more
artificial and unreal than to treat the sting of a whip as a
compound of two factors, an 'element of pain' and an element of 'smart' or 'excitement,' and insist that the former
lowers while the latter heightens activity? What evidence
is there of any such specialty? The only answer is found
in two hints given by Bain : 'to quicken an animal's pace,'
he says, 'the light smart is often the best application; to
arrest an excess of action, there must be greater severity':
surely it is a new rule for the driver of a four-in-hand, that
to stop his team he must whip it hard enough. Again, it
is said that, after a while, 'the acute smart is a cause of
reduced energy on the whole'; an assertion surely very
difficult to make good, and left at all events without the
shadow of a proof. Of course a horse, spurred into extraordinary activity, will become tired by the expenditure, and
flag; but so would he if he started at high speed from the
mere exuberance of health and the sniff of the morning
air; but that he slackens the sooner for having had a reminder from the lash, it would be difficult to show. No
doubt, with adequate brutality, you may break the spirit
and knock half the life out of any creature; but by adequate pampering and indulgence you may do nearly the
same; and in investigating the normal conditions of feeling and action, these extreme cases do not properly come
into view. I leave therefore 'the great law of self-conservation' where alone, I fear, it can be found, in the imagination of its ingenious discoverer.

(3) When once beyond these questionable beginnings of voluntary action, Bain's analysis of its ulterior growth is in a high degree acute and instructive; and needs only one or two slight additions or modifications to account satisfactorily for the gradual extension of our control over action and thought. One of these additions seems to be required in his explanation of the *imitative* tendency, which plays so important a part in all our training, and especially in the acquisition of language. The theory is that the vocal muscles, in spontaneous exercise, accidentally produce a particular syllable,—as *ba* : the audible impression which follows is thus associated with the muscular feeling involved in the act,—an association which is strengthened perhaps by the by-standers taking up the sound. The first time, the connection may be as yet too feeble to be of much avail; but after it has occurred a few times, it will become firm; and then, if the sound falls upon the ear, it will excite the voice to reproduce it [1].' This however is more than will follow from the Hartleyan law; for that law provides only for sequences of sensation, movement, and idea, *in the same order in which they originally occurred*; and here the order is inverted; and how little 'association' helps us to this we may learn by simply trying to say the alphabet backwards. Bain is not unconscious of this difficulty; but seems to think that associations have only to be strong enough, and they will read both ways. Any one who will endeavour to reverse his most familiar actions, for instance, to write or spell backwards, or conjugate a foreign verb in the inverse order of tenses, numbers and persons, may satisfy himself that this is an error. On supplying an omitted link, we escape the difficulty. The infant, in common with many young animals, has a tendency to repeat, immediately and over and over again, a movement once

---

[1] *Mental and Moral Science*, 1868, book iv. ch. ii. § 6.

performed. Whether we regard the tendency as original, or say that the active energy having taken a particular channel works in it more easily than in a changed one, the fact is indisputable, and cannot be regarded as a case of self-imitation, anticipating as it does all signs of any mimetic propensity: one stroke of the little arm, one spring of the legs, is followed by another; and so, a syllable, once flung out, is sure to come again with more or less of iteration. Every natural cry indeed is in itself continuous, i.e. a prolonged vowel; and when it is intersected by the appulses or pressure of parts muscularly agitated,— lips, tongue, larynx,—the continuity is broken into repetition by consonantal arrest of its regular flow; and thus are the first syllables produced. But, in every repeated act consisting of two terms, each type of term precedes the other; so that in the series A, B, A, B, etc., A no more takes the lead of B than B of A; if the muscular feeling of the vocal organs becomes in association the prior of the sound, so does the sound become prior to the muscular feeling; and either may excite the other. The sound however may be made by others; and when the child, hearing it thus, reproduces it, his lessons in imitation have begun. Rewarded by pleasant signs of encouragement, and helped by growing discoveries of what he can do with his machinery of noise, they soon supply him with new acquisitions; in gaining which, however, he could never reject his failures, or even be conscious of them, without *attention* to his experiments, and a frequent renewal of his *tentative efforts*; and these are already acts of intelligent will. There is a comparison between the sound which he misses and that which he makes,—a comparison which the phenomena cannot perform upon one another, but which he performs upon the two as related; and there is a direction of energy, more or less awkward, to avoid the one and make the other; a direction, other than that of the spontaneity which it aims

to deflect. There is an *initiative from within* which deals
with both the 'impression' from without and the memory
of the past, and uses them as materials for fresh attain-
ments. In the case of speech, where the mechanism is too
remote or delicate for parent or nurse to reach, the training
of voluntary control must be mainly self-originated, though
invited. In other cases, as in learning to clap the hands,
the process may be aided for the child by guiding his arms,
provided you leave the active operation, as much as possible, to him, and only prevent its going astray; so as to
let the succession of muscular feelings fall into the right
track. I have said that, throughout these processes, the
initiative is from within ; but, though this is essential, it is
not enough, to make them voluntary. Mere spontaneity,
be it ever so 'random,' is also from within ; and so are
routine movements of instinct on its one line ; and Will
does not come into play till the attempt *to control the spontaneity*, and make it do *this and not that*, i.e. till there is
some *selection*, and among possible strokes only one is a
hit : whoever can exclude the wrong and direct himself
upon the right exercises voluntary power.

I am the more anxious to emphasize this *selective or
preferential* function of will, because it is partly slurred,
partly denied by many modern psychologists, and the
means are thus lost of distinguishing instinct and habit
from volition. In Bain's illustrations of our growth in
voluntary power, it is indeed indirectly implied : we learn,
he says, to 'single out' the proper movements, to 'determine specific actions,' to bring about a 'successful coincidence,' and from among 'ideal representations of all possible movements' to perform some desired one[1]. But the
significance of this unavoidable language is so far from
fixing his attention, that he *totidem verbis* excludes its

---

[1] Mental and Moral Science, book iv. ch. ii. §§ 5-7.

meaning from his definition of voluntary action ; the specialty of which, he tells us, is ' that the antecedent and the consequent are conscious or mental states (coupled of course with bodily states) ; when a sentient creature is conscious of a pleasure or pain, real or ideal, and follows that up with a conscious exercise of its muscles, we have the fact of volition': 'the two phenomena are successive in time, the feeling first, the movement second.' ' Not unfrequently two, three, or four feelings occur together, conspiring or conflicting with one another ; and then the action is not what was wont to follow *one feeling by itself*[1].' According to this account, an animal urged upon action by any single feeling is exercising will, though there be no ' singling out,' no comparison, no exclusion, but only a rush forward upon a straight line : in this limitation of it Bain sees nothing to distinguish the case essentially from those in which conflict and deliberation may be present. His opinion is sustained by the authority of Mr. Sidgwick, who thinks that 'no clear line can be drawn' between actions ' originated unconsciously,' i. e. from instinctive impulse, and those which are ' conscious and voluntary[2].' And it is carried to its utmost extent by Mr. Hazard in his treatise on ' Freedom of Mind in Willing'; which abolishes all distinction, except in degree, between the human and the brute faculties, and treats the instinct of the beaver or the ant as a case of Will realizing a single end through intelligence knowing a single means, while our larger wants supply us with a plurality of ends, and wider intelligence reveals to us a variety of means[3]. In conformity with this identification of all action with Will and all skill with intellect, he dispenses with *choice* as an element of volition : whether it is present or not depends

---

[1] Mental and Moral Science, book iv. ch. xi. § 2.
[2] Methods of Ethics, book i. ch. vi. p. 60, 3rd ed. 1884.
[3] Freedom of Mind in Willing, 1864, book i. ch. xi. pp. 101–103.

on the accident of there being more ends or means than one, or only one ; and *if* it be present, it is a mere intellectual judgment upon compared prior conditions, and precedes the act of willing, which is confined to the *effort at execution*[1].

I cannot reconcile myself to a use of language which identifies phenomena so unlike as the blind instinct of the caterpillar and the foreseeing and discriminating intellect of man ; and which separates processes so allied, nay blended, as the moral choice of the higher principle of action and the moral effort to give it effect. Though we cannot plant the line exactly between animal skill and human intelligence, and can mark the former only by negative suggestion, it is impossible to doubt that the exclusions thus made are in the main well founded ; and that you cannot attribute to the insect, to the salmon, and to the migratory bird, a *knowledge* of what they are about, of the future, even posthumous, offspring they are providing for, of the distant latitudes they seek, and the relation between the ends they pursue and the methods adopted for their attainment. This absence of knowledge from operations which *we* could perform only by means of it, needs to be marked by some distinctive term ; and in calling them *instinctive* as opposed to *voluntary*, we mean to claim for the latter precisely the *elective* and *foreseeing* element which characterizes self-conscious agency. If a preconceived end and a selection of means are *not* necessary to volition, then, within the scope of conscious nature, there is no such thing as involuntary action ; and, to find it, we shall have to pass into the mechanism of the material world. If we assume and take into consideration the Divine Will, *all movement* is voluntary. If we omit this

[1] Freedom of Mind in Willing, 1864, book ii. ch. i, especially pp. 188 *seqq.*

consideration as transcendental, the question arises, how are the movements taken up which it relinquishes? Is it by one category,—*the mechanical,*—covering all that is not claimed by finite wills?—or by two categories,—*the mechanical,* for *insentient* things, and *the automatic,* for *simply sentient;*—leaving *the voluntary* for *the more than sentient, the self-conscious and reflectively intelligent*? Surely this triad is the only natural expression of differences which insist on taking the lead in our view of the world under its active and passive aspects. The last head alone gives us a complete causality, carrying its own directing power. The first gives us only *imparted* or *transmitted* changes through passive media that only hand them on (as the first law of motion itself asserts). The second gives us an intermediate order of facts, viz. the latter half of causal action without the first,—the conscious execution of an absent directing idea; the idea being at once undeniable, and yet not predicable of the creature itself, but left out in the transcendental sphere, to be claimed by Nature or by God. This classification, adopted by the common sense of mankind and incorporated in current language, there is nothing in our later knowledge to disturb; and we may rest content with the definitions of Locke and Edwards, who both of them regard *Choice* as the characteristic of Will[1].

By thus limiting the range of Will to the function of *determining an alternative,* we dispense with those earlier stages of the Hartleyan psychology in which single lines of associated feelings, ideas, and movements are formed by closing up their links; and we take up the problem at the point where first two co-present tendencies conflict. *There* it is that the hinge of our whole question is found.

---

[1] Locke's Essay on the Human Understanding, B. II. ch. xxii, §§ 5, 15; Edwards's Enquiry, Part I. § 1.

Prior to this, we may allow the law of association its claim to connect sensation, conception, and movement, and to make action dependent on suggested ideas : we are perfectly familiar with this process in the training of skill and the formation of habit ;—a process exactly the same as that of learning by heart, and exemplified also in the breaking-in of an animal. Here, in this passage from the 'automatic' to the 'secondarily automatic' or habitual, there is one definitely given path to be traced and smoothed, and no alternative presents itself except in the form, at once universal and negative, of the *all else* that is to be excluded ; so that the only entrance which Will can make is in the shape of *attention*, warding off the intrusion of lateral disturbance, and securing for each step the determination of the next. In this function, the Will only stands sentinel at the outposts to let the files be rightly formed within, and does not mix with them and direct them, so as to render them properly voluntary. And when once the connections have been strongly riveted, we regard an habitual action as no less involuntary than one that is instinctive ; and though, in both cases, we may hold the agent responsible for it, it is because, while not *issued* by his will, it was *preventible* by it. If it conflicts with some higher principle of action which ought to have been present, the cohesive force of habit will not excuse it ; choice holding a perpetual veto against mechanism.

Leaving these cases of transition from automatism to habit, let us fix our attention on the point where the line of usual association bifurcates into alternative possibilities. Suppose that you suffer under some calumny, admitting disproof ; your natural course would be, to give the exculpating statement. But if in doing so you must cast a shadow on some fair name, or embitter some precious friendship, your impulse will be arrested by a resistance equally natural. Consider what takes place in deciding

this conflict; for a true analysis of the process gives the
solution of our problem. The elements which are present
are (1) two incompatible springs of action, the desire to
save your own credit, and the desire to save that of others ;
and (2) what I will call *your own Past*, i.e. a certain formed
system of habits and dispositions brought from your previous use of life. The former head comprises the *motives*
that are offered ; the latter, the *character* that has come to
be. Do these settle the matter between them? Is the
character the arena on which the play, or rather the war, of
the motives fights itself out, and is the volition the flash of
the stronger sword? Or, inverting the parts of active and
passive, shall we say that the past character, instead of
lying still and *being influenced* by the triumphant motive,
comes in as umpire between them, *giving the ascendency* to
that which is the more consonant with itself? Or, is our
account of what is there still incomplete ; and must we
admit that, besides the motives felt, and besides our formed
habits or past self, there is also a *present self* that has a part
to perform in reference to both? Is there not a *Causal
self*, over and above the *caused self*, or rather the *caused
state and contents* of the self left as a deposit from previous
behaviour? Is there not a *judging self*, that knows and
weighs the competing motives, over and above the *agitated
self that feels them*? *The impulses* are but phenomena of
your experience ; *the formed habits* are but a condition and
attitude of your consciousness, in virtue of which you feel
this more and that less : both are *predicates* of yourself as
subject, but are not yourself, and cannot be identified with
your personal agency. On the contrary, they are *objects
of your contemplation* ; they lie before you to be known,
compared, estimated ; they are your data ; and you have
not to let them alone to work together as they may, but to
deal with them, as arbiter among their tendencies. In all
cases of self-consciousness and self-action there is neces-

sarily this duplication of the Ego into the *objective*, that contains the felt and predicated phenomena at which we look or may look, and the *subjective*, that apprehends and uses them. It is with the latter that the preferential power and personal causality reside ; it is this that we mean when we say that 'it rests with us to decide,' that 'our impulses are not to be our masters,' that 'guilty habit cannot be pleaded in excuse for guilty act.' If this distinction be lost sight of, and the word Self be used exclusively of the objective and phenomenal, the essence of the personality is erased, and nothing remains, in the absence of any cause which can settle an alternative, but to deny the alternative, contrive that one of its terms shall slink away, and leave the field to a linear series of jointed phenomena. No one denies that, with alterations in their data, i.e. in the intensity of our impulses and in the acquired cast of our habit and temper, the problems of right action become more or less difficult and weighted by temptation ; and, in formerly treating of the principles of Ethics, I have endeavoured to reduce these variations to definite rules. But, short of mania, they do not go so far as to usurp the whole causality for the mere conditions ; and the deciding Ego of a rational self-consciousness will never allow that it is *obliged to follow* the importunities of its feeling ; will insist, on the contrary, that it can *command them.* If my past alone predetermines my future, having settled both the motives that shall be suggested and the reception which I shall give to them, I in the present have no part or lot in the matter, except to play the stepping-stone of transition from the one to the other ; and the doctrine which involves such an utter collapse of the sense of personality appears to me self-condemned. Here it is that we touch the hinge of the whole question : whether we *are*, or whether we *have and partly produce*, the phenomena of our own life. If we are nothing but the growing sum-total of them thus far, then

the next term in the series is given by the preceding. But
if, instead of our equivalents, they are only our predicates,
they express, without exhausting, an essence and power
behind them, which may betake itself to other modes of
manifestation. I submit that the consciousness of self, as
an identical personality, is the consciousness of such power;
and that no one can sincerely deem himself incapable by
nature of controlling his impulses and modifying his
acquired character. That he is able to make them the
objects of examination, comparison, and estimate, places
him in a judicial and authoritative attitude towards them,
and would have no meaning if he were not to decide what
influence they should have. The casting vote and verdict
upon the offered motives is with him, and not with themselves ; he is 'free' to say 'Yes' or 'No' to any of their
suggestions : they are the conditions of the act ; he is its
Agent. In the typical case of inward conflict which I have
supposed, between your sensitiveness to unjust reproach
and your tenderness for others' reputation, you do not let
yourself sway to and fro with the varying fling of the
motives upon your character, like a floating log on an
advancing and retreating wave ; but address yourself to an
active handling of their pretensions ; and deciding that the
care for repute, however vehement, is lower than the sympathy, however calm, you force yourself to obey the better
claim. You yourself, as a personal centre of intelligence
and causality, are at the head of the transaction, and determine how it shall go ; though doubtless what you have been
about in the past, and what you feel in the present, enter
subordinately into the problem as its avowed data or its
tacit aspects.

To the force of this inward assurance Professor Sidgwick,
though almost borne down by the arguments on the other
side, has put on record the following emphatic testimony :—

'This almost overwhelming cumulative proof seems,

however, more than balanced by a single argument on the other side ; the immediate affirmation of consciousness in the moment of deliberate volition. It is impossible for me to think, at each moment, that my volition is completely determined by my formed character and motives acting upon it. The opposite conviction is so strong as to be absolutely unshaken by the evidence brought against it. I cannot believe it to be illusory. So far it is unlike the erroneous intuitions which occur in the exercise of the senses ; as, for instance, the mis-perceptions of sight or hearing. For experience soon teaches me to regard these as appearances whose suggestions are misleading ; but no amount of experience of the sway of motives even tends to make me distrust my intuitive consciousness that in resolving after deliberation I exercise free choice as to which of the motives acting upon me shall prevail. Nothing short of absolute proof that this consciousness is erroneous could overcome the force with which it announces itself as certain[1].

It is right to add that subsequent reflection seems to have reduced this firm and sharp-cut judgment to a more yielding condition ; on its re-appearance in more recent editions of the *Methods of Ethics*, it shows evident symptoms of incipient melting away. But still, in the third edition, it makes again a modest assertion of its rights : 'Certainly, in the case of actions in which I have distinct consciousness of choosing between alternatives of conduct, one of which I conceive as right or reasonable, I find it impossible not to think that I can now choose to do what I so conceive, however strong may be my inclination to act unreasonably, and however uniformly I may have yielded to such inclinations in the past[2]'.

It is not, however, to be supposed that the empirical

---

[1] Methods of Ethics, ch. v. § 3, p. 51, 1st ed. 1874.
[2] Ibid. p. 64, 3rd ed. 1884.

psychologists have not an account to give of this consciousness of elective power: and their exposition must
be compared with the foregoing. They all agree in dispensing with any contribution to the result from the *present
self*, over and above what is furnished by the two other
factors ; and undertake to account for each volition from
the play of the motives upon the habits and dispositions
formed in the past. Of these conjoint conditions, either
may be announced as determining the volition : Mr. Shadworth Hodgson prefers to treat it as consequent upon *the
character*[1]; Bain, more in conformity with usage, regards
it as the resultant of the combinations of *motives*. Neither
has the least intention to ignore the unnamed condition ;
and the different language merely indicates the element
ascendent, and tacitly endowed with activity, in the mind
of each. In bringing the case of *Choice* under the rule
that the strongest motive always prevails, Bain represents
the so-called chooser as passively at the mercy of the
objects that offer themselves ; each has a certain attraction ;
and that which has the greatest carries the day and gives
him his volition. When this happens *at once*, it shows that
there is no approach to equality in the strength of the
attractions, but that one has a decisive preponderance.
When, on the other hand, there is an interval of suspense,
it is because the motives are nearly balanced and are
trying their strength till the weaker are driven from the
field ; or else that, in view of the evils of precipitate action,
a 'deliberative veto is in exercise,' till the opposing solicitations have been sufficiently compared ; when this arrest
is withdrawn, the volition rides in on the back of the
victorious motive. You may call this *Self-determination*,
if you mean by 'Self' only 'what is resolvable into motive,'
and consent to define it as the 'sum of the feelings' that

---

[1] See his letter in the Spectator newspaper, Jan. 25, 1879.

'impel the conduct, together with the various activities impelled'; for thus you do but vary the phraseology, still claiming the causality for the motives, though referring to the particular motives of the present case only under cover of the sum-total of motives called 'Self.' But if, under this word, you think of any entity that meddles with the phenomena, or turns them into anything more than antecedents and sequents of the regular sort, and mingles with them that 'mystical' fiction named 'Power,' you confuse the phenomenon of volition by thrusting into it an illusory element[1]. In this exposition, let us consider (1) the fundamental maxim that, among conflicting motives (defined as 'pleasures and pains in prospect'), the strongest must prevail. If this proposition is to have any meaning, and be susceptible of verification, there must be some common measure of motives, enabling us to set them on a graduated scale of strength, and say 'this is weaker than that, and here is the weakest of all.' Yet it is confessed that we have no such measure; Bain himself saying that '*the only test of strength of motive*' is that the volition follows. That it is so, you may readily convince yourself by trying to arrange the motives which *you have rejected* in the order of their relative strength; you will find it utterly impossible to do so. Even kindred inducements that may come into rivalry, a visit to a picture-gallery, and a skating-excursion, and a ride on the downs, may prove incommensurable; and when the range takes in quite dissimilar ends, addressing themselves to different parts of our nature, some prudential, some sympathetic, some moral, the common application to them of terms of quantity becomes simply ridiculous. How am I to balance the 'attractions' of a festive evening among friends in health against those of the same hours given to a friend in dejection and sorrow?

---

[1] Mental and Moral Science, B. IV. ch. xi. § 3.

or of attendance upon him in infectious fever against those of security to my own life? or of a new carpet against those of helping a church or an hospital into existence? I might as well compare my sensibilities in eating a lobster-salad and in reading an epic poem. The Will has to live and move among objects which, in their pleasurable or painful aspects, are perfectly heterogeneous, and no more measure themselves by one common standard than light, weight, and electricity by the thermometer. If it is said that all these, in spite of their differences, have in this respect the same feature, that they are susceptible of more or less *intensity*; and that, through whatever channel they may enter our consciousness, they will report themselves there with corresponding degrees of *excitement*; it may still be doubted whether we can tell, in the case of different senses and affections, all susceptible of degrees of stimulation, what excitements are equivalent or to what extent they miss equivalence. But, waiving this doubt, we may surely affirm that, in our inward conflicts, it is by no means the motive most intensely felt and most exciting, that wins our volition. Often a vehement passion may be controlled by the mere tranquil memory of a resolve quite distasteful to us at the moment. What else indeed do we mean when we speak of the frequent opposition of in-clination and duty? If therefore by '*strength* of motive' be meant its felt intensity, (and, if it denotes a quality at all, this is the only possible sense), the proposition that the volition follows the strongest motive is false. If, as Bain admits, the only test of greatest strength is in the victory, we are simply landed on the tautology, that the prevailing motive prevails.

(2) The account given of *delayed choice* I find unintelligible on Bain's theory. The suspense, he tells us, is evidence that the opposite motives are nearly balanced; and time is occupied in trying their relative strength. How do they

manage this experiment? What is going on during this pause? He does not reveal the secret: it is a battle in the dark; or behind the scenes, as in the classic drama, that lets no horrors come upon the stage: all we know is that, at last, the door is opened, and the volition, stepping into the daylight, reports which is the victor and which is the slain. I have often been conscious of incompatible motives, but never of their behaving themselves in this way, and presuming to settle their quarrels on my field and without my intervention, and even to make me the prize for whose captivity they fought. If there be several of them, have they to try it all round, in a succession of single combats, till the last survivor can go off with me unmolested? That the period of suspense should work itself out in this way without betraying the transaction is inconceivable. But Bain offers us an alternative explanation: it may be that the time is spent in using judgment, instead of experimenting on strength: the 'deliberative veto' may be applied to stay decision, until the several motives have been surveyed, compared, and estimated at their value; and then withdrawn, to let the winner have its way. But *Who* exercises and withdraws this veto? *Who* compares and appraises the clamorous impulses? As there is no '*Self, irresolvable into motive*,' there is nothing but the motives themselves to do the 'deliberation,' the 'veto,' the 'comparison,' and then put an end to it all. If it be said that the 'Self' which deliberates is indeed a sum-total of feelings, impulses, and acts, but those of the whole previous life, and not the mere group of the immediate crisis, so that it is the 'formed character' up to date which examines and appreciates the solicitations of the moment; I reply with two remarks: (*a*) A sum-total of feelings, impulses, &c. cannot deliberate, any more than each feeling and impulse separately, but only *a Mind* that has them: nor is that mind superseded by any particular condition or 'formed

character' to which it may have been brought, so as to surrender to it the work of comparison and estimation.   The
habits contracted in the past may improve or deteriorate
the mind's capacity for right judgment, but cannot take its
place. (*b*) Deliberation as to an impending act assumes
that no one of the motives on the field is predetermined victor in virtue of its superior 'strength': for, if it
were so, the suspense on which we are insisting would
be illusory : in the state of character as defined by the past,
and the relative force of the motive, the conditions of the
volition are already complete.   The very fact therefore that
we pause and compare implies that consciousness repudiates
the determinist assumption, and recognises a tribunal with
jurisdiction over the pleas of motive and habit, and em-
powered to open new lines, and set new precedents, of
Right.

(3) In order to avoid recognising this personal causality,
Bain supplies yet another meaning of the word 'Self,'
besides that of the collection of 'motives,' and that of the
hitherto formed character.   It sometimes is used to mark
my '*permanent interests*' as distinguished from '*temporary
solicitations*': and 'self-determination' means no more than
that my idea of the former moves me more than my feeling
of the latter : but this in no wise disturbs the law of the
strongest or the necessary sequence of volition on motive,
by introducing any agency beyond these phenomena : it
simply *classifies my motives*, using the word 'Self' as a
name for the 'ideal' ones.   He adds that 'to neutralize, by
internal resources, the fleeting actualities of pleasure and
pain, is a great display of moral power.'   Two brief com-
ments comprise what I have to say on this phase of the
doctrine. (*a*) That 'Self' means something 'permanent'
as opposed to what is transient, there can be no doubt ; and
therefore self-determination is certainly the ascendency of
the permanent.   But permanent *what?*   Is it merely the

more durable, that is, frequently recurrent, among the
phenomena, as contrasted with the fleeting and occasional?
Am I myself in my digestion, and not in my toothache?
By no means: the 'Self' is not *some of our phenomena*, but
the Subject of them all: and it is the continuity and
identity of this subject that make 'permanence' predicable
of it, and not predicable of anything that happens in it: a
self constitutes a permanent: but a permanent order
repeated does not constitute a self. Self-determination
therefore is not determination of some phenomena by
others, but of phenomena by a subject. (*b*) So irresistibly
do we feel this that Bain himself cannot state his case
without confessing it. While reducing the whole inward
life, voluntary no less than involuntary, to a mere time-
order of sequence, and denouncing the words 'Will' and
'Power' as mischievous 'expletives,' serving as nests of
dynamic illusion, and fostering the idea of some 'mystical
or fictitious agency,' other than the occurrence of the
antecedent phenomenon, he yet tells us that 'to neutralize,
by internal resources, the fleeting actualities of pleasure and
pain, is *a great display of moral power.*' What is 'moral
power,' if there be no such thing as power at all and the
word is a misleading 'pleonasm'? *Who* displays it? is
it the *sequences*? *Who* neutralizes the fleeting solicitations,
by command of 'internal resources'? Is it the *ideas* of
something less fleeting? or are these just the 'internal
resources' by means of which the thing is done? Who
then *uses* these means, finding them among his 'internal
resources'? The author has evidently slipped into
phraseology more sensible than his doctrine, and having
no intelligible meaning except on the assumption of that
'mystical agency' which he denies. And so does he again
when he says 'The *collective* "I" or self can be nothing
different from the feelings, actions, intelligence, of *the
individual.*' If I am only *a collection*, I am a *divided*

aggregate: if I am an '*individual*,' I am a unit not divisible ; and the collection of feelings, &c. is not myself, but belongs to myself, the many in the one.

(4) One more attempt to take its meaning out of the phrase 'self-determination' is made by Bain. He tells us that '*Spontaneity*' is synonymous with it : that is, in comparison with action propelled or induced from without, any that springs up of itself from within may be regarded as 'self-determined,' that is, functional to the nature of the being and provided for out of its resources. When restricted to the voluntary acts of human beings, the word would denote the absence from them of any external pressure or prompting by others : as when a person unsuspected comes forward and confesses a past crime. Undoubtedly, both words, 'spontaneity' and 'self-determination,' denote *action from within:* but there is a difference between them which Bain overlooks : spontaneity denotes action from within *in the absence* of any counter forces or *irrespective of them*: self-determination, *in their known presence and in spite of them.* The latter word is never used except to claim for the Ego a jurisdiction over the solicitations to action whencesoever presented ; and we do not employ it to mark merely that the agent has no accomplices in his inducements. In no way can this term be appropriated by the Necessarian : it expresses precisely the relation between the motives and the personality which he desires to disprove.

I have mentioned that, while Bain rests the determinist case on the necessary connection between *motive* and volition, Mr. Shadworth Hodgson prefers to emphasize the necessary connection between the formed *character and the volition*: and I must not neglect the argument of so acute a metaphysician. He presents it as a comment on the following words of a Libertarian writer : 'I feel, when I have done wrong, that I have done something *I* could have avoided,—the accusation of conscience directed against that which I mean when I speak of myself.' 'Admirably stated,' says Mr. Hodgson, 'first expressing our *sense* of freedom in choosing, and then giving the interpretation of that sense, viz. (in the case of wrong-doing), the moral reproach against the *Self* as agent. Now I say that all the *Determinist* theory is therein contained. The reproach is ultimately against the *agent* [he means, as distinguished from the act]. The agent gives rise to the act of choice, not the act to the agent ; the act flows from, presupposes, and is evidence of, the *character* of the agent. We reproach ourselves for *being* such agents as to choose the good so feebly, or the bad so readily. We accept the responsibility of what we *are*, as evidenced by what we choose : and in this our moral responsibility consists.' He then proceeds to argue that if you make the responsibility depend on a supposed power, irrespective of character, to choose differently, you dissolve the connection between act and character, and practically treat the agent as characterless at the moment of action : and then his choice expresses nothing, and is destitute of moral quality. 'The whole validity,' he concludes, 'of moral responsibility depends on the necessary connection between the character of the agent and the character of his act[1]'.

I understand this to mean that *if the act were free and wrong*, the reproach would be directed against *it* : but, *since it is the necessary result of the agent's* character, the reproach is directed against *himself*. It would draw reproach, if free : it escapes it, through being necessary. Reproach therefore goes only with freedom ; and could not be transferred to the *self* but in the consciousness that the self was free. How could we 'reproach ourselves for *being* such agents,' how 'accept the responsibility of what we *are*,' if our 'being such,' were not our own doing, but

---

[1] Spectator, Jan. 25, 1879.

were, like the immediate act, the inevitable fruit of the retreating antecedents back to our nativity? Granting that from the character as it is nothing but this act could come, still, in upbraiding that character, I certainly exempt it from a like necessity, and assume that I could have determined it into a better form: else, I should as soon feel compunction for a hump-back or a squint. The Determinist, if he cares for it, may have the act: for, so much the more, in order to interpret the self-reproach, must he leave free the character. It is the abuse of a prior liberty that has brought us under the present necessity.

And here it is well to observe the ambiguity that lurks in the word 'character.' In order to work the determinist theory, that is, to refer the volition wholly to its antecedent phenomenal conditions, *it ought to mean* my collection of inward and outward habits gathered in the past: *these* it is which are affirmed to be, under the offered motives, the necessary determinants of my act. But these are not all that we usually intend to cover by the word '*Self,*' or the word '*character*' when employed as its equivalent: we think, not merely of a manufactured Ego, the resultant of its own experiences and therefore changing through their course, but of a permanent self-identical Ego living through all, responsible now for what it *is* because responsible all through for what it *does*. And when we say that an act gives evidence of the character, we mean, not that it is retrospective and reveals the past and established habits, but that it shows us the kind of use which the living Ego makes of its freedom. If the act were perfectly fresh, unencumbered by any antecedent acquired tendencies, it would express one of the mind's preferences, and so far tell us what it is and what it is not. The 'character' thus reported to us *includes the Will*; and so, while determining the act, leaves room for *self-determination*.

On the whole then, I submit, the empirical psychology does not dispose of our consciousness of personal causation, or succeed in reducing us to a theatre of felt antecedents and sequents. There remains the indelible conviction that we are not bound hand and foot by either our present incentives or our own past : but that, drag as they may, a power remains with us to make a new beginning along another path than theirs. It is matter only that moves out of the past : all mind acts for the future : and though that future operates through the preconception of it which is earlier than the act, and so might seem to conform to the material order, yet, where two or more rival preconceptions enter the field together, they cannot compare themselves *inter se* : they need and meet a superior : it rests with the mind itself to decide. The decision will not be *unmotived*, for it will have its reasons. It will not be unconformable to the characteristics of the mind, for it will express its preferences. But none the less is it issued by a free Cause that elects among the conditions, and is not elected by them. For what can be more absurd than to say, because an intelligent and moral agent is careful to bring his actions into correspondence with the conditions available for bettering the future, that they and not he must be credited with the causation ? If the conditions were different, the decision would no longer be the same, precisely because the mind is free to appreciate its problem and conform to its terms, by making the best of the possibilities it supplies.

§ 3. *Argument from the Axioms of Causality.*

While the modern determinist relies chiefly on the ingenuity of his psychology, the older writers trusted most to a higher method of metaphysical demonstration, established upon certain axioms of causality. Two self-evident propositions,—viz. that 'whatever begins to exist must have a cause,' and that 'different effects must have different causes,' were sufficient to establish their case: for a 'free will,' that is, a will to which either A or B is possible, would then be no cause at all, for want of definite and invariable effect: and the appearance of volition A rather than B, or B rather than A, would be an effect without a cause; in the former case contradicting the second axiom: in the latter, the first. The argument has its full strength in this compressed form, and it is needless to expand it. It will be readily seen that these axioms assume a very different aspect according to the meaning we attach to the word 'Cause.' Concentrating our attention upon this, we shall find how important is the distinction formerly drawn between its primary and its secondary or phenomenal sense.

The first of the axioms we adopt at once; subject only to a satisfactory interpretation of the word 'cause.' But this reservation is unfortunately inconsistent with our acquiescence in the second: for by *a Cause* I understand 'that which determines an alternative,' that is, with which it rests to produce either of two phenomena: so that, far from admitting that different effects cannot come from one cause, I even venture on the paradox that nothing is a proper cause which is limited to one effect. I will not repeat, but only recall, the analysis formerly given of our idea of causality; showing that it is identical with our self-knowledge of the exercise of will; and that that exercise, presupposing the presence of two or more possibles, consists in turning one of them into an actuality, and so replacing what was previously contingent by what is now necessary. This order, in which the definite issues from the indefinite, and the *will* passes into the *must*, is what we mean by the order of causation, and that alone is a cause which terminates the balance of possibilities in favour of this phenomenon rather than that. When from our own experience we pass out with this idea to seek its complement and counterpart in the cosmos, we find it only in a like *preferring power*, in a mind which, among many universes that might be, thinks out and institutes one that shall be and that is: after which (unless there be some exempted province where a plurality of possibilities is left open) all that was before uncertain becomes irrevocably fixed, and the several series of phenomena, shed forth and sustained by their causal Source, are pure *effects*, marching through time with regulated pace and irreversible succession, so that they can be reckoned by premonitory signs, which however only convey, without exercising, causality. Hence in nature, in contradistinction from the realm of mind, there is no such thing as *contingency*: it has passed the stage of Volition, and is now Will in process of execution: we rightly assume its habits to be uniform and its rules invariable: and this, in the sphere of mere observation and experience, is all that we can mean by *necessary*.

This physical world however has a way of *shamming* contingency, with such success as not only to bewitch the inexpert, but sometimes 'to deceive even the elect.' So long as we are in ignorance of one or more of the concurrent series of phenomena that will meet upon a point of time, our calculation of what will happen then will have more answers than one, like the values of an unknown term in an equation of variable data: and the uncertainty of our expectations will have all the effect upon us of a real contingency, though the issue, if we could only read the conditions throughout, is definitely settled. Chance and probability are not therefore attributes of natural events, though often treated as predicates or categories of them, but mere defects in our knowledge; with the increase of which they are continually retreating in favour of certain and distinct foresight. In what does

this increase of knowledge consist? Always in the discovery of some unnoticed line of antecedents, or the disen-
tangling of some that were confusedly blended together ;
in either case throwing forward into view the characteristic
symptom of one and not the other of the incidents between
which we wavered. The actual fact therefore is, that here
there was no alternative to begin with (one side being
already excluded except from our fancy), and there is no
removal of an alternative to end with ; but, through our
ignorance, both are successfully simulated ; and as the
subjective contingency is mistaken for an objective, so is
the cancelling of a subjective doubt mistaken for the
operation of an objective cause : the newly deciphered
'antecedent,' having determined our *mental alternative,*
receives an extravagant homage, and is treated as if it had
determined a real one, and is misplaced in the rank of
causes. Through an illusion of our imperfect insight,
a necessary system is enabled to mimic the contingency
whence it issued : its sham-alternatives are then resolved
by sham-causes : and finally, a hoodwinked philosophy
adopts the pretenders, and makes the title to causality to
be 'invariable antecedent.'

Now it is only of these pseudo-causes,—the regimented
terms of an instituted and now necessary system,—that
the second axiom holds : and precisely because it is true
of them, they are disqualified for being accepted as proper
causes at all. If however they are to retain the name in
its philosophical sense, the rules which are gathered from
that secondary sense are not applicable to it in the
primary : and it is surely the extreme of simplicity to
expect that a maxim expressing the special behaviour of
a determinist's world should prove demonstrative, or in
any way persuasive, to an indeterminist. It begs the question *ab initio.*

The mode in which a living Will, having real command

of several possibilities, may create a determinate system
which should yet present an appearance of contingency,
finds illustration in the most common-place experience of
life.   Suppose that I am at the head of a large School
or Hall, where a public dining table has to be provided
every day; and that, to save the worry of diurnal invention, I establish a sufficiently extensive rotation of dinners:
but, with a view to a little further variety, amuse myself
with giving this whimsical instruction to the steward : that
whenever, at full moon, the thermometer at 8 A.M. is below
45°, and the price of corn not more than 50s. per quarter,
there should be plum-pudding instead of apple-dumplings.
To the guests at the table the welcome apparition will
long seem to be a mere chance, and will excite no more
expectation at one time than at another.   But the moon-
beams through the hall windows, and the deep shadows in
the porch on the dispersion of the party, cannot constantly
recur on just this occasion without associating themselves
with it : and when the youths in their rooms get up a
dispute about the phenomenon, *a lunar theory* of it is sure
to be advanced.   It will of course not escape opposition ;
and the apple-dumpling that appears at the next full moon
will give the sceptics a mortifying triumph.   On this, some
meteorological youth who keeps registering instruments
outside his window, observes that these disappointments
of monthly expectation are rare in the winter ; and, after
adding a dinner-column to his weather register, he insists
that the phenomenon goes by the temperature quite as
much as by the moon.   But, provokingly enough, the
hypothesis is equally contradicted by a whole year of
monthly apple-dumpling, bringing back the reign of chance
again, and puzzling the young philosophers : till a country
gentleman's son, whose ideas are neither lunar nor meteoro-
logical, but exclusively agricultural, remarks that during
all that time high prices ruled at Mark Lane, and declares

his belief that when the corn market goes down, the monotony of their second course will cease. After long controversy, the three claims to determine the phenomenon will be made out and adjusted : and the *aggregate of the conditions* will be installed into the place of 'invariable antecedent' which, when perpetuated, constitutes the 'cause.' Yet it is obvious that they are only a combination of *signs* prefixed, for which any other might have been substituted : that the discovery of them only shows that what we had deemed a mere contingency really goes by a fixed rule : that this rule, when defined, clears our doubts, but is no agent and exercises no choice : and that the whole determinate system depends, in the last resort, upon an intending Will as its creative cause, to which it was equally open to institute more or fewer conditions. The detected constant antecedents get the credit of causality simply because they do for our *subjective alternatives* just what a real cause does for an *objective alternative*, viz. discharge one of its terms and leave the other as the only possible : and we overlook the momentous difference, that this is done in the one case by exposing an illusory contingency, in the other by terminating a real one. This difference renders the maxims borrowed from the former wholly inapplicable to the sphere of the latter, and even tantamount to a denial of its existence. Such argument is more energetic than convincing. Boldly to affirm as axiomatic the absolute reign of necessity is to convert your opponent by throwing him into chains.

Let us however suppose this maxim universally true, and see what comes of it. If it holds of mind as well as matter, and is co-extensive with causality itself, it applies no less to God than to us ; and all that has begun to be in his eternal life, the thoughts and acts that have written themselves out in the history of the universe, have been without alternative, the sole possibility of things. He could neither have withheld creation, nor created anything else. If in its immensity his nature is exempt from external constraint, it is because it swallows up and embraces all necessity within itself: he does not prefer, he does not choose, he does not divide and judge; he thinks what must be thought, he does what must be done, and perceives neither better nor worse that might be. Pessimism and optimism are each alike a vain jangle: the world had to be what it is, and stands in no degrees of comparison: there is no margin of the possible beyond the actual: they are identical. I never like to press the consequences of a doctrine from which I dissent, knowing well the happy ingenuity with which its dangerous tendencies are evaded by men's better affections: but, without some regard to them, it cannot be estimated as a logical whole: and if here a conclusion is legitimately drawn from the necessarian's premisses which he does not desire to admit, it is but a fair invitation to him to carry a fresh scrutiny to his first principles. He usually resents the imputation of *fatalism*: and with some reason, so long as the question is detained on the field of human life: for the fatalist imagines it to make no difference whether he bestirs himself or not: the necessarian, that it is just this that does make the difference, only that with the end the means also are no less ordained, and that God will not act *for* him but *through* him. But when the doctrine is carried into the Divine nature, does it leave anything there that is distinguishable from *Fate*? How can we call *that* a *Mind*, from which the alternatives, the problems, the comparisons, of thought are absent? and how, *that* a character which has no choice, and cannot help being and doing precisely what it is and does? Goodness cannot exist except under possibility of evil, or love except under conditions of preference, or perfection except as the superlative and crown of a better and a worse: and from an infinitude embracing nothing but necessities such predicates must be withheld. The determinist scheme is, in this aspect, the natural prelude to the Calvinistic doctrine of absolute sovereignty and irreversible decrees, and is developed into a consistent theology in the work of Jonathan Edwards ; but can never harmonize with a Religion which is in earnest with its Moral conceptions, and in their transcendent application does not suffer them to be crushed and paralyzed beneath the weight of infinitude and almightiness.

The argument which I have been criticizing shows very clearly that the question at issue is, in the main, a conflict between the physical and the psychological interpretation of the word '*Cause*.' On all hands it is agreed that, if all its meaning is obtainable by outward observation, and that nothing must be predicated of it that cannot be verified by the order of the material world, the phrases 'invariable antecedent,' and 'assemblage of prior conditions' must be accepted as its equivalents : the maxim that 'each cause can have but one effect' must be admitted ; and by its simple extension through every field must establish universal necessity. But the psychologist insists that we carry the idea of causality with us into nature, instead of taking it thence : that we do not discover it in the phenomena, but insert it behind them : that what we need from it is, to apprehend why they are so and not otherwise, and have the definite order into which they have set ; and that that apprehension is supplied in a determining Will which might issue other things but does issue these. This determining power alone is what he understands by Cause: and whatever necessity there is (other than logical) is but the product of its freedom, the self-imposed method of its own action. In external nature therefore we must not look for alternative causation : *there*, contingency has ceased : it is the realm of immanent volitions, already in the executive stage, and parted from the essence and act of

causality. From that field therefore the very object of our
quest is absent in its initiative : it is vain to seek the
living among the dead.

How are we to decide between the logical claims of
these two interpretations? the one making determinism
all-comprehending and eternal : the other, educing the
determinate from the indeterminate? Whence do we
obtain their respective assumptions? and what is their
relative authority? The former appeals, as we have seen,
to outward observation and induction, which (within their
province) abundantly establish the uniformity and persistency of natural laws. The latter appeals to an internal
consciousness of what, in our own case, causality is, viz.
the realization of one out of a plurality of possibles ; a fact
as intimately known to us as anything can be, all its
elements being within ourselves. If then we apply the
idea of causation to the cosmos at all, can we give a reason
for preferring either of these conceptions to the other? Is
there any evidence which, for instance, would invalidate
the second? Yes, there is. If Spinoza's dream could be
realized ; if the constitution of nature could be deduced
' *more geometrico* ' from necessary postulates (such as the
existence of Space and Time), involving no mind ; if its
actual laws turned up, one after another, in the working
out of equations constructed from these elements ; then,
no doubt, all open possibilities would be as effectually
excluded as they now are from the properties of the ellipse.
But so long as we are thrown upon inductive methods to
learn the ways of nature, and have to hold ourselves ready
for any tidings of them, however strange, it is evident that
we are not entitled to say that they could not have been
otherwise. We make out what they are by laborious cross-
questioning, precisely because no ground of antecedent
reason gives us the least surmise of them : nor, when we
have found them, can we assign any *ratio essendi* why they

are this rather than that. No one can affirm that the ratio of gravitation and distance, the rates and modes of ethereal undulations, the three forms of body with varying temperature, the number, the atomic weights, the movements, the combinations, of 'the chemical elements,' are the sole possible ones, like the equations of the parabola and the hyperbola. Here therefore, through the whole field of empirical and inductive knowledge, we are so far from having any proof of necessity that we are obliged to treat the laws of nature as contingent, and to deal with their present determinate condition as one out of several indeterminate possibilities. It is just the *absence of necessity* that compels our resort to empirical methods: and the fundamental principle of induction is that what, in point of fact, has become settled and uniform, is, in point of thought, alternative or contingent. Yet, strange to say, it is chiefly by the great champions of the inductive method, while insisting on it as the supreme organon of truth, that the proclamation of universal necessity is most emphatically made. They wait upon experience to believe in the uniformity of phenomena, thus acknowledging that it is unguaranteed in the nature of things; yet treat with contemptuous impatience every idea of an alternative possibility. They thus confess by their method what they deny in their conclusion. Under these conditions the logical advantage appears to me to lie on the psychological side.

Before quitting this argument from causality, it may be expedient for me to notice a difficulty started by the modern Physics in connection with it: though, as we shall see, it presses with nearly impartial weight upon both sides of our present question. We are asked what limit we put to the alleged power of the Will? Does our volition actually *create* the energy expended in its execution? or only *liberate* and direct it? If the former, we contradict the accepted proposition that the cosmic energy is a constant quantity. If the latter, where is the store released, and how does the will get command of it?

The answer to this inquiry will emerge more clearly if we carry it in the first instance to the Supreme Will: for no sooner do we try it upon this case than we perceive that the distinction vanishes between 'creation' and 'direction' of force. In instituting the different orders of attraction, gravitating, magnetic, chemical, God must be conceived by us not as *adding* to the total power previously existing, but as determining in particular lines, and applying to particular objective use, a portion of his own inherent Might; and so all that we call 'creation' is, on its dynamical side, only a conversion of the potential into the actual. The word, so far as it implies the origination of what previously was not, is applicable only to *things and their phenomena*, and not to the *power* whence they are born: that power is eternal and co-extensive with the almightiness of God. Whenever we speak of it as within limits, we refer to some detachment of it that is set apart for the production of this or that class of phenomena: or, as in asserting its quantity to be constant, we confine our attention to such force as is *invested in the cosmos*; beyond which we in no wise mean to deny *an infinite free store* in the transcendent reserves of the Divine nature.

Even if the force put forth by our Will were altogether new,—in the sense of being not reducible to any type named by us in the order of physical antecedents and consequents,—it would not on that account have emerged from darkness: it would merely be that, as free beings, we were permitted to draw on the free store of God. In this case, undoubtedly, our relation to him would escape the restrictions of physical-science rules, and lie on the other side of the dynamic boundary of nature: it would be in the proper sense *supernatural*: for all that, the power wielded by us would be as much *borrowed* as if it were heat expended in producing mechanical motion.

But there seems no necessity for treating the force exercised by the Will as altogether new. Of the fixed amount invested in the universe there is nothing to prevent our being intrusted with a certain store, which may be potentially wrapped up in our constitution, and on which our will may draw as occasions for it arise. There is no more difficulty in allowing to our organism such an available magazine of latent power than is inseparable from the whole conception of potential energy. And if you once allow such a provision, whatever purpose it serves for the Necessarian it would serve no less for the Libertarian. It is regarded by the physicists as a quasi-chamber charged with pent-up force: the nerve which carries the message of the will has but to lift a latch, and through an open valve the executive current rushes through the proper channel to its work, and the deed is done. So it is, when the only possible course is one. In order that either of two should be possible, we have only to furnish our chamber with two valves on its opposite sides; and whether the message is sent to the right latch or to the left, the energy is there, and the line is laid, which will realize the volition. If there be any difficulty in the free-will case which is absent from the other, it attaches to the prior stage of the choice of this or that message to the executive machinery, and not to the source or adjustment of the dynamical conditions of its work. On this score neither scheme can boast of any advantage over the other.

Notwithstanding this, I believe that the picture presented by physiologists of what takes place in reflex actions strongly influences the imagination in favour of the Necessarian doctrine. The steps of the process are well known: (1) some stimulus from without is applied to the peripheral extremity of the sensory nerve: (2) conducted to the

central extremity, it is handed over there to the imbedded
beginning of the motory: (3) along which it is conveyed
and transmuted into molecular motion and contraction in
the peripheral muscles.   Here, all has the aspect of a
mechanical series of changes : the more so, as they may
be produced and exhibited in animals deprived of consciousness by severance of the connection between the
spinal cord and the brain : and though we cannot represent to ourselves the conversion of functional neurotic
excitement into a spasm of fibrous masses, it has its
analogy among inorganic phenomena, in the transmutation
of heat into molecular and molar motion.   When therefore
it is said that such a series, unconscious and involuntary
when detached, is turned into conscious and possibly
voluntary by connection with the brain, it is hastily imagined that volition is *only consciousness of a mechanical
process,* and that man is simply a machine that feels its
own working.   Without disturbing the theory of reflex
action, a little reflection will show how it fails, in every
essential point, to illustrate the operations of will.

A lady who is a social favourite, is in lively conversation
at a dinner-party five or six miles from her London home.
A servant hands to her a telegram, 'the child has fallen
downstairs; he is seriously hurt.'   A convulsion of horror
passes over a face just bright with laughter, agitates her
pulse, takes away her breath : but, with the self-control of
benevolent tact, she contrives to withdraw with just adequate explanation ; orders her carriage and flies to her
boy: but on the way goes round to her physician's door
to take him with her ; and even remembers that there
may be need of a surgeon too, and bears the delay till she
can return provided with both forms of skill.   Reaching
home at last and going straight as pioneer to the child's
room, she covers the flutter of fear and pity with a bright
look and comforting words, till the way is prepared for the

friendly doctors ; and when it proves to be a broken arm, she insists on being their attendant whilst it is set, that she may strengthen his heart and quiet his cries, though herself feeling as if she were being torn limb from limb.

Now here is a system of actions and abstentions which, from the intense tumult of consciousness amid which they take place, are typical examples of the characteristics of Will. How far do they conform to the pattern of reflex action ? Simply in this : that there is a physical affection of a sensitive nerve to begin with ; and muscular movements to end with : but, all that lies between, wherein the whole essence of the history consists,—the flash of imagination, the rush of feeling, the conflict for its control, the hurry of thought, its reduction to order, the sharpness of instant decision, the strain of sustained resolve,—is wholly absent in the supposed parallel. Not only are the whole psychical contents a pure addition (for reflex action has none), but the physiological story itself must read quite differently. (1) The original stimulus is no longer *sensory*, measured by the keenness of the peripheral impression ; but *ideal*, depending on the *thought* signified by the signs given to the eye : not till the terrible meaning is seized, does the heart beat quicker and the passionate energy begin its course. The nerve-affection therefore, instead of having nothing to account for but the transmission of its own molecular movements to the molecules of its motory associate, has now to answer for (*a*) the conversion of its physical motion into intelligence, and, at the next step (*b*) the inverse translation of this intelligence into muscular activity. But these are states admitted to be so separated by an impassable chasm that neither of them can give any account of the other : 'between molecular motions and states of consciousness,' says Professor Tyndall, 'I do not see the connection, nor have I as yet met anybody who does :' 'if we are true to the canons of science, we must

deny to subjective phenomena an influence on physical
processes[1].' The substitution therefore of an *idea* for a
pressure or a puncture as the initial excitement brings at
once the reflex machinery to collapse. But (2) if we even
conceded to the idea the same influence as that assigned
to the sensory nerve, the physiologist would have to tell
us how it is to find the motory, or motories (for there will
be plenty of them) on which this influence is to be spent.
In the reflex arrangement the afferents and efferents are
already brought together, and so isolated that communication can pass unerringly from one to the other. But in the
brain no one has even imagined a corresponding adjustment, assigning both a locality to each idea, and a ganglionic connection with every motory nerve down which it
might have occasion to send a message to muscles: nor is
any such connection conceivable, seeing that ideas and
actions do not run in couples, like the reflex elements ;
the same impelling idea needing, under different conditions, the most various combinations of muscular service.
And this brings into view (3) the presence, in voluntary
action, of *an alternative element*, to which nothing corresponds in the reflex case. On the one hand, impelling
ideas themselves are liable to appear upon the field in
rivalry, and to need an umpire to pronounce upon their
relative claims. And on the other, each of them, when
left alone, may have several possible messages to the
organs of action, and must provide for some process of
decision. If we follow the mechanical model, we may
indeed by mere increase of complexity, contrive, for the
chamber of power, any number of retaining valves, and
latches to hold them : but discretion to determine *which
latch*, under existing conditions, it is fittest to lift, not the
most refined engineering can supply.

---

[1] Presidential Address before the Birmingham and Midland Institute, Fortnightly Review, Nov. 1, 1877.

§ 4. *The Foreknowledge of Voluntary Actions.*

In no aspect has the necessarian problem proved more perplexing, and at the same time more inevitable for every serious mind, than in its relation to the *foresight* of voluntary conduct,—by ourselves in regard to one another, by God in regard to us all. There are few who have not asked the Apostle Paul's question [1], 'if God hath mercy on whom he will, and hardeneth whom he will, why doth he yet find fault ? for who hath resisted his will?' and fewer who find themselves satisfied with his answer, that creative power has a right to be arbitrary and render no account of its doings. We will not however plunge into the theological depths of the 'eternal decrees,' till we have examined the same question on the modest scale of human experience. The facts of which we have to give the interpretation are of the following kind.

It is only in reliance upon an order of events fixed in itself and known to us, that we are able to reckon upon what is yet future : and the measure of our insight into the ways of nature is our success in predicting their results : nor do we ever hesitate, in case of failure, to attribute our miscarriage to our own ignorance of some needful condition, and not to any contingency in things themselves. Now we form expectations respecting the behaviour of men, not less securely than respecting the course of the physical world : varying, no doubt, in certainty, but, in these variations, following the same rules of gradation which are our guide in the study of nature : confident, where the elements are few and well defined, as in the eclipse, in the daily meal and the nightly sleep : doubtful, where they are many and entangled, as in the weather of next week, the particular people we shall meet in the Park, and the text of the next sermon we may hear

---

[1] Rom. ix. 18, 19.

at church. Our life depends, from hour to hour, on the persistent repetition of innumerable voluntary acts on the part of others : that the courts will sit, that the banks will be open, that the newspapers will appear, we feel as sure as that the clock will strike ; nor is the assurance perceptibly weakened, though the fulfilment of our expectations involves a long series of volitions on the part of many persons ; as, in the course which is run by a bill of exchange, or of a letter to Calcutta and its reply. If we enter a shop to make a purchase, if we promise a reward to the diligence of a child, if we build a prison for the reception of criminals, if we assume that a trade will not be permanently carried on at a loss, it is in reliance on the steady operation of motives : and we should think it but a poor compliment to our 'freedom,' if others did not reciprocate that reliance towards ourselves, and trust our constancy as we trust theirs. Even in cases where the play of motive is too complex for our reckoning in individual actions, the average of a sufficiently large number discloses the uniformity which the separate instances conceal, and proves that conduct of a given type varies with the balance of inducements and hindrances to it. Thus, the number of 'marriages bears a fixed and definite relation to the price of corn[1]': the suicides in London or Paris are represented by a figure that only slightly changes with the pressure of severer times ; and retains the proportion between the sexes and the different ages[2]: and every year 'we know from experience that not only do there occur nearly the same number of murders, but that even the instruments by which they are committed are employed in the same proportion[3].' Wherever

---

[1] Buckle's Hist. of Civilization in England, 1857, vol. i. p. 29.

[2] Ibid. p. 26.

[3] A. Quetelet, Sur l'homme et le développement de ses facultés, ou Essai de physique social, 2 tomes, 1835, tome i. p. 7.

statistical returns enable us to embrace a comprehensive aggregate of human facts, like evidence emerges of the regular control of the will by the application to it of impelling conditions.   Of the inference to be drawn from such averages Mr. Buckle speaks thus confidently: 'Suicide is merely the product of the general condition of society, and the individual felon only carries into effect what is a necessary consequence of preceding circumstances.   In a given state of society a certain number of persons (about 250 each year) must put an end to their own life.   This is the general law, and the special question as to who shall commit the crime depends of course upon special laws: which however, in their total action, must obey the large social law to which they are all subordinate.   And the power of the larger law is so irresistible, that neither the love of life nor the fear of another world can avail anything towards even checking its operation [1].'

The cases of forecast which are massed together in this general argument are of two very different kinds.   In one class we must place those in which we can depend upon particular actions of individuals, from the insight we have into their springs of conduct : in the other, those in which, while totally unable to say what this or that person will do, we yet feel sure that, among a sufficiently large number, a particular mode of possible behaviour will recur with nearly uniform frequency in the same society in equal times.   These two classes are explicable on totally different grounds : the first assuming the logic of invariable causality, and using it: the second (as will presently appear) dispensing with it.   We must take them therefore in succession.

In dealing with predictions of individual action, we must first remember that between the two opponents in this

---

[1] Buckle's Hist. of Civilization, vol. i. p. 25.

controversy there is a considerable amount of common ground. The libertarian, in refusing to surrender a free personal power, does not dispute the influence of either the immediate 'motives' or the 'formed character,' to which exclusively the necessarian attributes the action. And as these factors may, at different times, have very variable shares in producing the action, and the personal power may take its turn of remaining in abeyance, the field may often pass wholly into possession of the other conditions: and the necessarian reckoning will then accurately represent the fact. It is perfectly possible for a free mind to behave as it would if it were not free: and there is no small portion of human life in which it may legitimately do so : in which therefore there is no need to travel beyond the necessarian formula. The great mass of predicted actions will be found within this range ; and may be conveniently distributed under two heads, viz.

(1) *Habitual* acts, which simply repeat the usages of the past, scarcely needing any motive, and unopposed by any. In order to expect such acts, it is enough for us to have experience of their uniform recurrence : so long as no revolution disturbs the nature of the agent or his scene, we look for their regular appearance as for the alternation of day and night. Thus, we never doubt that people will dress, that the church bells will ring on Sunday, that the postman will give a double knock, and that we shall not see the officers of the guards in wig and gown and the barristers at Westminster Hall in regimentals. These are typical examples, and therefore unmixed and extreme : but whoever reflects on the vast tissue of mutually understood habits which spreads through an old civilization will perceive how large a proportion of our expectations is provided for under this head. They cannot be said to exemplify the foreknowledge of operations of Will ; for the acts in question are mechanical and not

voluntary, except in the negative sense of being *preventible* by the Will. Our faith in them is founded on the persistency of a working mechanism ; not on any insight into the future decisions of the Will, but on the assumption that the Will is safe out of the way.

(2) *Single-motived* acts, which are dictated by some uncontested want. That a thirsty man will accept a draught, that a captive will not refuse his liberty, or a lieutenant a step of promotion, that capital will flow into more profitable and secure investments, that high-priced food will diminish the consumption of manufactured goods, can be as certainly foretold as that an irritated mastiff will attack, and a frightened sheep will scud away. Such acts, simply instinctive in the animals, are quasi-instinctive in man : with whatever self-consciousness they may be performed, so long as their impelling feeling has the field to itself, without competitor, it rushes unhindered to its end ; and there is but one result to be expected. Here again, our confidence is founded on *absence of Will.* It is the *isolation* of a given appetency or passion or need, the assurance that there is nothing to stand in its way, that gives certainty to our reckoning. In order to give scope for the preventive power of the will and bring the action within the voluntary category, that assumed isolation must cease.

So much for the cases which are short of voluntary. Suppose that we now let in the will, and give it work to do among conflicting impulses soliciting the agent. Let us invest it, for argument's sake, with the active alternative power which the word freedom is intended to denote ; and consider whether, in presence of this new factor, uniformity ceases to be possible, and is lost in uncertainty. Does it follow that, because either of two courses is possible, neither can be repeatedly preferred ? When the mind is free to choose, may it not *choose to be uniform*, that is, determine itself in conformity with a rule? To say that this is impossible, and that to be free is to be wavering and oscillating, is to pronounce consistency attainable only by necessity. Yet what do we mean by a *conscientious person* but one who imposes upon himself a steady rule of choice, which is to be pushed at any cost through all solicitations, and who makes himself always follow the higher spring of action? and since there is nothing haphazard and fluctuating in the relative worth of these springs of action, but they constitute a definitely graduated system, his resolve, when carried out, cannot fail to produce an order of conduct on which reliance may be placed. Thus the foresight of voluntary action is not forfeited by retaining personal command of moral alternatives.

This freely chosen uniformity the necessarian, it is true, knows how to interpret in his own favour. It is not a choice, he tells us, without a motive : it is determined by the superior *rightness* of the selected spring of action : with the feeling which the agent has of this,—a feeling which makes it his strongest motive,—he could not determine otherwise. This brings us back to the old fallacy, already analyzed, of 'the strongest motive'; and raises the question again whether, in describing the relation between *the chooser* and *the object of his choice*, it is more correct to treat the object of choice as determining the chooser, or the chooser as determining the object of choice. Certainly, to a conscientious man the *rightness* of a spring of action may be his *reason* for siding with it : and if the will were amenable to reasons in the same way that the understanding is, their appearance would be conclusive with it : as it is impossible to withhold *assent* from the apparently superior term, so would it be impossible to withhold *volition*. But we know it to be otherwise : after seeing the right, we have ourselves something to supply ere it wins even the inward field ; and, failing this, we end with the ' Video meliora proboque, deteriora sequor.' We can neutralize our own approval and throw ourselves into the opposite scale, in spite of its wrongness: and *we* it is that settle whether, in our choice, we shall listen to the 'strength' of the lower principle or the 'worth' of the higher. You may call that which is finally preferred our 'motive'; but that the '*action follows the motive*' is simply because the motive is what *we prefix to the act.* The causation remains with the self-conscious and irresolvable personality.

Against every attempt, like this, to reserve for the mind an active function in regard to its own motives and internal decisions, an objection is brought which, from its frequent recurrence, is evidently regarded as conclusive. If you not only select your act, but, earlier than this, select your motive, there must be a will behind your will, rendering your volition, as well as your conduct, voluntary. And, for the same reason, your choice of motive, if necessity is still to be excluded, must be determined by a free consideration of its claims, and a voluntary preference of some and rejection of others. As this stage in its turn is subject to a like rule, there is nothing to stop our *regressus ad infinitum*; and, ere I could take a pair of shoes to put on this morning, there must have been an unlimited series of 'volitions from all eternity [1].'

This charge is founded on a transference to the libertarian of an idea of causation which is peculiar to the necessarian, and makes him responsible for precisely the very rule which he disowns. When both of them accept the maxim 'every phenomenon must have a cause,' the necessarian means it must have *another phenomenon* as *a determinate* antecedent: the libertarian means it must have a *determining* agent, *not another phenomenon.* The latter therefore, as soon as he has traced the phenomenon,

---

[1] Edwards on the Will, Part II. § v, end.

—in this case the act of choice,—to a mind that wills and decides alternatives, has got what he wants, and is pressed by no further question: there is no uncaused phenomenon remaining on his hands, for which he must go out in quest of another Will; for he has never maintained that the acts of one will were events demanding the operation of another: that one which he has found is itself a determiner of alternatives and is competent to the whole. *He* therefore is already at his goal and is urged to no regress. But the necessarian, who takes the word cause in the sense of *determinate antecedent*, cannot understand any escape from the sequence of phenomena into a source, other than phenomenal, in which they begin or take their direction: for him the act is from the volition, the volition from the motive, the motive from the prior education or the posture of circumstances: nor is it ever possible to arrest the retreat on the lines of the past. This necessity of *his* idea of causation he has unwarrantably imputed, in the foregoing objection, to that of his opponents; which has its whole origin, interest, and definition, in the protest against it. It is expressly to cut off the *regressus ad infinitum*, and establish an adequate causality on the spot, that the doctrine of the free mind is set up. There is no ground whatever for separating the selection of the motive from the selection of the act, as if they belonged to two consecutive wills; when, with a dinner in my satchel, I come upon a starving boy, and the question is forced upon me, 'shall I follow my hunger or my compassion?' the motive chosen carries the act, and the act includes the motive as one of its elements; and one decision tells the story from end to end.

This charge is the more curious, because it is not only illusory, but must evidently be retorted upon those who make it. They tell us that every uniform phenomenon must have its uniform antecedent; which, being also a uniform phenomenon, must have a similar predecessor, itself subject to the same rule: and so on, *ad infinitum.* All orderly phenomena being on that account derivative, it follows *that there is nothing original*; and each change which for a moment we took to be a cause turning out to be an effect, the search for causality is but a disappoint-ment running back through eternity.   Here therefore we encounter a real *regressus ad infinitum,* an absolute despair of any beginning.   If, to escape from this, you arrest the retreat by setting up the conception of a creative mind, then you acknowledge that intellectual Will supplies the missing condition,—of originating power which starts the determinate out of what was not determinate before. There is no *tertium quid*; either endless chain of physical necessity; or competency of volitional thought to settle alternative realizations.

From this survey of the conditions of voluntary action, it will be evident what inferences may be legitimately drawn from any assumed power of predicting them. (1) If they can be fore-announced with the same certainty and exactitude as the duration of an eclipse or the minute of high-tide, it can only be from an exhaustive knowledge and measurement of their predetermining means : and no room is left for free will.   We argue to the future from present necessitating forces.   (2) If they are merely objects of assured expectation founded upon usage, our knowledge of their causes is partial : we depend on the obvious presence of usual motive, and the continuance of the agent's experienced character.   But on these may be superinduced unknown dissuasives and new resolves, which defeat our reckoning, and bring down our foresight from certain to contingent.   No prediction of human action is exempt from this element of uncertainty, or competent to prove the determinist's position.   The irremovable con-tingency *may* indeed be quite compatible with his doctrine;

being due simply to our ignorance of the intruding forces which disappoint us. But it may also arise from an exercise of free will on the agent's part, in which he determines instead of being determined. Such foresight of conduct as we have is therefore neutral to the question.

Next, let us examine the meaning of the 'law of averages' from which Mr. Buckle draws such startling inferences. The peculiarity here is that, of a series of events quite irregular, taken one by one, the quotients or averages of large equal groups are uniform. The death-rate, for example, in our collective population varies but little from 18.7 per thousand in the year; and each age has its peculiar number of victims, though the uncertainty of life at every age is proverbial. Such facts as these have repeatedly been adduced to exclude the hypothesis of chance phenomena in nature: that is, to show that, if an event is incalculable, it is not because it stands detached and unconditioned and belongs to no particular point of space and time: but because its conditions are more or less in the dark for us, and, being complex, form shifting and untraceable combinations, which only at irregular intervals meet adequately for the effect. If each condition were definitely known and the rule of its occurrence ascertained, we could work out the sum of them all to the point of their concurrence, and predict the event. If, on the other hand, they were an indefinite and inconstant lot, and what was a condition yesterday was none to-day and *vice versâ*, the event might as well be unconditioned altogether: its re-appearance on equal areas or in equal times would present only a formless rabble. There is nothing to supply them with a rule; there is no roll-call for them to obey. But if the conditions be limited in number and determinate in character, they will be susceptible of only a restricted set of permutations, which, when pursued through groups of instances sufficiently vast, will equalize their frequency and yield a constant average. Every such result is a summary of large experience, and a guide to similar large experience in the future; by justifying our expectations with regard to which, it seems to take the place and serve the purpose of prediction in the case of particular events; and suggests the question whether it does not warrant the same determinist inference. ;This preconception is strengthened by the fact, that the first application of the method of averages has been to some of the more complex tissues of phenomena in the physical world, for example in meteorology and in physiological statistics, where necessary causation holds an undisputed place. It is not surprising therefore that the rules emerging from Actuary tables and the Registrar General's reports should be regarded as no less the expression of an inflexible necessity than the columns of the Nautical Almanac. And the idea is allowed to pass without resistance in its dealings with physical events, which men are always glad to rescue on any terms from the appearance of disorder. But when it is found that a similar rule applies to voluntary actions, that murders and suicides, when tabulated, are as little variable as births and deaths, there is a natural repugnance to draw the corresponding inference, and conclude with Mr. Buckle, that there can no more be free will in human conduct than chance in physical affairs, and that by predetermined necessity there is a fixed quantum of crime in every society, which the struggles of individual will are unavailing to change. If not too much stunned by his startling announcement, we should do well to consider, whether from persistent averages his inference of necessary causation is legitimately drawn; and if it fails, whether it be by simply pushing it too far, beyond the physical into the moral province of phenomena, or by a fallacious dealing with both.

In order to answer these questions we have only to consider, what are the conditions indispensable to the disclosure of a law of averages. If among these we have to reckon, not only an experience of a multitude of phenomena counted off on to their places in time, but also an apprehension or preconception of their 'invariable unconditional antecedents,' then every empirical percentage in the facts will carry in it a lesson of causation. But if, for an average, you want no more than the phenomena themselves, as loose items under numerical limits of repetition and variation, then any rule emerging from their series will be silent about their causation. Without entangling ourselves in the subtleties of 'the theory of probabilities,' we may safely specify the essential conditions of a law of averages as follows.

(1) A particular kind of contemplated event, liable to happen in a plurality of ways, as to time, place, order and frequency. Death, for example, incident to all, but at various ages, and with slower or more rapid inroads on the ranks of the living.

(2) Ignorance on our part of the cause (in the sense of premonitory antecedent) of the event in its particular instances. If we knew it, we should be in a position to foresee its cases, one by one ; and should have no need of a mere percentage. The life-assurance business would be superseded, if each one's day of decease were stamped upon his forehead.

(3) In the phenomenon's modes of happening there must be definite numerical limits. And, the narrower the limits, the shorter will be the series in which the varieties are run through, and only repetitions turn up, yielding an average in small figures. If you twice toss up a penny, the possible results are limited to four, viz. (if H = Head, T = Tail) HH, TT, HT, TH. If you twice throw a die, so as to deal with six faces instead of two, the possible

results are thirty-six, and the average recurrences will be much more infrequent. And were the variations without limits, no average could arise.

(4) Among the phenomenon's modes of happening there must be, under the same observed conditions, an equal frequency; or, as it is said, each must have as good a chance of presenting itself as any other. Your penny, for instance, must have both its faces alike; and your die must not be loaded; and the population whose death-rate you tabulate must not be made up of ordinary mortals mixed off with a race of Methuselahs.

(5) The experience must be large enough to exhaust the permutations over and over again, till their recurrences are approximately equalized; and must therefore be of wider range in proportion as the variations are more numerous. To ascertain the percentage of colour-blind people, you must carry your physiological catechism through, not a village simply, but a nation: or, if the percentage is to take in all varieties of abnormal vision, you will consult the optical statistics of a continent.

Let these conditions be fulfilled, and your law of averages will be gained. What then are their contents? They demand no more than empirical facts, counted and grouped as loose phenomena; and so little involve any causal assumption, that they would exist with the same results if there were no such thing as causation at all, over and above the simultaneous and serial distributions in time. A human mind, bereft of the category of causation, would not, so far as I can see, be disqualified for the computation of averages: and if so, they teach us nothing about causes, and can have no vote upon the rival claims of necessity and free will.

Once furnished with a number of empirical averages, we may of course deal with them as with any other materials of thought, and apply to them processes of comparison and induction involving causal ideas. Two cases of such procedure have some bearing on our present inquiry. When two similar empirical averages,—say the birth-rate or the death-rate of the two sexes,—turn out unequal, the fact affects us as a new phenomenon, and presses on us its demand for some differentiating cause. If our search is successful, we have rescued one element or more from the general ignorance of causes which is the second condition of all averaging: and this first inroad upon the darkness may possibly be but the beginning of discovery, tending to an ultimate power of predicting the particular events. Were this possibility to be realized, we should be landed, undoubtedly, in a predetermined necessity; but only because the average was gone.

On the other hand, you may contemplate the figures of an average through a series of years; and from their virtual identity you may infer, respecting the unknown conditions, *the persistency of their aggregate causality* through the group, in spite of its irregular distribution among the individuals. But equal aggregates may be made up of very different components, and include interchangeable alternatives, that vary the story and leap from item to item, without affecting the result. The percentage decides nothing about the necessary or free disposal of the working energy detailed through men and things. Whether the total amount be all parcelled off piecemeal into packets of labelled weight, or partly paid off in larger loans of manifold possibility, cannot be told by looking at its steady sum. We may therefore state the whole case thus: when you know all the conditions of an event and can measure them, you may foresee it, and be sure that it belongs to a determinist system. Where the conditions are not all in view, and some of them are known only as equally liable to be present or absent, you cannot predict the particular phenomenon, but you may determine its *average*, or constancy in the long run. This condition may be fulfilled in either of two ways: (1) by what I may call a *sham-contingency*, that is, ignorance on our part of the real determining antecedents of the incalculable phenomenon; so that they work out of the dark, and tell you nothing except their equal frequency of presence and absence: and (2) by a *real* contingency, that is, a dependence on fresh initiation by a self-determining *arbitrium*. By hypothesis, the phenomena open to the Will are limited in number, precisely as in the determinist case; and are equally possible, as conditioned by the chooser; so that the same prerequisites of constant averages are exactly reproduced.

In order to bring home the evidence to a concrete case of the problem, let us suppose our penny to undergo a change of constitution. Its uppermost face has hitherto been selected by a combination of several small forces, at whose resultant we can only make a guess; for example, the more or less perfect poise of the finger, the point and strength of the thumb's percussion, the exact place of the surface on which the coin drops. Instead of these incalculable determinants, suppose it endowed with a free will, to dispose of itself in falling with vote for head or tail. Between these equal possibilities the issue comes out of the dark: they present a balanced alternative, upset by an invisible agent: and the decisions will as often be given the one way as the other. The throws thus willed will evidently give the same numerical equalities with the throws previously determined by the composition of forces: and the tabulated results will carry no evidence against the presence of free will.

There remains one unanswered question respecting the statist's logic, to which a few words are due. However true it may be that averages may be extracted from a sufficient range of past experience, without committing us to any causal theory, we cannot put them to use, by taking them as our guide into the future, without assuming a continuity in the order of nature. What is this but a causal assumption? and how are we warranted in making it? It hardly needed Hume's acute analysis to convince us that no logical link connects the two propositions, 'Water freezes at 32° Fahrenheit at present,' and 'Water *will* freeze at 32° Fahrenheit next year.' The expectation expressed in the latter is not a *reasoned* expectation; but either exemplifies an 'intuitive assumption' of the 'uniformity of nature,' or is one of the inductive inferences which leaps from a limited experience to an unlimited conclusion. For reasons stated in a former chapter, preference must be given to this empirical explanation: anticipation, with us, is only memory shifted to the fore; and as the transference is but an act of the imagination, it is not secured as knowledge, and is never closed against the possible correction of fact. J. S. Mill rightly prohibits any absolute affirmation of the uniformity of Nature, and cautions us against carrying it too far beyond the cognizable spaces of the world; and the rule holds good of illimitable time as well. If this be so, it must be no less possible that the future should not repeat the past than that the terrestrial order should disappear in transstellar regions; and the continuity of nature is but contingent, and carries in it no 'necessity.'

Though however this is strictly true, it must be admitted that, in practical effect, a law indefinitely persistent in the past constitution of the world is, for us, equivalent to a Necessity; and the abstract possibility of its change will in no way relieve its pressure upon the affections and the will. In depending therefore on the continuous system of natural law, we certainly gain, on the one hand, an immovable reliance on the faithfulness of its promise, and, on the other, a consciousness of utter inability to escape the grasp of its terrible hand.

Yet stay: this is not all. What is this which we cannot escape? It is the constitution of the world, not excepting ourselves. If then that constitution includes within it our own investiture with free will, *that* also is one of the continuing things; and the very rule of continuity itself turns upon us with another face, and guarantees us against the universal reign of irresistible necessity. The average on which we rely is the joint product of a necessary and a contingent factor; the latter being qualified for partnership in a constant result, by the limits of its variation and the equality of its possibilities. The steadiness of the total is saved, while the freedom of the individual is reserved.

Mr. Buckle's premisses therefore are incompetent to prove his conclusion. And not only so: the Necessity which he describes as so crushing a tyranny can, on his own theory, have no existence in such a form. For, if it be there at all, it is there throughout, and pervades and carries the thoughts and will of every man, not less than the phenomena of the scene around: he has no causality, other than passes through him and moves the figures on and off the stage of his consciousness, and has nothing to set against the forces that constitute himself and his history. As no 'effort' which he makes, no surrender which he permits, can be without its determinate antecedent, neither can it be baulked of its appropriate effect. The personal part that he plays is that which he wills; and that which he wills is in accordance with his nature and the order of the world. Where then are we to look for the coerced 'persons who *must* put an end to their own life,' and who are selected by 'special laws' determining *who* shall commit the crime'? and who find the 'power of the larger law so irresistible 'that all counter motives and efforts 'can avail nothing'? may the fatalistic burglar plead that he had to kill his victim, to make up the murder-tables true to date? If not, what is the meaning of the dictum, that the requisite 'number of persons must' do the registered deed, and *that* by a necessity which is 'irresistible' and paralyzes all dissuasives?   The ascription of a dynamical resistibleness to a numerical law, the supposed reduction of intense human motives to impotence by the despotism of an average, and the implicit assumption of a helpless struggle of men marked out for ruin against the Nature-power with which they are identified, are gratuitous fallacies, which could hardly have escaped the acuteness of the author, had he not been betrayed by his love of startling paradox.

For these reasons the determinist inference extracted from the law of averages appears to me illegitimately drawn. I am alarmed at my own rashness in challenging an argument which has captivated the intellect of Laplace, De Morgan, Buckle, and almost the whole host of scientific men in our own day.   But *reasoning* is a matter which cannot honestly be taken upon trust, even from great men ; and where, as in this case, the logic, though somewhat subtle, is really not intricate and involves no elements that are the special property of experts, one must take courage to use one's own eyesight.   By the attempt to do so I am forced to believe that this statistical argument is a complete illusion [1].

Since the implication of necessity is supposed to lie in the bare fact that voluntary action can be foreseen, it can make no difference whether the foresight is human or Divine : and the whole plea might be regarded as discussed and discharged in the foregoing criticism.   The very limited foresight of man however covers so small an area, that, to supply an inference of universal necessity, recourse has been naturally had rather to the prescience of God, as

---

[1] See an able and acute discussion of this subject in Mr. Venn's Logic of Chance, 1866, ch. xiv, xv, where the treatment proceeds upon a different doctrine of causation from that assumed in the text, yet reaches a result nearly the same.

embracing everything, and as existing at the very fountain-head of whatever has been determined. We must there-fore devote some separate attention to an argument which has weighed, more perhaps than any other, upon the imagination of religious persons, and been regarded by philosophers of great name as the one insoluble difficulty of the whole controversy. Chief among these must be reckoned Descartes ; who, after stating that our first-hand assurance of free will is 'as certain as any knowledge we can ever have,' and also, that we cannot rightly suppose ourselves 'capable of anything which God has not fore-ordained,' owns that we embarrass ourselves in the greatest difficulties, the moment 'we attempt to reconcile our free will with his ordinances, that is, to define with our under-standings the whole extent of our free will and the order of eternal Providence.' 'Whereas,' he continues, 'we shall escape them without difficulty if we observe that our thought is finite, while the omnipotence of God, by which from all eternity he has not only known, but also willed what is or what can be, is infinite. Hence it is that, while we have intelligence enough to know clearly and distinctly that this power exists in God, we have not enough comprehension of its extent to know how it leaves the actions of men free and indeterminate : and that, on the other hand, we have also such assurance of our liberty and power of suspense that there is nothing more clearly known to us : so that the omnipotence of God should be no hindrance to our belief in it. For we should do wrong to doubt that of which we have inward consciousness and which we know by experience to be inherent in us, on the ground that we fail to comprehend something else which we know to be incomprehensible in its nature[1].' The position here taken up is that, of two propositions which we

---

[1] Principes de la Philosophie, §§ 39-41 ; Cousin, iii. pp. 87, 88 (first published in 1644).

cannot reconcile, we ought to consider that which is guaranteed by self-consciousness to have the extreme of certainty, but to retain our hold of both ; content with the separate evidence of each ; and leaving their harmony for higher faculties to apprehend. This is an attitude natural and reasonable to the modest common sense of mankind ; but involving a kind of despair of philosophy not likely to be a permanent humour with Descartes ; and we find him, accordingly, making the attempt against which he cautions us. 'I will try,' he writes to the Princess Elizabeth, 'to explain our dependence and our liberty by means of a comparison. Suppose a king who has prohibited duelling to know for certain that two gentlemen of his kingdom, living in different cities, are at enmity and so excited against each other that, if they meet, nothing can prevent their fighting. Suppose that he gives to one of them a commission to go on a given day towards the city where the other is, and to this other also a commission to go on the same day to the city where the first is. He knows for certain that they will not fail to meet and fight and so violate his prohibition : but, for all that, he is not chargeable with constraining them to do so ; and his know-ledge, and even the volition he has taken to determine them to it in this way, does not prevent their act, of fighting when they come to meet, from being voluntary and also free : it is what they would have done, if they had known nothing of it and it were some other occasion that brought them together : and they would also be justly punished for violating the king's prohibition. Now what a king may here do in regard to some free acts of his subject, God, with infinite prescience and power, does unerringly with regard to all those of men. Before sending us into the world he has known exactly what would be the inclinations of our will : he himself has planted them in us: he has also disposed all other things externally to us so that such and such objects should present themselves to our senses at such and such times: on occasion of which he has known that our free will would determine us to this or that ; and he has willed it thus: but, for all that, his will has put no constraint upon us to act thus[1].' No ; but he has taken good care, by exclusion or atrophy of all opposing desires, that our will should go along with his, and that conflict should be impossible ; he therefore bespeaks the decision and keeps it out of our hands, leaving one course alone open to us, just as completely as in the case of spontaneous instinct. This *precaution against an alternative possibility* is not liberty, but the denial of liberty: it is precisely that management of men by administration of motives, that assumption that they will give you any required resultant by mere composition of forces, which are the characteristic marks of necessarian doctrine. In Descartes' process therefore of reconciliation between 'dependence and liberty,' as in the treaty of peace between Prussia and North Schleswick, the latter has totally disappeared ; with the aggravation of a mean pretence of saving it.

The problem which Descartes first pronounces insoluble, and then tries and fails to solve, may well discourage less daring philosophers ; and against the arguments from the Divine decrees it has become common to take refuge in the mere plea of mystery. Dugald Stuart says, 'I do not think them fairly applicable to the subject [of free will] ; inasmuch as they draw an inference from what is altogether *placed beyond the reach of our faculties*, against a fact for which every man *has the evidence of his own consciousness*[2].' He would hardly have fallen back upon this state of suspense, had he been satisfied with the attempts of earlier

---

[1] Œuvres de Descartes, Cousin, ix. pp. 373, 374 ; Lettres à Madame Elizabeth, 1646, No. 2.

[2] Phil. of the Active and Moral Powers, Hamilton's Ed. of Works, vol. vi. p. 396.

libertarians,—Dr. Samuel Clarke[1], Dr. Whitby[2], Dr. Reid[3],
—to remove the appearance of inconsistency between the
freedom of human actions and the prescience of God :—
attempts which in effect resolve themselves into Origen's
remark, that 'God's prescience is not the cause of things
future, but their being future is the cause of God's prescience that they will be.' These logical variances between
different writers and even in the same are not confined to
one side of the controversy. Necessarians also, while taking
their stand together upon the foreknowledge of God as
making their doctrine of human action good, draw from it
the most opposite inferences respecting his moral attributes : Edwards, on the one hand, insisting on its inseparable connection with the holiness and righteous government
of God : J. S. Mill. on the other hand, admitting that 'not
only the doctrine of necessity, but predestination in its
coarsest form, that is, the belief that all our actions are
divinely preordained,' is, in his view, '*inconsistent with ascrib-
ing any moral attributes whatever to the Deity*[4].' Whether
any clear path can be opened through these manifold contradictions cannot be determined till we have settled (1)
the grounds for affirming the Divine prescience : and (2)
its relation, if established, to the will of human agents.

(1) To the theologians who have dealt with this question the Scriptures have supplied the main armoury of
proof for the doctrine of God's foreknowledge. Regarding
the Bible from beginning to end as a revealed account of a
continuous scheme for the governance of the human race,
opening with a 'Paradise lost' and closing with a ·Paradise
regained,' they have virtually read it all as *prophecy*; and
being destitute of any true literary chronology and sound

---

[1] Demonstration of the Being and Attributes of God, 1704.
[2] Discourse on the Five Points, 1710.
[3] Essays on the Active Powers, iv. ch. 10, 1788.
[4] Examination of Hamilton's Philosophy, p. 519.

method of interpretation, have found in it innumerable close-fitting predictions, of historical personages bad and good, of particular heroisms and crimes, of revelations depending on special character or single acts ; so that, in their view, the whole Providence of the world has been worked out by forecasting the exact moulds of every human will, and securing that, at the right time, every Pharaoh's heart should be duly hardened, and every people doomed to perish be punctually visited by some strong delusion or fatal snare. The great Hebrew conception, of the ever-living God thinking out and unfolding the contents of the ages, could not constitute itself without these concrete applications to individual men and incidents : and when the retrospective interpretations of pious hearts, resolved to see God in all, are taken for prospective announcements of things yet to be, there can be no lack of documentary testimony to the Divine foreknowledge. Edwards's proof accordingly consists of little more than a citation of texts, declaring future events which depend for their appearance on the voluntary acts of men, or speaking of human agents as implements of Divine purpose,—clay in the potter's hand. It is no doubt possible to produce an array of texts that present the other side. But the proof that the Scriptures contain Edwards's view is unanswerable ; and those who accept his premisses cannot stop short of his unqualified assertion of the Divine prescience.

If the mere recital of the scriptural doctrine is no longer convincing, we are thrown upon the grounds of belief supplied by philosophical Theism. And here it can hardly be denied that the idea of Divine foreknowledge is involved in both the sources to which we have referred our apprehension of God. If we know him as *intending Cause*, if we see in the universe an organized system of ends beyond ends, he comes before our thought as a prospective Mind, whose agency at every present moment has regard to an

anticipated future ; and to suppose that future invisible is
to suppose the present impossible. And if, again, we know
him as *Supreme authority of Right*, if we see in our own
conscience the reflection of his Will, we thereby place ourselves under a discipline of progressive character, and the
human race under a moral education, by which all life and
history are turned into a probationary scene of government.   Such a scene ceases, by the very light that shows
it, to be a blind jumble of accidents, and becomes a *Drama*,
in which the end is preconceived from the beginning, and
each act, as it passes, brings up the conditions and the persons needful to lead on to the consummation.   He without
whom there would be no future but his own, cannot create
a future of which he has not first the idea.   It is not without reason therefore that prescience has been assumed
by theologians as part of the conception of a perfect
being.

(2) Does then the Prescience, thus evidenced, involve
determinism in human actions ?   In the theological form,
as deduced from Scripture, it certainly does : in the philosophical form, as worked out by the Reason, I submit it
does *not*.   In the former the peculiarity is, that individual
acts of will are described as fore-announced, often ages
before the person is born : as the impieties of Antiochus
Epiphanes (Dan. xi. viii. 9, 14, 23) ; the reforming zeal of
Josiah (1 Kings xiii. 1-6) ; the restoring act of Cyrus (Isa.
xliv. 28, lxv. 13) ; the betrayal by Judas (Matt. xxvi. 21-25).
If it is uncertain beforehand whether there will even be a
Cyrus, a Josiah, an Antiochus, a Judas (and this depends
on innumerable volitions), or, if there be doubts how each
will deal with his opportunities and his temptations, prediction of his place and behaviour in history will be impossible : and if the prediction has been made and verified,
it can only have been by the exclusion of contingency : a
thing *known for certain* cannot *be* uncertain.   But the pre-

science required by philosophical Theism is not of this definite and individual kind, except in the domain of physical nature, where choice has no place. Beyond this, in the world of intelligences, a margin of freedom being allowed, the lines of possibility are not rectilinear, but divergent, and open a way into innumerable hypothetical fields, among which, as yet invisible, lies the actual. In the outlook upon this realm which embraces the future, what is needed, in order that the intending causality of God, and his moral government, may secure their ends and shape their means? Simply, that no one of the open possibilities should remain in the dark and pass unreckoned; and that they should all, in their working out, be compatible with the ruling purposes of God, not defeating the aim, but only varying the track. An infinite Mind, with prevision thus extended beyond all that is to all that can be, is lifted above surprise or disappointment, and able to provide for all events and combinations; yet, instead of being shut up in a closed and mechanized universe, lives amid the free play of variable character and contingent history, into which there is room for approval, pity, and love to flow. Is this a *limitation* of God's foresight, that he cannot read all volitions that are to be? Yes: but it is a *self-limitation*, just like his abstinence from causing them: lending us a portion of his causation, he refrains from covering all with his omniscience. Foreknowledge of the contingent is not a perfection; and if, rather than have a reign of universal necessity and stereotyped futurity, he willed, in order to prepare scope for a gift of moral freedom, to set up a range of alternative possibilities, he could but render some know-ledge conditional for the sake of making any righteousness attainable; leaving enough that is determinate, for science; and enough that is indeterminate, for character. 'There is no absurdity in supposing,' says Dugald Stewart, 'that the Deity may, for wise purposes, have chosen to open a source of contingency in the voluntary actions of his creatures, to which no prescience can possibly extend[1].'

§ 5. *Kant's interpretation of Free Will.*

In the foregoing section it has been admitted that if we had the power of accurately predicting the particular voluntary actions of a man, the proof of their determinate origin would be unimpeachable. This rule is recognized in the following statement of Kant's : ' Inasmuch as man's empirical character must itself be formed from the actions he puts forth and the rule to which experience shows that they conform, all his actions as put forth are determined by his empirical character and other concurrent causes according to the order of nature ; and if we could scrutinize to the uttermost all his volitional phenomena, there would be not a single human action beyond our power to foreknow and predict from its antecedent conditions. In regard to this empirical character therefore there is no freedom[2].' Had this assertion occurred only in treating of the ' antinomies of the Pure Reason,' it might have been set down to the account of the author's pleadings for sceptical suspense. But we meet with it again in the treatise on the Practical Reason : ' If it were possible for us to have so deep an insight into a man's way of thinking, evinced in both inward and outward acts, that every minutest motive to them should be known, as well as all the outward occasions influencing them, we could calculate his conduct for the future with as much certainty as an eclipse of moon or sun[3].'

All escape from determinism seems here to be cut off.

---

[1] Active and Moral Powers, Hamilton's Ed. of Works, vi. p. 401.

[2] Krit. der reinen Vernunft, Transcend. Dialektik, 2tes Buch, II. ix. 3 ; Ros. ii. p. 431.

[3] Krit. der prakt. Vernunft, 1er Theil, 1^{es} Buch, III. ; Ros. viii. p. 230.

Nor, apparently, is it less effectually barred by the author's warning, that the categories of the understanding must not be applied beyond the sphere of experience, and that to carry them as interpreters behind the veil of phenomena is a misuse of them involving transcendental illusions[1]. The notion of *causality*, accordingly, is available only within the limits of successive events in time; and these it presents under a law of necessary sequence, in which each change is determined by those which have elapsed before. Every human action is thus made dependent on an irrevocable past, and falls under the *Zwang der Naturgesetze*.

When we seek, in the pages of Kant, for an account of these determining antecedents, we find him answering in the familiar terms of the modern Necessarian. The agent's volition is what it must be from his character as already formed, together with the present motives played off upon it by the conditions of his life: with his sensibilities adjusted and appealed to as they are, no phenomenon can emerge but their natural resultant. It is precisely thus that Edwards, Priestley, Mill and Schopenhauer sum up their case.

Finally, the verdict seems conclusively pronounced, when Kant tells us that 'whatever events of an agent's existence in time, including his own actions, we propose to except from the law of Nature-Necessity, and reserve for Freedom, we simply surrender to blind Chance,' and reduce our 'Freedom' to 'a futile and impossible notion that can only be rejected[2].' This identification of free alternative with fortuity balances the identification of causality with necessity, and, as its counterpart, completes the apparent evidence of Kant's determinism.

But the metaphysic Vates is not less skilled than the Delphic in delivering *oracula ambigua*; and it is necessary

---

[1] Krit. der rein. Vernunft. Ros. ii. p. 240.
[2] Krit. der prakt. Vernunft. Ros. viii. p. 225.

to listen and ponder again before venturing on the interpretation.   With a pardonable surprise we then learn that
Man, in virtue of his rationality, is characterized by a
power of initiating from himself an unconditioned series of
events,—a power which, without any dependence on an
antecedent in point of time, is the condition of every
voluntary act; so that he is the self-determiner of his own
empirical character[1].

In virtue of this unconditioned initiative, Man is a '*free*'
Subject, able to live out of pure reason, which is his essential Self; and, in conforming to the law of reason, exercises
genuine Autonomy.   Here he has immunity from the
control of the *Naturnothwendigkeit* and the bonds of his
empirical character and his sensory instincts and *Antriebe*.
These indeed are in his consciousness and obtrude themselves upon his experience; but they are not his true Self,
and have no right to give the law to him; and so far as
they obtain sway over him, he is under a *heteronomy*.

To this power of self-determination, exempt from the
forces of inward impulse and external conditions, Kant
appropriates the name *Will*; which is therefore the practical expression of Reason alone, and is indeed the same
thing, only in agency, instead of in mere intelligence.   Far
from conceding the word to the persuasion exercised by
appetite, interest, or affection, and allowing acts so
prompted to be voluntary, he claims it as directly antithetic to these dictates of the sensitive nature and impressions of experience.   All these he sets apart as the imposed dynamics that play in or upon this or that individual
sample of life.   The following definitions exhibit this
fundamental peculiarity of his doctrine: 'the *Will* is a
kind of causality in living beings, so far as they are
rational: and *Freedom* is that property of this causality

---

[1] Krit. der rein. Vernunft. Ros. ii. p. 434.

in virtue of which it acts independently of foreign determining causes: while the causality of all irrational beings
has the property of *Nature-Necessity*, whereby they are
determined to activity by the influence of foreign causes[1].'
He adds, accordingly, shortly afterwards, 'only as belonging to the world of reason does Man call his causality
a Will[2].' Again he says, 'We think of Will as a power
of self-determination to act in conformity with the idea of
certain laws[3].' And once more: 'everything in nature
operates according to laws. But only a rational being has
the power of acting in conformity *with the idea* of law, that
is on principle; in a word, has *a Will*[4].'

The reader who feels the contrast between these two
sets of propositions may well ask whether such a 'fabula
bilinguis' can be told of one and the same Subject. What
sort of agent can he be, who is wholly determined by his
past, yet invested with new initiative, who is as hetero-
nomous and calculable as the moon, yet unconditionally
autonomous, who is at once an automaton and a creator?
How are we to gather up in a conceivable unity such a
paradoxical contrariety of attributes? Yet, strange to say,
they are affirmed not only of the same Subject, but of one
and the same act; so that everything which he voluntarily
does is determined by him, yet wholly determined for him,
and involves him in responsibility, while exemplifying his
subjection to necessity.

Kant seeks relief from these contradictions by virtually
assigning the same agent, and the same act, to a place in
two worlds, so severed from each other that no intellectual
engineer can bridge the chasm between them, and of every
proposition true of the one the meaning dies when transferred to the other. If it be possible for one agent to

---

[1] Grundlegung zur Metaphysik der Sitten, 3ter Abschnitt. Ros. viii.
p. 78.
[2] Ibid. p. 87.　　　　　[3] Ibid. p. 55.　　　　　[4] Ibid. p. 36.

occupy such a double position, we can make no use of his unity, but in all that we say of him there must be as much duality as if we spake of the subjects of two parted hemispheres; and if both could claim any single act of his, it must present itself, in default of any mark of identity, as simply tantamount to two. Where the possibilities have nothing in common, the actualities can never be the same.

These worlds that exist but cannot speak together are supplied to Kant by his imperfect idealism; which, resolving space and time into subjective forms of sense, turns all that is perceived or felt in them into phenomenal experience of ours; yet, refusing to forego the substantive existence either of objects affecting us, or of ourselves as subjects acting upon them, retains it for both, behind the screen of all their empirical contents, as *Ding-an-sich*. There, it is true, they are beyond our knowledge, which can deal only with the matter of experience. But they are assured to us as the indispensable correlative of experience; as Noumena demanded by the phenomena; and, however silent about *what* they are, we are certain *that* they are. As it is we who, through the make of our Sensory capacity, put what they do to us into Time, they themselves are timeless, and can be named only as being, not as happening.

Applied to the human person, this distinction supplies two interpretations to the *Self* of which he speaks. In virtue of his receptivity and retentiveness, he is conscious of innumerable images and feelings delivered upon every sense, recurring in memory, redreamt in fancy, marshalling themselves in order, grouped into concepts, linked into inseparables,' parted as opposites, and constituting in the aggregate the whole materials of life, distributed and turned into its scenery by his plastic illusions of space and time. While his understanding is busy upon these, parcelling them out among its categories, they fall also with various appeal upon his sensitive susceptibilities ; bringing pleasures and pains, stimulating impulses and educating desires, the natural spontaneity of which would carry him hither and thither and dispose of him from moment to moment.   Of all this internal history he is aware : he reads it as laid out before him and makes it an *object* of reflection.   It is his *experience* and makes the drama of his career ; and the habits into which it moulds him, with the motives and affections which it pushes into mastery over him, flow into his *'empirical character'* and determine its direction.   The total contents of this history form the *phenomenal Self*, the object of psychological self-knowledge.   It is studied on the same terms as any other series of changes, differenced only by their assignment to an inner instead of an outer seat ; and the study must result in bringing them under the same categories, viz. those of all natural experience, whatever its field may be. Among these is the law of determinate causality, from which no time-series in Nature can be exempt ; and which accordingly is unreservedly applied to the whole of the organic world, including the animal races, whose senses, instincts, passions and affections most nearly approach to the human.   The 'Natural man' therefore, considered as born in time and carried through its empirical conditions, must be under the universal rule, and, like all that is successive, be, from moment to moment, dependent on his past.   To be so ruled is to be under necessity.

But if the assemblage of *cognita* here described constitutes the contents of the *known* self, there must be, besides, a *knower* of them; for, a phenomenon has no eyes to see itself ; nor is the blindness mended by stringing on to it any number of similar incapables.   The receptivity which has a feeling is not the intelligence which apprehends it and makes an object of it : if it were, there would be as many intelligent subjects as there are felt objects ;

whereas of nothing are you more certain than that, however numerous and various may be your inward states, you who report them as your own are one and the same. In this unity of yours you are therefore a *non-phenomenal Self*, who, over and above *having* experience, *know* that you have it, and discriminate yourself *from* it, as well as from other things. Of this *Noumenal* Self, it is true, you can affirm nothing objective, to tell what it is; for this would be to negative its very essence, by turning it into phenomenon. As a pure activity behind all the changes of your nature it is for ever invisible, and cannot be brought to the front to be looked at and defined: the self-consciousness, as Schopenhauer aptly says, being in contact with it only *a parte post*, and not *a parte ante*[1]. And yet, precisely because it finds the phenomenal self and is not found therein, you are carried in it beyond the felt and perceptible world into a sphere of knowing without being known. 'Even of himself in his essential being a man must not pretend to gain the kind of self-knowledge which inward feeling gives. For since he certainly is not, so to speak, his own creator, and gets what conception he has not *a priori* but empirically, it is a matter of course that his acquaintance with himself also is due to his inner sense, and can be gathered only through the phenomena of his nature and the way in which his consciousness is affected. Nevertheless, he must of necessity assume, beyond this composite constitution of his subjective self out of mere phenomena, some underlying ultimate foundation, viz. his *Ego*, be its constitution as an entity what it may; and must therefore refer himself to the sensory world in regard to his mere perceptions and susceptibilities of feeling, but in respect to whatever in him is pure activity (coming into consciousness *immediately*, and not at all

---

[1] Ueber die Freiheit des Menschlichen Willens, § ii. p. 24, Frankfurt, 1841.

through affection of the senses), to the intellectual world ; of which however this is all he knows.   To a conclusion of this kind a reflecting man must be brought in the case of everything that comes before him.   And it may probably be met with in even the most ordinary understanding ; which, as we know, is much inclined to look behind the objects of the senses for an invisible somewhat essentially self-active ; but which forthwith proceeds to spoil the idea, by investing this invisible with sensible form ; that is, by wanting to make it an imaginable object ; and so comes out not a bit the wiser [1].'

This purely self-active Ego, the power by which Man distinguishes himself from other things and even from his empirical self as affected by objects, is Reason (*Vernunft*) ; which must be ranked higher than Understanding, on this account : that, while both exercise self-activity, that of the Understanding wins only such conceptions as reduce the presentations of Sense to the categories and rules essential to make them available for thought ; but the Ideas which Reason supplies indicate a spontaneity so pure as to go far beyond all that Sense can furnish ; and establish for it the pre-eminent function of distinguishing from each other the worlds of Sense and of Understanding, and so pre-designating the limits of Understanding itself [2].

Here then, in the pure spontaneity of Reason, pre-supposed in the understanding and the perceptions which are its objects, we reach our essential Self, and know ourselves to belong to a supersensible world, whither, at all events, we cannot carry our Sense-form of Time, with its phenomenal order and its Nature-Necessity.   In these inmost penetralia of Man as intelligent Subject, only his Noumenal essence is present : divested of his empirical conditions, he is simplified to a *Ding-an-sich*, with *Vernunft*

---

[1] Grundlegung zur Metaph. der Sitten. Ros. viii. pp. 84, 85.
[2] Ibid. pp. 85, 86.

as centre and no circumference : and as the pure spon-
tancity of Reason can give forth only the rational, his
Will, which is but his Reason in action, is uncontested
and free.   If this were his only Self, he would be wholly
free, and live out of his Will's own law.   If he were only
his other and recipient self, he would be wholly disposed of
by foreign pressures planted in him or put upon him, and
be subject to Necessity.   In his actual self, however, he is
a combination of both, and has a consciousness accessible
to their opposite appeals ; and the question on which we
still need Kant's reply is, how, in the sphere of human
experience, in which all events and actions are dealt out
by necessary law, he can save, for this composite agent,
any remnant of the freedom derived from the Noumenal
world.

The answer is to this effect.   The agent, as subject of
Reason, and as recipient of experience, is a being in whom
two causalities meet.   The pure activity which he has in
the former capacity can never be other than reasonable
and right : its essence must always particularize itself in
what is rational in character : what is rational and right is
so for ever and unconditionally : it does not stand under
the conditions of time, so as to begin and cease to be :
and so far as the agent's character conforms to it he is
exempt from the laws of time-succession, and has a
freedom unimpaired by Necessity.   This intellectual causality from behind the empirical character, though not
cognizable among the phenomenal conditions of action, is
always supplied in thought as its transcendental ground ;
and betrays its constant presence in the idea that, be the
realized actions what they may, there is something other
that they ought to have been and might have been.   We
have no answer to the appeal, 'You can, because you
ought.'   But though the agent's character is in contact
with this freedom in its timeless causation, all its history in

experience is made up of actions that are, as phenomena, mere effects of phenomena. The possible co-existence of this sequent causality with the timeless I must permit Kant himself to state:

'Suppose it permissible to say that Reason has causality in regard to the overt phenomenon : would this enable us to call the action free, while it is quite exactly determined in the empirical character (the mode of feeling), and necessary ? The empirical character is, in its turn, determined in the rational character (the mode of thinking). This last however we do not know, but trace through phenomena, which strictly give us no immediate knowledge, except of the mode of feeling or empirical character[1]. Now the action, so far as attributable to the mode of thinking as its cause, results thence not at all conformably to empirical laws, i. e. not so that its conditions in the pure reason, but that only their effects in the phenomena of inward feeling, are *antecedent.* The pure reason, as a mere noumenal power, is not subject to the Time-form, with its conditions of Time-sequence. The causality of reason in the noumenal character *has no origin*, and does not begin at a certain time to produce an effect ; for then it would itself be subject to the phenomenal law of nature, so far as it determines causal series in time ; and the causality would be, not freedom, but nature. We may therefore say, If Reason can have causality in regard to phenomena, it is a power of first starting the sensible condition of an empirical series of effects. For the con-

---

[1] At this point Kant appends the following important note : 'The proper morality of actions (Merit and Guilt) hence remains to us, not excepting that of our own bearing, wholly in the dark. Our accountability can refer only to the empirical character. None can fathom, so as to judge with thorough impartiality, how much of it is the pure effect of Freedom, how much of mere Nature, and to be set down to the account of some irresponsible defect or happier conditions of "temperament."'

dition which lies in the reason is not sensible and therefore has not itself a beginning. Accordingly, we here alight upon what we missed in all empirical successions, viz. a case where the *condition* of a series of events could itself be empirically unconditioned. For here the condition is outside the series of phenomena (in the noumenal), and therefore subjected to no sensible condition and no time-determination by an antecedent cause [1].'

If this passage betrays the difficulty felt in persuading freedom and necessity to lodge in the same person without contradicting one another, still harder must be the task of bringing them into close quarters in one and the same action without breach of the peace : yet this also the author courageously undertakes. He assigns a function in the doing to each of the two selves, with strict injunctions that neither shall encroach upon the other. The act, as belonging to the empirical self, is an event in time ; and under this aspect it is but a continuation of his past history, played upon by the appeal of passing incidents to his susceptibilities and inclinations : by its conformity to these it shows what he has come to be, and enables you to judge what are the persuasives that are now availing with him. On their causality then the act undeniably depends; and it cannot be the same that it would be if they were different. But in conforming thus to his empirical cast of habit and desire, is it conformable to his rational Will? And if this, his other Self, had been there alone, would he have done the same ? If so, its freedom concurred with the natural causality, and the act is but doubly provided for. If not, still the free noumenal self is not out of the game : it asserts on the spot the *de jure* claim of the law which has *de facto* been set aside : it makes the agent own that he has been tempted, and, in spite of the temptation, is

---

[1] Krit. der rein. Vernunft. Ros. ii. pp. 432, 433.

without excuse ; for it rested with himself to start a new
initiative: and it takes upon its own causality, as the timeless essence of the character behind its phenomenal history,
the responsibility for the whole series of its contents and
all that the empirical has become. And hence it is that,
whilst a moral agent 'does not consider himself answerable for the impulses and inclinations awakened in him by
the empirical world, and impute them to his proper self,
that is, his will, he *does* hold himself responsible for any
indulgence he may show them, when he allows them influence upon his maxims to the detriment of the rational
laws of the Will[1].'

Such, in its essential features, is the doctrine by which
Kant attempts to save the free will presupposed by the
Moral law, without trenching upon the universality of the
'Nature-necessity.'   Before proceeding to any critical
estimate of it, I will beg the reader's attention to the
meaning which it affixes to certain leading words, among
which are distributed, very unequally by different writers,
all the conceptions with which this controversy deals.

(1) *Will* is '*a kind* of causality,' viz. '*of living beings*':
not indeed universally, but ' so far as *they are rational*': for
'only as belonging to the intellectual world does man call
his causality *Will*.' By these limitations of its range, the
word is more hardly earned (its *comprehension* is greater)
than with Schopenhauer, who assigns it to all animal
activity. Whence this difference between the master and the
disciple? Kant's requirement of *rationality* in addition to
animality might have been (one would suppose) from his
wanting to make room for *choice*, to which reason alone
is competent. But this is not what he intended. The
causality of the rational will with him is exactly parallel
to the causality of the animal activity with Schopenhauer,

---

[1] Grundlegung zur Metaph. d. Sitten. Ros. viii. p. 93.

—the exercise of a determining power to its proper issue, with no more idea of alternative in the one case than in the other. Whether his language is always consistent in this respect is another question. But what he contemplates in his definition is, that the rational will, in its timeless world, determines as immediately its single possible consequence, as Schopenhauer's animal will turns up its necessary effect in time. Hence,

(2) *Freedom* is 'the property of this causality' in virtue of which it 'acts independently of foreign determining causes,' that is, (I suppose) is unaffected by their causality as incommensurable with them, so as to act all the same whether they be present or absent. Thus defined, the freedom of the rational will is a *negative* property in the activity, of being *unhindered* : that is, it is 'free' to go its own way, and let the essence of Reason express itself in something rational. To this sense the word is limited by determinists in general, and by Schopenhauer with particular emphasis ; who applies it accordingly to the flow of a stream, the sweep of the wind, the play of animal spontaneity, and other phenomena assigned by Kant to the opposite head of 'nature-necessity.' The reason why Kant insists on having Reason present before he will grant the word obviously is, that the absence of hindrance is good for nothing and virtually null for a creature that is not aware of it : the freedom may be *there*, but it has *no owner* till rational self-consciousness arrives upon the scene to appropriate it. He rightly judged that the word *free* marks, not only the outward fact, but the inward thought and feeling, of unimpeded power : but in the definition he does not name the feeling ; and the fact which he does name (the 'property of the causality') is certainly the same that Schopenhauer finds, *unfelt*, in physical objects and non-rational organisms. Both authors alike refuse to accept for the word the only meaning, viz. the power of

deciding an alternative,—which gives exactitude to the question they are discussing.

(3) *Necessity*, usually in the compound form, *Nature-necessity*, 'is a property of the causality of all irrational beings, whereby they are determined to activity by the influence of foreign causes.' This definition is evidently determined by that of the opposite word 'freedom'; as that was taken to mean the spontaneity of a being,—the acting *out of itself*,—it followed that 'necessity' can be nothing else than *being acted upon* by what is *other than itself*. The definitions therefore hang consistently together ; but they do not truly render the conception commonly embodied in the words. The effect B comes from the foreign cause A with no more necessity than the act or condition x from its rational essence X : on the contrary, there is nothing more disputable than the *nexus* between physical cause and effect, nothing that more surely *must be* than the activity or property constituting the nature to which it belongs. Given the nature, you cannot but have what it is and does. Yet this inner necessity, by which an acting nature acts after its kind, is precisely what Kant calls 'freedom.' Then again, when he comes to his 'irrational beings,' he finds them wholly disposed of by 'foreign causes.' Have the animals then no *home* causes ? no spontaneities, no appetites, no instincts, no passions ? Yes ; but with Kant these are all 'foreign,' because the animals have, in his sense, no *Self*, being without the Noumenal Will, and are flung out into the phenomenal world, to be the sport of its antecedents and sequents. This seems a highly artificial rendering of the terms. Necessity is really constituted, not by foreign causation, but by *limitation to one possibility*.

In order to judge whether Kant's solution of the problem of the Will can be accepted, we may direct attention, in the first place, to the relative evidence offered for its two co-existing terms, viz. *necessary causation* and *free causation*. Before we can pronounce on their existence together, we must have warrant for saying that each of them *is*: what assurance is offered us of this?

To answer this question, we must recur to the distinction drawn by the critical philosophy between what we may know and what we cannot know. The sphere of the former is that of possible experience; which is constituted of two elements, the sensory *material* of which we are recipient, and the sensory forms (space and time), and categories of the understanding, with which our percipient and organizing activity meets it. Where both these conditions are present, intelligence performs its function, and pronounces upon something as known. Where either of them fails, no cognitive state is reached; sensory matter, if alone, leaving on the recipient formless feelings which he has without knowing them; and the sensory forms and categories of understanding, alone and abstracted from experience, amounting to no more than the empty possibility of unrealized knowledge. Hence, space and time *per se* are not known objects, but activities in us waiting for objects, or rather for the opportunity of making them: but, when the opportunity comes, the resulting phenomena are known. Similarly, the categories of the understanding, for example, 'causality' and 'necessity,' are not things or facts in themselves that can either be learned or tell us anything, but mere heads of relation under which we have to think the changes which experience supplies. But, as soon as they have got hold of the changes and settled them in their appointed places, then the knowledge at once of them, and of their 'causality,' 'necessity,' &c. is constituted.

By this rule, our knowledge of the serial causation, or 'nature-necessity,' of the Time-world, is complete, having the *a priori* certainty of the ultimate forms of thought.

Experience is on no other terms possible for us : this is our law for all that arises. A phenomenon, for example, a human action, that is *not* under the time law and that is unconditioned by its antecedents, is a self-contradiction. For the empirical life therefore and all its contents the rule of causal Necessity is valid, with all the certainty attaching to our only possible knowledge.

Compare with this the grounds on which Kant rests the parallel assertion of *free* causation. Does he find any immediate consciousness of it ? Not so : for consciousness is with him the 'Inner *Sense*,' where the matter is feeling and the form is time, and the product phenomenal ; while the freedom we seek is in the timeless sphere. Does he even claim to know it as an operative agency at all ? On the contrary, he continually speaks of it as 'a mere idea,' ' whose objective reality can in no wise be proved,' nay, the bare ' possibility of which it is impossible to explain ': for ' Reason would overstep all its limits, if it undertook to explain how *pure* reason can be *practical* reason ; which would be tantamount to explaining how freedom is possible [1].' How then can he persist in upholding an idea which he thus despairs of verifying? All that he claims for it is, that it can as little be disproved as proved : that it admits of successful defence against objectors who charge it with asserting an impossibility ; and that, when necessary causation has done its utmost in explaining the moral phenomena in the empirical character, something still remains over whereof no account is given, and which carries the case for final solution to a super-sensible causality, invisible indeed to positive thought, yet intelligible as *other than* the necessary causality of the sensible world [2]. To this *hiatus* then in the explanation of the empirical character we must turn for the source of

---

[1] Grundlegung zur Metaph. d. Sitten. Ros. viii. pp. 94, 95.

[2] Ibid. pp. 97, 98.

Kant's 'well-grounded idea' of 'free causality in the Will.'
He bids us look at the consciousness of the Moral Law in
ourselves and in all men as the valid law of Reason; and
observe that, unlike the natural laws, it does not execute
itself, but appeals to us with imperative authority for the
realization of its contents. To this appeal we cannot but
respond with inward assent, which yet is quite different
from impulse or desire, and often opposed to inclination
and strangled by it. The demand thus made upon us is
unconditional, and can neither be set aside by any pleas of
reluctance and threatened pain, nor complied with through
motives of interest and liking: it will hear nothing of
pleasure or utility: it insists on being obeyed for its own
sake, that is, simply because it is the law of moral Reason.
Were the actions it enjoins the means to an end, the object
aimed at would be something in experience, and the law
would be empirical: but its emergence in consciousness as
binding *per se* shows the law to be *a priori*. It is impossible to mistake the implicit meaning of this constitution
of the practical Reason. The moral law is not found by
the understanding, but given in the Reason. It is, and is
recognised as being, for one and all. It is an imperative
rule of activity; the universality of which implies that
every one can obey it, for obligation cannot go where
power is not. And that it is unconditional, presupposes
that the Will to which it speaks is not in bondage to the
natural causality stored-up in propensions and habits of
the formed character, but *free* to act out of itself in conformity with known duty at any cost. Thus the freedom
of the rational Will, first in the order of being, comes out
last in the order of thought, as a postulate detected in the
consciousness and interpretation of the Moral Law. There
it lies presupposed, but silent; discovered as an indispensable cause, but else a blank to our knowledge.

If Freedom can support this constructive right of entry

by no more explicit title-deed, I fear that, on Kant's own principles, the necessary causation must be installed in sole possession.   For the claim depends entirely upon the *a priori* idea of Duty, that is, upon the inner constitution of the practical Reason, and not at all upon any objective contents which it takes up in its applied use.   To the moral law, as Law, and not to what is legislated, do the imperative authority and the absolute universality belong, just as to Space as space, and not to the things it contains, the corresponding irremovability from thought and infinitude belong.   In other words, it is a subjective form of our faculty of Will, precisely as Space and Time are subjective forms of our faculty of Perception and Representation : and in and by itself, under the enjoined isolation from material contents, it is no less empty and unmeaning than they ;   and must be pronounced a transcendental *Schein*, on the same grounds which establish the 'Ideality of Space and Time.'   If the ' law ' on which the case is made to hinge has this subjective vacuity, the ' freedom ' presupposed in it sinks back into a hypothetical possibility ;   and *that*, not without being encumbered by a difficulty of its own, viz. that, as a *form* of possible causality, it is in the Noumenal world, inherent in the self as *Ding-an-sich*, while the matter it has to take up in order to *be* an activity, is in the phenomenal world, on the other side of the chasm pronounced impassable.   It is otherwise with the subjective activities which elaborate our perceptions: *there*, both the inner forms and the given matter are related terms within the sphere of sense.

Suppose however the two causalities to be separately established on equally solid grounds : and consider next, whether they can live together on the terms of reconciliation deemed adequate by Kant.

Every human action, moral as well as unmoral, takes place in time and is a phenomenon.   It falls therefore under the law of all phenomena, and is conditioned by the aggregate of preceding and concurrent changes : it stands in the order of natural causality. The determining conditions may be summed up under the two heads of the already formed character of the agent, and of the motives appealing to him at the crisis of action. Both of these are in his time series ; the constituted character being his stored-up antecedents from the past ; and the motives, the immediate antecedents in the present. It is repeatedly stated that an observer who could read these elapsed and elapsing phenomena from end to end, would be able to predict the action about to be. This means that he has in hand all the determining conditions, and that the action is completely accounted for by the order of natural necessity. There is no room therefore for the intrusion of other causality out of the supersensible order, unless it could enter without bringing any additional effect ; which nullifies its causality. Where then is the 'something more' which Kant finds 'remaining over' after exhausting the empirical resources for explaining moral action? How can certain prediction be possible, unless the whole fact be covered by the computed causes?

Perhaps the overlapping margin that still lies in mystery is,—as indeed he himself intimates,—the consciousness of *guilt* inseparable from wrong action, with its attendant remorse for not having done otherwise ; and therefore, inmost belief that other action was possible to the Will. With all his foresight of the action as inevitable, the scientific observer may well be unprepared for this concomitant consciousness, and find it unaccountable. Certainly, if the agent took the same view of his own action that the observer takes, he could have no such feeling : it is explicable only by his additional belief in his obligation and therefore his power of determining himself otherwise. The presence of this 'something more,' in the shape of a sense of guilt, presupposes his belief in a free self-disposal; but does it presuppose the truth of that belief? No more than our belief in an infinite Space with finite contents really external to us precludes Kant's 'Æsthetic Idealism,' which tells us that it is an illusion. As he thinks it easier to account for sensory illusion than to account for such an entity as Space, so may the pure determinist make light of the alleged moralist's illusion, in comparison with the enigmas of a real free will. When once we begin to palm off our objective beliefs upon the inner make of our subjective activity, there is no reason why we should stop the process short with the perceptive or any other faculty, theoretical or practical, in order to save from wreck a plank or two from the phantom ship, that shall be real enough to float us to terra firma once more. But, apart from this, take the other side of the alternative: suppose the implied belief true. What becomes of the predicting determinist? A disturbing element turns up in his calculation, if the agent, in spite of definite and unaltered antecedents, may determine either so or otherwise: the freedom is there at the cost of necessity; and they cannot co-exist.

But of this 'something more,' over and above the record of necessary sequence, Kant gives yet another account. May it not be, he suggests, that although ' in the empirical character there is no freedom,' it yet contains more than the stored-up series or aggregate of antecedents, considered as effects, one from another? Its contents, besides their story as phenomena, have features due to the noumenal will whose causality they express: so that the whole empirical character is pervaded by the timeless essence of the real true Self, while phenomenally made up of successive acts determined in the play of natural causes. In what form then does the free causality leave its trace on the empirical character? Does it introduce rational acts of dutiful will which else would not be there? These would be so many inner phenomena, which would appear in the observed series and be counted in among the elements of prediction, just as if they were due only to their antecedents in the natural order. Either the prediction will be falsified by this intrusion of self-determined terms in the guise and in the midst of the otherwise determined, and the alleged foresight of moral action will be impossible: or else, the self-determination, claimed as a 'causality,' will be as though it were not. If the free causality contributes no rational acts, independent of the nature-causality, to the empirical character, it remains a transcendental dream which never realizes itself: it is withheld, by its noumenal character, from ever stepping into Time; and yet a reserved claim is retained on its behalf to some unintelligible share in the time-phenomena of character. Kant's theoretical and practical Reason constitute together a being of very peculiar duality: not so much an Ego with a double consciousness, as a single consciousness covering a double Ego; one, dealing with a world of phenomena, natural order, necessity: the other, with 'things in themselves,' with moral law, with free initiative, with eternal good: accessible by faculties for each, of knowing in the one, of willing in the other, but faculties curiously debarred from carrying their processes over from the empirical to the eternal; so that the one consciousness embraces unharmonized activities and irreconcilable beliefs. In no part of his philosophy is this characteristic more striking than in his scheme of partnership between necessity and free will.

So long as Kant is engaged in the mere negative task of preventing freedom and necessity from clashing, it is sufficient to throw a ring-fence round each, and insist on its never breaking bounds. If we had really two selves, it would be easy to stow away necessity in one and freedom in the other, and prevent them from coming to blows.

The man who contemplates himself as an intelligence, thereby plants himself in a different order of things and in totally dissimilar relations to the grounds of action, when he thinks of himself as an intelligence with will, consequently endowed with causality, and when he perceives himself as a phenomenon in the sensible world (as in fact he also is), and his causality subjected, in its outward determination, to natural laws[1].'   But, as he contemplates himself in both ways, the two systems have an observer above them, an Ego beyond the two selves, who will insist on unifying their relations ; who will not hear of the phenomenal world being all bespoken as the monopoly of necessity, from the frontier of which the free causality is turned back as a foreigner without a passport ; or who, if against rules entrance should be connived at, will want to know how the two heterogeneous powers, the spontaneity of Reason and the force of propension and habit, partition their determination of human action.   For, as the one goes in for only the rational, and the other for only the pleasant, and neither takes the least cognizance of the object of the other, it is difficult to see how the phenomenal field is to be divided between activities that have no common measure.   To pure Reason, desire, and to Desire, reason, is a power blank and dead ; they can neither negotiate nor fight together: what we do from desire is not owned by reason : and reason does not swerve from its course, however desire may change. Between two such selves no delimitation of their field can be made, any more than between two ambassadors ignorant of each other's language.   They need a superior that knows them both, and stands as plenipotentiary over them, and draws this line or that, by help of the judicial comparison impossible to either insulated energy.   And for that superior we need look no further than the self-conscious

---

[1] Grundlegung zur Metaph. d. Sitten. Ros. viii. p. 92.

person whom we have supposed as observer of the two
contrasted selves. With him, as the common subject of
them both, it rests to determine between them by an *arbitrium* of his own ; and this arbitrium is called *free*, not
because it is a single force with no resistance in the way,
but because it can start either this activity or that, irrespective of the forces of desire and the constraint of habit, and
all that belongs to the sentient department of what is
termed the 'nature-necessity.' And that this arbitrating
function under dual conditions, and not the mere unob-
structed spontaneity of lonely reason, constitutes what we
really mean by will, comes out in many an expression
unconsciously dropped by Kant himself : as when he says,
'The Will is a power *to choose that only* which reason,
independently of inclination, recognizes as necessary in
conduct, that is, as good[1].' In exercising this preference,
then, the will determines an alternative, one member of
which is in the Time world of sense, while the other is in
the eternal world of reason ; it must therefore have access
to both, and in setting aside the force of inclination must
directly apply its free causality to neutralize the necessary
causality of nature. Yet this is quite inconsistent with the
position that both causalities may and must co-exist without mutual interference.

Kant's attempt to save moral freedom without trenching
on natural necessity underwent an ingenious revision at
the hands of Schelling ; who presents it, however, as simply
a possible interpretation and completion of his predecessor's
doctrine. He accepts the position that the whole history of
the empirical character and each of its overt acts is subjected
to natural laws of sequence, and open to possible prediction :
so that from the agent, constituted as he is, nothing else
could be expected. But whence is that constitution of his?

---

[1] Grundlegung zur Metaph. d. Sitten. Ros. viii. p. 92.

Is that nothing but the necessitated product of his phenomenal life? Not so: he brought a nature with him into his
time-experience, a nature already definite from beyond
time, where nothing outward is, but only the free self-
determining grounds of Noumenal existence.   If that
essence of him were *given him* as a fabricated outfit ready-
made, if it were a foreign thing (*ein todtes Seyn*), all that
came of it in the way of action would follow by sheer
necessity, and responsibility would be out of the question.
It is no such *datum*, and is not *a thing*, but an activity: it
is his own essence, that is, of a self-active Ego that first
constitutes and then knows itself: for consciousness is
' Selbst*setzen*,' before it is ' Selbst*erkennen*.'   By substituting, as the centre of the noumenal Ego, this idea of inner
action for mere being and knowing, Schelling arrives at the
notion of unborn man as an original timeless *Will* (an *Ur-*
or *Grund-wollen*), which freely causes itself 'to be somewhat': and so fixes the initiation of the dependent empirical acts and character upon the prenatal self-determining
Ego.   The act which determines a man's life in time does
not belong to time, but to eternity; not that it is prior in
point of time, but that it is an eternal act, immanent in him
throughout, going back to the beginning of creation, and
itself an eternal beginning.   'Such as a man now shows
himself to be in act, that he was, and thus he did, from
eternity and already in the beginning of creation.'   His
action does not *come to be*, as he himself does not come to
be, but is by nature eternal.   The formative determining
act beyond time which settled the individual nature persists
through birth, because it shapes the type and constitution
of the bodily organization.   Though there can be no direct
consciousness of this timeless self-causation, yet indirectly
the moral experience is conformed to it; for, in spite of the
determinism of action, the good man has the peace of conscience which is possible only to free righteousness ; and

even a Judas Iscariot cannot, on the plea of an evil constitution of his nature, either escape remorse himself or accept
immunity from others, for guilt which he knows to be his
own. This murmur of responsibility is but the echo bespoken
before all time from the voice of duty in the eternal self,
and waked by impinging on the finite experience, and
bearing witness that the condition of free action is imperishable ; being the absolute nature of the man himself, the
essence of his essence, where action and being coalesce in
one.　If he is evil disposed, it is his own fault that he is
what he is; for by his own act *he has made himself.*　Let
him not fancy that he must have existed before he willed :
his existence consists in his Will, which has in it only what
is self-defined [1].

This culminating paradox of Schelling's affords a distinct
test of his theory as an interpretation of Kant : for in the
Metaphysic of Morals we meet with its direct contradictory
in the proposition that ' Man is *certainly not self-made* [2].'
His deviation from Kant is also apparent from his treating
the antithesis between the Noumenal and the Phenomenal
Ego as almost interchangeable with that between prenatal
and postnatal existence : so that he calls his doctrine a kind
of predestination ; only, refrains from allowing it that name
because *destination* implies a fatalized lot, that is, imposed
by external power ; whereas the pre-existing causality
which he wishes to indicate is within the essence of the
Ego itself.　But the name *Prädeterminismus*, which was
accordingly selected for the theory, equally marks the
tendency to divide the free from the necessary causality by
the date of birth ; and to refer the whole empirical series

---

[1] Philosophische Untersuchungen über das Wesen der menschlichen Freiheit und die damit zusammenhängenden Gegenstände.
Schelling's sämmtliche Werke, Stuttgart, 1860, Band VII. 383–389.

[2] 'Da er doch sich selbst nicht gleichsam schafft.' Grundlegung,
p. 85.

contained within the character to an act of will prior to the life in time. Kant's transcendental subject with its causality is certainly not separated from the empirical by any such chronological limit: all our acts of will spring from the supersensible rational essence as their ground, while, in their phenomenal aspect, they appear in the successive order of nature. The initiative which determines our character is not spent before we are born, and transmitted as a factor into experience ; but remains an immanent open possibility throughout.

Far from relieving Kant's problem of any difficulty, this Predeterminism introduces new contradictions. Professing to save its 'freedom' by carrying it off into the Timeless antechamber of creation, where no phenomena are, it nevertheless sets the noumenal Ego to perform there *an act* (*Handlung*) of self-determination,—nay, act upon act,— whereby it 'makes itself.' An act, it is not denied, is an initiation or beginning to be, that is, a phenomenon ; and to affirm such a thing is to quit the shelter of the timeless world. A retreat back into it is vainly attempted by calling the act 'eternal' and simply identical with the acting being, a mere '*contradictio in adjecto.*' For what possible meaning can be attached to an act which does not happen, a beginning which is not in time, a determinant which posits nothing new, a ' making ' where all is just as it was before ?

Nor is the advantage which Schelling hoped to secure by converting the essence (*Wesen*) of the noumenal Ego from Being (*todtes Seyn*) into Act (*Grundwollen*) gained, but at the cost of another contradiction. The 'Absolute act' is called 'free,' because it is purely from *out of the essence.* Yet it is this absolute act, this ' Urwollen,' that '*makes itself something,*' and so *constitutes* the essence. The two propositions are irreconcilable. If the first be true, the essence is given *a priori*, and the act it delivers is necessary and nothing else. If the second be true, the Ego enjoys the peculiar privilege of acting before it exists. We are thrown upon the former as the only conceivable branch of the alternative: then we find that the pre-existent essence of the Self, brought with us into this life, leaves as little room for human responsibility as the Divine decrees, and that predestination is not yet deposed.

It is instructive to notice the transformation given to the leading terms of this problem by Schopenhauer, in review-ing the foregoing doctrines of his predecessors. He is able to expound his rigorous determinism without discarding any of the antitheses on which they have relied for saving the conditions of moral accountability. *Ding-an-sich* and the *Erscheinung*, the noumenal and the empirical Self, Will-causality and *nexus naturae*, freedom and necessity, all reappear, and play accurately-distinguished parts in a theory strongly contrasted with theirs. All these phrases are with him but various expressions of the two factors of moral action which alone are there to be expressed, viz. the actually formed character, and the motives which at present appeal to it: the former is the inner Self, regarded as now the permanent datum of each rising problem: the latter, the outward influences which the crisis combines. The sense of responsibility, wakened even in the necessarian by the commission of wrong action, merely lays the fault at the right door, as between these two, and owns that he himself is the doer of the deed: that is, that the motives need not have occasioned it, had his character only been different; and it is a sorrowful surprise to him to find, by unmistakeable fact, that he is what he is. It is the experience of his fall under the motives administered, that first reveals to him the cast of his 'empirical' or realized 'character': and by the 'Noumenal self' nothing more is to be understood than the character prior to the application of this practical test: its *a priority* is simply its existence in the undisclosed condition. Or, if we push the abstraction further, and undress the conception till we have laid *all* experience aside, the *Ding-an-sich* thus reached becomes the individual type of susceptibility to motives, which the agent brings into the world at birth,— his humanity with its idiosyncracies of genius and temperament. This is his native constitution, the distinctive essence of the man, the thing that he *is*, which will come out in what he *does*,—his *Esse* which is prior to his *Operari*. Now, among the terms thus defined, which is it, if any, that rightly claims the predicate *free*; and which, the predicate *necessary?* The former we have seen assigned, by both Kant and Schelling, to the causal *activity*, the essential self, as passing into unchallenged expression; that activity being so emphasized by Schelling as to devour the *esse* and be alone. And the latter they have charged upon any pre-existing *datum* or *nature* of the Ego behind the initiatory acts of Will: and it was to avoid such 'predestiny' that Schelling insisted on planting Will before all. Schopenhauer disapproves and inverts this rule: he says:

'The operation of our freedom we must no longer seek, as the common view would have us, in our particular actions, but in the whole existence and essence of the man himself, which must be regarded as his free doing (*That*), which presents itself in a plurality and variety of actions only in relation to our modes of cognition or conditions of time, space, and causality: though these actions, in virtue of the original unity of the subject coming up in them all, must have exactly the same character, and hence appear strictly necessitated by the motives which elicit and determine them in each individual case. Hence, for the world of experience, the rule *operari sequitur esse* holds without exception. Each thing operates according to its constitution, and the effect resulting from causes reports its constitution. Every man acts according to what he is; and the action necessary in conformity with this, at the time being, is

determined by the motives alone. And so, the *freedom*
which is not to be found in the *Operari* must lie in the *Esse*.
It has been a fundamental error, a ὕστερον πρότερον, of every
age, to assign necessity to the *Esse* and freedom to the
Operari. On the contrary, in the *Esse* alone does the
freedom lie: and out of it and the motives the *Operari*
follows of necessity; and by what we *do* we know what we
are [1].

If freedom is predicable of existence only and not of
action, it is curious that Schopenhauer should find no
better means of claiming it for a man's 'whole existence'
than by calling that existence 'his *free doing*' (*seine freie
That*). His slip into such a phrase might have convinced
him that his new rule had evicted freedom from its only
possible abode, and left it to perish as a homeless exile.
As a predicate of *existence* freedom has absolutely no
meaning, unless and until the existence *acts*: and then,
he tells us, it is excluded by *necessity*. The word names
an attribute of *movement* or *change*, apart from which it
falls dead without remains. Suppose even that a thing
was declared *free to be* this or that: this would imply that
as yet it was neither, and therefore that its liberty was
limited to *becoming* one or the other: and that is *action*.
Hence, freedom is predicable only of a *Cause*, considered
as the activity whence all change or becoming can arise.
Yet Schopenhauer insists that causality is identical with
necessity. Is it urged that with the *esse*, as the seat of
freedom, he associates the *essentia* (*Wesen*), and so perhaps
may only mean, with Kant, that the essence spontaneously
comes out in pure expression? If we take him so (as
sometimes we may), still, in coming out, the essence *acts*,
and it is precisely that *agency* that is free. Besides, this
very outcoming of the essential character is coupled, in the

---

[1] Ueber die Freiheit des Menschlichen Willens, pp. 95, 96.

foregoing passage, with the motives, as exercising *necessary* causation. And this is the only consistent view : for, in the process of mere evolution out of an essence, there is no more variation of possibility, than in the same evolution compounded with a successionary *nexus naturae*. Monistic spontaneity, and dualistic causality without alternative, are alike the negation of freedom. Schopenhauer's allocation of freedom and necessity is only a misstatement of the position insisted on in a former chapter, that by a law of thought, a *Will* is prior to a *Must* ; combined with another, that a cause has to *exist* before it *operates*. This Cause alone can be free : the effect is necessary. It is not however in the *esse* of the cause, but in its *velle*, that the freedom lies, to carry the *operari* to determinate necessity.

From this review it will be evident that freedom, in the sense of option, and will, as the power of deciding an alternative, have no place in the doctrines of the German Schools. And so long as will is taken as single-pathed spontaneity, and freedom as its immunity from check, it matters not whether they be proved to exist, or disproved : determinism is assumed, and is maintained in possession of the field, and the conditions of moral responsibility are absent. An agent who cannot, at will, determine himself to either branch of an alternative, may be an *automaton spirituale*, but not a competent subject of a law of duty. A philosophy which disallows the possibility of such an agent may, with Kant, emphasize, as a human fact, the idea and the imperative feeling of moral law, and show how to evolve from it, in its applied form, a character of Stoical rigour and elevation ; but can never deliver it from the imputation of illusion. The unconditional mandate of the Right postulates, not the freedom of spontaneity, but the freedom of choice. Schopenhauer saw this clearly enough ; and, though treating the notion of a *liberum arbitrium indifferentiae* with the usual metaphysical ex-

communication as 'inconceivable,' pronounces it 'the only
clearly defined, solid, and decisive ground on which to
stake what is called the freedom of the will: so that you
cannot quit it without lapsing into hazy, vacillating ex-
planations, behind which shuffling half-thought seeks
shelter [1].' The form of the *terminus technicus* here used
to denote the optional power of the Will is, in part,
answerable for the ban under which the conception itself
has been put: for the word *indifferentiae* stipulates that the
object presented for choice shall be indistinguishably related to the chooser, or, as it is said, recommended by
motives in exact equipoise: in which case preference
would have to be awarded without any ground of preference. To no such doctrine is the advocate of free will
committed: if he were, he would be admitting what it is
his characteristic to deny, that 'motives' are 'forces'
having a common measure, and dominating the mind by
quantitative weight. It is not between equal incitements,
but between equal possibilities, that the alternative lies:
and the question for the moral agent is, whether he will
give himself over to his receptivity, or seize the initiative
by his activity. Between these two there can be no *in-
differentia*, except that both are possible; and of possible
selection only by a Subject knowing the law for their comparison, and invested with the Will for their determination.
Is even this deemed 'inconceivable'? Of course, it is inconceivable: to have it otherwise, you would have to get
it spread out before you as an objective process within
your psychological microscope; and into that position
nothing can come except what belongs to your receptive
self-consciousness: whereas here you stand behind all that,
at the well-head and native moment of intelligent and
causal activity, where knowing and being are still one.

---

[1] Uber die Freiheit des Menschlichen Willens, p. 9.

However far back you may carry your self-analysis and scrutiny, you come at last to what you can no more get to see, than you can hide yourself in your own shadow. The whole illusion of Necessity springs from the attempt to fling out, for contemplation in the field of nature, the creative new beginnings centred in personal Subjects that transcend it.

§ 6. *Ethics of Necessity and Free Will.*

The last test to which we must submit the claims of the opposing doctrines of volition is their relative agreement with the fundamental conditions of the moral life. The application of this test is rendered difficult by the extreme statements on either side : on the one hand it is contended, sometimes even by its own advocates, that determinism abolishes all moral, as distinguished from natural, differences ; and on the other, Professor Sidgwick maintains that an ethical system may be wrought out without any reference to the topic of this controversy, and need not be perceptibly affected by the author's view of it. Both these opinions appear to me to need considerable qualification.

The dictum, that volition is invariably determined by the strongest motive, is usually accompanied by the assumption that the only motive is prospective pleasure or pain. Hence we are accustomed to identify the necessarian with the egoist, and to charge him with the consequences of a rule of life founded wholly upon self-interest. There is nothing, however, in his determinism, which obliges him to adopt this theory of human nature. He may, without inconsistency, recognise among its springs of action affections that are not self-regarding ; compassion and attachment to others ; zeal for self-perfection ; even devotion to right. These disinterested impulses he may find assembled in the mind ; and may regard the will as always serving the most intense for the time being : nor is he called upon to feel

any surprise, when he meets with self-forgetful heroism, and
unflinching tenacity of duty.   All that he is concerned to
maintain is, that, be the motive passions that are implanted
in us few or many, that which turns up the hottest will
have its way.   His difficulty will begin when, passing beyond this supposed psychological fact, he tries to make a
relative estimate of these hap-hazard impulses, and find for
them an ethical principle of order ; to say when and why
the altruistic should have place rather than the egoistic, or
the sense of right than both.   If they are not to be left
upon a level, any one being legitimate that can get a footing, they must be reducible to some scale.   Say that there
is nothing worth having but pleasure, and you set up an
intelligible eudæmonist scale ; with the result, however, of
erasing the altruistic affections and sense of right, except
as instruments of egoism.   Say that, besides this, there is a
second scale, of higher and lower in some other quality;
and you will find it impossible to name that quality without assuming an authority over the will other than the
sway of the 'strongest motive' ; and no less so, to settle
terms of adjustment between the eudæmonist and the
qualitative scales, and define what gain in the one is
equivalent to each loss on the other.   From this difficulty
it results that, although, in theory, the doctrine of necessity
may be held in conjunction with *any* ideal of character, in
fact it is found in close combination with the *utilitarian* ;
happiness being treated as the sole possible end of action
to each, i.e. *his own* happiness ; whence it would seem to
follow, that other people's is not and cannot be his end ;
whereas the very opposite inference is drawn, viz. that,
since my neighbour's happiness is worth as much to him
as mine is to me, I must take no less account of his than
of my own.   By this enormous leap of false inference,
egoism is transformed into a 'greatest happiness system' ;
and, under Epicurean disguise, a postulate of Duty sur-

reptitiously enters, totally at variance with the alleged necessary sway of personal pleasure and pain. Supposing therefore the determinist to start with the recognition, in our nature, of several original impulses, benevolent as well as selfish, I do not see how he can ever reduce these heterogeneous principles to a common standard of motive strength other than the eudæmonist;—how therefore he can properly avoid having his ethical system, so far as it is consistent, shaped by his determinist philosophy.

Further, if the moral distinction of actions is resolved into the sentient, and the happiest are *ipso facto* the best, what we do is approved by others because they are benefited by it: they praise it, in order to encourage its repetition: a social sentiment crowns it with favour; and the satisfaction with which we ourselves come to regard it is but the reflection of this foreign applause. This theory,— that self-judgment is a copy of the verdicts pronounced by others, that the sentiments of conscience are an enforced adoption of the public view of interests in place of our own,—is inseparable from the eudæmonist assumption. We have seen reason, however, to discard it, as quite at variance with our moral experience; and to adopt the reverse order of deduction, as the prime characteristic of all coherent ethical doctrine. Whatever therefore pledges determinism to this assumption gives a false direction, *ab initio*, to its moral speculations ;—a direction, at all events, entirely opposite to that which would commend itself to a libertarian.

Two doctrines which give quite a different account of the origin of moral obligation and the nature of its authority, can hardly be expected to be identical in their practical effects; and a slight examination will suffice to reduce their alleged ethical equality within very narrow limits. Let us consider what room is left under each for the several elements of the moral life.

Under a determinist constitution of things, full scope is left for the right education of habits, internal as well as external ; nor need there be anything special in the discipline resorted to for forming them. It will consist in a systematic administration of influential motives to counteract deflecting temptations and sustain the flagging energy of pre-formed purpose. A necessarian school, not less than any other, will quicken industry by the prize and the rod, by the emulation of the class and the word of public praise or rebuke ; and as the scholar's culture proceeds, new leverage is gained for lifting him from lower levels, in his growing literary feeling and deepening thirst for knowledge. His will can be moulded, by fitting pressures, to take the form, intellectually, of accomplishment and art, and ethically, of self-restraint and sympathy. And what is true of private training is true not less of public polity : so long as men are amenable to ' motives,' civil society wields its essential powers ; Law, armed with due sanctions, will speak not without effect ; and patriotic services will be commanded by the assurance of social sympathy, honours and rewards. If it is said that, on this theory, we shall be punishing the criminal for what he cannot help, the answer is ready, 'We punish him *in order that he may help it* ; and in order that others too, under like temptation, may rightly reckon both sides of the account. That we treat him as responsible means simply this,—that we give him fair notice of our intention to make him smart for any mischief he may do.'

Regarded in this light, as an organisation of motives for the formation and control of character and the protection of social life, Education, the penal code, and the unwritten law of honour and dishonour, may certainly have a place at least as indispensable in a determinist world as elsewhere. Nor will their form be very materially different. It is in their inward meaning and interpretation that the peculiarity will be found: they are computed purely by a prospective calculus, measuring what they are likely to do; and lose the element of retrospective justice, awarding its due to what has been done. They are prudential, remedial, disciplinary; applied to the minds of men, as medicine to their weak or ailing bodies, not so much relying on internal support as directed to overcome internal resistance. In short, the moral evil, to the prevention or cure of which they address themselves, is undistinguished in this theory from natural, provided both are probably remediable; they assert, as Professor Tyndall says, 'the right of society to protect itself against aggressive and injurious forces, whether they be bond or free, forces of nature or forces of man[1].' They are therefore no more in need of any inspiration of moral sentiment than the physician's prescription or the mole-catcher's trap, or any other provision for warding off the troubles of life. The treatment of mankind which they establish is perfectly analogous to the skill of the beast-tamer, who, by adroit use of the nose-ring and the lash, the threatening or the coaxing voice, knows how to break in the wild animal's humour and reduce it to docility. The highest institutions of society are thus but an engine of management, playing upon the weaknesses of the creatures ruled, and so applied by its cooler and more diplomatic heads as to produce surprising results of civilization in the least promising subjects,—to make the bear dance and the raven sing, and, by anodynes to all conflicting passions, cage up the most opposite natures into one 'happy family.'

Now, if this disciplinary theory supplies an adequate rationale of written and unwritten law, it remains untouched when we step across from the determinist to the freewill territory; for here also the influence of motives, though not allowed to usurp an exclusive place, is ad-

---

[1] Science of Man, Fortnightly Review, Nov. 1, 1877, p. 612.

mitted and claimed as an object of careful estimate. But the mode of estimating them is materially affected by two additional beliefs or conceptions which the necessarian has cancelled as illusions ; and in the ethical bearing of these points of difference lies the crisis of the whole controversy. The first of them we find in the consciousness of the moral agent himself ; the second, in that of the outward observer.

Take the child or the natural man, to whom the secret has not yet been told that he cannot help being what he is and doing what he does ; and from every considerable struggle of temptation you see him emerge, if victor, with a look of heroic joy, if vanquished, with the blush of insufferable shame. He is not merely happy or distressed, as the winner or loser of some recognised advantage, but conscious of *good or ill desert*, at peace with himself from self-approval or cast down in self-contempt. If you give him your sympathy, and greet him with a ' Well done ! ', he can accept it as fairly *earned* ; if, in the other case, you visit him with reproach and alienation, you do but treat him as he treats himself, and act out his own remorse. There is an internal and self-administered justice which is beforehand with you, which expects you to be its minister, and already invests you with judicial power. The sentence of this inward justice must, it is evident, be retrospective, pronounced upon what has been done in the past, not with a view to what is to be got out of the future ; for the conscious offender cannot concoct a dose of anger in his heart against himself, in order to alter the balance of his motives another time ; he is putting himself, not under regimen, but under retribution. In the view which he thus takes of himself, is one deviation from the determinist theory of ethical treatment.

The other is found in the corresponding view of his conduct taken by the spectators. They look upon it, if it be heroically right, not with judicious applause intended

to patronise and reproduce its benefits; but with an enthusiasm of admiration and reverence, obviously directed
on the living agent as he is and the thing that he has
done. Or, if it is a cruel crime that startles their attention, they meet it with a burst of moral indignation, certainly not measured out as a medicine for cure or a device
for prevention, but expressing a horror of perpetrated
wrong inconsistent with impunity in the present. They
adopt, that is, and re-echo the agent's own conviction of
his inward merit or demerit: they hold him to be the
author of his own conquests, and responsible for his own
defeats. Their feeling is out of all proportion to any
service rendered or any mischief done, and is kindled, not
by the extrinsic effects of his action, but by the intrinsic
quality of character which it expresses. If, with Tyndall,
we put the wickedness of men in the same category with
the devastations of nature, moral abhorrence would be
impossible; and if noble minds rose upon us as necessarily
as lengthening summer-days, we might indeed 'rejoice in
their light'; but could not be penetrated by them with
the flash of a new self-knowledge, and carried away by an
uplifting veneration. These sentiments, which would be
absurd towards an implement, a machine, a transmuter of
heat, a magnetic engine, a conductor of electricity, are
however the great powers of character, the supreme direc-
tors of life; and education which fails to appeal to them,
legislation which does not assume them, will raise up no
strength and grace in the family, and produce nothing
stable and magnanimous in the state. If the efficacy of
punishment lay only in the deterring power of pain, Draco
would be the prince of legislators; and the rule would
hold good, that in proportion as the temptation to an
offence increases, must you countervail it by added severity
of treatment. Why do these methods notoriously fail?
Because they are in defiance of the sentiments of natural

justice; and, instead of speaking the thought of the inward
conscience and repeating its anger and its pity, super-
ciliously deny all good or ill desert, and pedantically
pursue their calculus of discipline. The motive force of
Law and opinion is to be sought, not in its mere command
over sentient pleasures and pains, but in its correspondence
with the retributory awards of the common moral sense;
and wherever, from disbelief in justice and the substitution
of management, this correspondence is disregarded, it may
be possible to organise some sort of human menagerie, but
not a civilised society great among historical States.

The language of Ethics, then, when translated into
necessarian formulas, parts with all conceptions distinctly
moral, and becomes simply descriptive of phenomena in
natural history. It tells us what has been, what is, what
probably will be; but not (unless in an altered sense)
what *ought to be*. Responsibility, obligation, merit, guilt,
remorse, forgiveness, justice, drop from its vocabulary, or
remain there only to mislead. We may well excuse the
modern determinist's reluctance to admit this incontestable
fact, and his efforts to disguise the loss of significance from
terms consecrated by the experience of mankind. That it
is no fancy, no trumped-up charge of his opponents, I will
endeavour to show by placing side by side two passages,
dealing with this aspect of the question, one by an eminent
assailant of the doctrine of necessity, the other by a no
less eminent upholder of it; on comparing which we shall
find that nothing is urged in the attack which is not
accepted in the defence, and that no logical consequence
which we have deduced is repudiated by either. The first
passage runs thus:

'Take liberty away, and you utterly subvert human
nature and efface every vestige of order in society. If
men are not free in the good and evil which they do, good
is no longer good, or evil, evil. If an inevitable and in-

vincible necessity makes us will what we will, our will is
no more responsible for its volition than the spring of
a watch is responsible for its movement : in this case it is
absurd to blame the will, which wills only in so far as
another cause distinct from it makes it will.   By rights,
you must go back to this cause, as I go back to the hand
which wields a stick, instead of stopping at the stick which
strikes me only as this hand impels it.   Again, take liberty
away, and you leave on the earth no vice, no virtue, no
merit ; rewards are absurd, and punishments unjust ; every
one does as he should, because he acts conformably with
necessity ; he has no duty to avoid the inevitable or to
conquer the unconquerable.   All is in order ; for the only
order is that all yields to necessity.   The fall of liberty
brings down with it all order and police, confounds vice
and virtue, legitimates every prodigy of infamy, extin-
guishes all shame and all remorse, and hopelessly mars
the whole human race.   A doctrine so monstrous is fitter
to be punished by the magistrate than examined in the
schools.'

This is a stern indictment ; and we naturally expect an
indignant disclaimer in reply.   Let us hear what the
opposite advocate says :

'Here I mean, if I can, to exchange the tone of the
preacher for that of the philosopher.   Look at it closely,
and you will find that the word Freedom is a word without
meaning ; that there neither are, nor can be, free beings ;
that we are but shaped into conformity with the common
order, with our organisation, our education, and the chain
of events.   These dispose of us irresistibly.   We can no
more conceive of a being acting without motive than of a
balance-beam without a weight ; and the motive is always
something external and foreign to us, fastened upon us by
some natural cause other than ourselves.   An illusion is
put upon us by the prodigious variety of our actions,

together with the connate habit of confounding the voluntary and the free. We have so often received, so often
given, praise and blame, as to have passed into a fixed idea
that we and others will and act freely. But if there is no
freedom, there is no action deserving praise or blame;
there is neither vice nor virtue; nothing that should be
rewarded or punished. What is it then that constitutes
the distinction among men? ill-doing and good. The ill-
doer must be destroyed, not punished; the doing of good
is luck, not virtue. But though the good or evil doer is
not free, man is nevertheless a being that you can modify;
and hence it is that you must destroy the evil-doer before
the public gaze. Hence also the good effect of example,
of intercourse, of education, of pleasure and pain, of splendour and poverty. And hence a kind of philosophy full of
pity, strongly attached to the good, yet no more provoked
against the wicked than against the whirlwind that fills our
eyes with dust. In strictness, there is but one kind of
causes, viz. physical causes; but one kind of necessity, the
same for all beings, whatever distinction, real or unreal, we
may set up among them. This it is that reconciles me to
mankind; that makes me exhort you to philanthropy.
Adopt these principles, if you find them good, or show me
that they are bad. They will reconcile you also with others
and with yourself; you will be neither pleased nor displeased
with yourself for being what you are. Upbraid others for
nothing, and repent of nothing: these are the first steps
to wisdom. Besides this, all is prejudice and false philosophy.'

Here, in the 'tone of the philosopher,' we have the very
same doctrine commended which before was denounced as
fit only to be punished by the magistrate; and, what is
curious, commended for the very same qualities for which
previously it had been denounced. Is it perhaps that I
have selected extreme representatives of the opposite sides,

the one vehement in invective against the rival opinion, the
other in laudation of his own, and neither able to appreciate
the position of the other? The explanation is natural, but
unfounded ; for, to complete the oddity of the contrast,
both passages come from the same hand, and express the
two states of mind which, at no long interval, successively
characterised *Diderot*[1]. I quote them, in order to show
that the modern disposition to acquit the doctrine of
Necessity of all ethical consequences receives no support
from its history in the last century ; when both the attack
and the defence turned in a great measure on the allegation
common to both,—only revolting to the one and acceptable
to the other,—that it abolished 'vice and virtue,' and threw
contempt on the sentiment of duty, and the language of
praise and blame. So frankly was this admitted, even by
those who deemed the admission morally dangerous, that
they sometimes prided themselves on having wrested from
Nature a secret which the Author of Nature had not
intended mankind in general to know : he had put them
under Necessity ; but, for their good, he had practised a
benevolent fraud, and implanted in them an illusory consciousness of freedom. In a letter to Madame d'Épinay
the Abbé Galiani says, ' A letter is always acceptable, were
it only to hear that people are still disputing about the
liberty of Man, and that there is a M. de Valmire[2] who is

---

[1] The first is from his article Liberté in the Encyclopédie ; the
second, from a letter to Baron Grimm of 1756 : Œuvres de Diderot,
Paris, 1818, tom. iii. p. 127, and iv. p. 716. The exact date of the first
I cannot fix ; the publication of the Encyclopédie extended from 1741
to 1772.

[2] A *nom de plume*, assumed by M. Sissous of Troyes, author of a
book entitled *Dieu et l'homme*, Amsterdam, 1771 ; respecting which
Voltaire, who had two years before published his *Dieu et les hommes*,
said in a letter to the author, Dec. 27, 1771, ' I find in it much depth
and subtlety of thought. By the penetration of your mind you have
been able to resolve problems above the reach of most of our reasoners,
and even of people of sense.' (Note to the passage in the *Lettres*,
ed. 1882.)

not M. de Voltaire.   Would you know my opinion on this
question?   The conviction of his freedom constitutes the
essence of man : he might even be defined ' *an animal that
believes himself free,*' and the definition would be complete.
Why does M. de Valmire himself tell us we are not free?
In order that we may believe him about it.   Then he
believes other men free and able to determine themselves
to believe him.   It is impossible for man to forget for a
single instant and relinquish the conviction he has of being
free : this is the first point.   The second is the question,
whether a conviction of freedom is the same thing as being
actually free?   I answer, it is not the same thing, but produces absolutely the same effects in morals.   Man is free,
then, because he is inwardly convinced that he is so, and
that is tantamount to freedom.   Here then is an explanation of the mechanism of the universe, clear as water from
the rock.   If there were a single free being in the universe,
there would no longer be any God ; no longer, links connecting being with being ; the universe would fall into disorder.   And if, in the essence of man, the inward conviction
were not fixed that he is free, human morals would never
again go as they ought.   The conviction of freedom is all that
is wanted to establish a conscience, remorse, justice, rewards
and punishments ; it answers every purpose.   Here you
have the world explained in a couple of words[1].'

If these frank utterances exhibit the ethics of Determinism, the doctrine, it is plain, is as little compatible with
veracity in God as with Duty in man ; and simply excludes all righteousness from the universe ; and the moral
faith and nobleness of the necessarian becomes an intellectual inconsequence.

[1] Correspondance inédite de l'Abbé Ferdinand Galiani, Conseiller
du Roi de Naples, avec Mme d'Épinay, le Baron d'Holbach, le Baron
de Grimm, et autres personnages célèbres du XVIIIe siècle, 2 tomes,
Paris, 1818, tome i. pp. 339, 340.   In the enlarged edition (*Lettres*),
Paris, 1882, tome i. pp. 300, 301.

With these repulsive oracles of the eighteenth century philosophy it may be interesting to compare, in conclusion, the attempt of two living representatives of physical science to save the moral responsibility of man without sacrificing the universal sovereignty of God. 'Assuming the existence of a Deity who is the creator and upholder of all things,' (say Professors Stewart and Tait), 'we further look upon the laws of the universe as those laws according to which the beings in the universe are conditioned by the Governor thereof, as regards time, place, and sensation.

Nothing whatever lies, or can even be conceived to lie, outside of this sovereign and paramount influence. There is no impression made upon the bodily senses,—no thought or other mental operation,—which does not take place in conformity with this expression of the will of God.

If it be asked how we can imagine any free will or moral responsibility to exist consistently with this doctrine, we may reply that we cannot tell in virtue of what peculiar constitution of things the sovereignty of God is consistent with our moral responsibility, nor can we even conceive the possibility of our obtaining the knowledge required to reply to this question. But it may, we think, be shown that the doctrine of the sovereign power of God, as above defined, is not inconsistent with moral responsibility. For, in the statement made, three things are spoken of. *In the first place*, there is God, the source of power : *secondly*, there are the conditions which he imposes ; and *thirdly*, there is the Ego, the being who is thus conditioned. Now, the laws of thought absolutely forbid our dismissing this Ego. It may possibly be argued that we consist of a bundle of sensations bound together, just as a bundle of threads are, by something which is no less a sensation, viz. the impression that we have an individual existence : to which we would reply that, even if this be granted, we must submit to impressions from which there is no escape.

Now, it appears to us that we cannot possibly have any impression more deeply seated or more impossible to up-root than this,—that we ourselves exist: it is something which we continually carry about with us, even into the grotesque regions of thought where all individuality is denied. It is into these regions that the materialists invite us to accompany them in order to perform, or rather to delude ourselves with the idea that we have performed, this singularly unhappy despatch! But, just as we cannot conceive of a man devouring himself, so neither can we conceive of his getting rid of his own individuality by any legitimate process of thought. Can we conceive of consciousness without a being who is conscious? or of sensation, without a being who feels? We may perhaps take it for granted that the statements we have now made, acknowledging at once a sovereign power and our own responsibility, will commend themselves to a large body of thinkers who will virtually agree with our conclusions [1].'

[1] The Unseen Universe, Introduction, pp. 14–16, 4th ed.

BOOK IV.

THE LIFE TO COME.

IT is by a somewhat abrupt transition, I am well aware, that I now pass from the grounds of Theism to the inquiry, whether man has any life in prospect beyond his present term of years. Were not my purpose constructive and practical, rather than critically systematic, I should follow up the statement of the true and permanent sources of religion by a review of others, no longer operative with us, which have played a considerable part in stages of civilization remote from ours ; should trace the working of these several principles in the religious grouping and history of mankind ; and try to find the natural order of their succession and of human development under their influence. I should further give some account of the chief systems of religious philosophy which have engaged the attention of modern times, and characterize the theodicies of Spinoza, Leibniz, Schleiermacher, Hegel. And, after adequate notice of such sources and schemes as I cannot accept, I should be glad, in returning to the positions already gained, to find the living links which connect them with our historical religion, and to determine the relation between the schools of philosophy and the schools of the prophets. But these several subjects,— of comparative theology, of modern philosophies of religion, of biblical literature and ecclesiastical life,—though in various contact with the topics already discussed, are too large for subsidiary and episodical treatment. And by leaving them to their rights of separate and independent study, no serious disadvantage will be incurred in dealing with the one remaining question which seems to press most upon natural feeling for a reasonable answer.

It is not at first easy to say, why we regard the faith in a life beyond death as a part of our *Religion.* Other expectations of a future similarly possible, yet incalculable,—of old age for the now young, of a purer literature and a wiser civilization for Europe in the centuries to come,—we do not thus consecrate, but place them on the secular side of our existence, though they too are out of sight and definite knowledge, and touched with lights of tender hope and high enthusiasm. I believe the reason is, that that ulterior life, as an object of thought, is *transcendental*, like God ; apprehended by us neither in the immediate consciousness by which we know ourselves, nor in the sensuous perception by which we know the world ; but in virtue of an intuitive third idea, of a Divine universal power which relates and unites them both. Were that life present to our experience, or did we witness it in others, it would pass into our biography or the scenery of our being, and occupy the level of familiar fact : its consecration is due to its being lifted *beyond experience*, withdrawn from the field of *vision*, and yet more real than either, because secured in the eternal ground of both. Not till we read the *causality behind phenomena*, does the universe look at us with a grandeur that is divine : not till we find our Duty invested with a supernatural light, does it subdue us with its sanctity : it is the embrace of the All-comprehending God in his energy and his perfection, which transforms each into a religious object : and it is the same transition of conception, from the empirical which is ours to the transcendent which is His, that brings the Future Life under the cognizance of religion. With death, the Self is sealed, and the personal record becomes a blank to the survivors ; the interchange also with the outward world, the play of action and passion, sinks to silence : there remains the third relation, into which all is now concentrated, viz. to Him in whom both the Self and the world have their separate being and their reciprocal life. It is on these lines of thought, I am persuaded, and by no means in the mere ' perception of the Infinite,' (and least of all when this is confounded with the Indefinite), that we must seek for the essence of Religion. It is not a quantitative affair, constituted by any boundlessness of space, time, and number ; and did these contain nothing but their own magnitudes, neither the heavens nor the ages would suggest anything divine ; and when tribes of men have worshipped the vault that holds sun and stars, or the Eternal Past, it has been as the abode of *creative Mind and living Power*, the wonder of which the immensity only serves to enhance. And so, it is not the idea of passing into ' Eternity,' but that of entering upon more intimate Divine relations, that consecrates the faith in a future life. It is difficult to estimate the misleading effect of these mathematical conceptions, when taken as the source or type of human religions.

The question of a Life to come centres in the interpretation of Death, as affecting the individual. To find its true significance, we must examine it in three points of view : physiological, metaphysical, and moral ; and gather our conclusions from a conspectus of all these relations.

CHAPTER I.

Death in its Physiological Aspect.

To the naturalist, Death presents itself simply, in antithesis to birth, as the opposite terminus in the history of an individual organism, necessarily incident to it as a product which, having arisen, cannot always stay, but only linger through an ascending and declining cycle of changes. At the beginning, he finds the constituents of the organism and the forces which build it up, to be not new creations: they are in the field around, and do but gather themselves together to work at a fresh centre, and, by special intensities, set up a focus of temporary detachment from the environment of the world. And at the end, he notices that these same constituents and forces do but lapse back from their concentration into the general storehouse whence they came, and, abandoning one completed task, disperse on commission for many another. He sees that the story is continuous, and that the growth and decline are out of and into the seamless tissue of nature, an episode in Time's enduring record: but the episode he says, is over: the tale is told: the individuality is gone; and leaves its place empty as before it came. He looks on the evanescence of each life as the condition and mode of the permanence of all.

This impression, that every separate being is but a transient ripple on a universal deep, gains strength from the wide sweep of the law of mortality. Were it a human fact only, it might perhaps admit of more constructions than one, and its darkness be made to recoil before the brilliant powers it threatened to engulf. But it embraces no less all other races of animals, and even all plants; and as no one in our time will claim an unseen survivorship for these, it follows that either we must relinquish it for man also; or else affirm that death, in spite of its similar aspect and contents, is not one and the same event to all, but under apparent identity conceals a difference truly infinite. This second side of the alternative it is impossible for the naturalist, as such, to adopt. The fundamental conception of his science so defines the relation of *organs* and *functions* as to make the latter *the act which the former has to do*: to require therefore the organ as antecedent to the function as consequent; so that, when the organ is spoiled and gone, the living function cannot remain. If this conception is to pass unquestioned, and if, under the word 'function' as applied to man, is to be included the whole of his thought, affection, and character, there is no room even to raise the question whether he has anything to expect beyond the day of his death. But the postulates of the special sciences at any given time have no authority in philosophy: they are merely relative to a particular group of phenomena: they are made up of abstractions liable to prove artificial and deceptive; and they often involve convenient, but provisional assumptions, which, after serving to push forward the lines of orderly survey, give way of themselves as the horizon enlarges. There will be no want then of the deference due to our naturalist, if we look a little closely into the physical principles on which he proceeds.

Function, he truly says, is that which an organ characteristically does; and by watching it as it works, by observation direct or indirect, its action can be traced from step to step. The stomach with its appendages, for instance, is found to be a chemical chamber for reducing the food and delivering its chyle, at a proper temperature, into the returning blood : pumped by the pulmonary heart into the lungs, the current wins its needful oxygen from the air, and rids itself in the lungs of superfluous carbon and water, and, after this combustion, returns to the remaining heart, ready for distribution throughout the body, as the bearer of nutriment and heat. Every part of this process involves a series of mechanical movements, controlling the flow of the fluids, and changing the doses of air. The muscles which perform this work are set to it by nerves reaching them from the spinal cord, one from the organ to ask for help, the other from the cord to give it ; or, where the action is to be voluntary, the headquarters are transferred to the brain. Though, in the reflex case, we can no longer perceptibly trace the successive stages of change, as in the history of the food and blood, yet we can follow it with the 'scientific imagination'; because the galvanic current, sent through the same nerves, even after death, will imitate the whole process. We know therefore that we are still within the limits of physics, and have to do only with a mechanical, chemical, and electrical engine. Within these limits, we have simply to follow the propagation and conversion of motion from point to point, from form to form, of matter, a story of molecular transition, of which each step is but a modification of its predecessor : they are all known to us on similar evidence and as belonging to the same sphere. But, the moment we touch *the conscious and voluntary case*, this smooth transition is abruptly cut off : our 'scientific imagination' stops short, completely baffled : we are flung upon facts not known in physics, and accessible only in quite another field, the experiences of which are as little interchangeable with molecular movements as a compunction is interchangeable with a timepiece. This distinction is repeatedly admitted by Professor Tyndall. Comparing the deflection of a magnetic needle by an electrical current with the sequence of consciousness on a state of the brain, he says: 'the cases differ in this, that the passage from the current to the needle, if not demonstrable, is thinkable, and that we entertain no doubt as to the final mechanical solution of the problem. But the passage from the physics of the brain to the corresponding facts of consciousness is unthinkable. Granted that a definite thought, and a definite molecular action in the brain, occur simultaneously: we do not possess the intellectual organ, nor apparently any rudiment of the organ, which would enable us to pass, by a process of reasoning, from the one to the other. They appear together, but we do not know why. Were our minds and senses so expanded, strengthened, and illuminated, as to enable us to see and feel the very molecules of the brain; were we capable of following all their motions, all their groupings, all their electrical discharges, if such there be; and were we intimately acquainted with the corresponding states of thought and feeling, we should be as far as ever from the solution of the problem " How are these physical processes connected with the facts of consciousness?" The chasm between the two classes would still remain intellectually impassable [1].'

Under these conditions, I presume it will be physiologically correct to say that, in the supposed molecular motions, their groupings, their electrical discharges, we have the *function* of the brain : they are the actions it is fitted to perform, precisely as the chemical resolution of food is the business of the stomach, and the burning of carbon that of the lungs, and the contraction of fibre that of the muscles, and the conducting of stimulus that of the

[1] Fragments of Science. Scientific Materialism, p. 420, 5th ed. 1876.

nerves. The organ then finds its function in a class of
phenomena separated by 'a chasm intellectually impassable' from consciousness and will : with what sense then
or consistency are we to charge it with these also as a part
of its business ? They are confessedly but co-existences
turning up in a different and unapproachable world, not
only unlinked as yet with their physical concomitants,
but, we are assured, intrinsically and for ever incapable
of being brought into intelligible relation with them. If
the organic and the mental phenomena lie thus apart, how
can any legitimate inference carry us from the one to the
other ? If we could not say, 'Given the first, the second
must follow,' how can we say, 'Take away the first, and
the second cannot be '? If no one can discern their connection to be necessary, who can affirm their disconnection
to be impossible? If the structure, when seen through
and through to its minutest changes, brings us no nearer
to consciousness, the cessation of these changes takes us
no further from it. It is a mistake therefore to imagine
that the mere organic history covers the whole field of
this problem, and by its termination demonstrates consciousness to be extinct : we are not entitled to say more
than that the signs and evidences of consciousness have
vanished ; but beyond or behind the 'physics of the brain'
there is another world, of invisible phenomena, whose relations to the former are unknown, and on the possibilities
of which we are not qualified to pronounce.

This check to the over-confident haste of the mere
naturalist will be corroborated, if we apply to the human
being, in life and death, the physical law of the conservation of energy. First, take the case of cerebral
excitement leading to voluntary action. I am seated, let
us suppose, at church, quietly attending to the service,
when someone steals in behind me, and whispers that
my library is on fire. I quit the church, spring into the

cab before the door, send one messenger to the police-
station, and another to the fire-engine house, and, as I
come to the spot, organize a plan for saving the contents
in the order of their value ; and, finally, move hither and
thither, from base to roof, to see it, as far as possible,
safely carried out.   Follow out the metamorphoses of
energy that run through this process, and try to mark
the successive equivalents.   The whisper which begins it
consists of aerial undulations of faint intensity : reaching
the auditory nerve, they are exchanged for molecular
movements there, at the rate of seventy feet per second :
in the brain, these are delivered over to the motor filaments
which communicate with the required muscles.   So far,
I presume, each of these steps may be held to register the
same amount of energy, which, if expressed in terms of
heat, would need no variation in the figure.   But now, we
suddenly come upon a wonderful accession, sufficient to
wield the whole weight of my body, and fling it hither
and thither like a cork, not only with level velocity, but to
considerable altitudes.   This conversion of molecular into
molar movement is referable, we are told, to the ' potential
energy ' stored up in the muscles, and dormant there till it
is unlocked and released from its tension by the trigger-
touch of the nerve thrill.   An enormous increment therefore
is here thrown into our system of equations ; but having
once passed from potential to kinetic, it follows through
its further course the same law of equivalence ; and the
cycle of voluntary movements completes itself without
either creation or waste of energy.   Now, in reviewing this
analysis, do we notice no omission from the reckoning ?
All the physical elements have, I believe, been stated with
exactness, and their quantities fairly described ; but are
they wholly unaffected by what is taking place on the
other side of the ' impassable chasm ' ?   Has my *consciousness of the meaning* of that whisper nothing to do with the

amount of energy thrown into the transaction? Is the difference between 'The library is on fire' and 'The library is all right' only that of aerial undulation in two words? If not, then there is a difference,—a direct dynamic difference,—*made by thought alone*: one idea leaving me quiet in my seat, another snatching me impetuously from it. Doubtless, the molecular action in the brain, if such there be, is disparate in the two cases; but this difference itself is due, not to the dissimilar affection of the auditory nerve, but to the different sense of the words, and therefore seems to present a case where the 'chasm' is bridged, to the discomfiture of the physical law. Professor Tyndall, true to the last to his 'physics of the brain,' holds manfully out against this inevitable inference; but only to leave on hand a problem which he pronounces incomprehensible, simply because he cannot think it out in physical pictures, and render it as apprehensible to the Imagination as it is intelligible to the Reason. 'Do states of consciousness,' he says, 'enter as links into the chain of antecedence and sequence which give rise to bodily actions, and to other states of consciousness? or are they merely *by-products*, which are not essential to the physical processes going on in the brain? Speaking for myself, it is certain that I have no power of imagining states of consciousness interposed between the molecules of the brain and influencing the transference of motion among the molecules. The thought 'eludes all mental presentation'; and hence the logic seems of iron strength which claims for the brain an automatic action, uninfluenced by states of consciousness. But it is I believe, admitted by those who hold the automaton theory, that states of consciousness are *produced by* the marshalling of the molecules of the brain; and this production of consciousness by molecular motion is to me quite as unthinkable as the production of molecular motion by consciousness. If, therefore, unthinkability be the

proper test, I must equally reject both classes of phenomena. I however reject neither, and thus stand in the
presence of two incomprehensibles instead of one incomprehensible. While accepting fearlessly the facts of
materialism dwelt upon in these pages, I bow my head
in the dust before that mystery of Mind, which has
hitherto defied its own penetrative power, and which may
ultimately resolve itself into a demonstrable impossibility
of self-penetration[1].'

Let us look into this 'logic of iron strength' which is
claimed for the automatic theory. In the process we
have described, the transmission of energy, preserving its
equivalence from step to step, either is or is not exact and
complete within the cerebral and muscular limits, apart
from what is felt and thought.

If it *is*,—if the mental concomitants might be omitted
without disturbance to the dynamic equations,—then, as
mere 'by-products,' they cost nothing in the way of
energy: they are not therefore physical effects, drawing
upon a physical cause. They are exempt from the law of
conservation which pervades the physical sphere: they
belong to another universe : and Mind emerges as something independent of Matter.

If the transmission of energy is *not* complete within the
bodily system, then (1) a part of it is expended on the
production of consciousness and thought; and accordingly,
by the law of Conservation, this part must (2) be capable
of transmitting its action in ulterior effects, and of returning
by an inverse path into the physical world ; if not by
immediate movement, at least by becoming potential, and
lying in wait for the production of future phenomena.
In this case Mind is not independent of Matter : neither
is Matter, of Mind : Causality passes from either to the
other.

[1] Fragments of Science, p. 561.

The automatic theory, therefore, which is ambitious of establishing the self-sufficiency of physics, results in either liberating mind from them altogether, or surrendering to it the prerogative of acting within their sphere. Nor is there any escape from this result, unless by repudiating the law of Conservation.

In the face of these inconsistencies I should say that 'logic of iron strength' is the last claim that can be set up for the Automatic Theory. But every reader of Professor Tyndall's picturesque writings must be aware that he habitually identifies *clear images linked in conceptual succession* with '*rigorous logic*'; and will feel no surprise at the strange reason which he gives for his compliment to the automatists, namely, that he cannot *bring before his imagination* 'states of consciousness interposed between the molecules of the brain.' Need I say that if our reasoning lost its 'strength' whenever our representative faculty could not accompany it, it would be impotent for all its most characteristic achievements? It is only of objects of perception that images can be formed in the mind; and the perceived world is immeasurably less than half of the universe we have come to know. Of 'states of consciousness,' however unembarrassed by the neighbourhood of molecules, we can form no pictures, though we can compare, identify and distinguish them. Nay, of the very physical forces which are the subjects of Tyndall's luminous and fascinating expositions, he must own that he can have no image: *that*, for example, which carries the message along the nerves or from point to point within the brain is entirely unpresentable as a *thing* before the mind: it is not the molecules themselves, but an assumed power in, among, or between the molecules, a power inaccessible to the thinker's senses and supplied by his Intellect to do the work of Cause. Imagination may embrace Space with the movements of its sensible contents; but it is the

Reason only that supplies the idea of their source and dynamic interaction ; and self-consciousness alone which gives us the whole inward world of feeling, thought, and will. The demand to have only a series of picturable phenomena offered to you, is simply a negation of all scientific conception ; a mere chain of imaged objects tells you nothing but that they are there : the mere notion of invisible forces gives you fruitless causes without the conditions of effects : it is precisely by a mixture of the two, an insertion of unpicturable power between the successive picturable things, that you first connect and rationalise your apprehensions and experience.

The 'iron strength' of the automatic logic proves, however, after all, insufficient to hold the Professor's versatile faith. He will not, at its bidding, reject the interaction, both ways, of cerebration and consciousness ; only, whichever way you take it, it is 'incomprehensible.' Be it so. Then if the *union* of the ' physics of the brain ' with the trains of thought be so profound a mystery, their *separation* can hardly be regarded as out of possibility : if the one is barely credible, the other ought not to be incredible. There is at all events, no such known necessity of conjunction between the physical organism and the mental life as to blend their fates in indissoluble unity.

Next, let us follow the law of conservation of energy into the phenomena of death. In its physical aspect, death presents simply a case of transformation of energy : the organic compounds of oxygen, hydrogen, carbon and nitrogen losing their precarious equilibrium and resolving themselves into more stable inorganic combinations, themselves destined hereafter to be partially taken up into new living forms. In crossing the mortal line, the total energy which had manifested itself in the heat and whole 'work' of the body is not altered, though every organ is cold and every function at rest : part of it has become potential, locked up in durable substances that may remain idle for ages; and part is busy in setting up new chemical arrangements on a vast scale. This latter part is the exact equivalent of the muscular contractions which have ceased, of the combinations which have gone out, and the nervous tension which has subsided, and, were it tested by a dynamometer, would give account of these alone. But we should miss in it any element answering to *the thoughts, the affections, the volitions*, which were the concomitants of these in the living man : they are unrepresented in the transformations. Consider the significance of this absence. If these mental activities are included in the category of 'energy,' then, since they are not transformed, they still continue ; for, were they extinct, the law of conservation would be broken. If they are not included, if the cycle of energy is perfect without them, then they lie outside the physical world, and are foreign to its fates. To treat consciousness as at once a superfluous appendage, and yet a liable partner, of the perishable organism, is pure self-contradiction.

I conclude therefore that in the physical phenomena of death there is nothing to prejudge the question of life beyond. They amount only to a vanishing of the prior evidences of life ; and leave it open to us to consider whether there are any other indications or reasons to replace them.

This conclusion however, though only defensive, guards too wide a field. It applies, not to the human mind only, but to the whole range of *conscious life* : for the sensations, the passions, the instinctive intelligence, of other animals are separated from molecular physics by the same 'impassable chasm' as the mental experience of man. We are dealing here with one of the most ancient of antitheses, —between *physics* and *more than physics*,—between ὕλη and ψυχή,—between the material of which organic structures

are built, and the animating power which occupies and uses
them.   And in maintaining that from the transient combinations of the former we cannot infer the perishableness
of the latter, we do but recur to the idea, pervading many
an old philosophy and mythology, that the universe is a
living frame, whose total vitality is eternally identical,
whose separate souls are numerically constant, while the
distribution of them here or there may variously change
through unending ages.   What is now taught as the *conservation of energy* was then conceived as the *conservation
of life*: the forms of which might baffle us by their Protean
diversity, but the principle of which is for ever the same,
with nothing added to it and nothing taken from it.
This theory, it is obvious, involved an immunity for souls,
not from extinction only, but from genesis: birth was but an
incarnation, and death, a release from prison : both of them,
mere incidents of a pre-existent and post-existent subject.
And, as so long a history could not be filled without many
a birth, the belief in transmigration naturally followed, and
passed the souls through the whole scale of supposed living
natures, from the insect on the ground to the stars in
heaven.   Such a doctrine it was easy to enlist in the
service of something like a moral or progressive theory of
the world : banishment into lower species, or promotion
into higher, being held in prospect as the recompense of
guilt or righteousness ; and, as many a human hero and
genius would thus become tenant of the inferior kinds, it is
no wonder that, so wielded, they get a lift into ' favourable
variations' and cleverer instincts, and exhibit in short all
the Darwinian evidence of a struggle upwards towards
man.   The fantastic aspects which this mode of belief has
often assumed have removed it from modern regard, except
as an obsolete curiosity; but its main principle, that the
ground of conscious life in the Universe is not phenomenal,
but uncreated and imperishable, Divine in its nature, though

not infinite in amount, is not an obvious absurdity, and is not less admissible as an hypothesis than our current speculations on matter and force. A deliberate refutation of it would be no easy task ; and some expressions still in frequent use, seem, however unconsciously, to look back towards it. We constantly hear of the 'competition for existence' that quickens all nature, and that, on the retreat of one species, eagerly fills the gap with others ; as if conscious life were a given quantity, which could let in fresh claimants only as it was vacated: nor have we ceased to seek, in the living Mind of the universe, the source and aliment of our own, and to rekindle our languishing flames at that undying fire. But the general conception, however defensible, does not avail for our immediate purpose. Even if all life were drawn from an eternal given stock, the sameness, the continuity, would belong only to the whole, and imply no unbroken identity between the torch that is quenched and the successor that is alight in its place: the lion in which, according to Plato's myth, the soul of Ajax was reborn, would not remember his defeat about the armour of Achilles : or the swan, tenanted by Orpheus, look back upon his visit to the shades, and the joy and despair of the won and lost Euridice. The plain of Lethe that had to be crossed, and the waters of its river 'Careless' that had to be tasted, before the second birth, effectually severed the unity between life and life[1]. And we must acknowledge the justice of Lucretius's criticism,

> Si immortalis natura animai
> Constat et in corpus nascentibus insinuatur,
> Cur super anteactam ætatem meminisse nequimus,
> Nec vestigia gestarum rerum ulla tenemus?
> Nam si tanto operest animi mutata potestas,
> Omnis ut actarum exciderit retinentia rerum,
> Non, ut opinor, id a leto jam longiter errat ;

---

[1] Plato, Rep. x. 621 ; Virg. Æn. vi. 714, 715.

Quapropter fateare necesse est quæ fuit ante
Interiisse et quæ nunc est nunc esse creatam[1].

The faint traces of ἀνάμνησις by which Plato's own speculation tries to link our present experience with anterior existence are insufficient to unite the two as successive actions of the same drama: and a future life as little related to the present as the present to a possible antecedent would have for us only the interest of an external history. What we are concerned to determine is not whether, when one chapter of consciousness closes, another is opened, which so little refers to the former as to be taken for entirely new and to reveal its connection only to an observer outside them both; but whether death leaves the felt personal identity untouched, and permits the story of the past to flow on in continuous sequel. This problem hangs on the nature, not of the *animal consciousness*, but of *human self-consciousness*: and the question is, 'Have we here any new element which can claim to modify our physiological estimate of death?'

In seeking an answer to this question I am anxious to keep, as far as possible, to undisputed scientific ground and avoid at present all appeal to Theistic *purpose*. This restriction will hardly be transgressed if I assume, as is common with physiologists, that, in living beings, we are justified in expecting a due proportion between organ and function, between faculty and range of life. It is true that such harmonious accordance is hardly conceivable apart from the idea of adjusted ends and means: but it is freely

---

[1] De Rerum Nat. iii. 670–678. Thus translated by Munro: 'If the nature of the soul is immortal and makes its way into our body at the time of birth, why are we unable to remember besides the time already gone, and why do we retain no trace of past actions? If the power of the mind has been so completely changed that all remembrance of past things is lost, that methinks, differs not widely from death: therefore you must admit that the soul which was before has perished and that which now is has now been formed.

admitted, under the name of *correlation*, by naturalists pure
and simple. Under the protection of this acknowledged
principle we are enabled, from a survey of the instincts,
perceptions and affections of an animal, to define approximately the scope and character of its life: just as, inversely, from the study of its organs and surrounding
conditions, we may form some preconception of its
directing impulses and aptitudes. Such rule of measurement we have to apply to the self-consciousness of man.

It is evident that the whole drift of the system of animal
instincts is the maintenance of the individual organism and
of its kind. That organism is worked by its spontaneous
energy, fed by its appetites and predatory skill, protected
by its fears or daring, sheltered by many burrowing or
building arts : while other impulses and affections secure
the continuance of the race, directing when and how to
build the nest, to warm the eggs, to care for the brood, to
steer the migratory flight. If we marvel at the wonderful
ways of insect intelligence and industry, it is for their
obvious adaptation to the needs of their individual or
collective life: by this standard it is that we judge them ;
and if they come up to it, we deem them perfect ; and ask
no more. The organism prescribes what they are to be ;
they subsist as its servitors, and when they have seen to
its wants, their limit is reached and their work is done.
The animal body, in short, is a machine charged with
powers, unconscious and conscious, for preserving, regulating, replacing itself : there is not a propensity or a sagacity
that is not subservient to this system of ends : so that
when the structure goes to pieces, the very *raison d'être* of
all its associated passions and perceptions is gone ; and the
term of the organic and that of the conscious life naturally
coincide.

This rule of judgment, it is evident, will still hold good
for our own nature, so long as we do not look beyond its

zoological springs of action. Nor does it immediately
desert us on our entering the secondary or self-conscious
list ; for, the transformed propensions which make money,
pleasure, power, objects of human pursuit, may be regarded
as only a more refined provision for the ease and security
of man as the 'paragon of animals,' and as exhausting
their function in the superiority of his place within the
fauna of the globe. And yet, not infrequently, even
these tendencies take to themselves so much of an ideal
character and betray such intellectual magnificence, that
already their scale appears more proper for a larger life ;
and the very fact that what is only hunger and want in
other creatures, and dies with each meal till it is needed
again, becomes in man the continuous spring of industry
and invention, the source of property and all its rights, the
basis of contract and exchange, and the incentive to social
ambition, exhibits an interval startling enough to surprise
us, if the destinies are the same. For, do we not here see
the very impulses which most obviously begin as menials
and purveyors for the body, ending with a conquest over
its importunities and a subjugation of it to rational if not
unselfish aims? And, the moment we enter the inner circle
of human characteristics, the interpretation of them as
instruments for working the organism utterly fails us. Who
would ever think of referring the sentiment of *Wonder* to
its physiological use? It neither helps the digestion nor
regulates the temperature : it succours no weakness, it
repels no foe : the labour to which it incites, the enthusiasm which it kindles, often detract from the animal
perfection and consume the organic powers that serve it ;
and only elevate the level and widen the relations of life,
opening to it intellectual interests and possibilites unlimited
in extent and inexhaustible in duration. The sense of
Beauty may perhaps play some rudimentary part in other
races, shaping some lines of grace, and enriching the

plumage of the bird : but, in its human maturity, it emerges from the sphere of Sense and takes possession of an ideal world, moulding thought into literature and character into drama.   It is not physically that we are nobler and more complete for our libraries, or theatres, or 'schools of Athens.' Compassion, sympathy, attachment, also serve in us, no doubt, the same ends for which they more or less exist in other creatures.   But how soon and far do they transcend this simply useful function, and claim a good upon their own account ! Surely it is no romance to say that human love reaches a pathetic depth and rises to a sublime height, which make it greater than its uses, and ally it with the proportions of more enduring being.   If you judged these features of humanity by a prospective instead of a retrospective measure, and asked yourself *whither they look* rather than *whence they come*, could you hesitate to say,—' it is for these that we are made ; these it is to which we must yoke our physical power in humble service, by which we are to rise above it, and pass into a life of larger dimensions ' ?

In the foregoing argument a higher destiny is claimed for man on the strength of his higher nature.   In the presentation of this argument he and the other animals are exhibited simply in their contrast with each other, as it might appear if they were separate creations, moulded upon a different idea.   Into this form the reasoning naturally fell, before the ' Origin of Species ' had given extension to the family affinities of the human race.   But the interval between the bestial and the spiritual life is none the less striking and fruitful in promise, when it lies between two stages of one genealogy, than when it sets off two natures as opposites to each other ; and it is no wonder therefore that it still tells its tale to the philosophical Darwinian.   It was with no slight satisfaction that I found Professor Fiske, the eminent American expounder of the law of evolution, drawing nearly the same inference from the premisses to which appeal has just been made. A parallelism of independent lines of thought is so pleasant a variety upon the endless divergencies of the critical intellect of our time, that I am tempted to quote a few sentences, on the '*growing predominance of the psychical life*,' which will powerfully reinforce our plea for great hopes.

'Let us note,' says Professor Fiske, 'one further aspect of this mighty revolution. In its lowly beginnings the psychical life was merely an appendage to the life of the body. The avoidance of enemies, the securing of food, the perpetuation of the species, make up the whole of the lives of lower animals, and the rudiments of memory, reason, emotion, and volition were at first concerned solely with the achievement of these ends in an increasingly indirect, complex, and effective way. Though the life of a large portion of the human race is still confined to the pursuit of these same ends, yet so vast has been the increase of psychical life that the simple character of the ends is liable to be lost sight of amid the variety, the indirectness, and the complexity of the means. But in civilized society other ends, purely immaterial in their nature, have come to add themselves to these, and in some instances to take their place. It is long since we were told that Man does not live by bread alone. During many generations we have seen thousands of men, actuated by the noblest impulse of which humanity is capable, though misled by the teachings of a crude philosophy, despising and maltreating their bodies as clogs and incumbrances to the life of the indwelling soul. Countless martyrs we have seen throwing away the physical earthly life as so much worthless dross, and all for the sake of purely spiritual truths. As with religion, so with the scientific spirit and the artistic spirit, —the unquenchable craving to know the secrets of nature, and the yearning to create the beautiful in form and colour

and sound. In the highest human beings such ends as
these have come to be uppermost in consciousness, and
with the progress of material civilization this will be more
and more the case. If we can imagine a future time when
warfare and crime shall have been done away with for
ever, when disease shall have been for the most part
curbed, and when every human being by moderate labour
can procure ample food and shelter, we can also see that
in such a state of things the work of civilization would be
by no means completed. In ministering to human happiness in countless ways, through the pursuit of purely
spiritual ends, in enriching and diversifying life to the
utmost, there would still be almost limitless work to be
done. I believe that such a time will come for weary and
suffering mankind. Such a faith is inspiring. It sustains
one in the work of life, when one would otherwise lose
heart. But it is a faith that rests upon induction. The
process of evolution is excessively slow, and its ends are
achieved at the cost of enormous waste of life, but for
innumerable ages its direction has been towards the goal
here pointed out ; and the case may be fitly summed up
in the statement that whereas in its rude beginnings the
psychical life was but an appendage to the body, in fully
developed Humanity the body is but the vehicle for the
soul[1].'

The inference here drawn from the dominance of the
spiritual activities in Man is not indeed the same that I
have claimed ;—not the immunity of the individual soul
from death, but the continued progress of psychical development for future Humanity on earth. Both beliefs,
however, are, in the author's view, warranted by the same
premises ; and that which is passed in silence here, is thus
expressly affirmed as the crown of his whole argument :

---

[1] The Destiny of Man, London, 1886, pp. 62-65.

'From the first dawning of life we see all things working together towards one mighty goal, the evolution of the most exalted spiritual qualities which characterize humanity.' 'Has all this work been done for nothing ? Is it all ephemeral, all a bubble that bursts, a vision that fades? On such a view, the riddle of the universe becomes a riddle without a meaning.' 'The more thoroughly we comprehend that process of evolution by which things have come to be what they are, the more we are likely to feel that to deny the everlasting persistence of the spiritual element in Man is to rob the whole process of its meaning. It goes far toward putting us to permanent intellectual confusion, and I do not see that any one has as yet alleged, or is ever likely to allege, a sufficient reason for our accepting so dire an alternative. For my own part, therefore, I believe in the immortality of the soul, not in the sense in which I accept the demonstrable truths of science, but as a supreme act of faith in the reasonableness of God's work[1].'

---

[1] The Destiny of Man, pp. 113-116.

CHAPTER II.

Death in its Metaphysical Aspect.

THE *Metaphysical* interpretation of Death, to which we must next turn, presses upon us the question, 'What is it that survives the perishing organism, if survival there be?' If we call it '*the Soul*,' whence have we the idea of such a possible prisoner escaped? Is it from any source which renders it legitimate, and justifies our acceptance of it as trustworthy? Or is it due to the mere imagination, continuing to picture what has vanished from perception?

A very obvious and ancient conjecture attributed the conception of a soul outlasting the body to the images of departed friends that haunt our memory by day and our dreams by night. On this principle it is that Lucretius expounds to us—

> quæ res nobis vigilantibus obvia mentes
> Terrificet morbo affectis somnoque sepultis,
> Cernere uti videamur eos audireque coram
> Morte obita quorum tellus amplectitur ossa [1],

and warns us not to suppose that such experiences guarantee any objective reality, or justify the belief—

> aliquid nostri post mortem posse relinqui,
> Cum corpus simulatque animi natura perempta
> In sua discessum dederint primordia quæque [2].

---

[1] De Rerum Nat. i. 132-135. Thus translated by Munro: 'What thing it is that meets us and frightens our minds when we are awake and under the influence of disease and when we are buried in sleep, so that we seem to see and hear speaking to us face to face them who are dead and whose bones earth holds in its embrace?'

[2] Ibid. iv. 39-41. Thus translated by Munro: 'That any part of

This ancient explanation of the belief in a Soul,—separated
however from the Epicurean doctrine of εἴδωλα or films,—
has been revived by Mr. Tylor[1], and Herbert Spencer[2];
the chief stress being laid upon the phantasms of dreams,
which are as vivid as any realities, and freely fetch back the
past into the present. This is the theory of *Animism*. If
it be true, the idea of a 'spirit in man' is identical, in
its origin, with that of a *visible ghost*; and it is first applied
by us *to others*, as a means of construing our external
experience of them, as objects of knowledge or imagination.
It thus expresses the same philosophical tendency which
seeks all our fundamental notions upon objective lines;
deriving, for instance, the principle of causality from observation of external phenomena, and moral sentiment from
estimates of the behaviour of men. The same reasons
which led me, in these cases, to treat the objective applications of the idea as secondary, and dependent upon
a prior subjective cognition, induce me here also to resort
to the self-consciousness for the ultimate ground of the
thought which we seek. If the belief in the permanence of
life through death depended on the scenery of memory and
of sleep, it would hold no less of other perishable objects
than of man:

Οἵη περ φύλλων γενεή, τοιήδε καὶ ἀνδρῶν[3].

And when the wintry winds have stripped the forest of its
leaves, and the snow has buried them, we can dream ourselves back into their summer shade, precisely as we can

---

us is left behind after death, when the body and the nature of the
mind destroyed together have taken their departure into their several
first beginnings.'

[1] In the Journal of the Ethnological Society, April, 1861, and in
Primitive Culture, 1871.

[2] In Principles of Sociology, vol. i. pp. 154 seqq. See also a review
of Mr. Spencer's volume by Mr. Tylor, in Mind, vol. ii. pp. 141 seqq.

[3] Hom. Il. vi. 146.

place beside us there the forms of the departed ; yet we
surrender the foliage to decay, and save the humanity for
existence. The permanence does not lie in the *simulacrum* ;
that is but a phenomenon, transient alike in all its varieties ;
and did we know of men only what we see and can reproduce in vision, our ancestors would be as much lost in the
past as the harvests which they witnessed or the trees which
they felled. The changeless element which we ascribe to
them is that of which we are aware in ourselves, and which
is given to us, not by our eyesight or our imagination, but
by our personality : the conscious self-identity which we
have as abiding subject of variable phenomena, and unitary
cause of multiform activities. The sameness which we thus
claim is quite different from that which we predicate of
outward things. A physical object, in order to retain
its name, must preserve a certain selection of its perceptible
characters, though the remainder of the group may change ;
we do not go behind the phenomena, but only run a line
across them, and call what lies on one side *essential*, what lies
on the other *non-essential*,—essential, that is, to the genus
of which the name has charge. A personal being, on the
other hand, may remain the same under a total change of
all perceptible attributes : the identity consisting, not in
partial similitude at different times, not in a reserve of
stereotyped phenomena, but in the Unity of the *Ego* or *Self*
to which all the attributes and phenomena belong,—a unity
undisturbed by the greatest contrasts of experience and
revolutions of character. This durable *selfdom* attaches to
us, not as *conscious*, but as *personal* (i.e. self-conscious)
beings ; as is evident from our different treatment of
domestic animals and of men, in case of injuries received
from them : an offending human being we call to account
for a detected crime, though it be a dozen years after its
perpetration ; but a dog we cannot punish to-morrow for
the offence of to-day : for, his sameness is only objective, to

us, not subjective, to himself. This constant centre to
which we refer all our acts as their source, and all our
experiences as their receptacle, is what we mean by the
Soul. The conditions of which it is successively conscious
are so many phenomena ; but, in its continuous capacity for
being conscious of them as its own, it is itself an entity,
which,—being deserted by phemomena, is not on that
account lost as a possible subject of them. Hence, the
Self or Soul stands for us as the permanent term in a
relation of change ; abiding as the patient background,
indifferent to the rates of succession, now rapid, now tardy
and interrupted, that pass across it ; not therefore necessarily affected by long blanks of silence, be it in the suspense
of a swoon, a sleep, or death. Since it is known to us only
as member of a relation, there is certainly a limit beyond
which, in the absence of the other term, we cannot well
hold it in existence as a mere sleeping potentiality. But
the limit is not a very near one ; nor are we driven to it ;
for the absence of conscious states is only negatively suggested by the failure of the usual signs ; and under the
reticence of all positive evidence, it is competent to the
permanence of the Ego to pursue the vanished phenomena
into the invisible and recover them there.

The personal unity which we thus know at first hand
in ourselves we attribute at second hand to others : that is,
we believe that they in like manner know it of themselves ;
precisely as we undoubtedly credit them with an apprehension of the same moral distinctions as our own conscience reveals to us. In this external application of the
idea we add nothing to it, and learn nothing new : we no
more see the souls of others than our own ; and in thinking
of them *as there*, we do but repeat, with that local difference,
the thought of our own as *here*. We do but provide, in
every case, a *permanent principle of personality*, in virtue of
which each, separately, exercises causation and has ex-

periences. Of these phenomena it is the necessary condition ; but it is not conditioned by them.

From this subjective and noumenal origin of the idea, it
is evident that of the Soul *as an object* we predicate nothing
beyond the bare Space definition of here and there, by
which one is discriminated from another.   As a constant, it
is indifferent to time, and there is no sense in asking for the
date of its entrance into the organism.   As known to us
only in relation to living feelings and actions, it has nothing
to say to us of its ultra-organic history : *there* we can think
of it merely as the possibility of phenomena which we are
unable to affirm.   As it is not a thing offered to perception
and open to the tests of analysis, no meaning can be
attached to any assertion of its simplicity or composition :
nor can we rely on such propositions as means for determining its indestructibility or evanescence.   In short, it
evades almost all the reasonings constituting what was
called 'rational psychology,' or the ontological doctrine of
the Soul ; and leaves on our hands only the negative assurance that it is not amenable to phenomenal laws, but is the
persistent ground on which they operate within us.   This
self-identity however we do affirm : nor, when we would
mark the felt unity of the cosmos through all space and
time and change, have we any way of doing so but by
planting there a universal Soul, as the centre whence its
energies flow and whither its phenomena look.   Holding to
the anchorage of this idea, we can look calmly on any
amount of world-waste and secular revolution : every lapse
has its re-instatement, every vanishing its new birth : all
discontinuity is partial and apparent : the continuity is
eternal and real.   This dominant *Self* of the universe we
discriminate from the *physical* which it animates ; we oppose
to the *phenomenal* which it puts forth ; and we claim as the
reality of both.   It is the All in its idea and its causality.
Thus the Soul is individual. God the cosmical aspect of the

inward principle of existence ; and they are homogeneous in our thought, except in the spheres at their disposal.

If by 'the Soul' we mean only our own subjective identity, if it is not itself an object known but merely that which knows objects, how, we may naturally ask, does it come to be designated by words of objective description, and assimilated to physical things ?   Do we not call it *'anima'* and *'spiritus,'* likening it to a breath, a wind ? or *'umbra,'* as if it were a shadow ? or *'imago,'* an empty but resembling form ?   It is so : nor could we proceed otherwise, if that which we do but inwardly feel and know to be, is to be made the topic of speech and communication.   Subjective consciousness is incommunicable ; and upon no element in it can we fix the attention of another, through verbal indication, unless by substituting for it some sensible symbol which most nearly influences us in the same way and may be present to both of us at once.   In the mysterious continuity of the Self, nothing so affects us with certainty as its inapprehensible presence, and its looseness from objective conditions ; and our best chance of referring a hearer to it by way of language is to choose some word which denotes what is all but empty and invisible, yet can breathe an influence and betray an existence : and such is a wind, a mist, a flitting outline on the wall.   These ghostly terms therefore, far from indicating the objective and perceptive origin of our idea of the Soul, are a sign of exactly the reverse : they are selected precisely because they verge upon the very zero of objectivity, and mark the extreme but vain struggle of language to take the final step into the purely subjective.   Instead of first turning other people into ghosts and then appropriating one to ourselves by way of imitation, we start, I apprehend, from the sense of personal continuity, and then predicate the same of others under the figures which keep most clear of the physical and perishable.

Let it be assumed then that we have first-hand knowledge of a Self or Soul, whose permanence as a possible
subject of experiences is not contradicted by any organic
phenomena, including those of death : and further, that
this individual Ego has been set up by the universal Mind
in whose embrace it lives, and which it reflects in its
miniature powers. How are we to conceive of the relation
between these two ? And especially is it in its nature such
that death must dissolve it ? Two metaphysical reasons
are urged from the pantheistic side why it must be so : (1)
the relation has begun, therefore it must cease : (2) the
egoistic personality is finite, and cannot hold its ground
amid the infinite.

(1) So strong a grasp of the modern imagination has the
first of these objections taken, that Immanuel Fichte, in
order to vindicate the doctrine of immortality, has deemed
it necessary to couple with it the pre-existence of the soul,
and so to replace the problem where Plato left it. But
surely this is a needless concession to a rule which has no
title to universal application. Within the limits of organic
life, whose history consists of a cycle of chemical changes,
it is true that birth is the invariable precursor of a series
leading to death ; but beyond this range it cannot be
shown that either mechanical or mental genesis must run
its course and come to an end. What indeed does Newton's first law declare, but that a particle once set in motion
in empty space will continue to move in a straight line
with uniform velocity for ever, unless some external force
supervenes ? And if we can think of the law of gravitation
as having been given to the material of the universe, surely
we are not on that account compelled by any logical
necessity to anticipate its cessation : nothing can less carry
the marks of a temporary character, or be more easily conceived to be eternal. Nor can I see that it is otherwise
with the case of intellectual and moral natures. If, at

a certain stage in the development of the cosmos, the Supreme Mind set up at a given centre a personal subject of thought and will like his own, with adequate assignment of causality, what is to prevent this from being a freehold in perpetuity, and to reduce it to a terminable loan? Why may not the communicated Divine nature endure as long as the uncommunicated Source on which it lives? So far as thought, and love, and goodness, are related to Time, their relation is not cyclical, but progressive, not returning to their beginnings, but opening out into indefinite enlargement and acceleration. The dictum therefore that whatever begins must end is one to which we are not bound to surrender: and the only pre-existence which we need allow to the Soul is latent within its Divine Source, ere yet its idea has taken effect and the personal monad been set up.

(2) The other principle assumed, viz. that personality is a finite phenomenon and must sink back into its infinite ground, plays a much larger part in the reasoning on this subject since the time of Spinoza; and in our own day is more and more treated as an axiom which is safe from challenge. The kind of sentiment and language to which it leads will be best estimated by a few citations. The following sentences are from Schleiermacher, and leave perhaps the most favourable impression of the doctrine which I desire to describe. 'When our feeling nowise clings to the individual, but is wholly made up of relation to God wherein all that is individual and perishable vanishes, then does it also cease to have in it aught but the imperishable and eternal; and we are warranted in saying that the religious life is that in which we discard and sacrifice all that is mortal and actually enjoy immortality. But the way in which most men represent it and their yearning for it seems to me irreligious, directly at variance with the spirit of piety: nay, their longing for

immortality has no other ground than their aversion to what constitutes the end of religion. Bear in mind how all its aspiration aims at enlarging the sharply defined boundaries of our personality and gradually losing them in the infinite, and, through consciousness of the All, becoming as far as possible one with it. But this is just what they strive against : they do not want to quit the familiar limits : the conditions of phenomenal existence are alone welcome to them : they are full of concern for their personality; so that, instead of being eager to seize the solitary opportunity which death offers them of transcending it, they are rather anxious to take it with them over the confines of this life, and long at most for wider vision and better limbs. But God says to them, as it is written, "Whoso loseth his life for my sake shall find it, and he that will find it shall lose it." The life which they would keep cannot be kept : for if the question with them is about the eternity of their individual personality, why are they not as anxiously concerned about what it *has been* as about what it *will be* ? and what is the good of the *a parte post*, if the *a parte ante* is out of their reach ? The more they long for an immortality which is no such thing and of which they cannot so much as form an idea (for who can manage to conceive a temporal existence as everlasting ?), so much the more do they miss the immortality which they can always have, and the mortal life as well, through thoughts that vainly vex and torment them. Let them try to surrender their life from love to God. Let them endeavour, while yet here, to sink their personality and live in the One and All. He that has learned to be more than himself knows how small the loss, to lose oneself. He alone who, in such self-abnegation, has as far as possible melted away into the Universe as a whole, and in whose soul a greater and holier yearning has arisen, has any legitimate place in it ; and with him alone can we really say a further

word of the hopes which death gives us, and of the perpetuity to which by its means we unfailingly mount[1].'

Whatever obscurity there may be in this passage,
Pfleiderer rightly interprets it[2] as rejecting the doctrine
of personal existence after death. If this were otherwise
questionable, all doubt would be removed by the published
correspondence which lays open to us one of the most
touching episodes of Schleiermacher's life. Among the
many hearers who were excited and carried away by these
very 'Discourses' and the 'Monologues' which followed
them, was an enthusiastic young preacher, Ehrenfried von
Willich, of Stralsund ; with whom and his wife, Henrietta
von Mühlenfels (still almost a child, for she was only six-
teen), Schleiermacher entered into intimate relations and
correspondence. Within three years of their marriage, between the birth of their first and their second child, Stralsund was besieged by the French, and at the same time
Willich was carried off by an eight days' fever. In the first
hours of her bereavement his young wife poured out the
whole passion and tumult of her soul to Schleiermacher, in
a letter of intense yet thoughtful pathos ; in which may be
seen, side by side, in conflict truly terrible, the native trust
of her heart that her own Ehrenfried yet lives and waits
for her in the Unseen, and the lesson of the Monologues,
that his soul was no longer hers, but resolved back into the
great All. She vehemently presses her doubts between
these two beliefs upon her fatherly counsellor and con-
soler : insists upon his clearing them up ; and so, draws
from him statements distinct enough to show that in the
immortality which he contemplated all personal identity
was lost. Let us follow the question and answer through
a few sentences. First comes the cry of pure natural love :

---

[1] Reden über die Religion. Zweite Rede ad fin. p. 119, Berlin, 1831.
[2] Religions-Philosophie, 1878, p 712.

'Oh Schleier, in the midst of my sorrow there are yet
blessed moments when I vividly feel what a love ours was,
and that surely this love is eternal, and it is impossible that
God can destroy it ; for God himself is love.   I bear this
life while nature will ; for I have still work to do for the
children, his and mine : but Oh God ! with what longing,
what foreshadowings of unutterable blessedness, do I gaze
across into that world where he lives !   What joy for me to
die !   Schleier, shall I not find him again ?   Oh my God !
I implore you, Schleier, by all that is dear to God and
sacred, give me, if you can, the certain assurance of finding
and knowing him again.   Tell me your inmost faith on
this, dear Schleier : Oh ! if it fails, I am undone.   It is for
this that I live, for this that I submissively and quietly
endure : this is the one only outlook that sheds a light on
my dark life,—to find him again, to live for him again, to
bless him again.   Oh God ! it cannot be destroyed.'
'Speak to my poor heart : tell me what you believe.'

Then, after awhile, comes the chill shadow upon this
light of hope :

'Do you know when it is that I feel the grasp of the
sorrow too bitterly ?   It is when I think,—" In that future
the old things will go for nothing : whoever is worthiest of
him will be nearest to him : and oh ! many of those who
love him are worthier than I " : and when I think—" His
soul is resolved back,—quite melted away in the great All ;
the old is quite gone by, it will never come to recognition
again " :—Oh Schleier, this I cannot bear : oh ! speak to
me, dear[1]'.

Here there is no escape for him, it seems.   How fast she
holds him, and will not let him go !   He cannot wrap his
thought, like a speaker on his own account, in some glow-

---

[1] Aus Schleiermacher's Leben.   In Briefen, B. II. 82, Berlin, 1858.
The letters are given in extenso in the *National Review*, vol. viii.
pp. 529 seqq.

ing cloud that may seem to give light, yet conceal what it
will : but must fit it to the shape of her sharply defined
agony of yearning doubt. Fluctuating between his sympathy and his philosophy, his words are tremulous and
unsteady, and try to put the joy of ' Yes ' into their inevitable ' No ' :

' You come to me,' he says, ' and tell me I am to dissipate
your doubt. *It is only however the images of fancy in her
hour of travail that you want me to confirm.* Dear Jette,
what can I say? Certainty is not given us as to what lies
beyond this life. Mistake me not : certainty, I mean, for
the imagination, which insists on seeing everything in definite forms : but else it is supremely certain, and nothing
would be certain if this were not, that there is no death, no
extinction for the spirit. True it is, that in the personal
life the spirit does not find its essence, but only makes its
apparition,—to be renewed, we know not how : all here is
beyond our knowledge : we can only imagine.'

' Ah then,' she thinks, ' the apparition has vanished for
ever,—that dear personal life which is all that I know : he
is Ehrenfried no more : gone to God, not to be kept safe,
but to be eternally lost in him.' Reading this lament of
her heart, Schleiermacher thus expostulates with it :

' When your imagination brings before you the idea of a
melting away into the great All, let it not, dear child, lay
on you any touch of bitter sorrow. Do but think of it as
a merging not into death but into life, and that the highest
life. It is indeed *that* after which we all strive in this life,
only that we never reach it, viz. to live simply in the Divine
whole to which we belong, and to put away from us the
pretension to set up for ourselves, as if we could be our
own. If he now is living in God, and you love him eternally
in God as you loved and knew God in him, can you think
of anything sublimer and more glorious? Is not this the
highest end of love, in comparison with which everything

which clings only to the personal life and arises thence is
nothing'?

Is her problem solved? Does she open her arms and
cling no more to 'personal life'? May she not rather
think thus within herself? 'When I loved and knew God
in my Ehrenfried, there were two objects of my love; for
one of them was by my side, and prayed with me to the
other in the unseen. Now that he has left me alone, and
'is living eternally in God,' are they still two lives or only
one? And when I love my husband eternally in God, am
I to have two objects of affection, or only one? If two,
then have I still the same dear soul to cleave to that has
upheld me here: and the love which passes to him, will he
not reciprocate? and if there is this interchange, what is it
but the inmost essence of the personal life? Love,—knowledge,—where persons are not; can there be a greater contradiction? If I am to have but one object of affection,
the human being merged in the Divine, then how is it that
I shall not vanish too, but still remain capable of apprehending and loving what is higher than myself? To tell
me that I shall then reach the perfection of insight and
devotion, is to save my personal life in all its power: and
if one is saved, why should any perish?' Did such a train
of thought pass through her mind, would it not indicate a
pupil wiser than her teacher?

The pantheistic disparagement of 'personal life,' though
very ill-defined, seems to depend upon two preconceptions,
widely different in character, one moral, the other mathematical; neither of them justifying the conclusion which it
is employed to introduce. The former insists, with Schleiermacher in the sentences just cited, that, in proportion as we
are faithful, we strive to surrender all self-regarding aims
at variance with the integral perfection of which we should
be ministering servants: and that, thus, when we have
completely attained, our separation dies away, and God is

all in all. But who can be blind to the fallacy of ambiguity which lurks in this language? Doubtless there is here a ' *self*' which is sacrificed : but by whom? By another ' *self*' that lives and loves the more intensely, when that foe is slain. The will which disciplines itself into harmony with God's does not cease to be a will when its goal is reached and the concord is entire. Is it not a *voluntary* relation, perfected between spirit and spirit, and consciously present in the affections of both? 'To live simply in the Divine whole to which I belong,' so far as I can 'strive after' it, is to know myself a part, and what part I am, in this ' Divine whole,' and fling away every desire disproportioned to my place. But to know, to measure and compare, to suppress and fling away,—these are all *personal activities*, the putting forth, from my own centre, of thought, of effort, of love : and in the consummation which is said to extinguish them they actually have their highest realization. To deny this is to confound *harmony between two* with *absorption in one.*

But still more misleading, I believe, has been the mathematical preconception that the infinite, instead of admitting any finite side by side with it, must embrace and merge it. Personality is represented as an outline artificially drawn round a small enclosure, within which lie the individual experiences of a human life : to set up a living individual is simply to establish such a centre of special consciousness, and fence it off by a containing periphery, and let it for awhile assert and discriminate itself as against the boundless environment from which it is cut out. Even while it lasts, this self-protection from the integral field is but an illusion : for the infinite is the All from which nothing can be withdrawn ; and whatever pretends to be another entity must recant and be content with a place as its phenomenon. And as it is birth into this world which traces the limit of apparent separation, so is it Death which wipes it out and

surrenders the individual back into the universal. This
mode of conception, borrowed altogether from the relations
of geometrical figures in space, confounds the *infinite with
the total*, and erroneously assumes that the infinite is
denied if we speak of anything besides. Of mere extension
this will doubtless hold : and we cannot say that the
universal field of things is made up of infinitude *plus*
the size of the Sun : that size you have already mentioned
when you have named the infinitude. But this rule has no
truth except where both terms are quantitative and homogeneous. Without quitting the category of magnitude,
one infinite does not avail to exclude another : for the
predicate belongs to time as well as space : neither of
them puts any bound upon the other : nor, in affirming
a square yard, do I encroach upon the prerogatives of
eternity. When we carry the infinitude from quantity to
quality, it ceases altogether to be a totality and becomes
an intensity : and far from embracing all that is less than
itself, completely excludes it. Infinite *knowledge*, for
example, is perfect thought of all that has been, is, or
can be, and does not comprise among its contents a partial
knowledge in which truth and error both have their share :
in order to meet with *this* you must resort to another
thinking Subject, a mind of limited range. And what is
there to prevent such finite intelligence from co-existing
with the infinite? How does the affirmation of the one
prejudice the reality of the other? The range and depth
of a great human mind does not exist at the expense of
lesser intelligences around ; and Newton who weighed the
planets could live under the same roof with the house-
keeper that prepared his porridge : nor does the infinitude
of the Divine Mind, that is the absence of all limit to
the functions of thought which it may perform, in any
way interfere with the ' broken lights ' of incipient reason
in us. Moreover, if it be metaphysically impossible for a

finite subject to coexist in antithesis to the infinite, it is not an impossibility that begins with death ; it must have place now as much as then, and then no more than now. Yet here we are, holding the very relation supposed to contradict itself ; conscious of ourselves, conscious of God : and if the wonder has not been too great to arise, what harder conditions forbid it to abide ?   Once at least have we been disengaged from the infinite, and emerged from non-existence. In comparison with this, is it not a small thing to emerge from Death? For there is now, at all events, the ready-made Ego, the established unit of formed character and practised powers, instead of blank nothing-ness, a mere zero of potentiality : there is no need to provide both field and agent : let the field be reopened, and the agent is there.

The pantheistic habit of depreciating *personality* and all individual finite existence as transient, if not unreal, over-looks, I cannot but think, an important contrast between the physical and mental hemisphere of the universe of God. In the former, and therefore in the sciences which interpret it, the tendency is ever towards *unity*. The immanent energy which starts from His will seems at first to break and diverge into dynamic varieties according to the field of conditions of which it takes possession ; and to each we give its name and appropriate its science for separate pursuit. But, after awhile, the several investi-gators, on coming together and comparing their notes, discover strange coincidences in the formulas which they have worked out ; and by following them out and scruti-nizing their meaning, they find it possible to establish equations that cross the boundary between the sciences. One mode of energy can be construed in terms of another : and as inquiry pushes further and further along the apparently spreading meridians of force, they are plainly seen to converge again, and advance towards some polar point of identity. The differences are phenomenal, the causality is one: the forms of power constitute a cycle that returns into itself, and can be read either way, being in truth only the rules of action and apparition of the Supreme Will. Here, of this sole reality all else is but the interchangeable manifestation: thither, whence all goes forth, must all return: the movements are for ever centripetal, and nothing can find a footing to set up for itself. Physical speculation itself acknowledges and expresses this tendency in its own way, when it tells us that, with the equalization of heat, first the solar system, then the whole visible universe, will be rolled together into one dead black mass. In the ultra-physical sphere, the whole tendency is precisely the reverse, viz. away from the original Unity of power into differentiation and multiplicity: the end pursued by the will of the Creator is here, plainly enough, to set up what is *other* than himself and yet akin, to mark off new centres of self-consciousness and causality, that shall have their separate history and build up a free personality like his own. We have seen how conceivable it is that, without prejudice to the Providential order of the world, he should realise this end, by simply parting with a portion of power to a deputed agent, and abstaining so far from necessary law. Now this Divine move, this starting of minds and characters, making the universe alive with multiplied causality, is quite different from the transitory waves of physical change that skim their deep and lapse: it brings upon the stage, not an event, but an existence: not an existence merely, but an ordering and electing and creative existence: a thinking power which is not a mere phenomenon of the Supreme Mind, for *that* would not constitute a mind at all: how can a state of one conscious subject be another conscious subject? We are here in contact with something greater than the succession of the seasons and the phases of the moon, with the very crown and culmination of the world's process : and though its scale be finite, yet, in comparison with it, the *impersonal* power in the universe is immeasurably lower : so that if, in virtue of its infinity, it really swallowed up the personal life at the end of the mortal term, it would be more like the sacrifice of children to Moloch than the taking of Enoch by God.   Personality is not the largest, but it is the highest fact in the known cosmos : and if death has power over it, there is nothing which death spares : it can undo the utmost which the Divine will has wrought.

The disposition to disparage the 'personal life,' and let it go as an 'individual accident of the universal' probably arises from an unconscious confounding of it with the bodily form ; on the break up of which, the spirit was supposed to have no retaining walls, but to escape as a vital breath and mingle with the general air.   With all its lofty pretensions and abstract speech, philosophy is not beyond the influence of mere images like these : and I am the more inclined to suspect their operation here because, when they are removed out of the way, I find it impossible to form any idea of that promotion to 'highest life' which Schleiermacher assigns to Willich when divested of *the self* now dropped in death.   Without thought, without love, without reverence, without will, without objects (and none but personal beings can have these), what remains to fill the phrase 'highest life'?   Psychologically, there can be no greater descent than the steps from the personal to the impersonal : and no one could imagine it a beatific advancement, unless he deceived himself by some false analogy to physical expansion.

From these considerations it results that metaphysical scrutiny, like the physiological, places the Ego in a category to which Death is neutral, beyond the limits of its known dissolving power.

Yet this side of our problem still presents us with a

difficulty. We can interpret the Soul as the permanent identity of the subject through all its acts and changes; and so assign to it a place in our ontology. We can there hold it apart and save it from subjection to the physical laws which affect its implements and media. But there is one geometrical condition from which we cannot exempt it, involved as it is in the very idea. The subjective Ego is always *here*, as opposed to all else, which is variously *there*: at its own centre it receives the messages of experience: from its own centre it sends forth its energy in reply. Without local relations therefore the soul is inconceivable. In thinking of our own, there is nothing to perplex us; for we are always at home, and carry our moving tent of measurement about with us. And, in thinking of another's, we are at no loss for its *locus*, whilst his visible form is there. But when this has vanished in death, we have no help towards that Space-condition, which yet is no less indispensable than before: and we have to cast about for some possibility of fixing the soul in a definite seat of existence. That possibility we cannot reasonably deny. If Boscovich and Faraday ask for only points of space in which to lodge and from which to direct the attractions and repulsions that constitute the cosmos, no more is needed for the concentration of consciousness and will. And if we even demand some imaginable objective changes corresponding with these, surely within the ether which already quivers into light and electricity there is scope for countless other undulations, and the enclosure of them within myriads of individual rings. Such speculative possibilities do nothing to dissipate our ignorance: they only expose the absurdity of saying that the universe contains no means of individualization except the present human body. In view of them, we can say perhaps with a deeper quiet respecting the departed, 'We rest assured *that* they live: but *where* they live we cannot tell.'

CHAPTER III.

ALL that has thus far been advanced aims at no more than to ward off unfavourable presumptions against the future life, drawn from alleged canons of possibility. Were the problem surrendered to physics and metaphysics, it could never quit its state of suspense ; there would be nothing to forbid the future : there would be nothing to promise it; and in such a question, this intellectual balance would be tantamount to practical negation. Not till we turn to the *Moral* aspects of Death, do we meet with the presiding reasons which give the casting vote : here it is that, having got the conditions of the case into right form, we call the real evidence and weigh the probabilities to which it points. And when I speak of '*Moral*' aspects, I mean all that are relative to the character, either of God as the ordainer, or of man as the self-knowing subject, of death. As between beings, Divine and human, standing in spiritual relations to each other, what place does this institute hold, and what significance does it apparently possess ?

I have already pointed out the obvious fact that, with us human beings, the usual animal order of means and ends is inverted ; the inner springs of action, instead of merely serving the organism, dominate it and use it : our faculties are set up on their own account, and carry their own ends. From this position I now advance a further step, and say that the divine ends manifestly inwrought in our human nature and life are continuous and of large reach ; and, being here only partially or even incipiently attained, indicate that the present term of years is but a fragment and a prelude. In order to estimate this general thesis, let us look at some features characteristic of our nature and of the scene in which it is placed.

§ 1. *Vaticinations of the Intellect.*

Is the *constitution of the human mind* what we should expect, if it were constructed for a lease of a single life like ours? or is it compacted and fitted up for an ulterior term ? The answer depends in part on the *scale* of its powers. And I am well aware that when we try to estimate this scale, we come across incommensurable terms ; for how can we compare capacity of reason with decades of years? how discriminate the amount of memory, of invention, of affection, of will, that shall be adequate for four-score years, from that which will answer for four hundred? Had we to deal with small and definite differences, this want of any common measure would present an insuperable difficulty. But, though mental faculty carries on its face no exact measure of its duration, yet it would be strange if we could not distinguish the provision for half a century and that for an unlimited existence. Some sort of proportion we expect, and never fail to find, between the endowment of a nature and the persistency and range of its achievement ; just as, in human productions, the material selected and the refined pains spent in perfecting them, are no uncertain index of the service expected from them. The parcel to be delivered in the next street the tradesman does not wrap up in water-proof and fasten with wire ropes ; for a week's encampment, you spread your canvas and do not build of stone ; nor is it for a summer's lodging, but for your ancestral house, that you set up fountains and plant oaks.

When, on this principle, you place side by side the needs of human life, taken on the most liberal estimate, and the scope of the intellectual powers of man, I shall be surprised if you do not find the latter to be an enormous over-provision for the former. This is the real ground of the 'practical man's' complaint against the higher mental culture, as a superfluous refinement. He says, truly enough, it is of no use for either the interests or the duties which must occupy all our years; and, except so far as it is demanded for a place in the skilled professions, and can be realized in the arts, it is a mere barren dreaming, that does no service at home, or in the warehouse, or at the council-board, or in parliament. Were his ideal,—viz. the perfect administration of affairs,—the right and adequate one for us, the 'Philistine's' judgment would be not far wrong; that we feel it to be false and narrow is due to our consciousness of capacity for larger and ulterior ends. These it is that permanently fix themselves in our imagination and reverence as the supreme glory of humanity: when we think of Newton, it is not at the mint, but in his study; of von Humboldt, not in the Geheimerath, but on the Andes; of La Place, not at the Ministry of the Interior, but in the observatory or at his desk. Nor, in turning to such illuminated names of the world's history, are we influenced only by gratitude for the benefits to mankind which must be set down to their account. Of these, equal genius may confer very unequal amounts; and their visible measure gives no clue to the order of our natural admiration; but the moment we take our standard, not from use but from worth, and are far enough off to see things as they are, we are aware that as the Reason rises and expands, the true end of our being is approached, and that its speculative light far transcends the small allowance needed for our temporal life. In our day, the naturalists have so persistently reminded us of our affinity with other animal races, and dwelt upon the border phenomena of an incipient humanity, that we are apt to lose sight of the immeasurable interval between the intelligence of man and that of any other tenant of the earth ; and it may be well to recall some of his mental characteristics.

Other creatures live in Time : Time lives in him alone. Made for the present, they are delivered over from hour to hour, intent only on the immediate, and, even when urged by prospective instincts, acting from the pressure of some instant want : their central light is *perceptive*, with brief and faint support from memory and anticipation. They see no more than the little range around them within which they are imprisoned, and to the conditions of which their move-ments must conform. This is their world ; and it is enough that they fit into it as it comes. We, on the other hand, not only remember our personal experiences through scores of years, and reckon them at equal distance beforehand, but contemplate our whole life here as a mere tick of an ever-lasting chronometer ; and *that* too, not with terror at our insignificance or any feeling that we are lost in the hurrying stream. but with reverent sympathy for the historical prelude to our own days, with intense curiosity respecting the long ages ere history had begun, and a glance of serious wonder down the indefinite vistas of the future. What means this vast outlook, if we have nothing to do but with the affairs of our own period? If our human relations are limited to our contemporaries, why do we so fling our passions into the struggles of dead generations, clasp the knees of their heroes, and join in the prayers of their saints? For the sweetness and harmony of life it would be enough, if the voices of our companions were music to our ear, and their faces a light to our eye : but we have need, it seems, of a wider capacity of fellow-ship that takes no notice of the barriers of death : for, what is literature, but the appeal of thought to thought

and heart to heart through silent ages ?—an appeal that is
for ever forming new friendships, quickening young genius,
and drawing forth fresh tears?   And that we are not made
to say 'this will serve our time,' and be careless of all
beyond, let all the prophets testify: for, what audience
could they find, except with a race eager to pierce the
limiting darkness of their immediate vision, and claim for
their thoughts a place and part in the invisible? This
feature therefore, look at it as you may, seems to imply
that we are in living relations with all time, and have
personal interests not only in contemporary things, but
wrapped up also in what has been and what will be
through an infinite perspective.

It is the same with the other infinitude.   Space lies
open, I suppose it will be admitted, to us alone of creatures
on this globe ; and though others too have their retinas, on
which also the starry vault shines in, it tells its depth and
looks its meaning to no night-watcher but man.   For their
own ends, there are no keener eyes, no nicer skill, no more
workmanlike architecture than theirs.   But only on *his*
domain do you find, from the days of Hipparchus to those
of Airy, vast graduated circles raised and swung, and
towers built and quadrated, and time-measures provided,
and all the exactest arts exhausted, merely to look into
the skies.   Few more expressive symbols of the human
characteristics present themselves than Tycho's castle of
Uranienburg, erected to shelter his six-foot globe and all the
huge mechanism for keeping his record of the stellar
heavens and the planet Mars ; and, still more, the modest-
looking dome beneath which the modern astronomer sits in
silence, his eye upon his transit-instrument, his ear upon
his clock, or pursuing the gliding star at his equatorial, or
resolving a nebula at his great reflector ; his patient figure
here upon the spot, his thought in that ether-field whence
the light he sees started half a million years ago.   Whence,

for an existence limited to a point, this insatiable interest in objects and movements, on the margin of infinitude?—an interest so absorbing as to take no denial, but determine the whole life-work of the votary whom it once possesses, enabling him, in dark ages, to pass unswerving through his persecutors with the steadiness of his own stars; and, in softer times, to go apart from the haste and despise the ease and ambitions of the world, in order to gain the calm and mingle with the mystery of the universal order. Is it that, like the traveller before a journey, he likes to study the country whither he is bound, and not be wholly without a key to its contents and laws? If you found a ploughboy taking lessons in navigation and poring over maps of New Zealand and Fiji, you would guess that he was about to take to the sea, and become a colonist at last; and if we have but to till our own earth for a season, what can be the fascination of sailing through the skies? Is it not that we have vaster relations than with our immediate surroundings, that the mind's estate is greater than we had conceived, and that in these excursions we feel the outskirts of a problem that is to engage larger meditations and maturer powers? and that the Science which transcends the demands of one life is the propylæum of another? This contrast between the absolute limitation of our position and the boundless range of our intellectual desires has long and often moved the wonder and the hope of thoughtful men. Colin Maclaurin especially, the interpreter of Newton, who brought the theory of the tides within the compass of his law, lays stress upon it in the following sentences:

'We cannot but take notice of one thing, that appears to have been designed by the Author of nature. He has made it impossible for us to have any communication from this earth with the other great bodies of the universe, in our present state; and it is highly probable that he has

likewise cut off all communication between the other
planets and betwixt the different systems. We are able
by telescopes to discover very plainly mountains, precipices, and cavities in the moon ; but who treads these
precipices, or for what purpose those great cavities (many
of which have a little elevation in the midst) serve, we
know not; and are at a loss to conceive how this planet,
without any atmosphere, vapours, or seas (as is now the
common opinion of astronomers), can serve for like purposes as our earth. We observe sudden and surprising
revolutions of the great planet Jupiter, which would be
fatal to the inhabitants of the earth. We observe in them
all enough to raise our curiosity, but not to satisfy it.
From hence, as well as from the state of the moral world
and many other considerations, we are induced to believe
that our present state would be very imperfect without a
subsequent one, wherein our views of nature and of its
great Author may be more clear and satisfactory. It does
not appear to be suitable to the wisdom that shines through
all nature, to suppose that we should see so far, and have
our curiosity so much raised concerning the works of God,
only to be disappointed in the end. As man is undoubtedly
the chief being upon this globe, and this globe may be no
less considerable in the most valuable respects than any
other in the solar system,—for aught we know, not inferior
to any in the universal system ; so, if we should suppose
man to perish, without ever arriving at a more complete
knowledge of nature than the very imperfect one he attains
in his present state ; by analogy or parity of reason we
might conclude that the like desires would be frustrated in
the inhabitants of the other planets and systems ; and that
the beautiful scheme of nature would never be unfolded,
but in an exceedingly imperfect manner, to any of them.
This therefore naturally leads us to consider our present
state as only the dawn or beginning of our existence, and

as a state of preparation or probation for further advancement; which appears to have been the opinion of the most
judicious philosophers of old. And whoever attentively
considers the constitution of human nature, particularly
the desires and passions of men, which appear greatly
superior to their present objects, will easily be persuaded
that man was designed for higher views than of this life.
These the Author of nature may have in reserve to be
opened up to us, at proper periods of time and after due
preparation [1].'

If from our cognitive and reasoning faculties we turn to
the creative, the same impression is repeated,—that they
are above the measure of our present lot. The reflective
mind of man, it has been said, alone is the mirror of
nature; but more than this, it is a retaining mirror, where-
on the images, once left, remain, and shine in the dark;
and, most of all, it is a redisposing, a beautifying, a
quickening mirror, that drops the matter and keeps the
meaning of things, freshens their colours, deepens their
expression, and so shifts their scenery as to shape a drama
from a chronicle. Well may the poet be called by the half-
sacred name of *Vates*; for the ideal transformation of the
actual is as divine a miracle as the turning of dust into
dew-drops; and the moulding of language into an instrument for this end, that its rhythm and its fire may sweep
through the ages, still waking up wrath and love and pity
wherever it alights, is a marvel surpassed only by our
blindness to it. There are two classes of permanent products raised and transmitted by human activity; one of
them is *co-operative*, and has its parallel in the life of other
creatures; as the coral-reef is deposited in increments
contributed by a constant animal succession, so the city,

---

[1] Account of Sir Isaac Newton's Philosophical Discoveries, B. IV.
ch. ix. § 16, 3rd ed. 1775.

the harbour, the aqueduct, the road, enlist and attest the
labours of many generations, and owe their solidity and
grandeur to prolonged experience and multitudinous skill.
Such monuments record the power of the *social* spirit, and
measure for us the greatness of *nations*. The other class is
purely *individual and personal*, and has no place except in
human kind : an Iliad, an Agamemnon, a Divina Commedia,
a Hamlet, a Faust, a Madonna di San Sisto, a Sinfonia
eroica, is a unique birth in which no second mind can bear
a part ; and, go where it may, speak to what myriads it
will, it is still the appeal of one soul to one, eliciting response as sharp and single as the echo to a solitary voice.
Flowing forth from a single creative nature, it acts by its
touch as an experiment in spiritual friendship, and gathers
an ever-increasing group, held fast in fellowship of enthusiasm, and owning a common obligation to the genius
which has discovered for them their true soul. What and
where then are the two members of this relation ? Is the
first of them nothing and nowhere ? and is the homage it
wrings from me paid to a blank ? or to a dead book only,
—to blotted paper, or coloured canvas, or an orchestral
score ? Heart-worship, like God, is 'not of the dead, but
of the living' ; and that, in the thought-glance with which
we look up to a Homer, a Dante, a Shakespeare, there
should be no reciprocity possible,—that, in reverencing the
prophets, we do but decorate their tombs,—that the touch
which wakes such fires within us should be that of a
quenched torch, would expel their chief meaning from the
noblest relations subsisting among human minds. A great
creative personality may be lonely and neglected in his
day ; and only when the reflection which he leaves of himself travels down the ages, does he select and gather together his natural associates and lovers : and shall he never
hear the chorus of that great company, or know of that life
which began for him when life had ended ? Can a word

that is immortal come from a speaker that is ephemeral?
Between the aspirations of high Art and the intimations
of Religion there is a hidden but indissoluble affinity.   It
was a touching thing to see how Strauss, bereft of his ' Old
Faith,' thought to crown his ' New ' by lifting the theatre,
the concert-room, the picture and sculpture-gallery into
the place of the church, and making aesthetics do the work
of devotion.   He rightly felt their kinship ; he wrongly
assumed their equivalence.   Beauty does not stop where
his sharp and definite thought arrested it, with form and
colour and sound, and living action and proportion ; but
goes down, beneath these sensible media, to indefinite
depths of inner expression, contiguous, if not identical,
with the penetralia of religion.   When these are cut off by
a floor of hard negation, the aesthetic material shapes itself
in vain ; the symbols are starved of their best meaning ;
and by their mere surface-play reduce to a diversion that
which might breathe a sanctity.   The ultimate root of Art
strikes downward till it feels and drinks the life-giving air
of the infinite and divine ; and, once severed from this, it
shrivels into a husk and semblance, a subjective pleasure
of our senses, not a report of the real soul of things.   Of
those who thus lose its essence, Jean Paul Richter says,—
' As there are idealists of the outer world who believe that
our perceptions constitute the object, instead of the object
constituting our perceptions, so are there idealists of the
inner world, who get their *real* from the *apparent*, their
sound from the *echo*, their *substance* from the *perception*,
instead of inversely explaining the apparent by the real,
or consciousness by its objects.   Our analysis of our inner
world we take for its genesis : i.e. the genealogist assumes
the place of progenitor and founder of the line[1].'   The
ideal faculty, as a perpetual vision of higher possibilities, is

---

[1] Kampaner Thal, Stazion 507, p. 112, Erfurt, 1797

perfectly intelligible, if the realization lies before it ; though it visits the heart with a 'noble discontent,' the light upon the future balances the shadow on the present. But it is utterly unintelligible, if, like Plato's interior eye-light when the lids are closed, it spends itself in weaving dreams ; so that every creative genius must live, either in a fool's paradise, or, if disenchanted of its illusions, in sadness unrelieved. If it is said that the possibilities unfulfilled for the individual who conceives them may prove true forecasts for the race, we must still ask whether a race, however progressive, can be credited with success, every generation of which is haunted by the consciousness of failure. Minds cannot be used up as mere material for foreign or collective purposes ; each carries its own end, and only in approaching this falls into consonance with others, and reduces the distance to the goal of all. Who can believe that the Everlasting Mind fulfils its end by disappointing every other? and that each age is to spend itself in lamenting its inheritance from another and its own short-coming? Is the eternal design of Perfection to be gained by the frustrated aspirations of countless ephemeral generations? Or, to the rule that 'one soweth and another reapeth,' is there not the compensating sequel, 'he that soweth and he that reapeth shall rejoice *together*'?

I will only add, ere I turn away from the consideration of the intellectual powers, that, in spite of their dependence on organic media of action, there is clear evidence of their being adequate to indefinitely more than the present term of life allows them to accomplish. The student of Nature, or the servant of Art, is indeed obliged to put a limit to his aims and be content with small achievements : but what is it that arrests his attempts? Simply the consciousness expressed in the maxim, 'Ars longa, vita brevis'; not that he could go no further and do no more ; but only that he has a short loan of time and tools, and

must reckon his piece-work by his hours. The very fact
that he sees what he must relinquish, and resigns it with
regret, shows that he could conquer it, if he had the
chance ; and it is precisely at the end of life, that, from
the vantage-ground of a lofty elevation and a large survey,
he most intently turns to the horizon and best discerns
the outline of the promised land on which his eyes are
about to close.   I do not know that there is anything
in nature (unless indeed it be the reputed blotting-out
of suns in the stellar heavens) which can be compared
in wastefulness with the extinction of great minds : their
gathered resources, their matured skill, their luminous
insight, their unfailing tact, are not like instincts that
can be handed down ; they are absolutely personal and
inalienable ; grand conditions of future power, unavailable
for the race, and perfect for an ulterior growth of the
individual.   If that growth is not to be, the most brilliant
genius bursts and vanishes as a firework in the night.
A mind of balanced and finished faculties is a production
at once of infinite delicacy and of most enduring constitution ; lodged in a fast perishing organism, it is like a
perfect set of astronomical instruments, misplaced in an
observatory shaken by earthquakes or caving in with decay.
The lenses are true, the mirrors without a speck, the
movements smooth, the micrometer exact ; what shall the
Master do but save the precious system, refined with so
much care, and build for it a new house that shall be
founded on a rock ?

What has been said of the powers of Thought applies,
with at least equal truth, to the force of Love. This also
reaches in our nature a depth and intensity far beyond
the exigencies of our present life ; and, after providing
for them all, is capable of passing into a transcendent,
almost an infinite function of character. I speak, of course,
only of a *capacity* given us,—of the possibility for which

we are made, and which we see realized in scattered cases, historical and actual. For alas! if we judged from the average distribution and level of mutual affection among men, we could by no means say that it adequately met their wants and sufferings. The canker of selfishness is deep lodged in a thousand parts of the social structure, and, wherever it has hold, eats away the vital fibres of all fair and happy growth. But, to measure the power of Love, we must look at it where it is, instead of where it is not; and in what it *can be*, rather than in what it *ordinarily is*. In attempting thus to estimate it, I am not so much impressed by its most commanding forms,—the parental tenderness on which young life reposes, and the quick compassion which receives suffering into its embrace, as by the relations into which it brings congenial souls that kindle and supplement each other, and easily rise together to an altitude inaccessible to each apart. To the former there clings so much of instinctive impulse and transient elasticity, that they may plausibly be treated,—especially since they appear in other creatures too,—as provisions for temporary and special emergencies; though we cannot fail to see that in human nature they expand and endure and establish a motive preponderance vastly in excess of the needs which call them forth. But when we quit the inter-dependencies of circumstance, and turn to the pure attachments of thought and character, begun, it may be, in the home, or in the college, or even between the reader and the author that have never met, we are in presence of a very different and simply human phenomenon, the influence of which, being inward and spiritual, evades the accidents of place and time. The brother and sister that have long walked hand in hand together, and let each see the spreading verdure and opening blossoms of the other's heart, have to be parted that he may go upon his manly way; and desolate are the moments when she watches

his receding ship and waves the silent adieu, and cannot
see him through her tears. But is there any break in the
charm and power of that personal relation? Not so; for
see! they speak across the world; the letters come and go,
that picture the separate lives and exchange the watch-
words of the still deepening love; and soon, they scarcely
heed the space between, so little can it intercept of the joy
of their communion. The image of each, periodically
enriched by some tender lineament or fresh colour, is never
far from the other, and by many an unfelt glance mingles
a secret suasion with the movements of the will. And is
this the limit of its power? Follow them a little further:
for the absent brother, let us suppose, there is soon a
longer voyage to be taken, over a sea from which there is
no message and no return. The fatal news has come: the
sorrow has been met: his books, his dress, his papers have
come home [1]: the intercourse is over: but has the relation
ceased? On the contrary, it now first reveals its true
essence and contents: his image, a little paler and a little
graver, it may be, but suffused with a diviner light, is
nearer to her than before, and guides her into higher ways,
and by a mere look allays every inward storm. The ideal
power of such an affection, often presiding over long
reaches of lonely life, is surely too much for the mere
residuum of a dead relation, but is the natural continuance
of a partially suspended one. If it be not so, our nature is
not framed in harmony with our condition, but is over-
charged with spiritual intensities that run to waste. If we
refuse this anomaly, we are entitled, when otherwise
without light, to judge of what we shall be by what we

---

[1] Πολλὰ γοῖν θιγγάνει πρὸς ἧπαρ·
οὖς μὲν γάρ τις ἔπεμψεν
οἶδεν, ἀντὶ δὲ φωτῶν
τεύχη καὶ σποδὸς εἰς ἑκάστου δόμους ἀφικνεῖται.
Æschylus, Agamemnon, 421.

are.   The great mountain-chain of Death bounds our
external view, nor are any seen approaching us thence ;
for the passes are all one way.   But if our mutual affections
are computed only for this cisalpine province in which
our lot is cast, why do we so follow with our looks the
travellers that leave us by the ascending tracks, and,
instead of losing them in the everlasting snows, trace them
into the transalpine valleys under fairer skies, and never
cease to converse with them, the visible with the invisible ?
Affection, in its very nature and idea, is *reciprocal* ; and to
suppose that, the reciprocity being for ever extinguished,
it can yet have a life-long survival,—nay, centuries of
impassioned homage, like that of Christendom for Christ,
is to match the fate of an ephemera with the soul of a
seraph.   We cannot consent thus to treat the supreme
aspirations of our nature as a delirious disease.   How can
it be,—as Jean Paul asks, 'that our breast is parched and
fretted and at last crushed by the slow fever-fire of an
infinite love for an infinite object, and must be assuaged
by nothing better than the hope, that this heart-sickness,
like a physical heat, will sometime be removed by laying
on it the ice-slab of Death [1] ? '

I have been careful, in the foregoing remarks, not to
appeal to the widespread hope and belief of a future life,
which has prevailed in the world ;   for it is hardly warrant-
able to argue from the mere prevalence of a belief to its
truth, unless it can be classed with the primary assumptions that are the conditions of all inference,—a position
which cannot be claimed by the doctrine now under consideration.   I have no doubt, however, that the faith in
immortality owes its large extension among men, in no
slight degree, to the secret feeling that in the nature of
man there is more contained than the measure of the

---

[1] Kampaner Thal, Stazion 507, p. 120.

present life requires and satisfies ; and so far, the historical
and ethnological existence of this faith bears witness con-
firmatory of the arguments I have endeavoured to unfold.

§ 2. *Vaticinations of the Conscience.*

Let us now fix attention on another part of our nature,
viz. on the *Law of its Powers*. This, if I mistake not,
speaks with even distincter voice. The prospective aspect
which we have noticed in the intellect and affections
depends on their range and intensity, as overpassing the
functions of our being here ; and as their measure may be
variously taken, a cynical estimate may always run the
evidence down, and accuse us of first over-glorifying our
nature, that we may then immortalize it. This precarious-
ness, which must always attach to an argument from
degree, we leave behind us, when we present our question
to the *Moral Consciousness* ; for here, if there be any
oracle at all, it is contained in the very essence of the
faculty, and may be heard from first to last, in the faint
and feeble tinklings of childish self-reproach, and in deep
bell-strokes of the full-toned conscience.

Impelled by conflicting impulses, we are not left in the
dark respecting their relative worth ; nor can we doubt
that we have the power, and are, in every case, under the
obligation, to turn away from the worse and put ourselves
at disposal of the better. This alternative problem we
know to be the trust committed to us. Is it faithfully
discharged ? we are in harmony with the righteous
authority that sets it. Is it wrongly answered ? we have
fallen into variance with the supreme law, and deserve
ill in the sphere where it rules. This is what we mean
when we say that we are here on our *probation*. But
liberty to go right,—liberty to go wrong,—can it be a
mere haphazard gift, an unmeaning institution of con-

tingency, as if from some curiosity to see what will turn
up? And when the experiment is over, are the actors
dismissed, the curtain dropped, and the theatre closed?
Such an issue would contradict the very essence of moral
freedom, which surely loses all significance if no difference
is to be made between those who use it well and those
who misuse it. When the two possible ways are thrown
open to human choice, it is already anticipated that not
all will take the same ; and provision must be made for
treating those who do as they like otherwise than those
who do as they ought. We are not upon our trial, unless
there is a future that depends upon ourselves. The alternatives of a trust have a sequel in the alternatives of a
reckoning. So that wherever Conscience is, there we
stand only in the fore-court of existence ; and a Moral
world cannot be final, unless it be everlasting.

It will perhaps be admitted that the conditions of a
responsible existence *do* involve these two stages,—a probationary term, and a retributory sequel; but it may be
said, there is no need to separate these and assign them to
different lives; both may be provided for within the present experience of the agent's own personality. Not only
has he time enough here to reap in later years according
as he has sown in earlier; but, from moment to moment,
each choice, as it is made, may pay him its own dues: the
same Conscience which goes before his will as its monitor,
may come instantly after it as its judge. And so, the
moral constitution may contain its statutes, its judiciary,
and its executive, all in one; and the offender, ere the act
is well over, may be hurried to the bar to hear his sentence,
and to the dungeon to bear it, without sensible change of
place or time. And that the two conditions do really fulfil
themselves *pari passu*, and make sure of justice as fast as
the cases for it arise, is said to be sufficiently evidenced by
the inward award of compunction to guilt and peace of

mind to faithfulness: for these, in themselves, constitute just the opposite treatment required to verify the prior warning and invitation of the moral sense, and stamp the true characteristics on wrong and right; nor is there any need of other and external recompense. From this point of view, it has become not uncommon to regard the claim for accurate retribution as having no bearing on the question of a future life, and to find all that is demanded in the self-consciousness of man. Thus Pfleiderer says, 'The requirement of a precise correspondence between the merit of the individual and his lot rests on moral and metaphysical assumptions from which the higher religious view of the world enables us to emerge, by leading us to discern in the inward blessedness of peace with God the highest and incomparably most precious good, beside which all external good and evil sink to superfluous appendages. The more a man can say, with the Psalmist, "If I have God, heaven and earth are nought to me," and with Jesus, "Not my will, but thine be done," i.e. the more divine he is, so much the more will he recognize the good and wise will of God in all that outwardly befalls him, and also regard and use the outward ill as a means to what is really best: he will therefore have no ground for complaint or for claiming future compensation; and none either for envying the wicked their external prosperity and invoking on them future retribution; inasmuch as he knows them to be already sufficiently punished in the present unhappiness of their pravity [1].'

This may be a good answer to those who resort to the future life as a means of external compensation for the apparent misadjustments of this world's goods: but the argument to which it is applied asks for nothing of the sort; far from seeking in heaven for outward recom-

---

[1] Religions-Philosophie, 1878, II. ii. 7, p. 717.

penses, through losing sight of the fact that the equities are already settled in the inward experience of the righteous and the wicked, it never looks beyond the inner experiences; alleging simply that, so far as they are carried here, they are obviously incomplete, it infers a continuance of the soul hereafter, to deepen its moral insight and press on to its harmony with God. The question therefore does not lie in the sphere of outward things at all; but is simply this; whether the present inward experiences of the good and the bad are already in satisfactory conformity with the relative worth of their character, so that justice has its perfect work; or whether the sweet and bitter fruits of tendency in them are still unripened by the seasons of this life and remain to be gathered under other skies.

When Pfleiderer wishes to place before us the intrinsic blessedness of the good, it is observable that he takes us up at once to the summit-level of character, whence all is seen glorified in the light of God, and the soul rests in a conscious peace with him. Doubtless the picture is true of this ultimate stage of goodness; but is it so often realized by mortal men as to be set down among the moral promises of this life? Is it the experience given while the battle lasts? or is it the saint's rest, when the strife is over, and the hymn of redemption breaks from the heart? Precisely because this beatific state is hardly reached by human faithfulness here, yet is the goal to which it plainly tends, are we justified in prophesying a future that shall carry it to its perfection. If we want to determine whether the moral law works out its whole history within us, including both probation and retribution, during our average of years, we must withdraw our eye from those rare heights, and restrict our view to the middle ground of experience, where the conflicts of temptation take place and the discipline of character is yet in full play. These intermediate altitudes constitute the proper field of Conscience; which, above them, emerges and becomes latent in a divine repose; and, below them, dies away and is lost out of all reach of moral pain. Now, between these extremes, i.e. during the whole probationary term, there is no proportion, on the one hand, between moral faithfulness and inward content, or, on the other, between immoral preference for the wrong and inward misery. That 'the good man is satisfied from himself,' and that there is 'no peace for the wicked,' may perhaps be suitably affirmed by poet or prophet with eye fixed on the ultimate tendency of things; but cannot be accepted as a true account of men as they are. The rule of ideal justice in the award of recompense is, that the greater excellence should have the ampler recognition, and the deeper guilt should have the most to bear. Is this rule then traceable in our inward experience? On the contrary, it is only the young catechumen of moral life that feels any elation at his conquests over temptation, and can attach much meaning to the phrase 'the pleasures of a good conscience.' As he grows older, and gains a deeper insight into the contents of Duty and the conditions of true holiness, a very different feeling comes over him : his little rudimentary virtue which had looked so bright and pleased him as a morning star, touches the sun and is swallowed up,—nay, is visible only as a black spot that in itself does not shine at all. The more he attains, the more sensible is he of the unattained; and, though none may have less to reproach themselves with than such as he, from none does the language of contrition flow with a significance so deep. Thus the satisfactions of conscience are least known where they are best earned.

Turning to the opposite side, we find the same story repeated in the incidence of penalties. It is a dictate of natural justice to show some mercy at a first offence, but

with every repetition to pass a heavier sentence, till the
whole rigour of the law is visited upon the hardened criminal. See whether, in the inward court of conscience,
any such judicial principle prevails. Is the first great
sin treated lightly there? Is not the offender, on the
contrary, terror-stricken by his sentence of shame and
remorse, and would he not flee from it, if he could, as
greater than he can bear? But if he falls again, it is
with a less surprise of horror; the burden of compunction
is more tolerable now. And each time that he is brought
again to the bar, he gains the ease of familiarity, and finds
some successful plea of mitigation; till, at last, he contrives
to corrupt the whole procedure, to suborn the judge, and
turn the very chamber of justice into a council-room of
guilty conspiracy. There is thus a process of gradual
escape from the weight of inward retribution, as the transgression becomes habitual; and it is precisely on this
account that upon offences again and again repeated the
outward punishment is increased. So long as the moral
sense is fresh and tender, it will itself effect, it is supposed,
a good part of the work of law, and lenient treatment may
perhaps suffice; but the frequent delinquent, who has
hardened himself against the reproaches of his higher
nature, must be brought under the heavy hand of society.
It is not true therefore that Conscience, in its retrospective
action, adequately administers its own law: were that the
only justice, the greatest criminal would have completest
impunity. The function which it really performs in our
nature corresponds, not to the judge's sentence on the past,
but to his prospective warnings addressed to the young
offender for whom he would yet save 'a place of repentance';—warnings grave and earnest at first, but fainter at
every repetition, and at last relinquished as a mere waste
and mockery of right. So is it with our natural contrition;
it startles us with a fearful vision of what we are and may

become. Treat it as a *premonition*, and it comes to us with all its intensity at the moment of happiest promise for its full effect; but treat it as a *punishment*, and where it is most wanted, it entirely fails.

For these reasons it is impossible to admit that our Moral nature runs through its own cycle, and fulfils its own idea, in our experience here. It announces a righteous rule which again and again it brings to mind and will not suffer to be forgotten, but of which it does not secure the execution. It is a prophecy, carrying its own credentials in an incipient foretaste of the end, but holding its realization in reserve; and if Death gives final discharge alike to the sinner and the saint, we are warranted in saying that Conscience has told more lies than it has ever called to their account.

§ 3. *Vaticinations in Suspense.*

From the constitution of the human mind let us now turn to that of the scene in which its part is played ; and see whether, in the treatment which it there receives, the halting justice overtakes its fugitive, and repairs the defective equities of the inward experience.

That there are provisions in the organism of the world for making us feel the difference between right and wrong ways of living, is conspicuous enough. That there is a Law given for our conduct we might know, even when it is illegible within, by the *sanctions* attending it, both (1) physical, at the hand of Nature, and (2) affectional, from the sentiments of men. We stand here, undoubtedly, upon a theatre of *character*, and work out upon it of ourselves, and experience from the very elements on which we live, a certain rough but significant justice : the only question is, whether, in its awards, there is any such exactitude and completeness as to satisfy the claims of a righteous administration, and leave no case open for more finished treatment and supplementary redress. On the former supposition, the court in which we are is final ; on the latter, it is a tribunal of first instance, subject to a judgment more searching and august.

Sensible and benevolent physiologists have taken good care that we should not be unacquainted with the gospel of 'natural laws.' If you sup on crabs, you will be sick ; if you don't wash, you will have eruptions ; if you decline fresh air and exercise, you will get the gout ; if you resort to stimulants, you will hurt your brain, and lose the evenness of your spirits. Far be it from me to deny the value of such rules, or their bearing on the conduct of life. Whoever, by disregard of them, weakens the energies and wastes the time entrusted to him for the duties of life, is guilty of a heinous moral offence. *Hindrances* to faithfulness are piled up without end by habits of negligence or excess, till every noble possibility may be buried beneath them. But do they, with equal certainty, bring the *penalties* due to unfaithfulness ? If a man is willing to incur them as the price of his indulgence, do they settle his account, and can he thus buy off the whole charge of his moral obligations ? The very attempt to do so, and to earn the right of escape into Epicurean egoism, is itself a new and enormous guilt, which cries out for ulterior and more effective retribution. Or, to vary the case and bring it to a more common type ; may not a cautious observance of these very physiological laws co-exist with immoralities, and be applied to render them safe ? Is there no such thing as *prudent* profligacy, that contrives, by art and vigilance, to slip the noose of threatened capture, and roam at large ? It cannot be pretended that health and vigour, that quick faculty and bright spirits, are any certain index of a temperate and blameless course ; and too many have been ruined by being the spoilt children

of nature, allowed to run wild with impunity in the plea-
sure-grounds of life, and snatched from this world at last
as naked of duty as they came into it. It is in vain then
that, for the moral government of men, we place reliance
on the mere response of their physical constitution to their
moral character. Besides, though it were ever so exact,
the very same collapse of health and strength which may
be incurred by evil courses, may be no less earned by
heroic self-devotion to others, or the service of some inspiring duty; and if such sufferings, invested with a penal
character, are rightly allotted to selfish vice, they must be
wrongly annexed to disinterested virtue; and we cannot
appeal to them as fulfilling the ethical conditions of our
existence.

A nearer approach to exact retribution is certainly found
in the remaining sanction,—the favour and disfavour of
mankind. The spectators of our conduct, morally constituted like ourselves, and looking at it from an impartial
point of view, seem likely to be affected by it truly, and to
judge it as would our own uncorrupted conscience; so that
their sentiment may be expected to rectify the distortions
of our own, and place us under the rule of perfect equity.
How little this abstract statement corresponds with the
facts of individual experience is obvious on the slightest
reflection. It is true only under conditions that cannot be
realized, viz. that some of our contemporaries have faultless
moral insight and judgment; that our actions are performed in no presence but theirs; and that we are dependent
for our peace of mind on their approval. Wherever such
conditions prevail, there must already be a moral consensus
so complete that the very need could scarce arise for
compressing the individual conscience into coincidence
with the social; and the court of public opinion, if opened,
would only find an empty calendar. It is no such ideal
tribunal before which we are actually brought. The critics

who think it worth while to pronounce upon our behaviour
are immediate neighbours, be they friends or enemies; and
they alone it is whose feelings towards us constitute an
important element in our well-being : if we can stand well
with them, why should we trouble ourselves about imaginary observers, whose applause is inaudible, and whose
frowns we never see ?   What then is the law by which a
man's associates will judge him ?   The average standard
of purity, of probity, of disinterestedness, of elevation, on
which they have tacitly settled as contenting them : everything allowed by this will be held permissible ; everything
transcending it will be held eccentric ; and whether he
drops below or rises above the established line, he will
equally feel the smart of social persecution.   Hence men,
no doubt, black-ball the cheat ; but so will a gang of
thieves jeer at the scruples of some novice in rascality ;
and the dissolute, scoff at the better mind of a companion,
starting back from some new flagitiousness.   The whole
tendency of felt opinion is therefore conservative of the
morality which places him where he is : it upholds him
against declension ; it weights him down against ascent ;
and punishes him indifferently for abnormal meanness and
exceptional heroism.   And suppose that, in the exercise of
its best power, it visits him for some lapse by a loss of
social caste and virtual expulsion from his clique ; the
sentence, penal in its momentary operation, can be stifled,
just like self-reproach, and got rid of, by simply stepping
down to the next level.   Handing himself on to associates
of a lower grade, he is in a circle of bright faces again, and
wins his reputation upon easier terms ; nor need he ever
be at a loss for society tolerant of the latitude in which he
suffers himself to live.   It is *class*-opinion alone that holds
the seat of effective judgment over men ; and, like any
other provisional government, it may get itself together out
of all kinds of accidental material, righteous or unrighteous ;

with the possible result of either a league of iniquity, or a ministry of perfect justice.

The only form in which human opinion assumes a character approximately judicial, is that of the final historical verdict pronounced upon recorded action by retrospective ages. When disturbing passions have adequately subsided and contemporary factions fallen asleep, the permanent moral elements, so long disguised, stand clearly out, and present the great figures of the past in their true elements and proportions ; to the discomfiture of many a glittering charlatan or imposing pontiff, dismissed from fame, and the canonization of not a few that had been treated as the offscouring of the earth. It is not wholly without reason that public men, conscious of faculty and of integrity, but condemned by ignorant ostracism, have appealed to the judgment of posterity : give it only adequate materials for piecing together the marred and broken images of the past, and its ultimate estimate will probably be the truest that is not Divine. But how seldom can this condition be secured ! how few are the reputations that are safely framed and glazed, beyond the critic's retouching hand to deform or idealize ! The more the ancient records are turned to the light and scrutinized, the more do the passions of the day appear to wake from their sleep, and reproduce, in the wrangling of historians, the controversies that had died away. What hero's form can lie quiet on its tomb, without fear of the chaplet of honour being chipped from its brow ? What reputed monster need despair, after centuries of execration, of some enamoured biographer to glorify him ? And even were there not these uncertainties, what have the mass of mankind to do with the verdicts of history ? It is only to the πρωταγωνιστὴς in each drama that they can ever be applied : the rest of us belong only to the crowd of citizens or army of infantry outside, of which perhaps he may speak, but which makes no appearance even at the

back of the stage ; and for us there are no future sentiments
that can in any way qualify the pressure of opinion close
at hand.   And if, for even the great actors on the scene, it
is not till after the lapse of ages that any justice can be
expected,—if the scourges of mankind are escorted to death
by voices of adulation and wait for dishonour to be wreaked
upon their bones, while the benefactors, hunted and hooted
out of life, are first re-instated, like exiles recalled when only
their ashes can be brought home, in monuments they never
see and a chorus of homage which they never hear ; what
further evidence can we ask of the aberrations of human
sentiment, and the need, under a moral administration of
things, of an ulterior provision to redress its wrongs ? And
the cry and prayer of the conscience for this are the more
emphatic, because, in almost every age which has stoned
its prophets and loaded its philosophers with chains, the
ringleaders of the anarchy have been, not the lawless and
infamous of their day, but the archons and chief priests
and decorous men of God, who could protect their false
idols with a grand and stately air, and do their wrongs
in the halls of justice, and commit their murders as a
savoury sacrifice ; so that it has been by no rude violence, but by clean and holy hands, that the guides,
the saints, the redeemers of men have been poisoned in
Athens, tortured in Rome, burned in Smithfield, crucified
in Jerusalem.

From this survey of the great lines of human experience
two inferences seem to force themselves upon us : (1) That
everywhere,—in our conscience, in our physical nature, in the
sentiments of associated men,—there are indelible marks
of a morally constituted world, moving towards righteous
ends : (2) That *nowhere,* within us or out of us, do we find
the fulfilment of this idea, but only the incipient and often
baffled tentatives for realizing it by partial approximation.
This is what we should expect to see, from the first station

of an unfinished system ; and it irresistibly suggests a justifying and perfect sequel. The vaticinations of our moral nature are thus in harmony with those of the intellectual and spiritual ; distinctly reporting to us, that we stand in Divine relations which indefinitely transcend the limits of our earthly years.

INDEX OF SUBJECTS.

INDEX OF NAMES.

THE END.